Vol. 1

Story & Art by
Ao Mimori

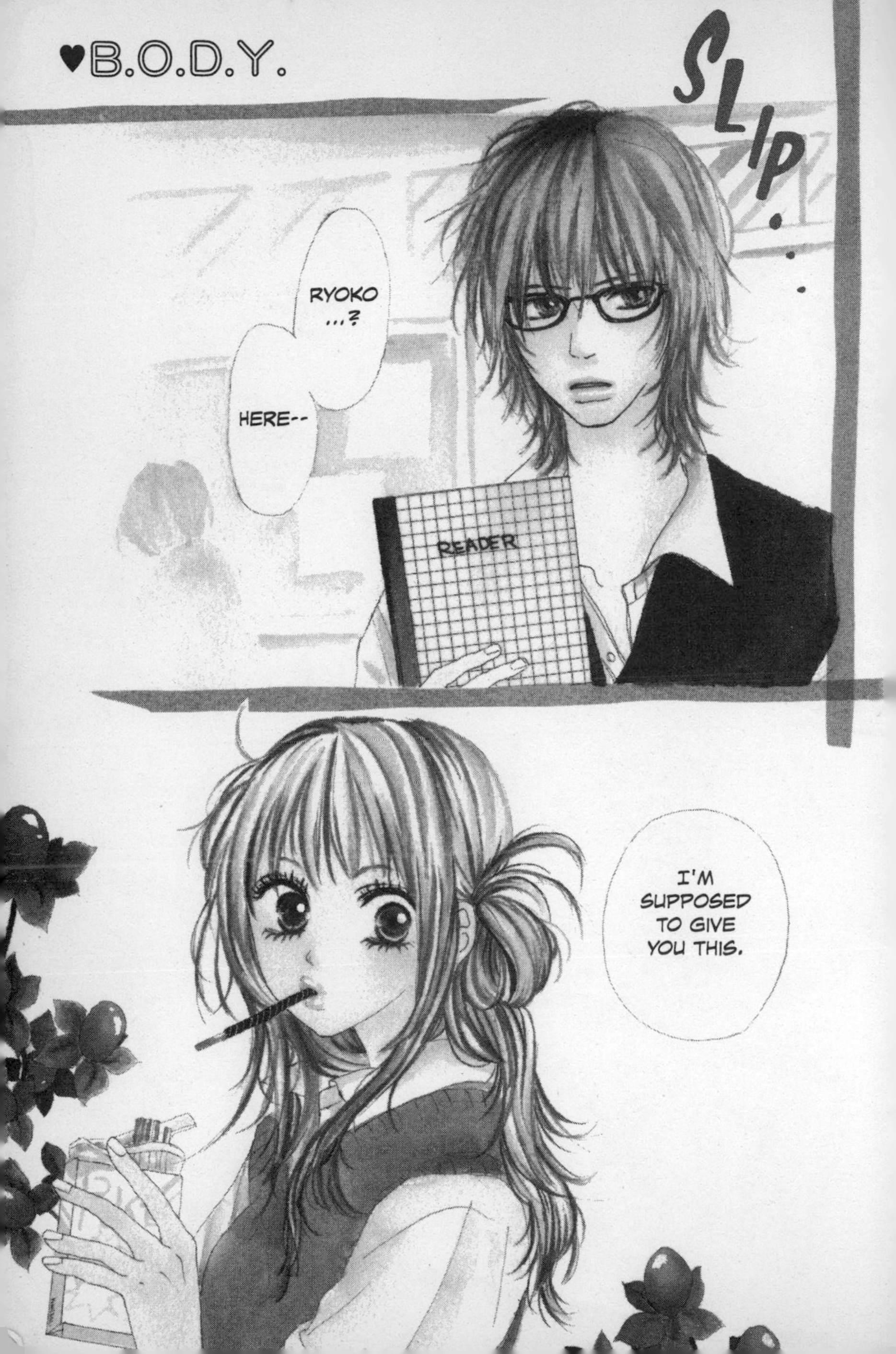
SLIP...
RYOKO ...?
HERE--
READER
I'M SUPPOSED TO GIVE YOU THIS.

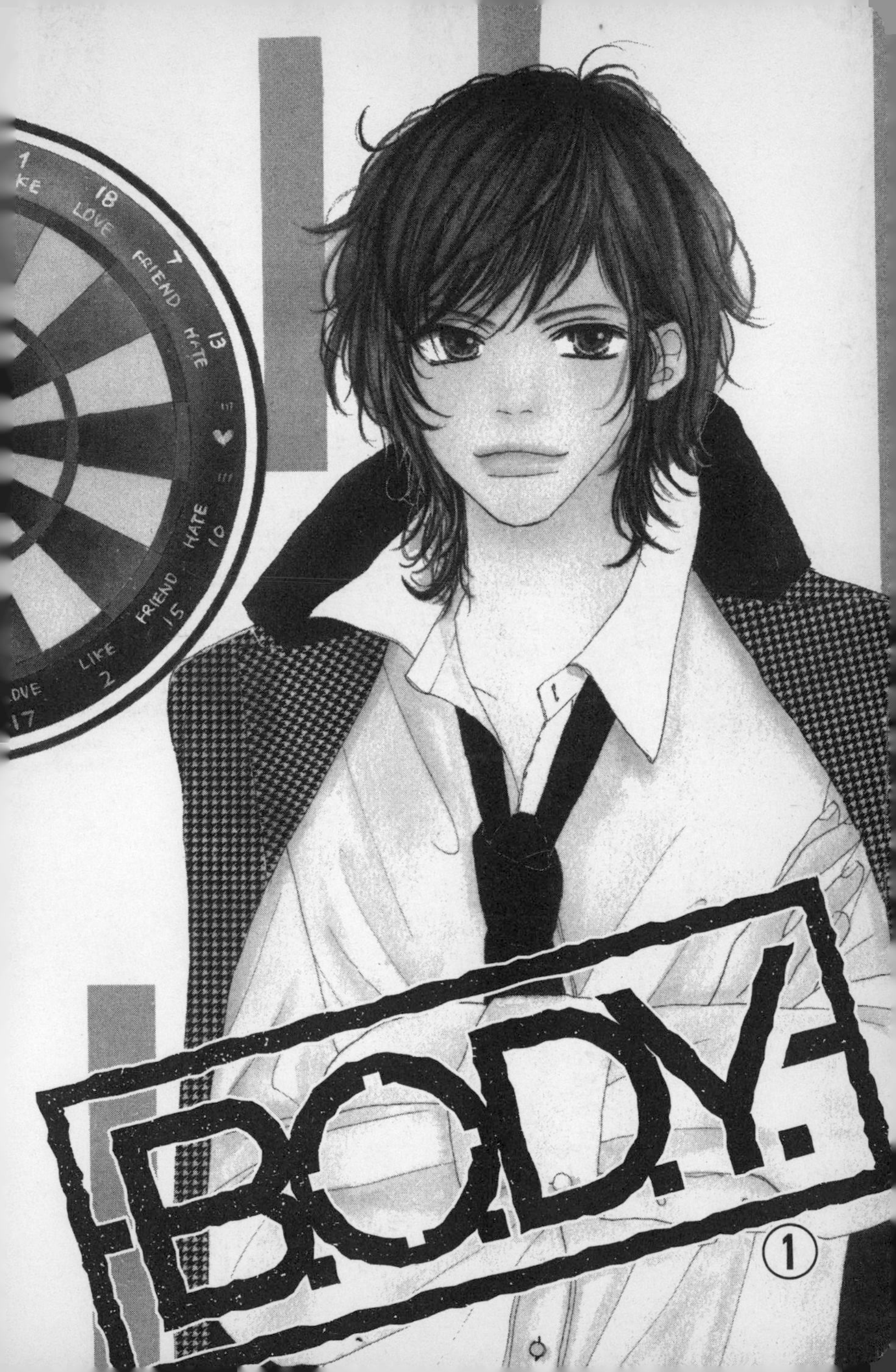
18
LOVE
7
FRIEND
13
HATE
HATE
10
FRIEND
15
LIKE
2
B.O.D.Y.
1

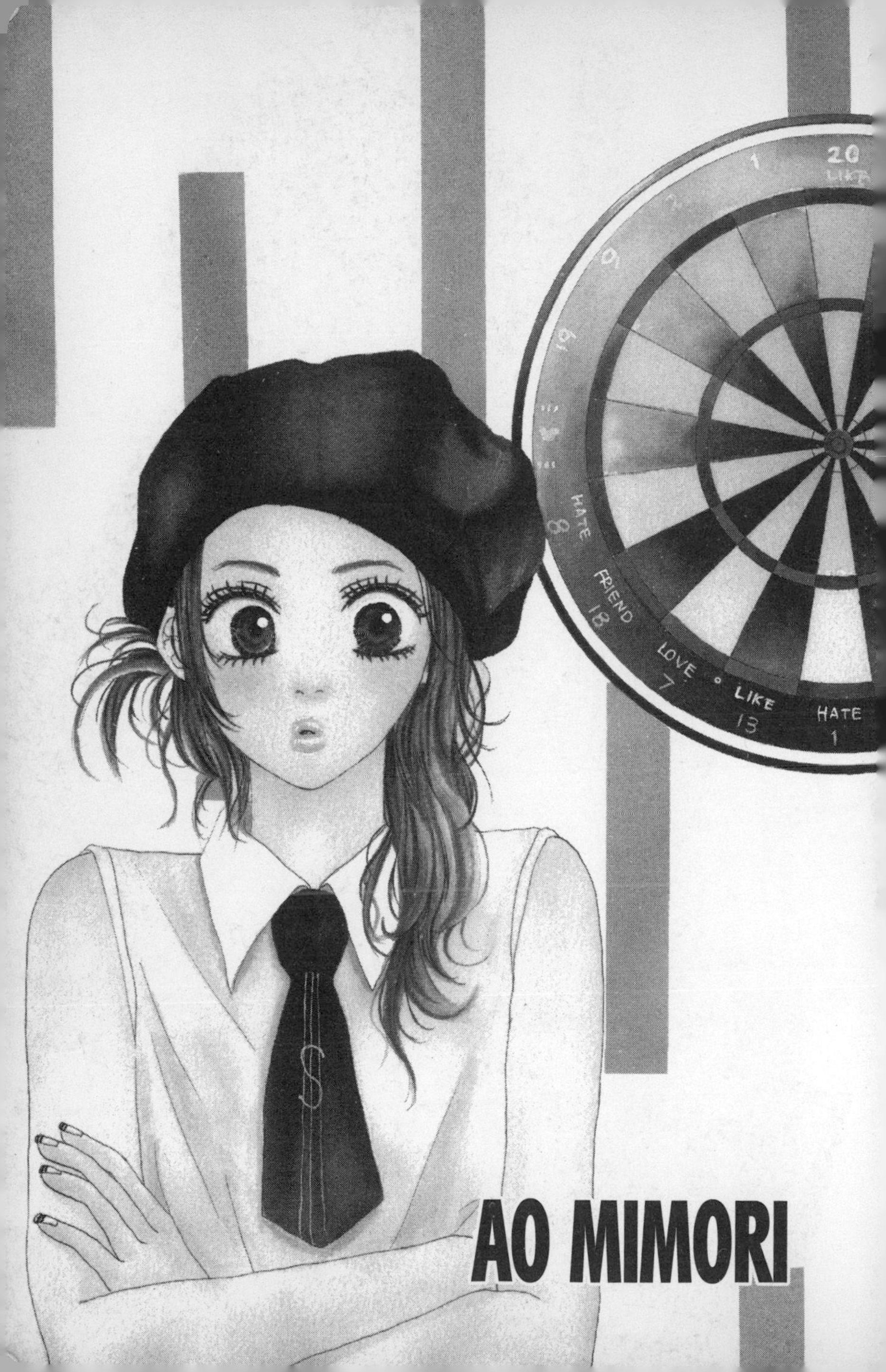
20
HATE
8
FRIEND
18
LOVE
7
LIKE
13
HATE
1
AO MIMORI

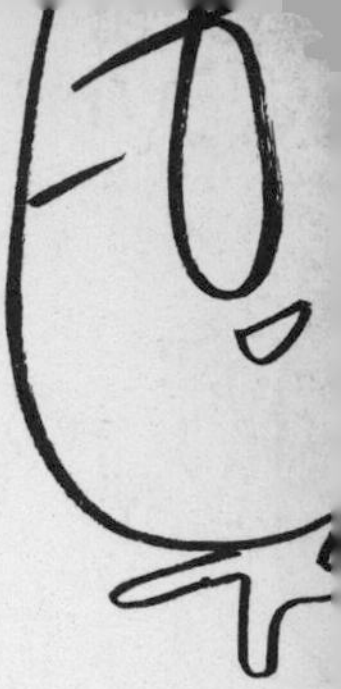

Hello—

Mimori here!

They say the third time's the charm and this is my third series, so here's hoping you're charmed!

Psst! Confession time: I have no idea where this story is headed. I'm totally fumbling my way through-- but I'm doing my best!

There are a few bonus pages scattered here and there, but they're not vital to the story. You don't have to read them unless you've got extra time on your hands. (Of course, I hope you do!)

Thank you for reading B.O.D.Y.!

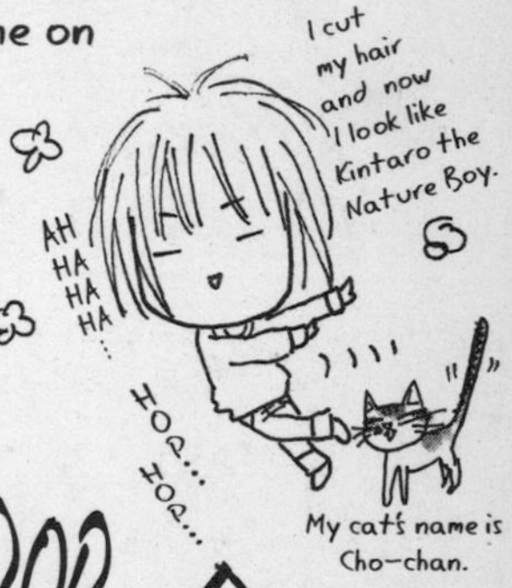

I cut my hair and now I look like Kintaro the Nature Boy.
AH HA HA HA...
HOP... HOP...
My cat's name is Cho-chan.

And other useless banter...

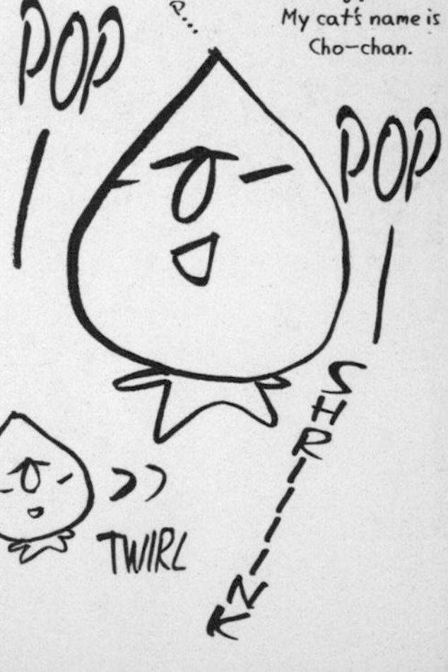

POP
POP
SHRI-I-I-NK

This is it, huh?!
Well then, let's get started!

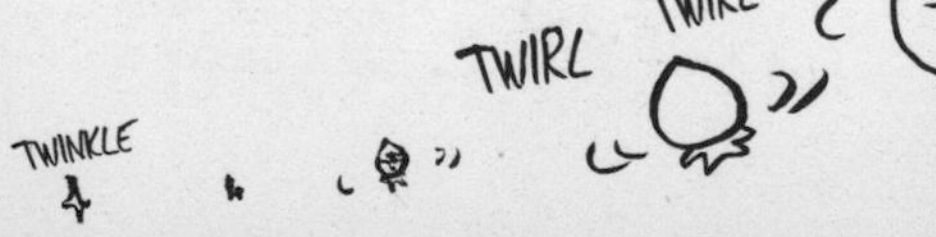

TWIRL
TWIRL
TWIRL
TWINKLE

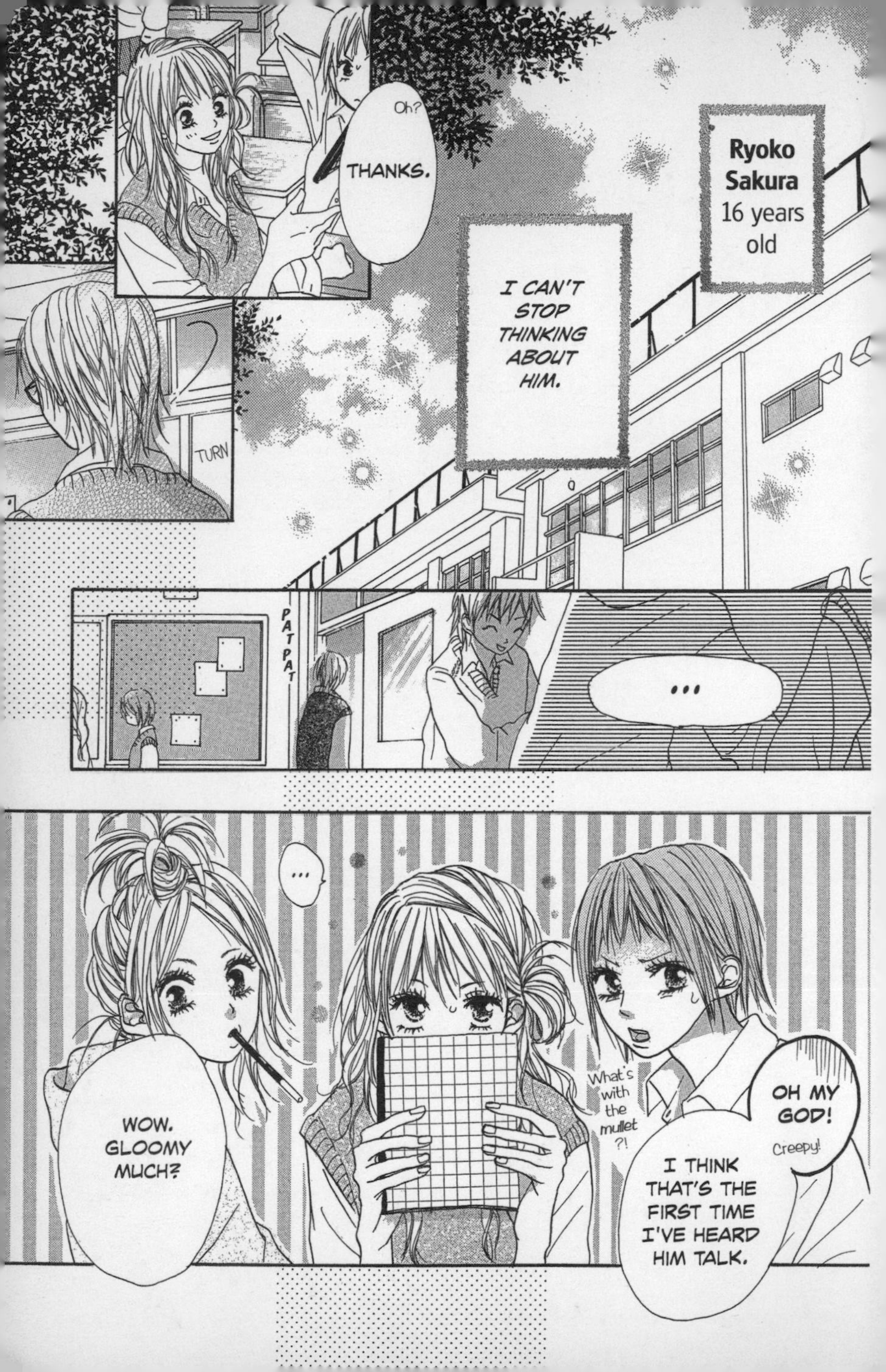
Ryoko Sakura 16 years old
I CAN'T STOP THINKING ABOUT HIM.
Oh?
THANKS.
TURN
...
PAT PAT
OH MY GOD!
Creepy!
I THINK THAT'S THE FIRST TIME I'VE HEARD HIM TALK.
What's with the mullet?!
...
WOW. GLOOMY MUCH?

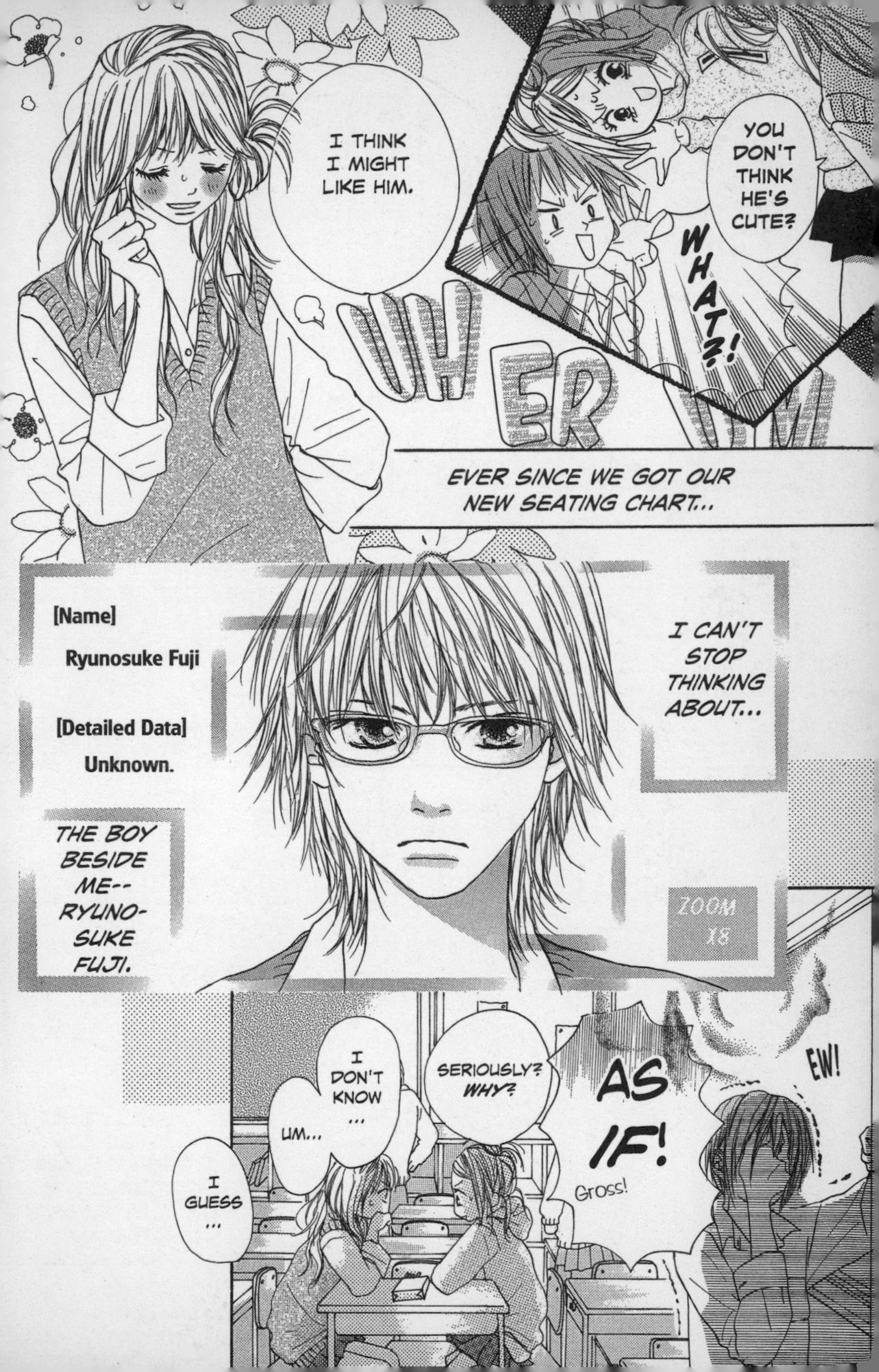
YOU DON'T THINK HE'S CUTE?
WHAT?!
EVER SINCE WE GOT OUR NEW SEATING CHART...
I THINK I MIGHT LIKE HIM.
UH
ER
I CAN'T STOP THINKING ABOUT...
[Name]
Ryunosuke Fuji
[Detailed Data]
Unknown.
THE BOY BESIDE ME-- RYUNOSUKE FUJI.
EW!
AS IF!
Gross!
SERIOUSLY? WHY?
I DON'T KNOW...
UM...
I GUESS...

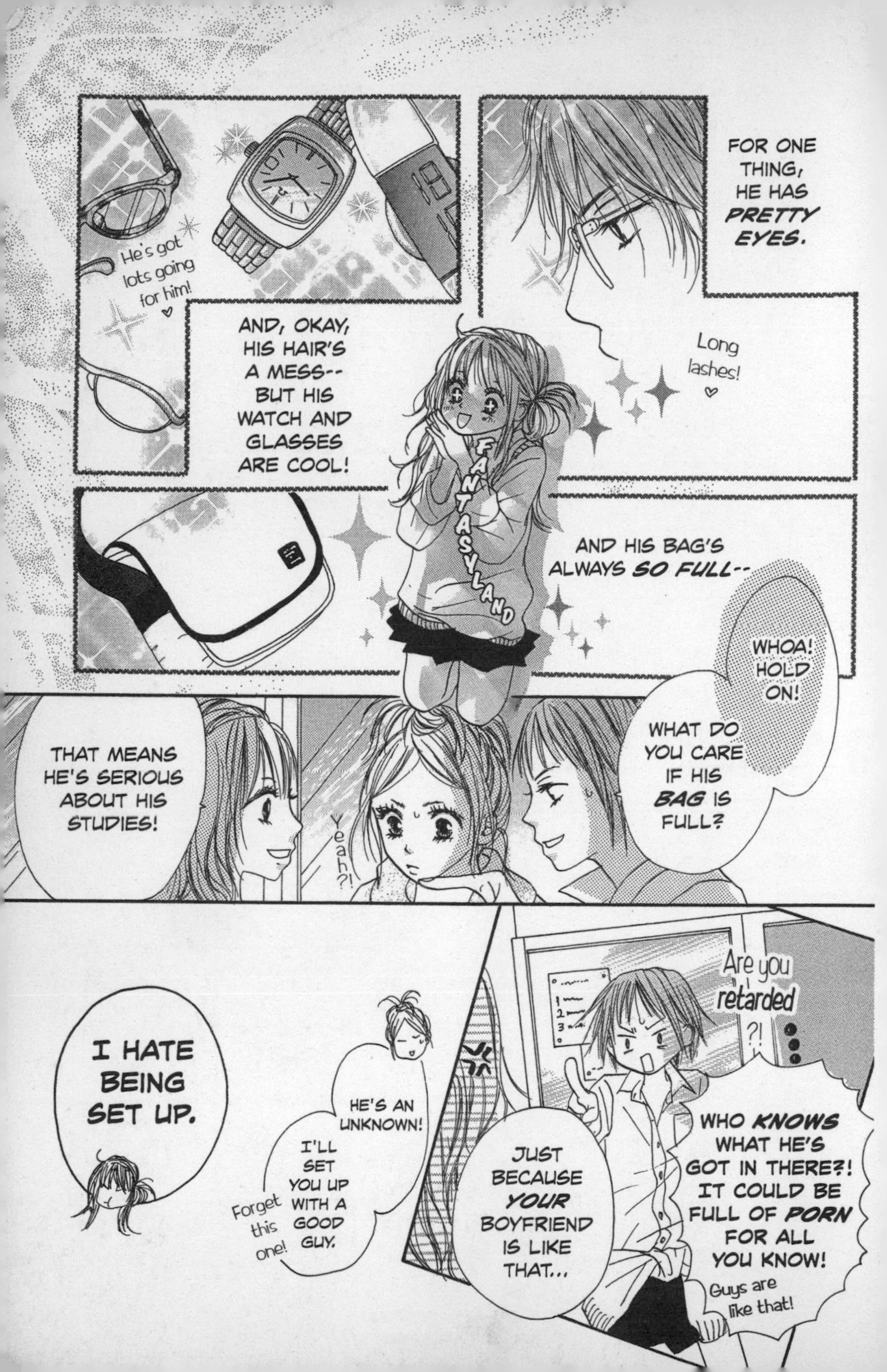
FOR ONE THING, HE HAS PRETTY EYES.
Long lashes! ♡
He's got lots going for him! ♡
AND, OKAY, HIS HAIR'S A MESS-- BUT HIS WATCH AND GLASSES ARE COOL!
FANTASYLAND
AND HIS BAG'S ALWAYS SO FULL--
WHOA! HOLD ON!
WHAT DO YOU CARE IF HIS BAG IS FULL?
Yeah?!
THAT MEANS HE'S SERIOUS ABOUT HIS STUDIES!
Are you retarded ?!
WHO KNOWS WHAT HE'S GOT IN THERE?! IT COULD BE FULL OF PORN FOR ALL YOU KNOW!
Guys are like that!
JUST BECAUSE YOUR BOYFRIEND IS LIKE THAT...
HE'S AN UNKNOWN!
I'LL SET YOU UP WITH A GOOD GUY.
Forget this one!
I HATE BEING SET UP.

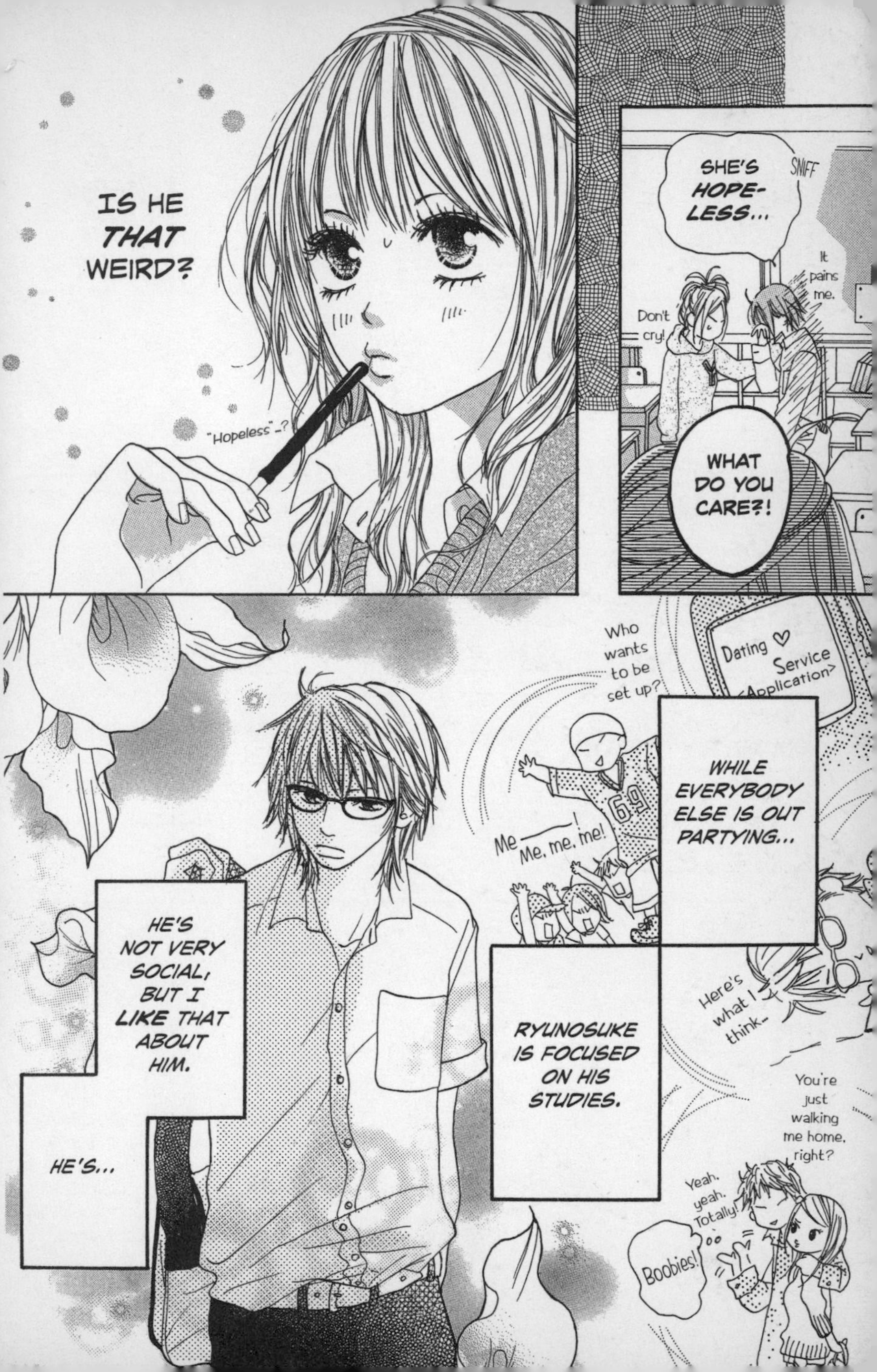
SHE'S HOPELESS...
SNIFF
It pains me.
Don't cry!
WHAT DO YOU CARE?!
IS HE THAT WEIRD?
"Hopeless"...?
Who wants to be set up?
Dating ♡ Service <Application>
WHILE EVERYBODY ELSE IS OUT PARTYING...
Me——!
Me, me, me!
Here's what I think...
RYUNOSUKE IS FOCUSED ON HIS STUDIES.
You're just walking me home, right?
Yeah, yeah. Totally!
Boobies!
HE'S NOT VERY SOCIAL, BUT I LIKE THAT ABOUT HIM.
HE'S...

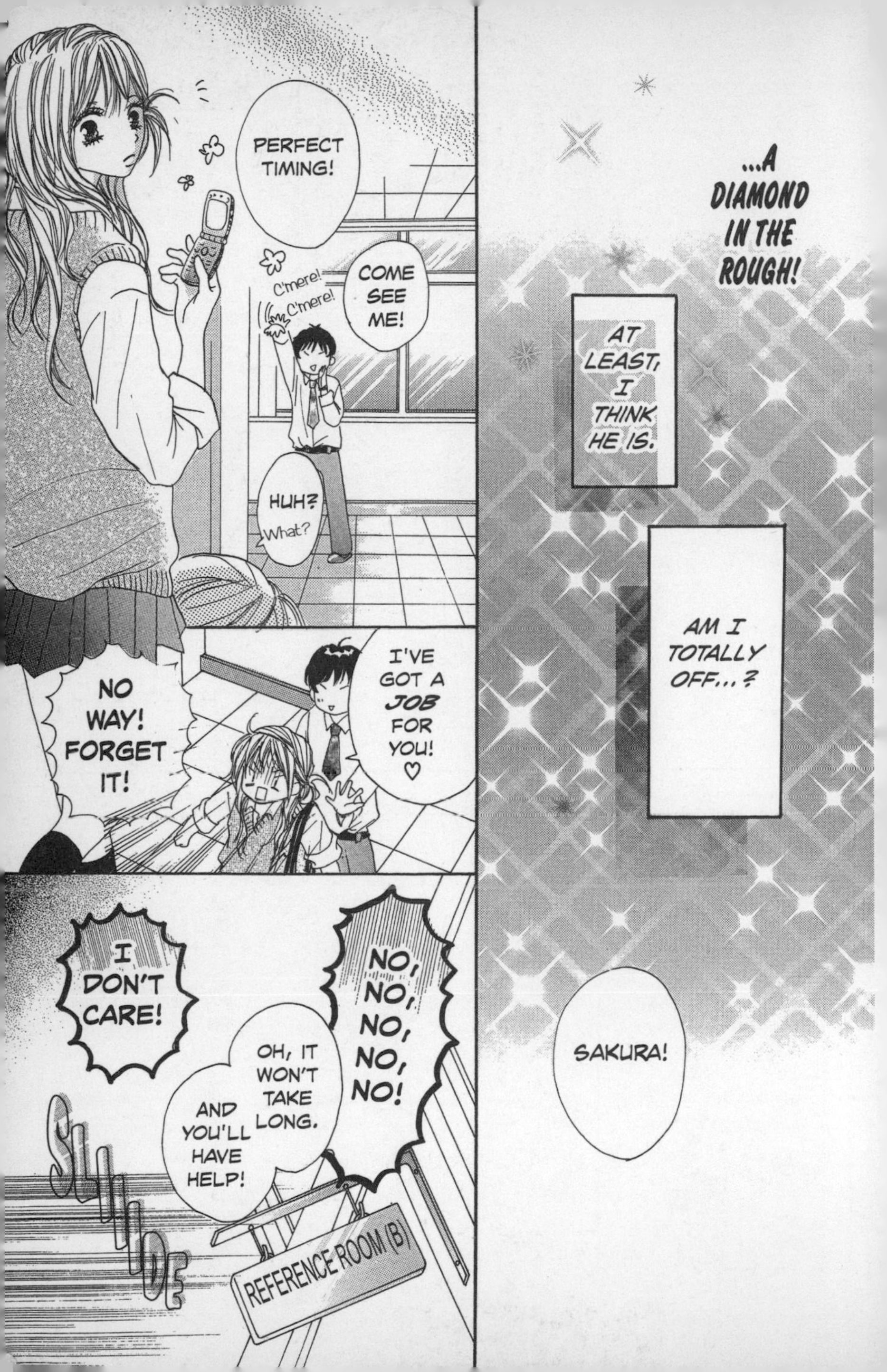
...A DIAMOND IN THE ROUGH!
AT LEAST, I THINK HE IS.
AM I TOTALLY OFF...?
SAKURA!
PERFECT TIMING!
COME SEE ME!
C'mere! C'mere!
HUH? What?
I'VE GOT A JOB FOR YOU! ♡
NO WAY! FORGET IT!
NO, NO, NO, NO, NO!
OH, IT WON'T TAKE LONG.
AND YOU'LL HAVE HELP!
I DON'T CARE!
SLIIIDE
REFERENCE ROOM (B)

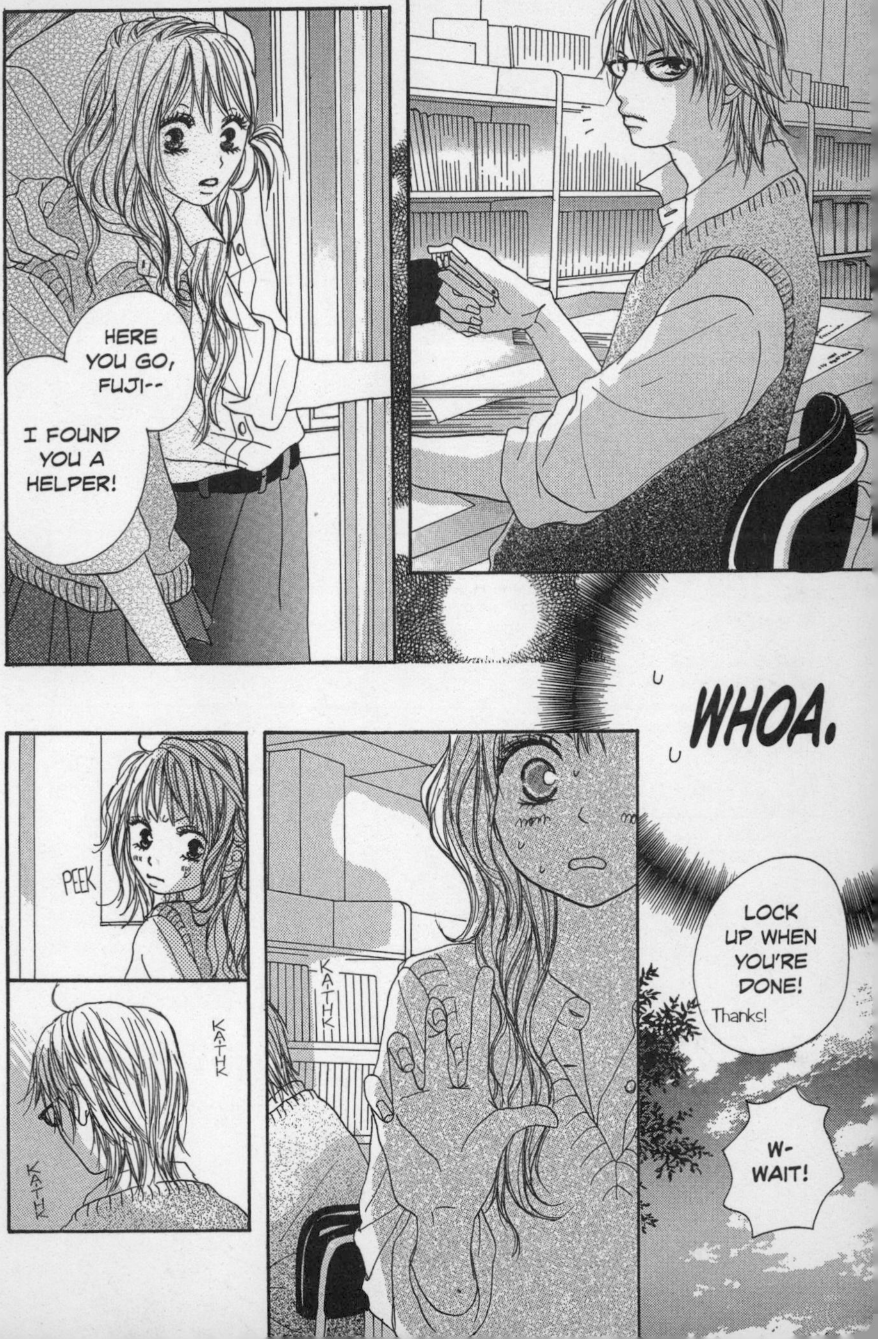
HERE YOU GO, FUJI--
I FOUND YOU A HELPER!
WHOA.
LOCK UP WHEN YOU'RE DONE!
Thanks!
W-WAIT!
KATHK
PEEK
KATHK
KATHK

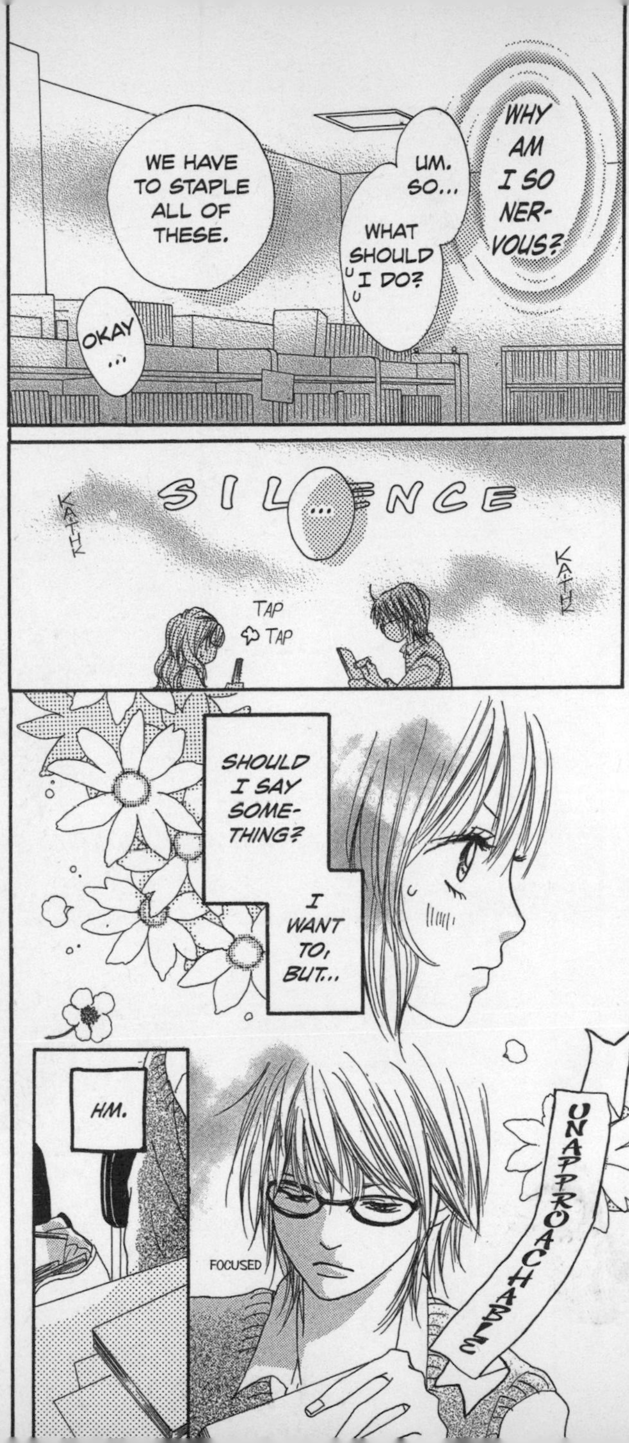
WHY AM I SO NERVOUS?
UM. SO...
WHAT SHOULD I DO?
WE HAVE TO STAPLE ALL OF THESE.
OKAY...
KATHK
SILENCE
...
TAP TAP
KATHK
SHOULD I SAY SOMETHING?
I WANT TO, BUT...
UNAPPROACHABLE
FOCUSED
HM.

About Karuho Shiina, without whom I could not have done this series...

She's--how should I put this?--she's just like a character in one of her books! She's this totally hip, modern woman who just loves to laugh. Whenever I talk to her I'm like, "Why am I so uptight? Why can't I be more like her?!" We're both in the middle of different series right now and we're always texting each other stuff like, "How many pages so far?" It's great motivation.

I talk to her about everything--my problems, my manga, my love life--I mean everything! I owe her so much!

Thank you for putting up with me, Karuho, and I hope we stay friends...! ♥

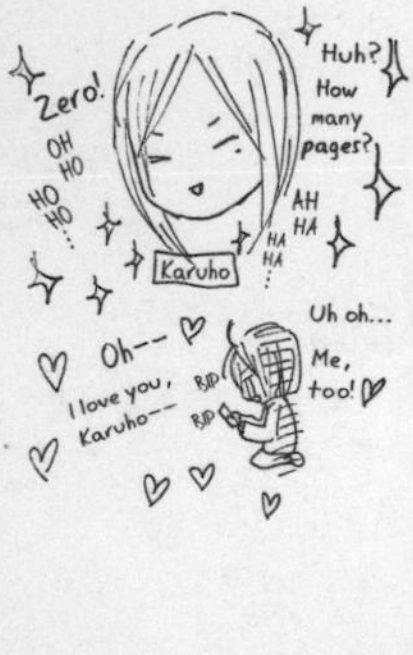
Huh? How many pages?
Zero!
OH HO HO HO
AH HA HA HA
Karuho
Uh oh... Me, too!
Oh--
I love you, Karuho--
BIP BIP

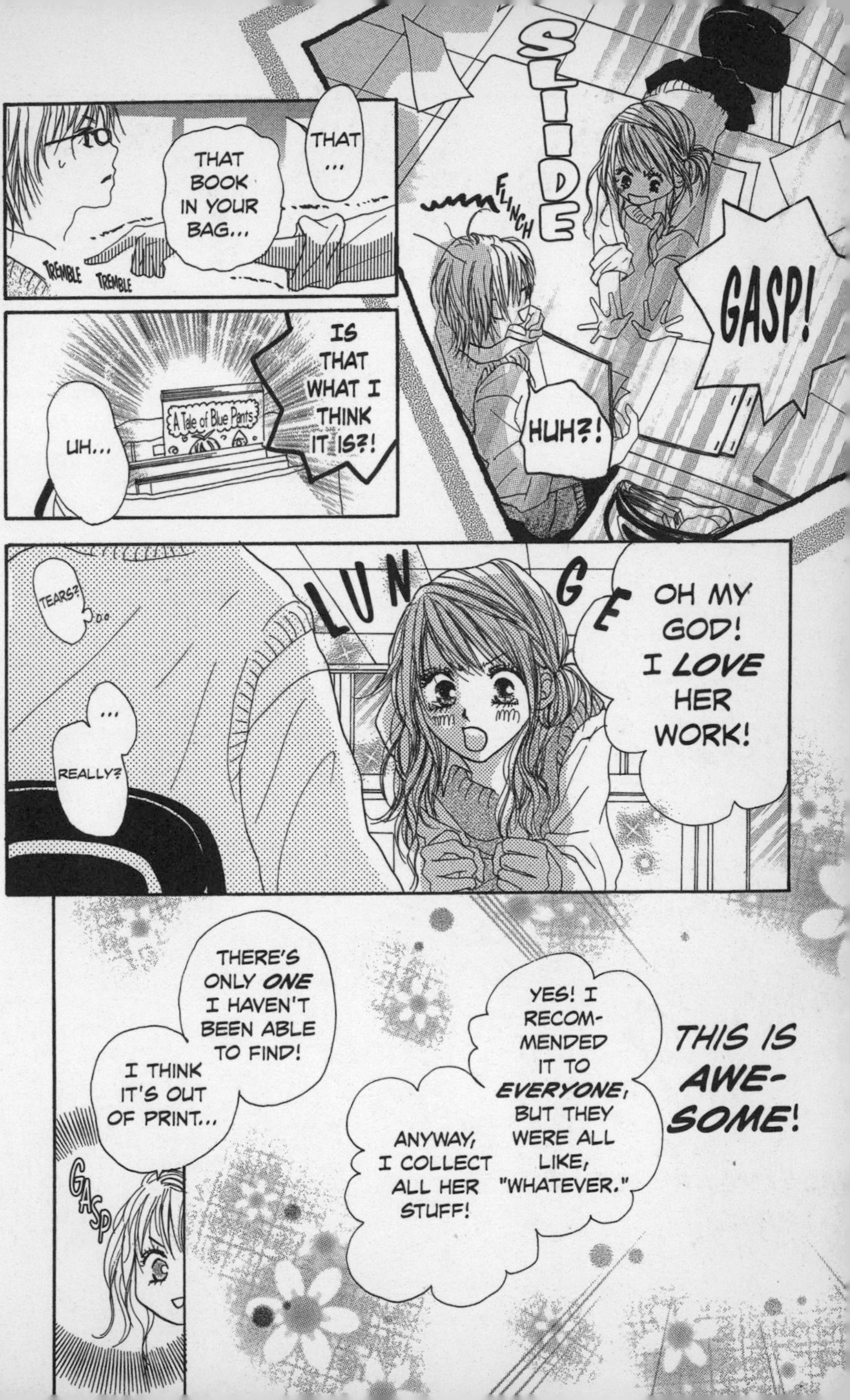
SLIDE
GASP!
FLINCH
HUH?!
THAT ...
THAT BOOK IN YOUR BAG...
TREMBLE
TREMBLE
IS THAT WHAT I THINK IT IS?!
A Tale of Blue Pants
UH...
OH MY GOD! I LOVE HER WORK!
LUNGE
TEARS?
...
REALLY?
THIS IS AWE-SOME!
YES! I RECOM-MENDED IT TO EVERYONE, BUT THEY WERE ALL LIKE, "WHATEVER."
ANYWAY, I COLLECT ALL HER STUFF!
THERE'S ONLY ONE I HAVEN'T BEEN ABLE TO FIND!
I THINK IT'S OUT OF PRINT...
GASP

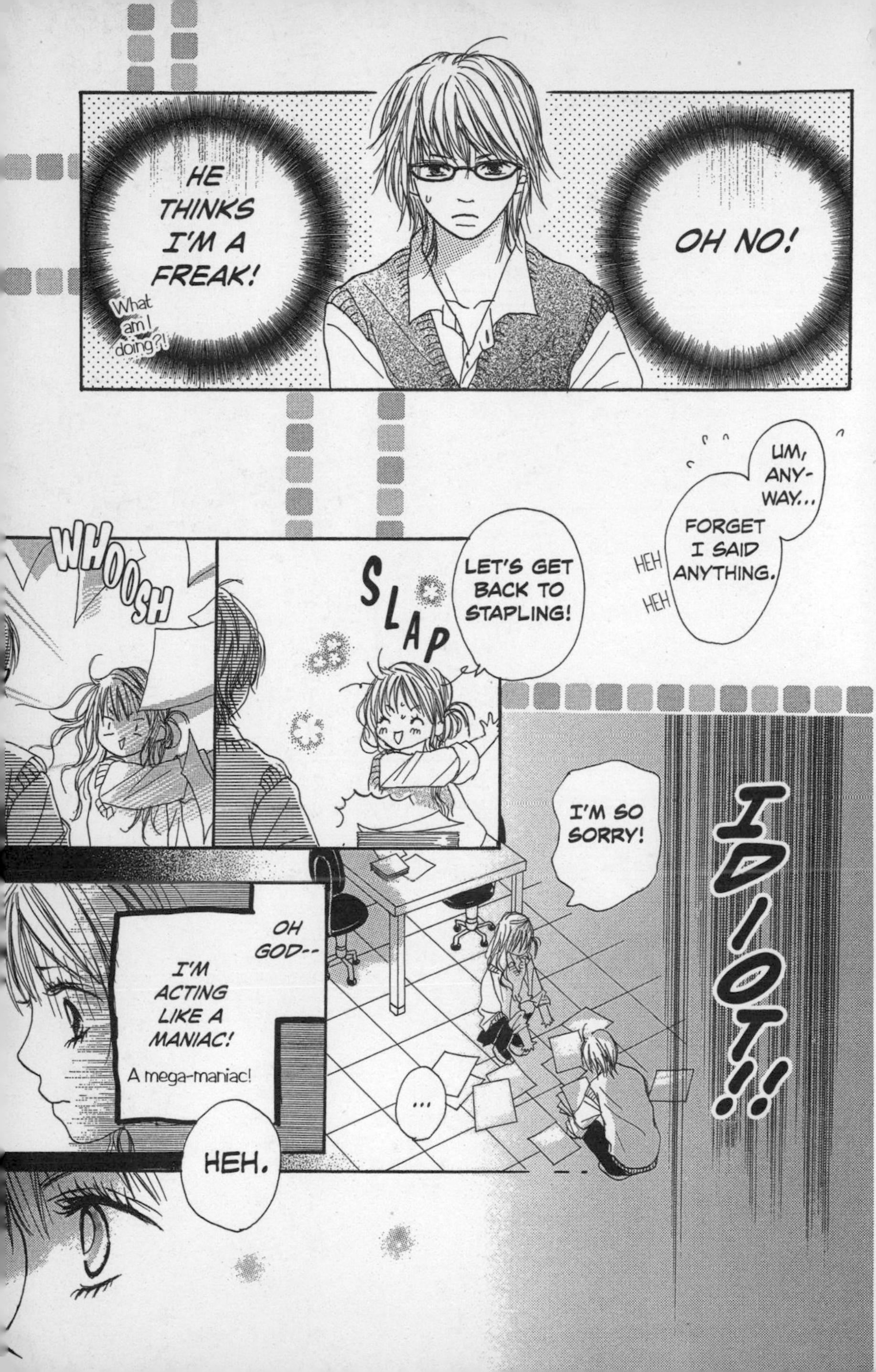
OH NO!
HE THINKS I'M A FREAK!
What am I doing?!
UM, ANYWAY... FORGET I SAID ANYTHING.
HEH HEH
LET'S GET BACK TO STAPLING!
SLAP
WHOOSH
IDIOT!!
I'M SO SORRY!
...
OH GOD-- I'M ACTING LIKE A MANIAC!
A mega-maniac!
HEH.

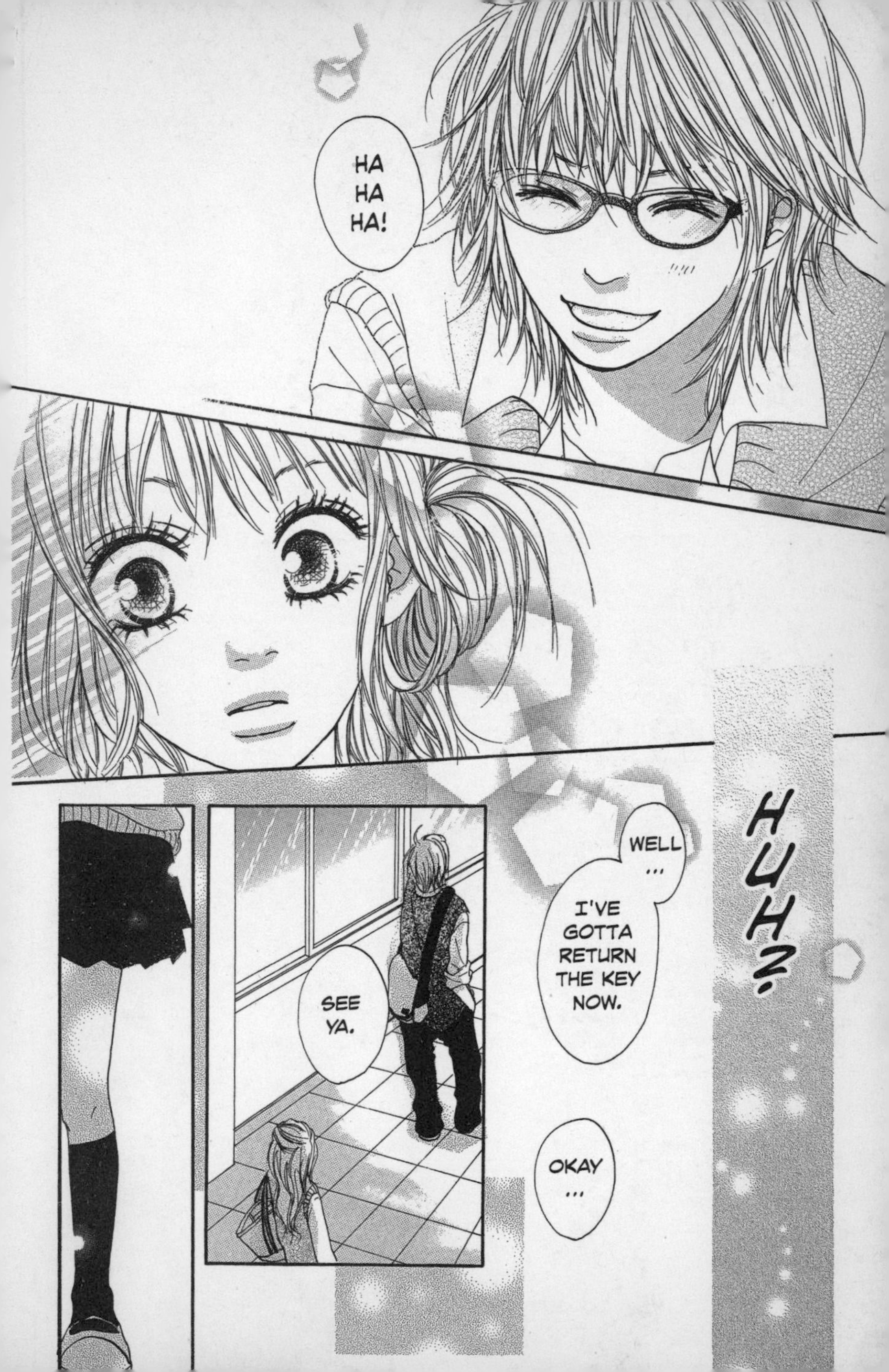
HA HA HA!
HUH?
WELL ...
I'VE GOTTA RETURN THE KEY NOW.
SEE YA.
OKAY ...

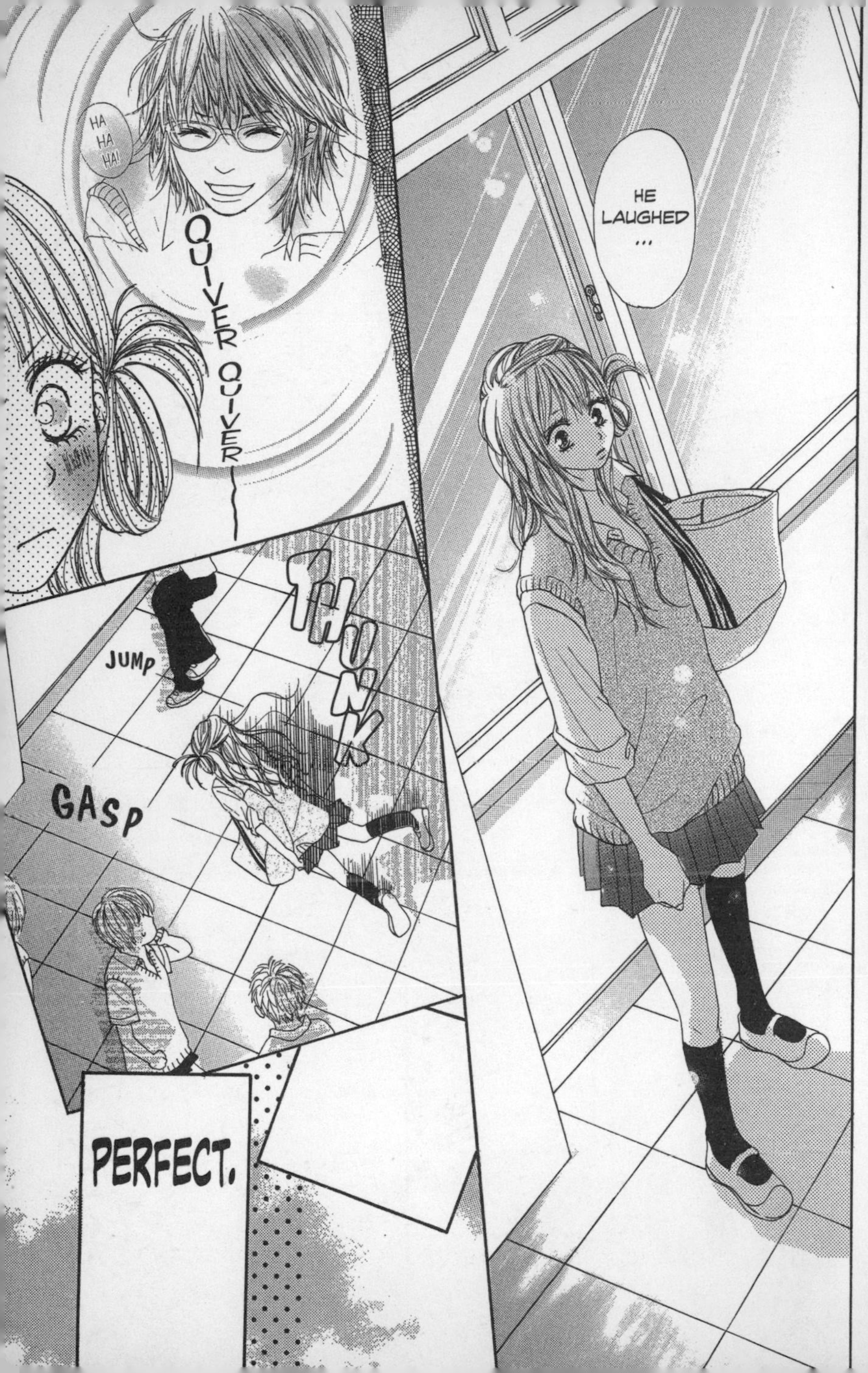
HE LAUGHED ...
HA HA HA!
QUIVER QUIVER
THUNK
JUMP
GASP
PERFECT.

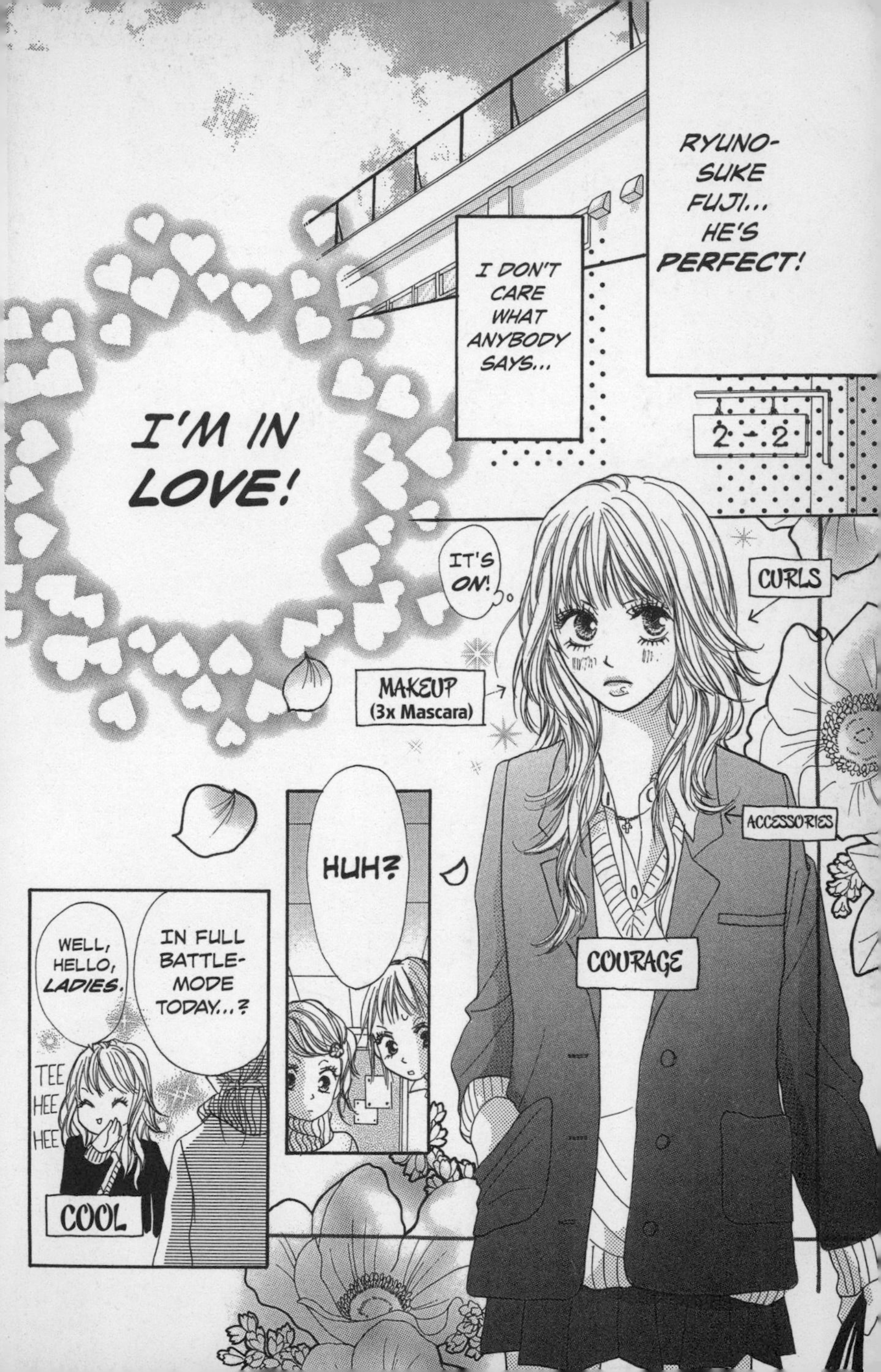
RYUNO-SUKE FUJI... HE'S PERFECT!
I DON'T CARE WHAT ANYBODY SAYS...
I'M IN LOVE!
IT'S ON!
CURLS
MAKEUP (3x Mascara)
ACCESSORIES
COURAGE
HUH?
IN FULL BATTLE-MODE TODAY...?
WELL, HELLO, LADIES.
TEE HEE HEE
COOL

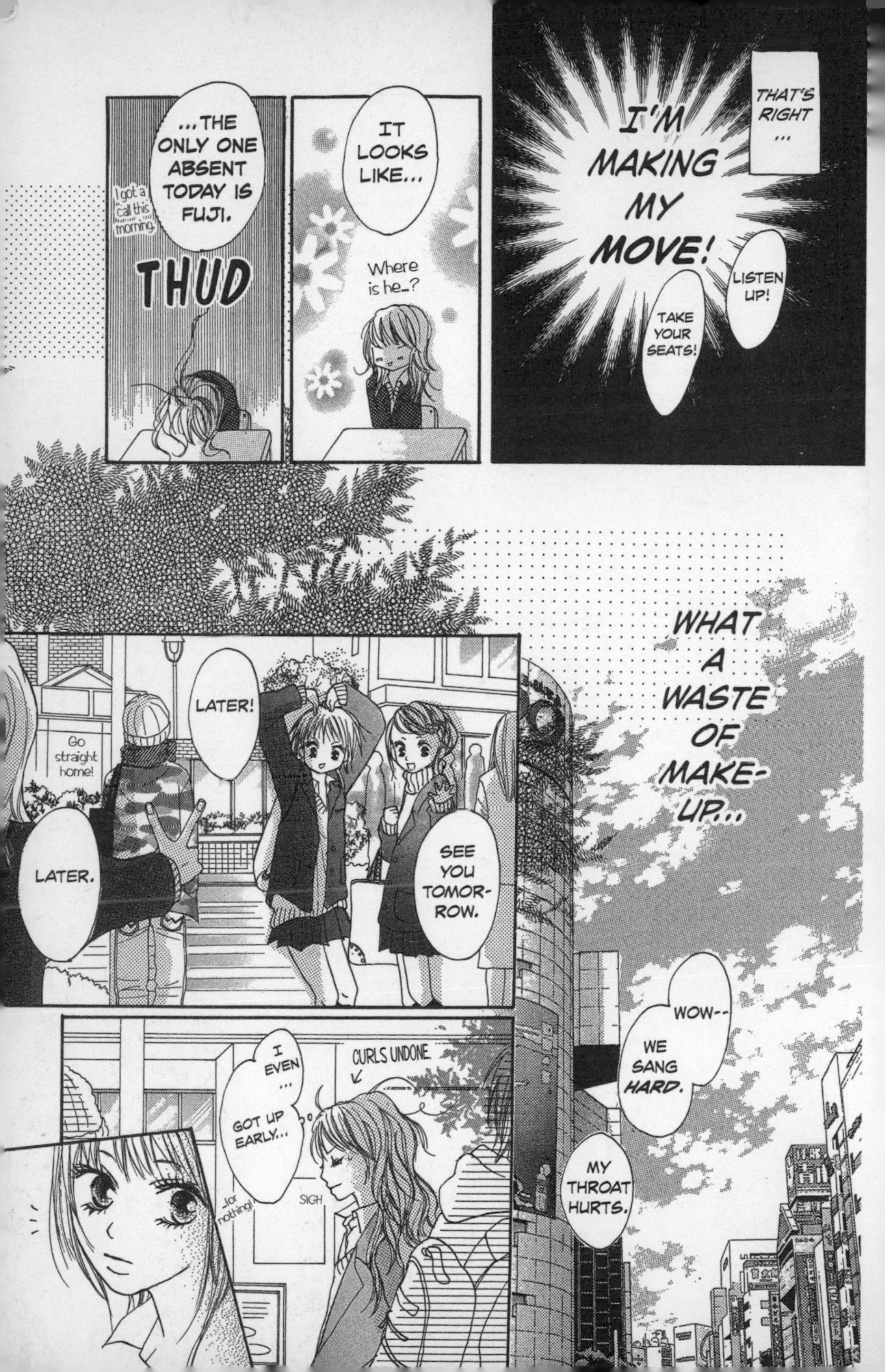
THAT'S RIGHT ...
I'M MAKING MY MOVE!
LISTEN UP!
TAKE YOUR SEATS!
IT LOOKS LIKE...
Where is he...?
...THE ONLY ONE ABSENT TODAY IS FUJI.
I got a call this morning.
THUD
WHAT A WASTE OF MAKE-UP...
WOW-- WE SANG HARD.
MY THROAT HURTS.
LATER!
SEE YOU TOMORROW.
Go straight home!
LATER.
CURLS UNDONE.
I EVEN ... GOT UP EARLY...
...for nothing!
SIGH

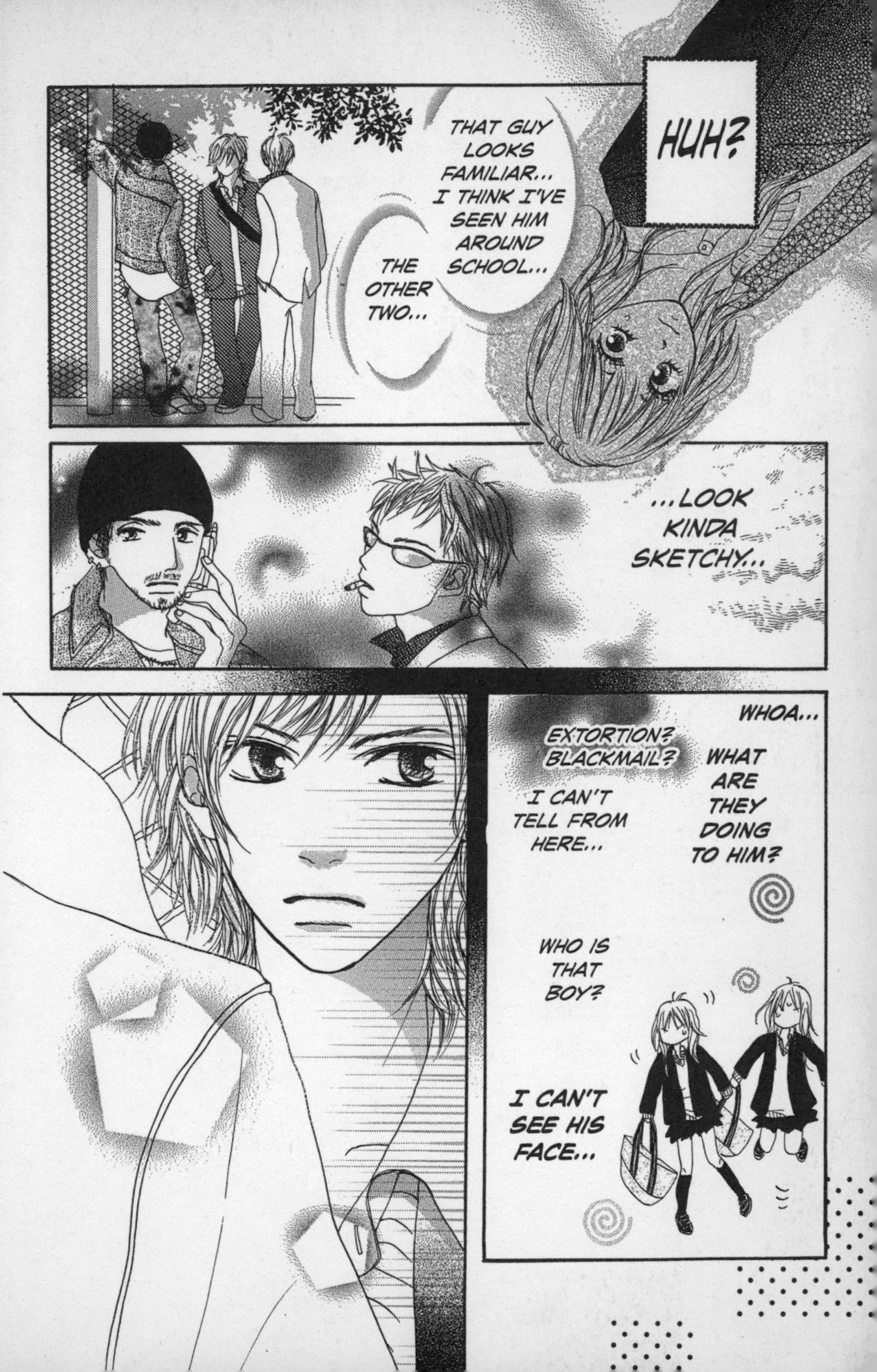
HUH?
THAT GUY LOOKS FAMILIAR... I THINK I'VE SEEN HIM AROUND SCHOOL...
THE OTHER TWO...
...LOOK KINDA SKETCHY...
WHOA...
WHAT ARE THEY DOING TO HIM?
EXTORTION? BLACKMAIL?
I CAN'T TELL FROM HERE...
WHO IS THAT BOY?
I CAN'T SEE HIS FACE...

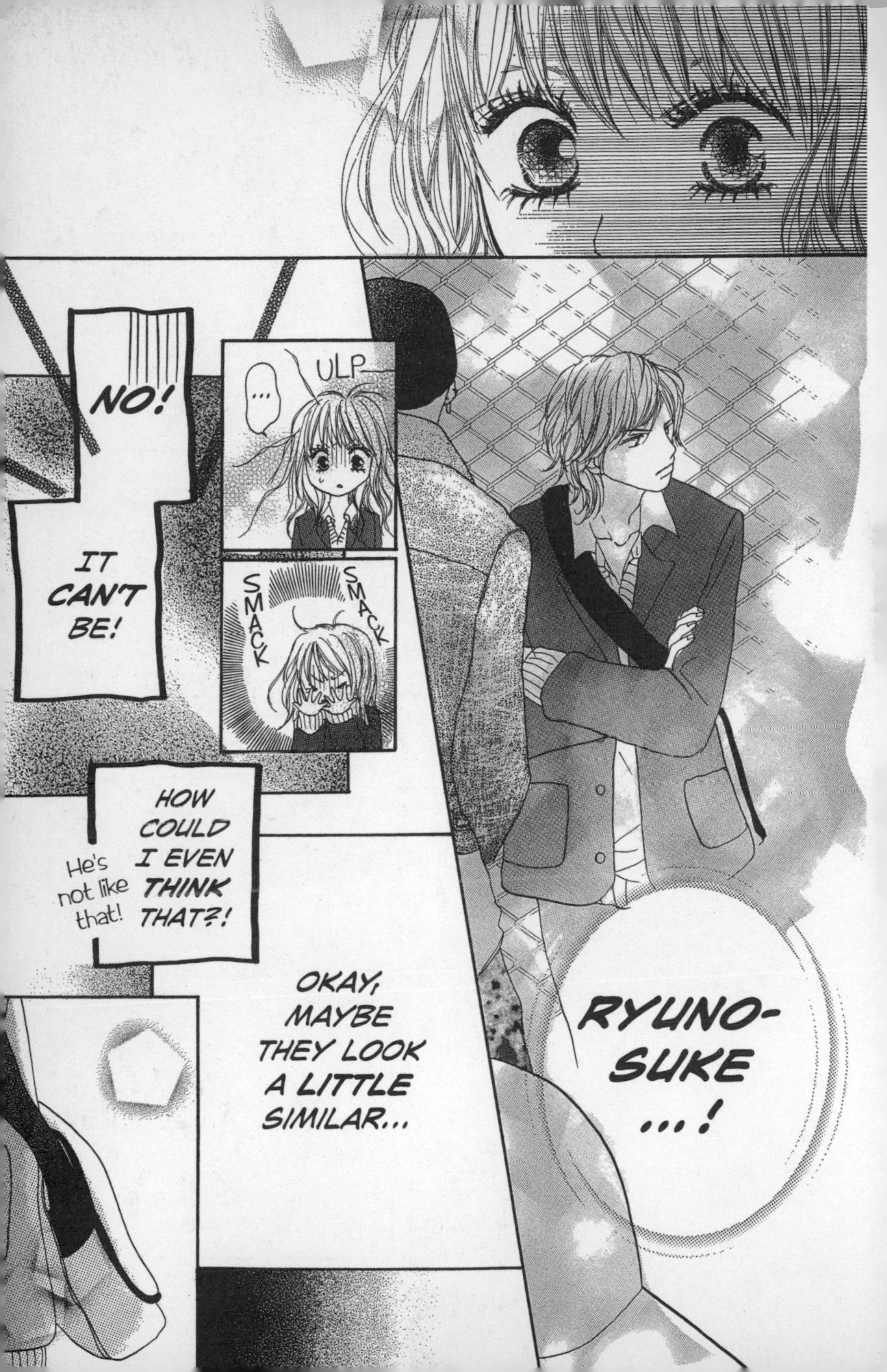
RYUNO-SUKE ...!
OKAY, MAYBE THEY LOOK A LITTLE SIMILAR...
NO!
...
ULP
IT CAN'T BE!
SMACK SMACK
HOW COULD I EVEN THINK THAT?!
He's not like that!

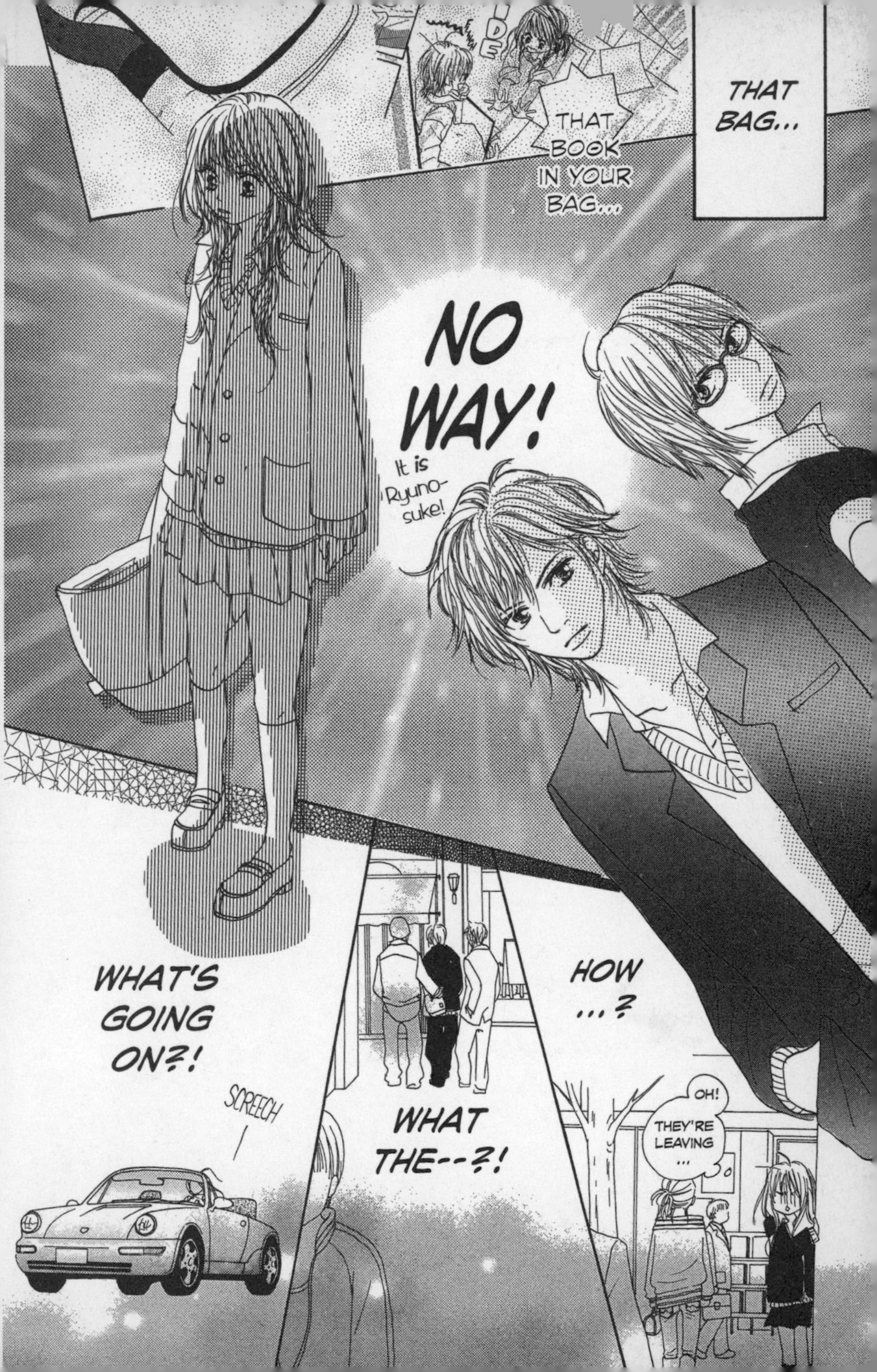
THAT BAG...
THAT BOOK IN YOUR BAG...
NO WAY!
It is Ryuno-suke!
HOW ...?
OH!
THEY'RE LEAVING ...
WHAT THE--?!
WHAT'S GOING ON?!
SCREECH

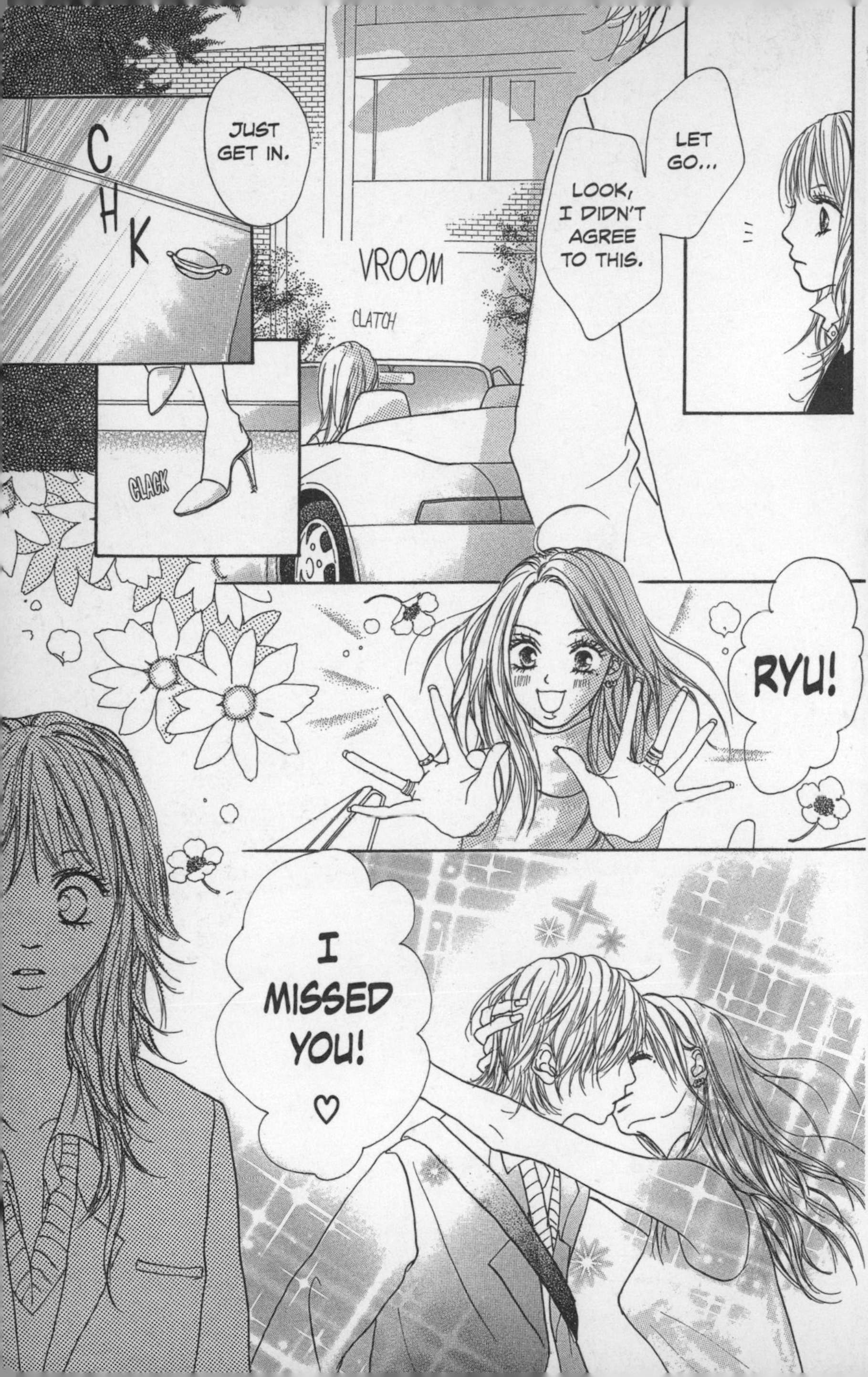
LET GO...
LOOK, I DIDN'T AGREE TO THIS.
JUST GET IN.
CHK
VROOM
CLATCH
CLACK
RYU!
I MISSED YOU! ♥

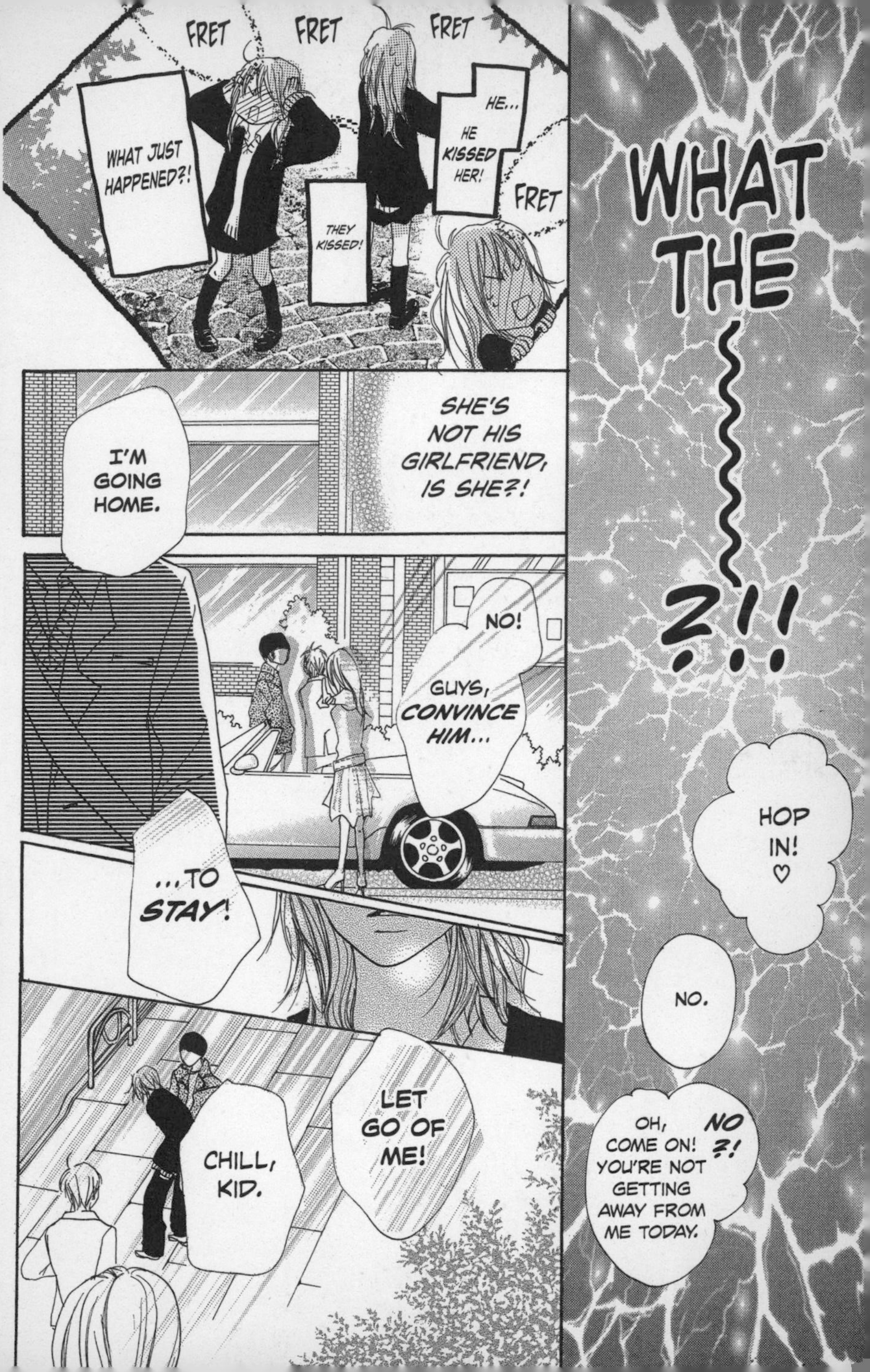
WHAT THE~?!!
HOP IN! ♡
NO.
NO?!
OH, COME ON! YOU'RE NOT GETTING AWAY FROM ME TODAY.
FRET FRET FRET
HE... HE KISSED HER!
THEY KISSED!
WHAT JUST HAPPENED?!
FRET
SHE'S NOT HIS GIRLFRIEND, IS SHE?!
I'M GOING HOME.
NO!
GUYS, CONVINCE HIM...
...TO STAY!
LET GO OF ME!
CHILL, KID.

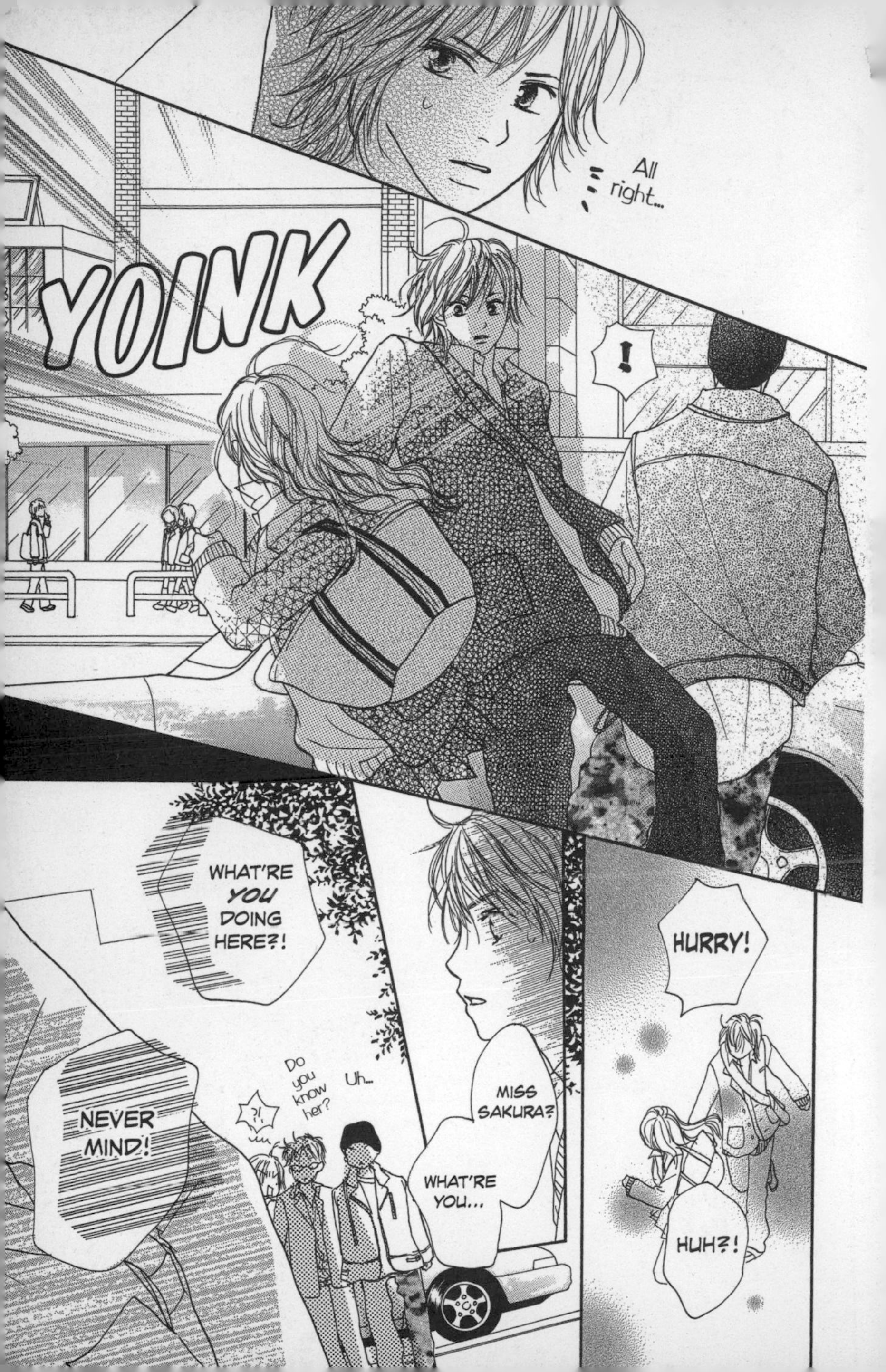
All right...
YOINK
!
HURRY!
HUH?!
MISS SAKURA?
WHAT'RE YOU...
Uh...
Do you know her?
?!
WHAT'RE YOU DOING HERE?!
NEVER MIND!

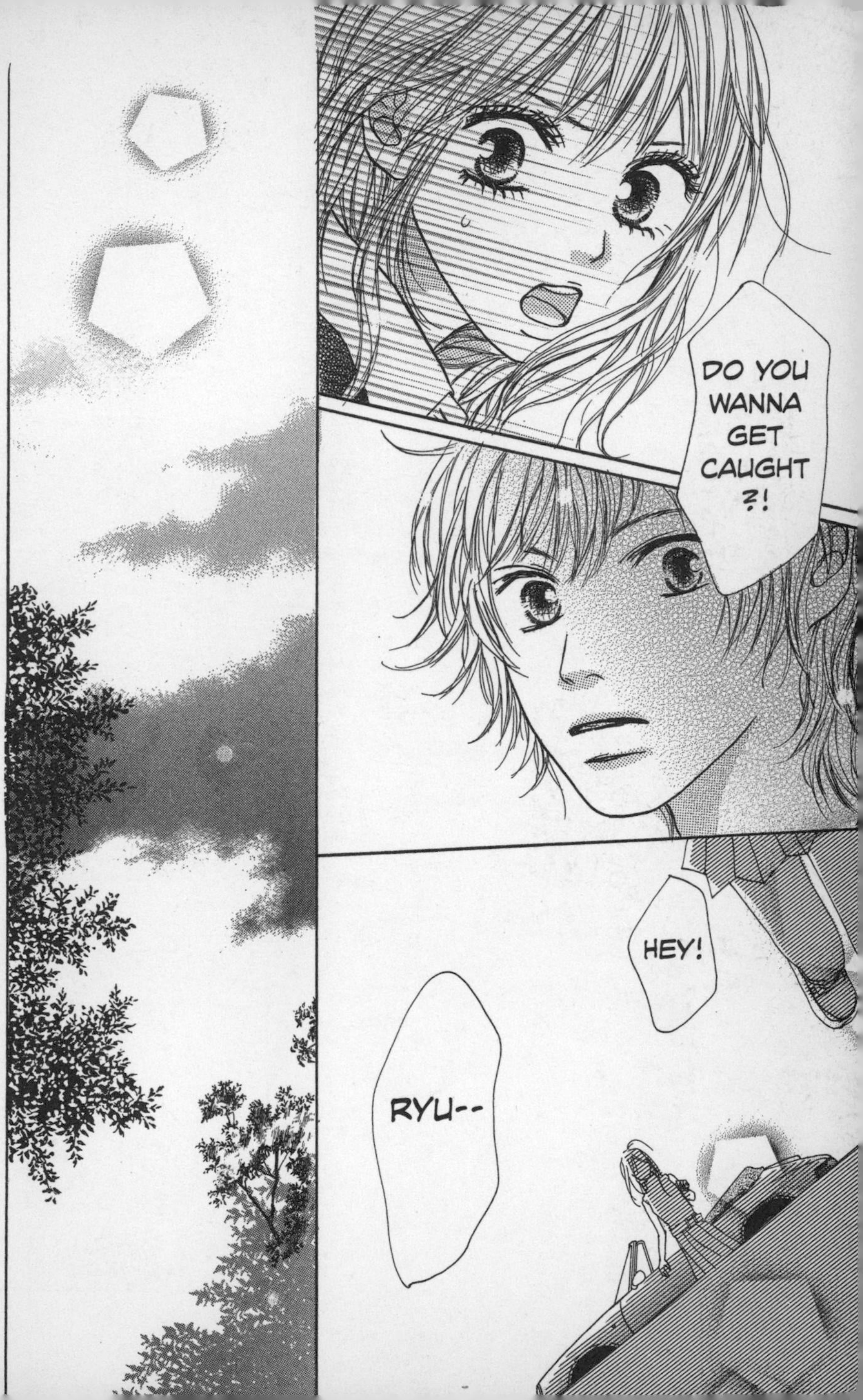
DO YOU WANNA GET CAUGHT ?!
HEY!
RYU--

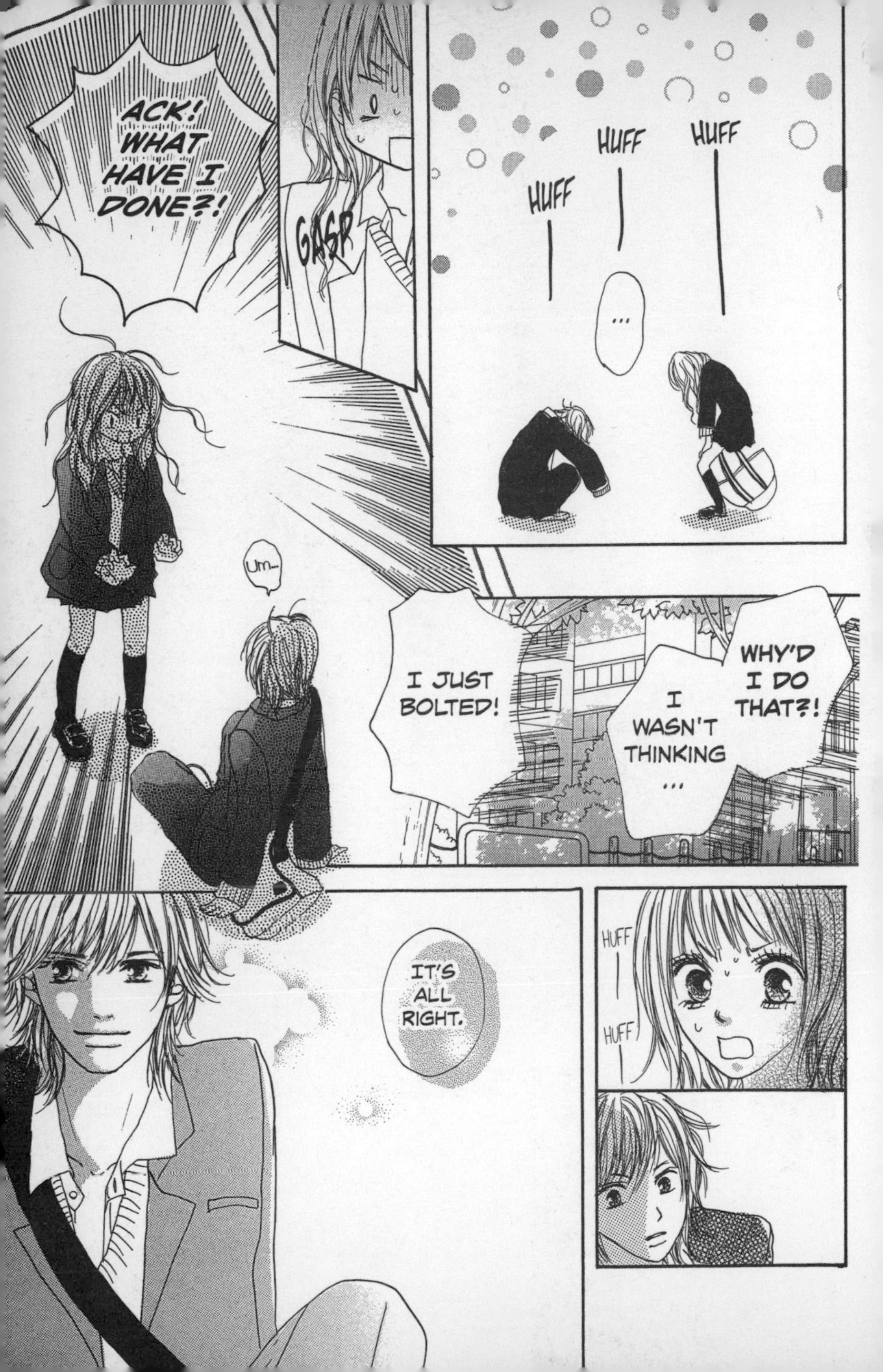

HUFF
HUFF
HUFF
...
GASP
ACK! WHAT HAVE I DONE?!
Um...
WHY'D I DO THAT?!
I WASN'T THINKING...
I JUST BOLTED!
HUFF
HUFF
IT'S ALL RIGHT.

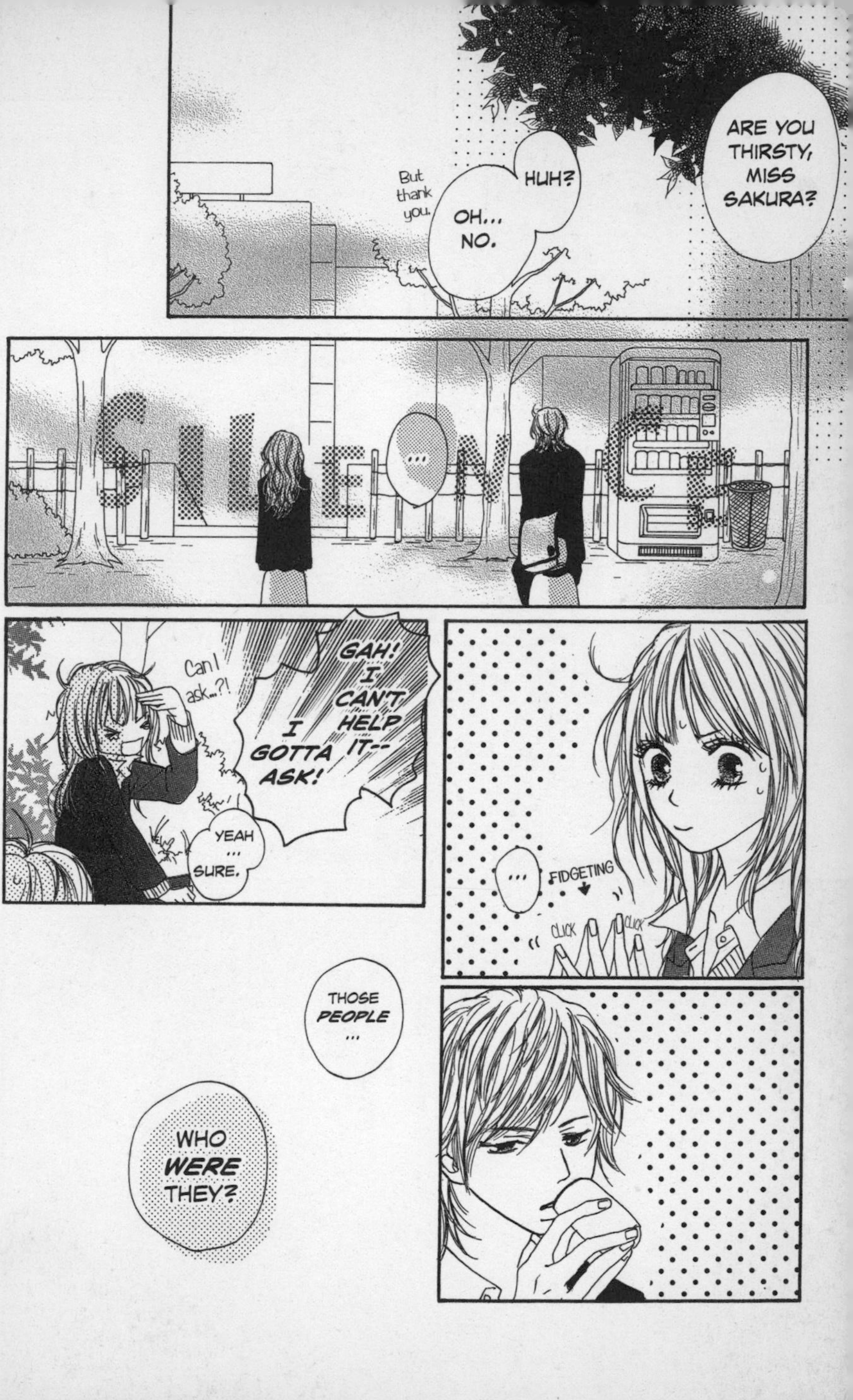
ARE YOU THIRSTY, MISS SAKURA?
HUH?
OH... NO.
But thank you.
SILENCE
...
...
FIDGETING
CLICK
CLICK
GAH! I CAN'T HELP IT-- I GOTTA ASK!
Can I ask...?!
YEAH ... SURE.
THOSE *PEOPLE* ...
WHO *WERE* THEY?

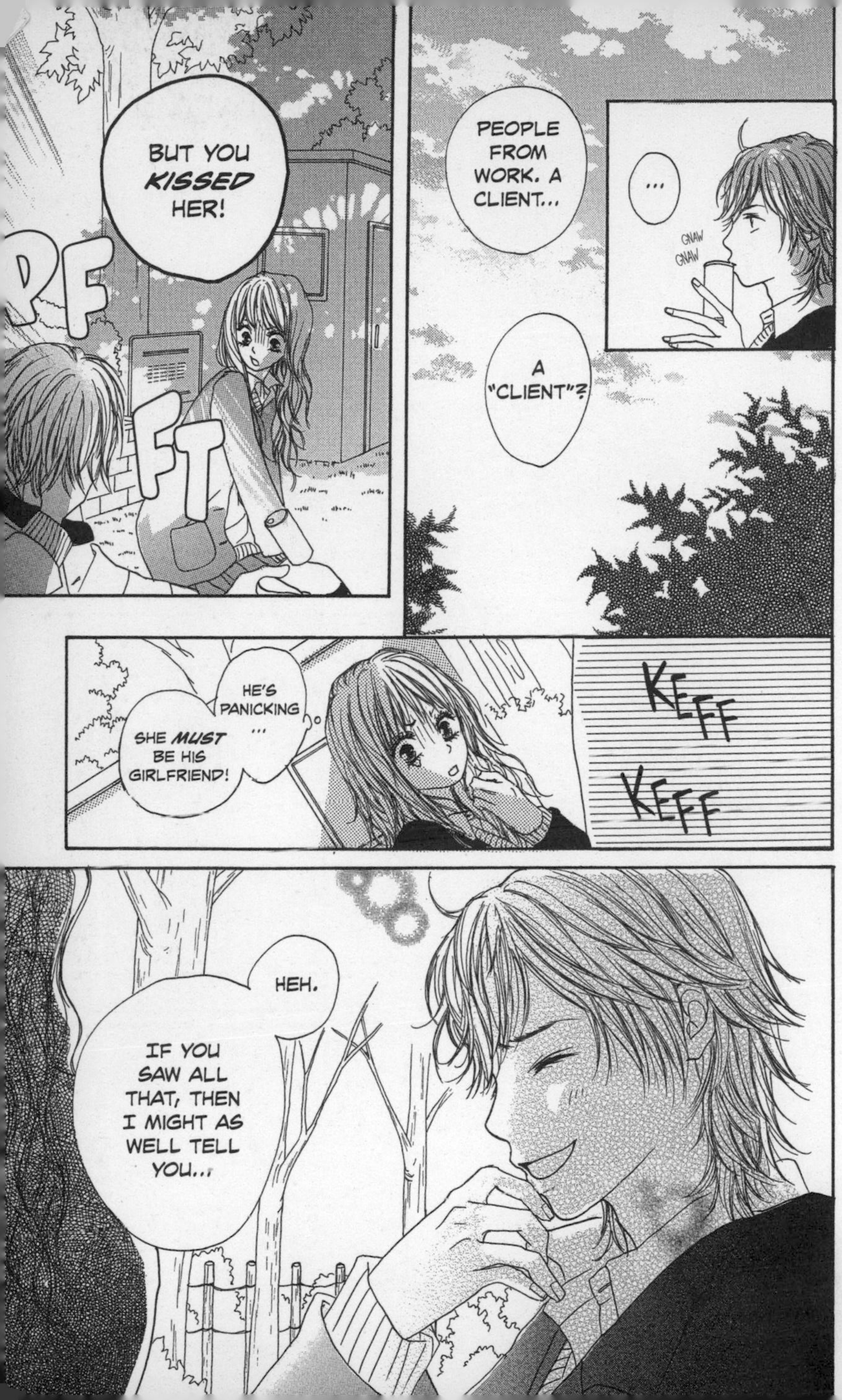
PEOPLE FROM WORK. A CLIENT...
...
GNAW GNAW
A "CLIENT"?
BUT YOU *KISSED* HER!
PFFT
KEFF KEFF
HE'S PANICKING...
SHE *MUST* BE HIS GIRLFRIEND!
HEH.
IF YOU SAW ALL THAT, THEN I MIGHT AS WELL TELL YOU...

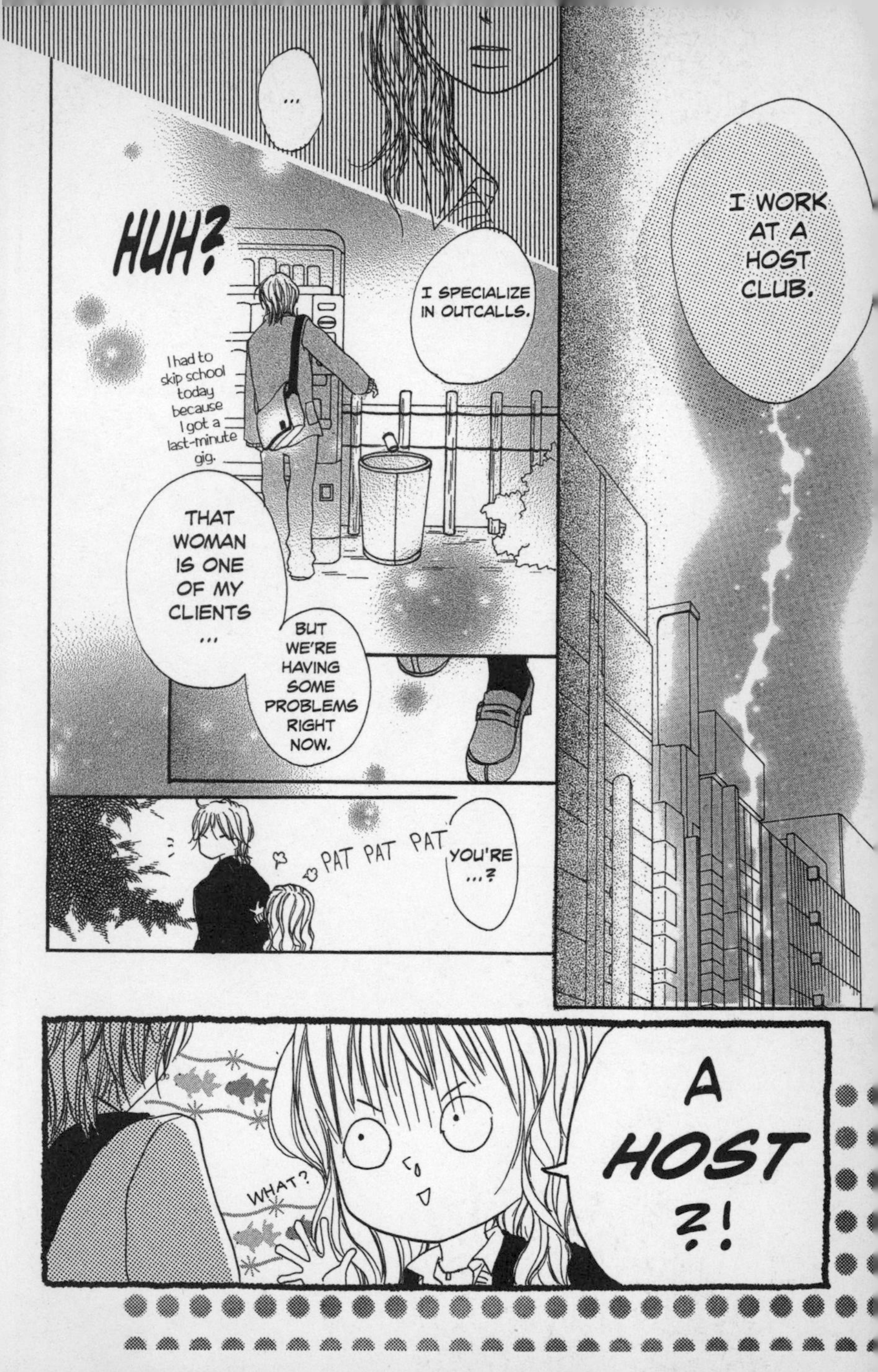
I WORK AT A HOST CLUB.
...
HUH?
I SPECIALIZE IN OUTCALLS.
I had to skip school today because I got a last-minute gig.
THAT WOMAN IS ONE OF MY CLIENTS ...
BUT WE'RE HAVING SOME PROBLEMS RIGHT NOW.
YOU'RE ...?
PAT PAT PAT
A HOST ?!
WHAT?

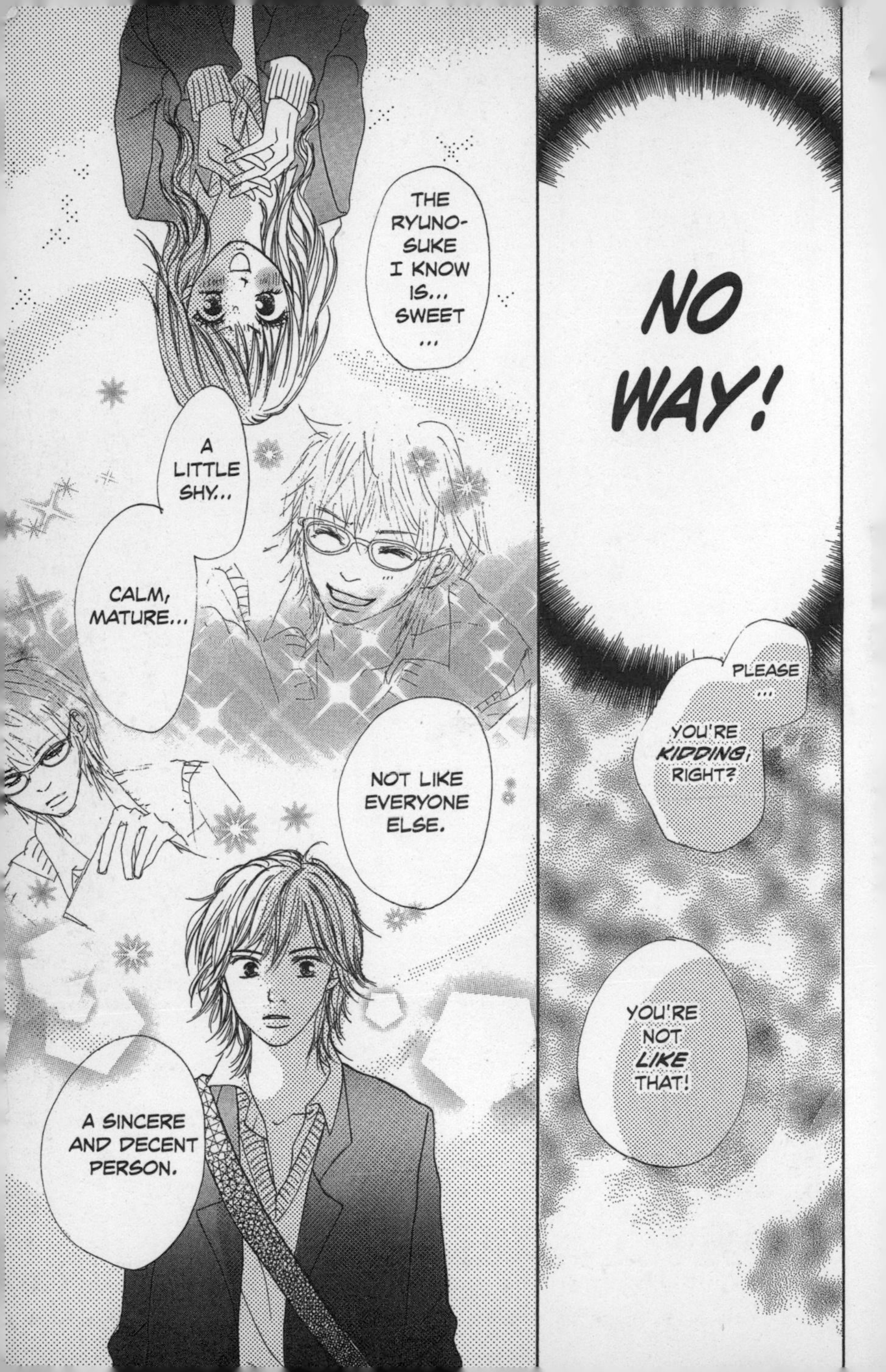
NO WAY!
PLEASE... YOU'RE KIDDING, RIGHT?
YOU'RE NOT LIKE THAT!
THE RYUNO-SUKE I KNOW IS... SWEET...
A LITTLE SHY...
CALM, MATURE...
NOT LIKE EVERYONE ELSE.
A SINCERE AND DECENT PERSON.

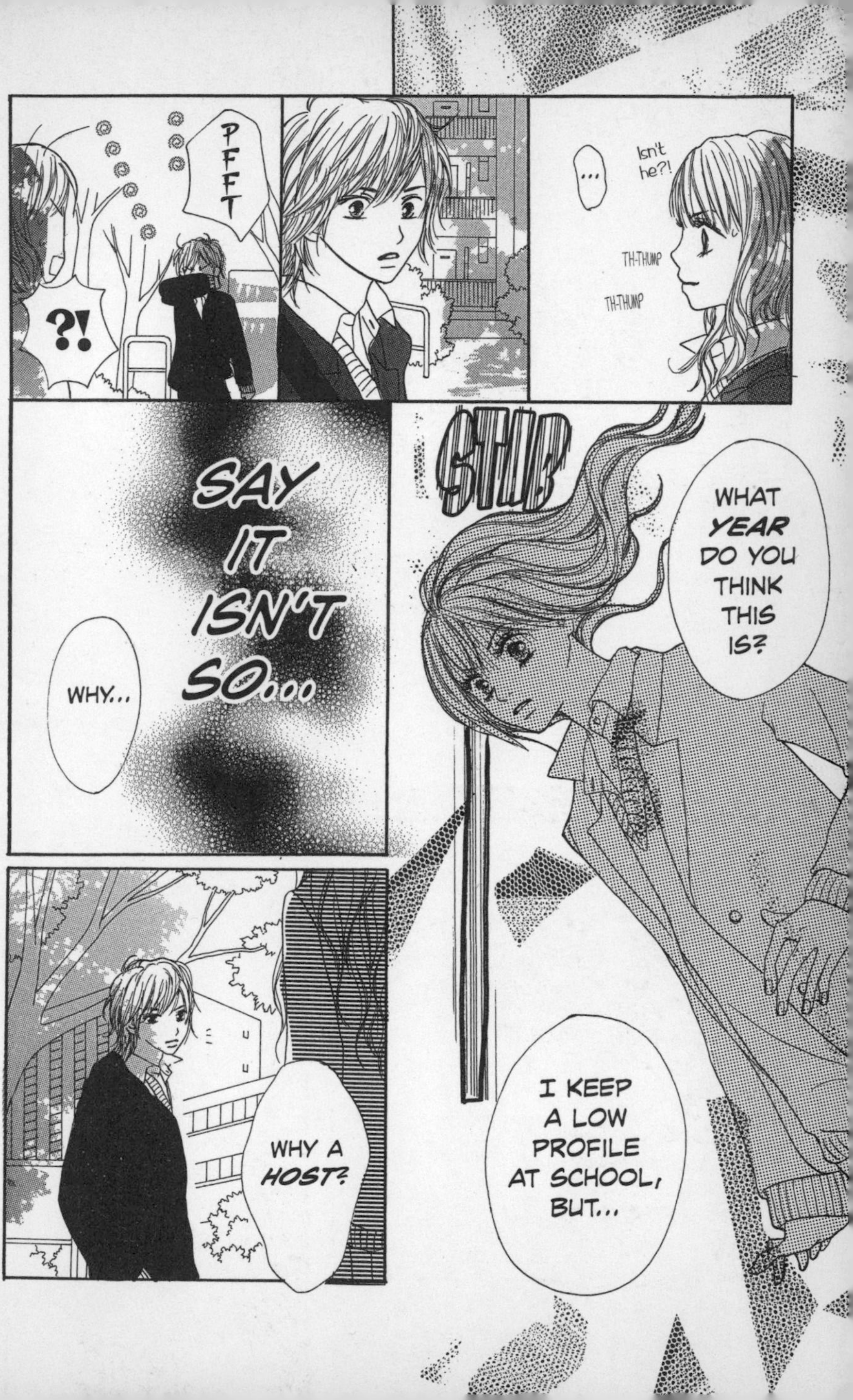
...
Isn't he?!
TH-THUMP
TH-THUMP
PFFT
?!
STAB
WHAT YEAR DO YOU THINK THIS IS?
SAY IT ISN'T SO...
WHY...
I KEEP A LOW PROFILE AT SCHOOL, BUT...
WHY A HOST?

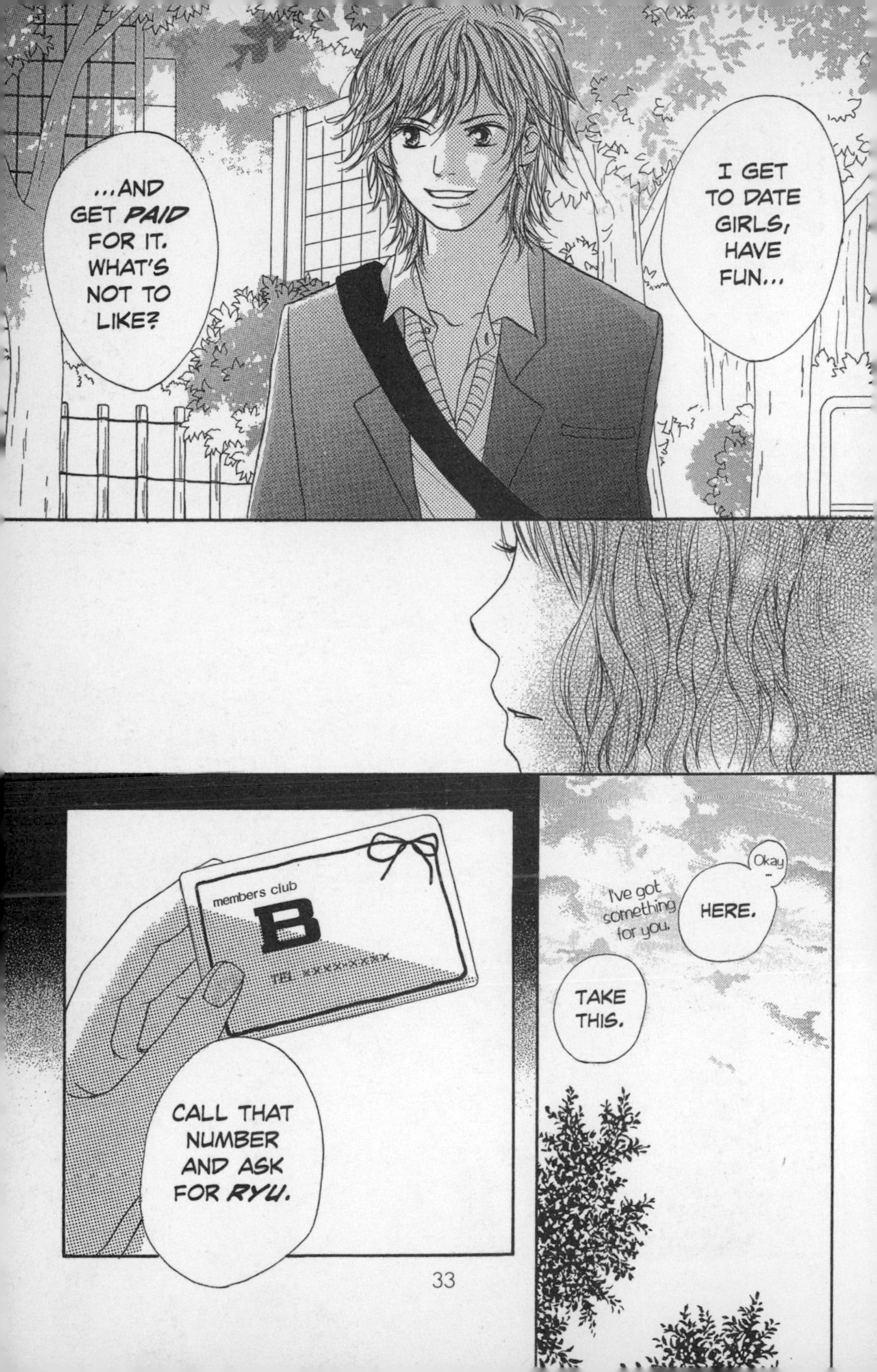
I GET TO DATE GIRLS, HAVE FUN...
...AND GET PAID FOR IT. WHAT'S NOT TO LIKE?
Okay...
HERE.
I've got something for you.
TAKE THIS.
members club
B
TEL xxxx-xxxx
CALL THAT NUMBER AND ASK FOR RYU.

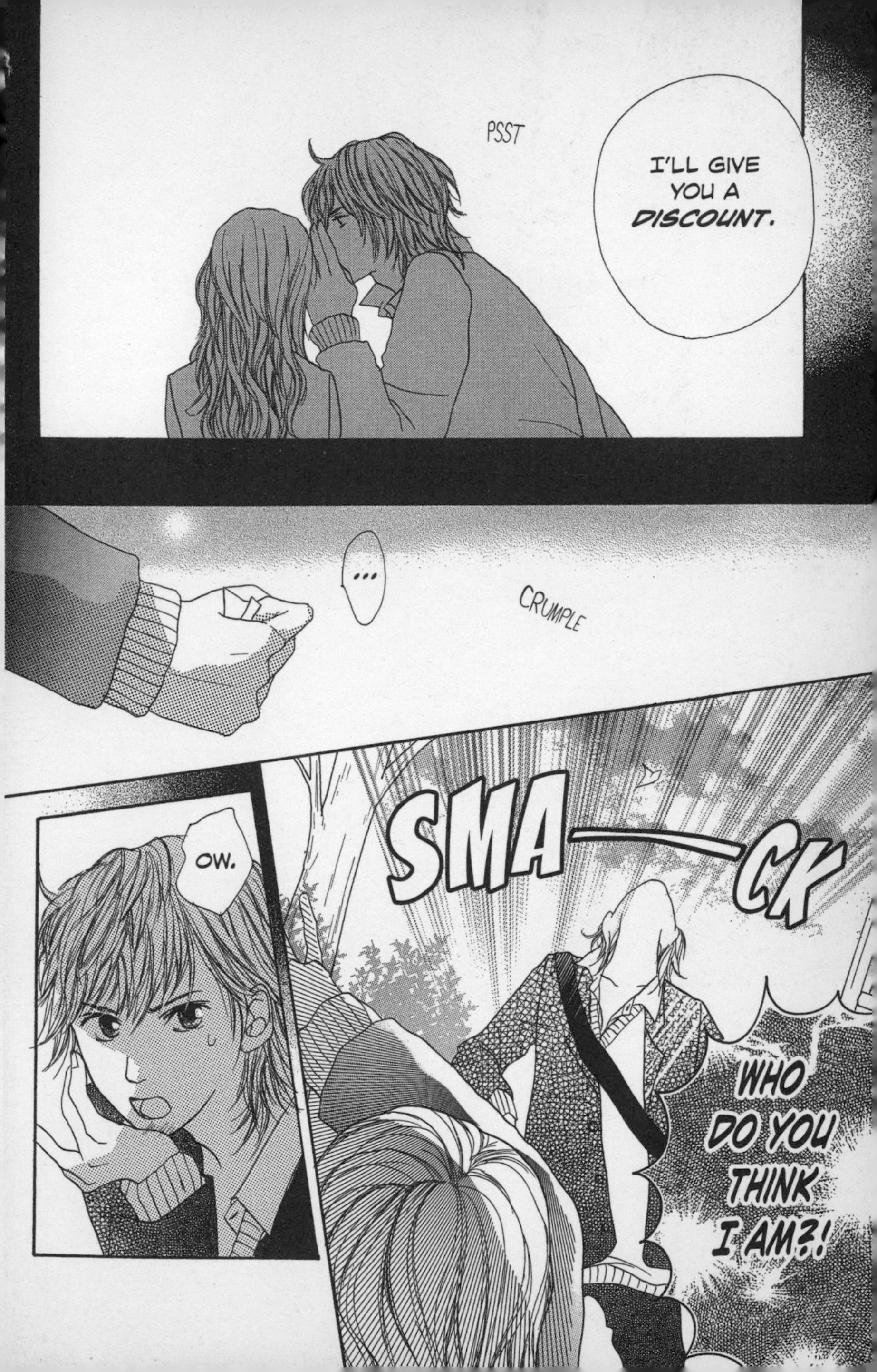
PSST
I'LL GIVE YOU A DISCOUNT.
...
CRUMPLE
SMA——CK
WHO DO YOU THINK I AM?!
OW.

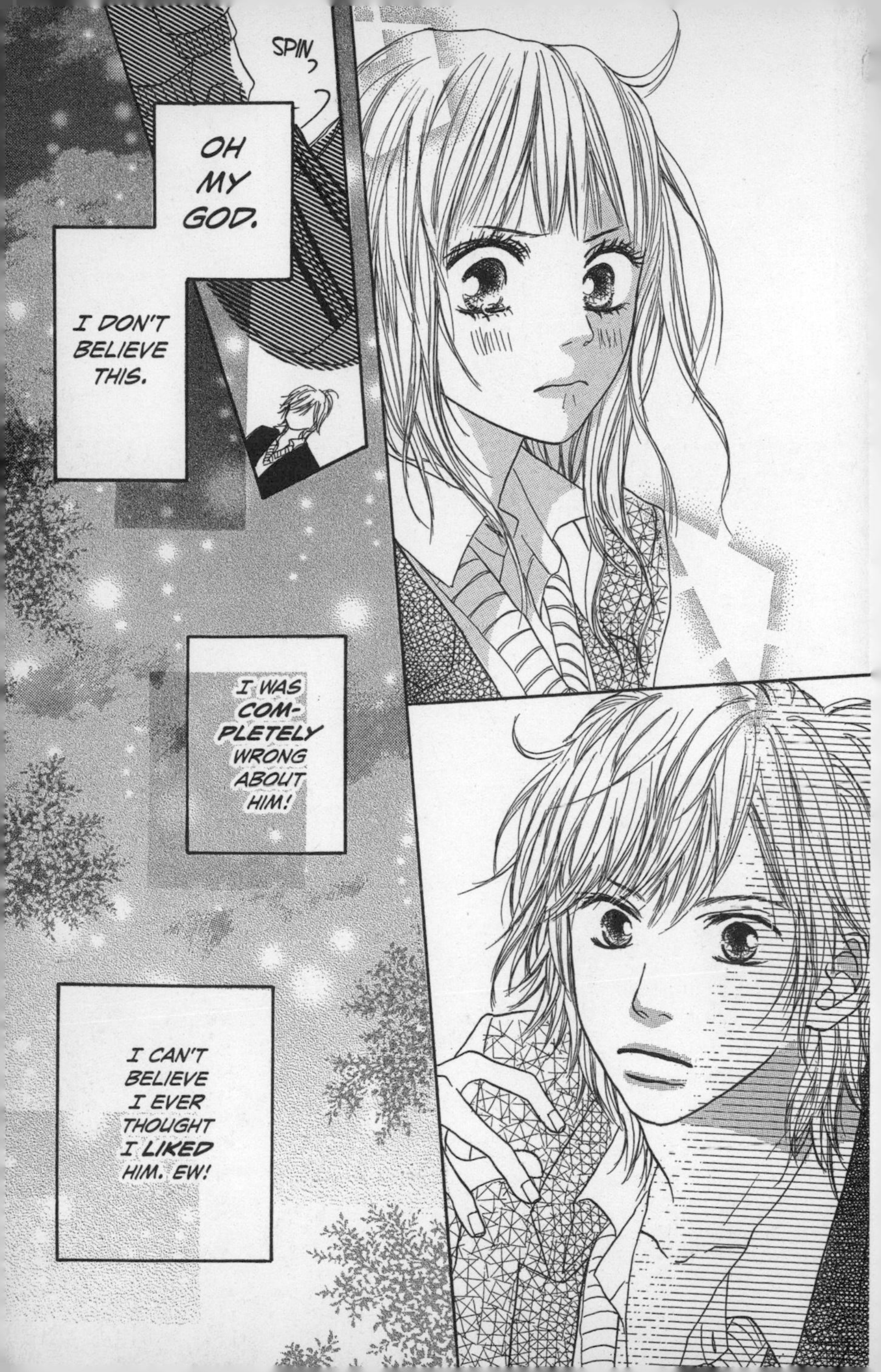
SPIN
OH MY GOD.
I DON'T BELIEVE THIS.
I WAS COM-PLETELY WRONG ABOUT HIM!
I CAN'T BELIEVE I EVER THOUGHT I LIKED HIM. EW!

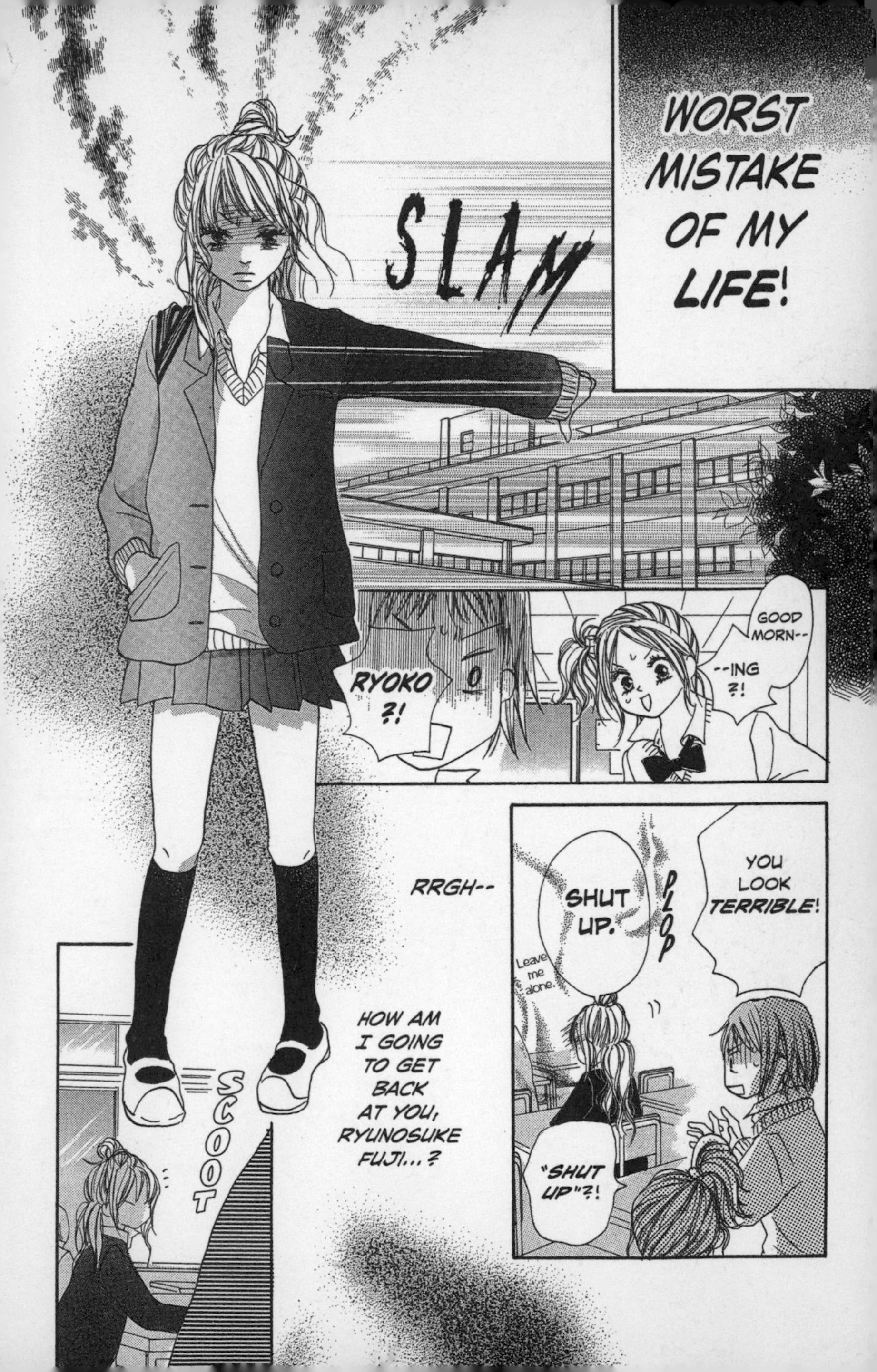
WORST MISTAKE OF MY LIFE!
SLAM
GOOD MORN--
--ING?!
RYOKO?!
YOU LOOK TERRIBLE!
PLOP
SHUT UP.
Leave me alone.
RRGH--
"SHUT UP"?!
HOW AM I GOING TO GET BACK AT YOU, RYUNOSUKE FUJI...?
SCOOT

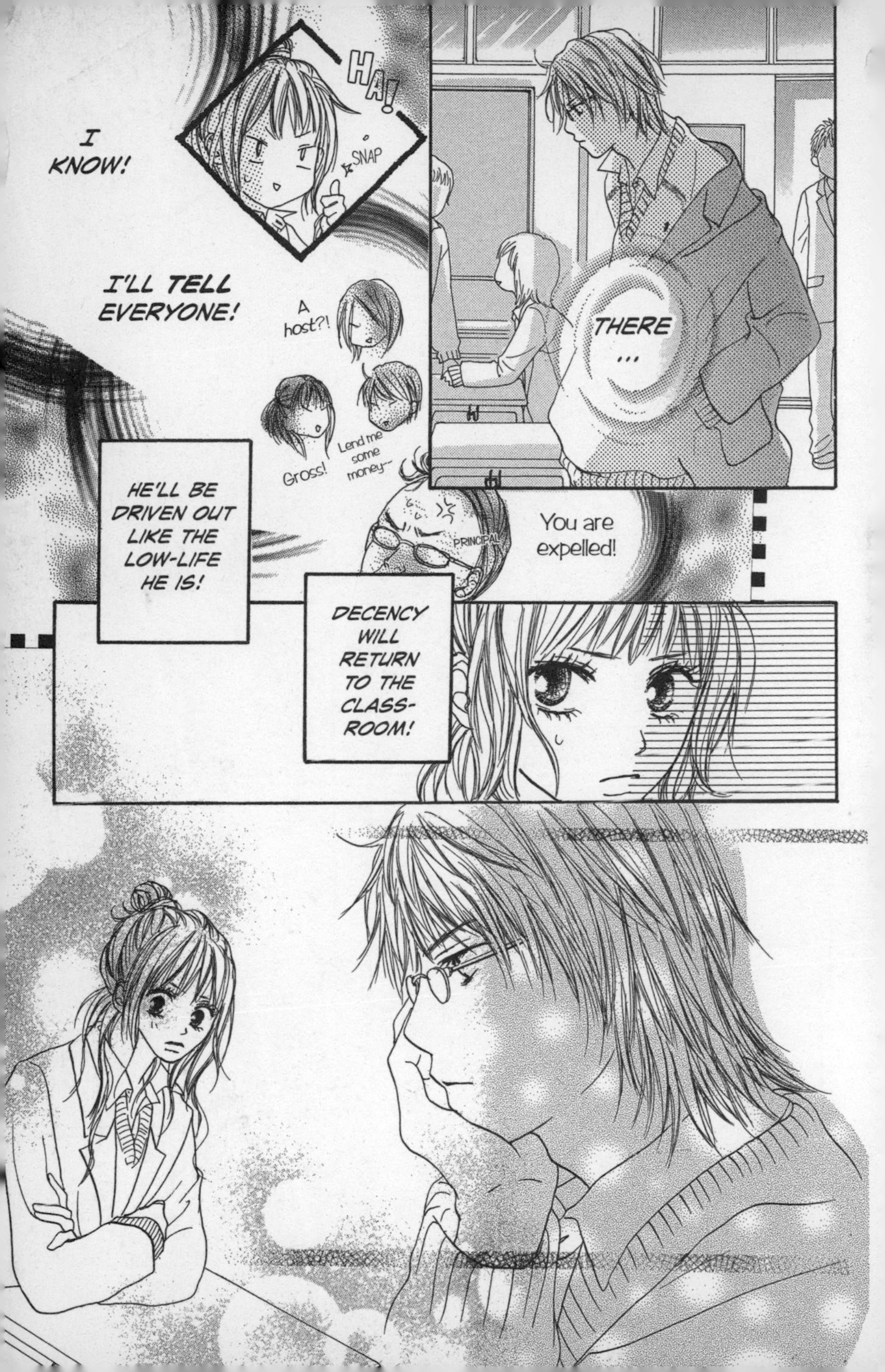
THERE ...
HA!
SNAP
I KNOW!
I'LL TELL EVERYONE!
A host?!
Lend me some money~
Gross!
You are expelled!
PRINCIPAL
HE'LL BE DRIVEN OUT LIKE THE LOW-LIFE HE IS!
DECENCY WILL RETURN TO THE CLASSROOM!

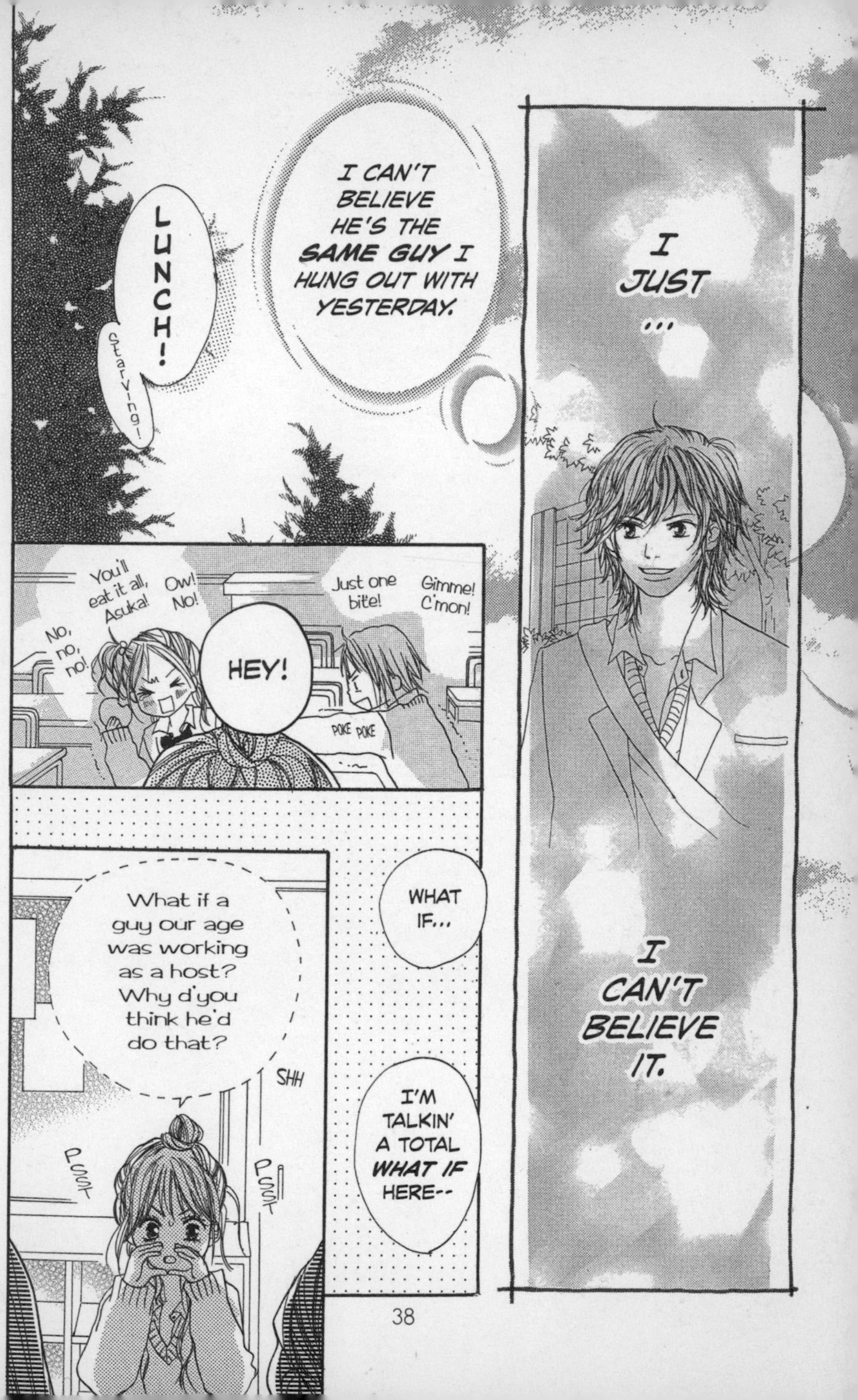
I CAN'T BELIEVE HE'S THE SAME GUY I HUNG OUT WITH YESTERDAY.
I JUST...
I CAN'T BELIEVE IT.
LUNCH!
Starving!
Gimme! C'mon!
Just one bite!
POKE POKE
HEY!
Ow! No!
You'll eat it all, Asuka!
No, no, no!
WHAT IF...
I'M TALKIN' A TOTAL WHAT IF HERE--
What if a guy our age was working as a host? Why d'you think he'd do that?
SHH
PSST
PSST

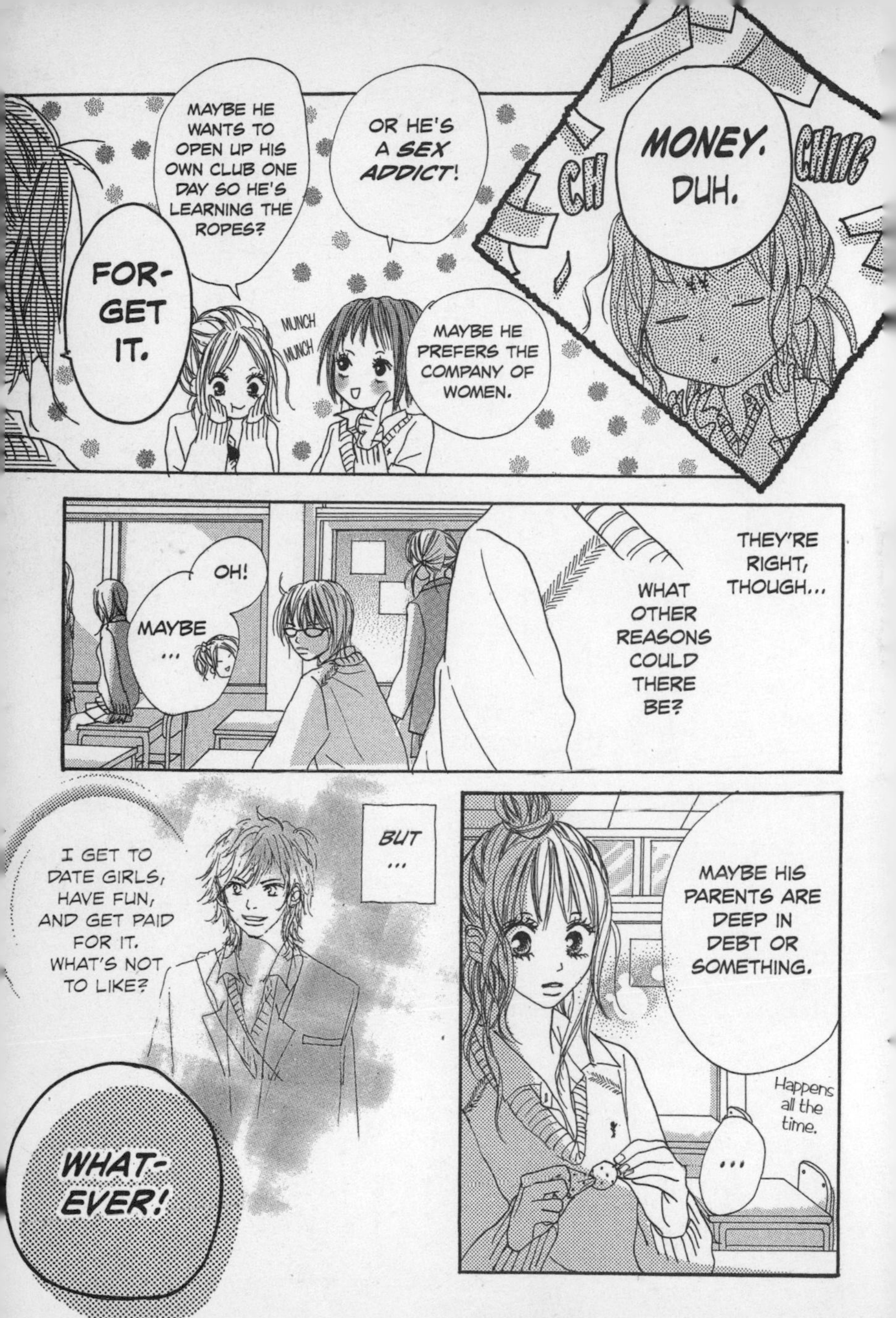
MAYBE HE PREFERS THE COMPANY OF WOMEN.
OR HE'S A SEX ADDICT!
MAYBE HE WANTS TO OPEN UP HIS OWN CLUB ONE DAY SO HE'S LEARNING THE ROPES?
MUNCH MUNCH
FOR-GET IT.
CH
CHING
MONEY. DUH.
THEY'RE RIGHT, THOUGH...
WHAT OTHER REASONS COULD THERE BE?
OH!
MAYBE ...
MAYBE HIS PARENTS ARE DEEP IN DEBT OR SOMETHING.
Happens all the time.
...
BUT ...
I GET TO DATE GIRLS, HAVE FUN, AND GET PAID FOR IT. WHAT'S NOT TO LIKE?
WHAT-EVER!

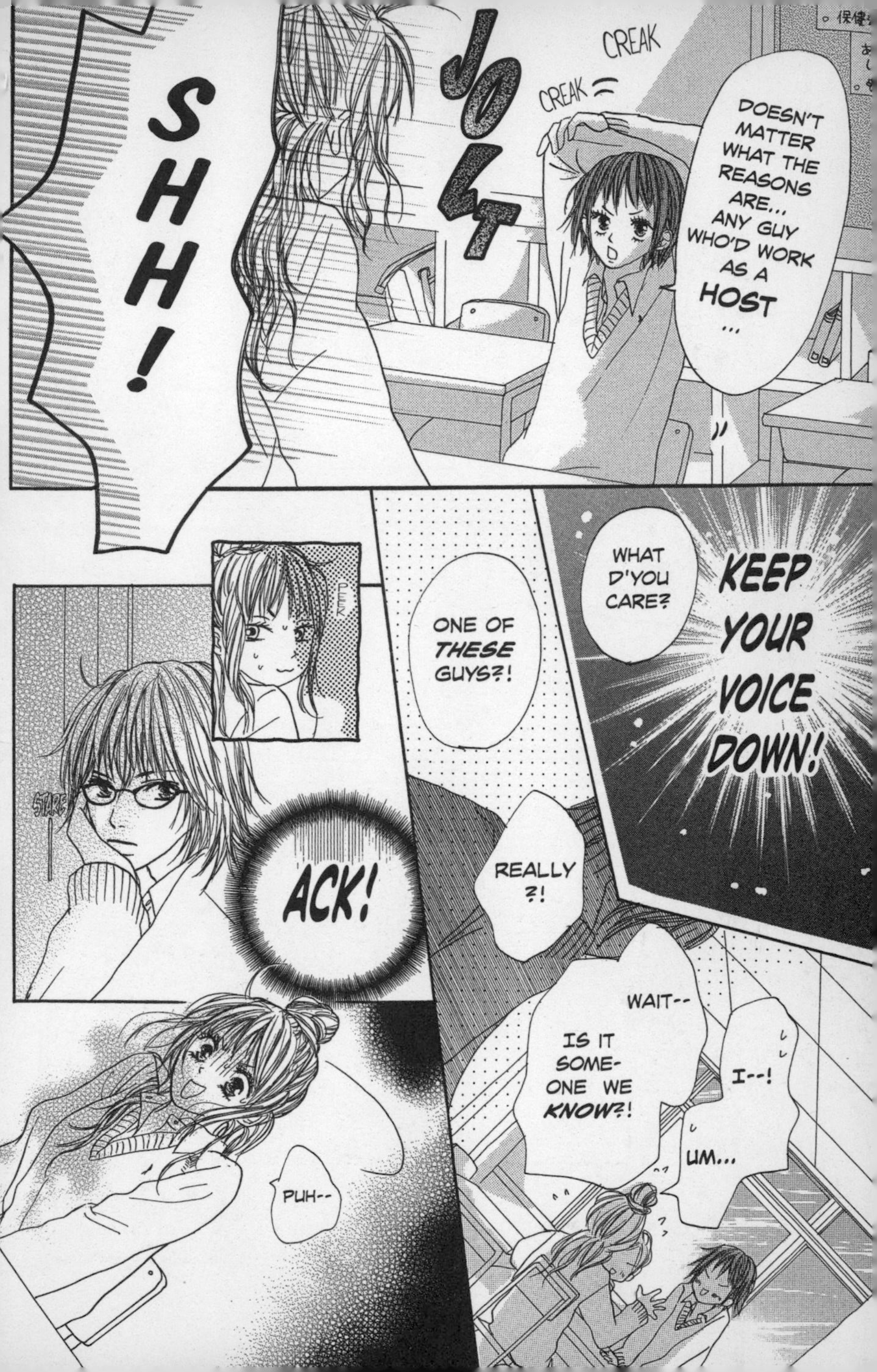
CREAK
CREAK
DOESN'T MATTER WHAT THE REASONS ARE... ANY GUY WHO'D WORK AS A HOST...
JOLT
SHH!
KEEP YOUR VOICE DOWN!
WHAT D'YOU CARE?
ONE OF THESE GUYS?!
REALLY ?!
WAIT--
IS IT SOMEONE WE KNOW?!
I--!
UM...
PEEK
STARE
ACK!
PUH--

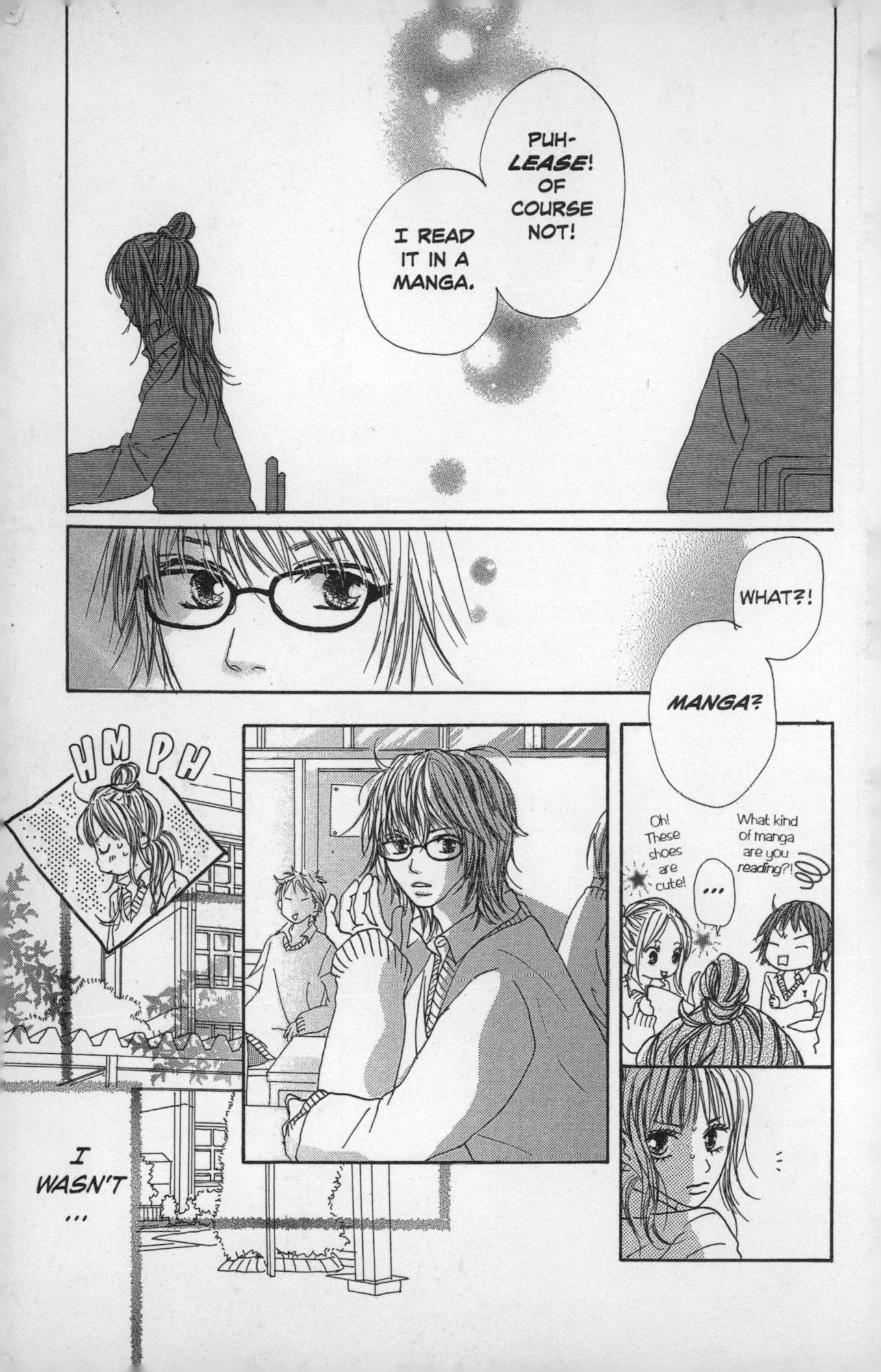
PUH-LEASE! OF COURSE NOT!
I READ IT IN A MANGA.
WHAT?!
MANGA?
What kind of manga are you reading?!
...
Oh! These shoes are cute!
HMPH
I WASN'T ...

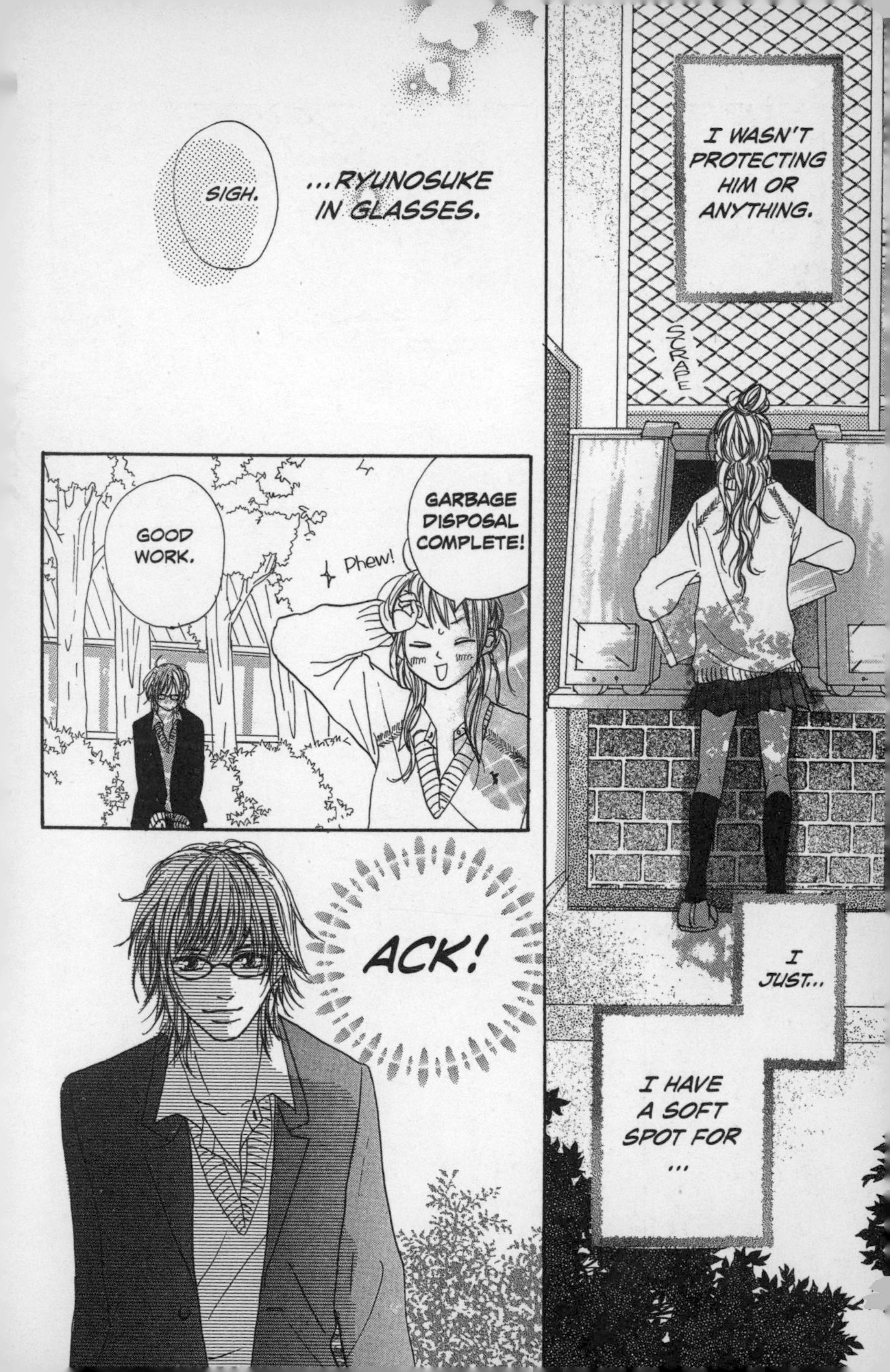
I WASN'T PROTECTING HIM OR ANYTHING.
SCRAPE
I JUST...
I HAVE A SOFT SPOT FOR ...
...RYUNOSUKE IN GLASSES.
SIGH.
GARBAGE DISPOSAL COMPLETE!
Phew!
GOOD WORK.
ACK!

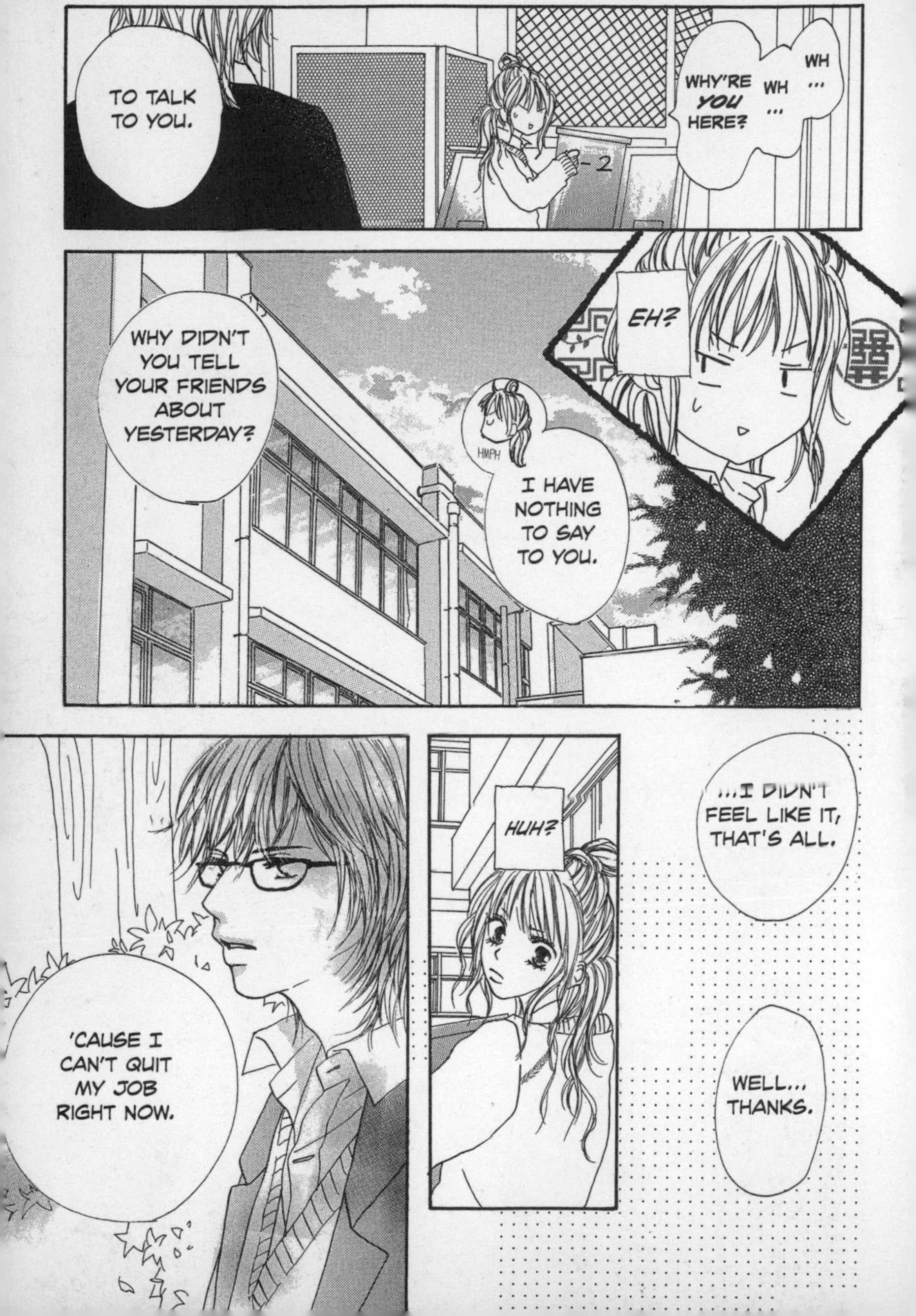
WH ...
WH ...
WHY'RE YOU HERE?
TO TALK TO YOU.
HMPH
I HAVE NOTHING TO SAY TO YOU.
WHY DIDN'T YOU TELL YOUR FRIENDS ABOUT YESTERDAY?
EH?
...I DIDN'T FEEL LIKE IT, THAT'S ALL.
WELL... THANKS.
HUH?
'CAUSE I CAN'T QUIT MY JOB RIGHT NOW.

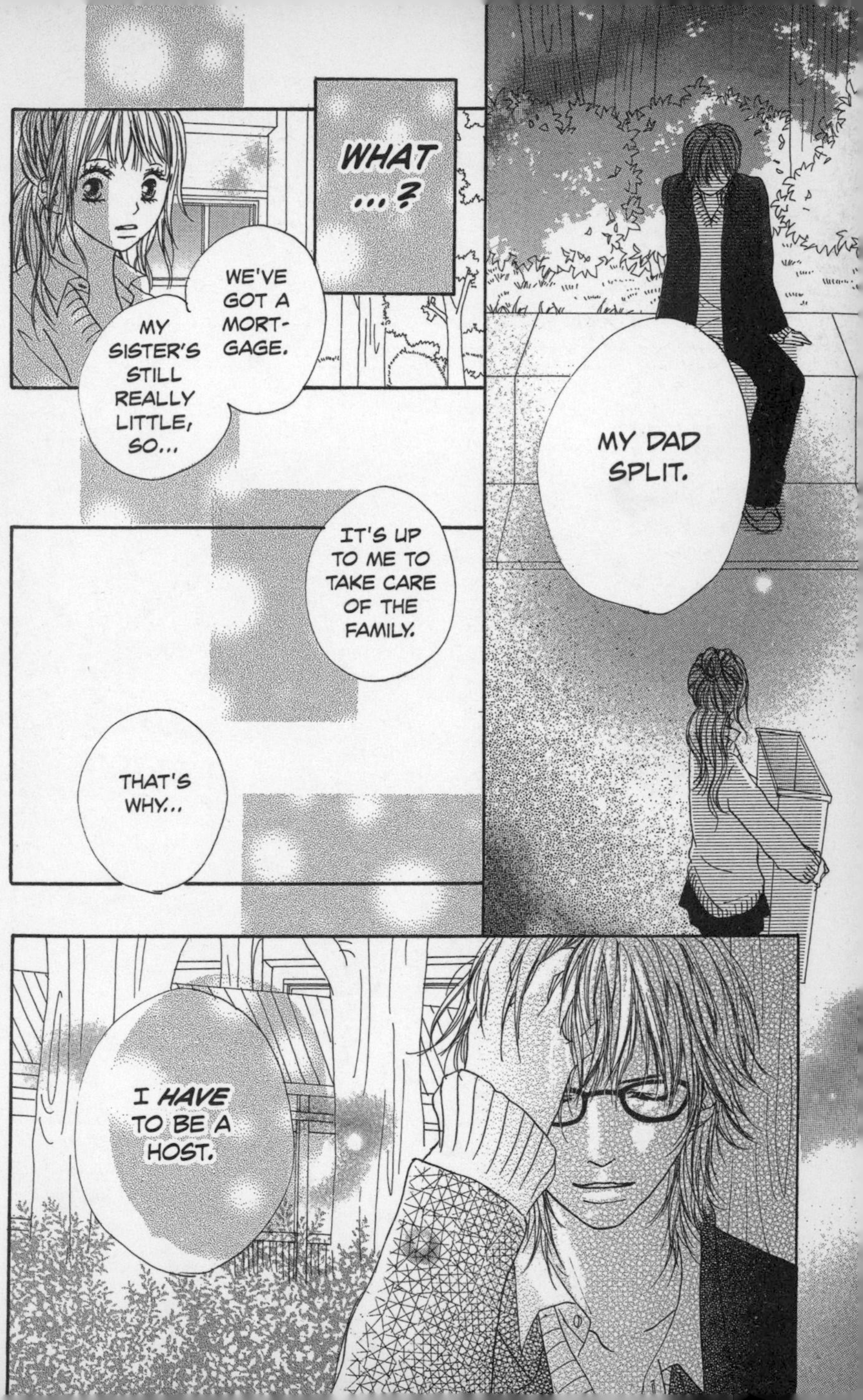
MY DAD SPLIT.
WHAT ...?
WE'VE GOT A MORT-GAGE.
MY SISTER'S STILL REALLY LITTLE, SO...
IT'S UP TO ME TO TAKE CARE OF THE FAMILY.
THAT'S WHY...
I *HAVE* TO BE A HOST.

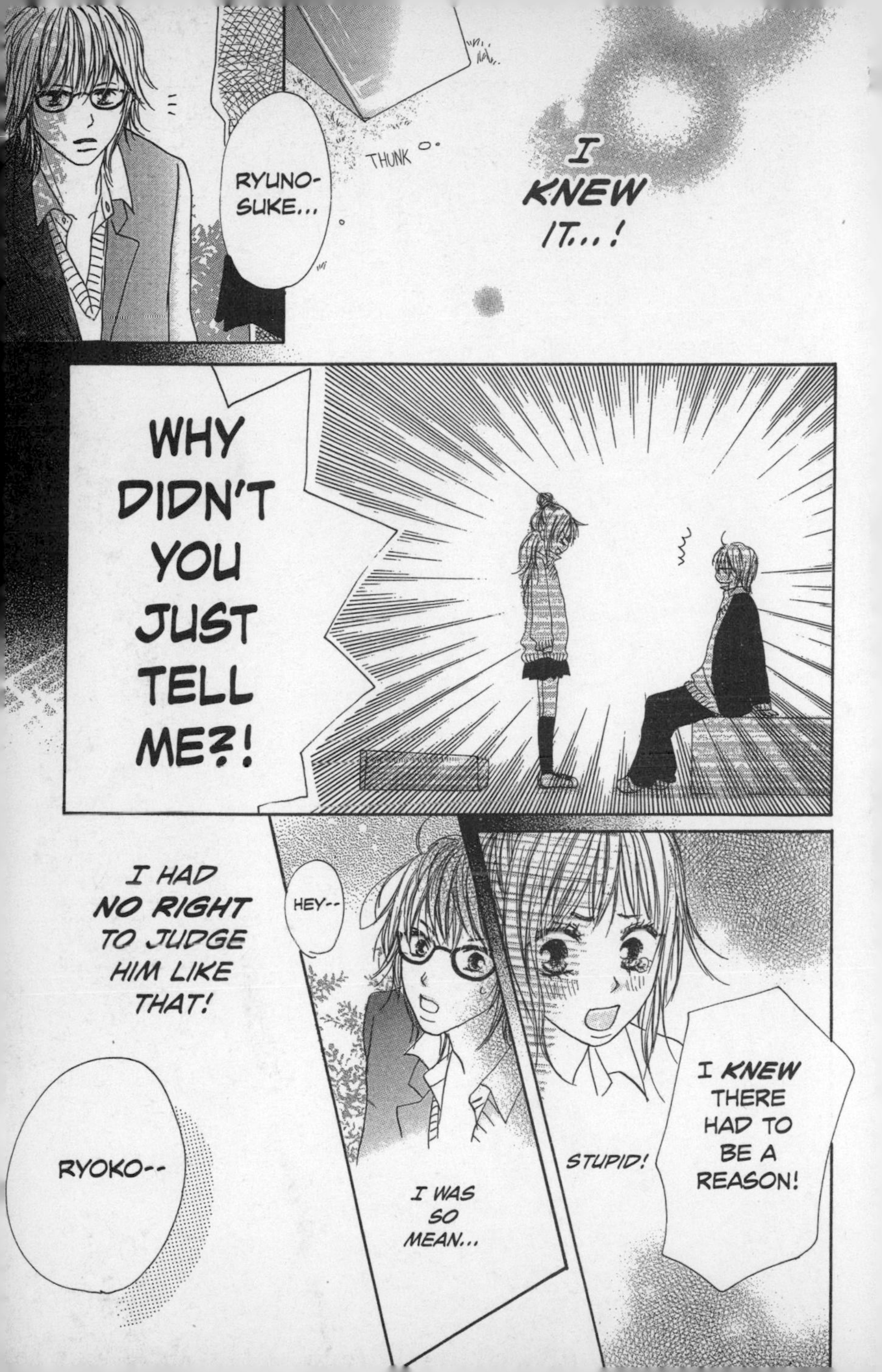
I KNEW IT...!
THUNK
RYUNO-SUKE...
WHY DIDN'T YOU JUST TELL ME?!
I KNEW THERE HAD TO BE A REASON!
STUPID!
I WAS SO MEAN...
HEY--
I HAD NO RIGHT TO JUDGE HIM LIKE THAT!
RYOKO--

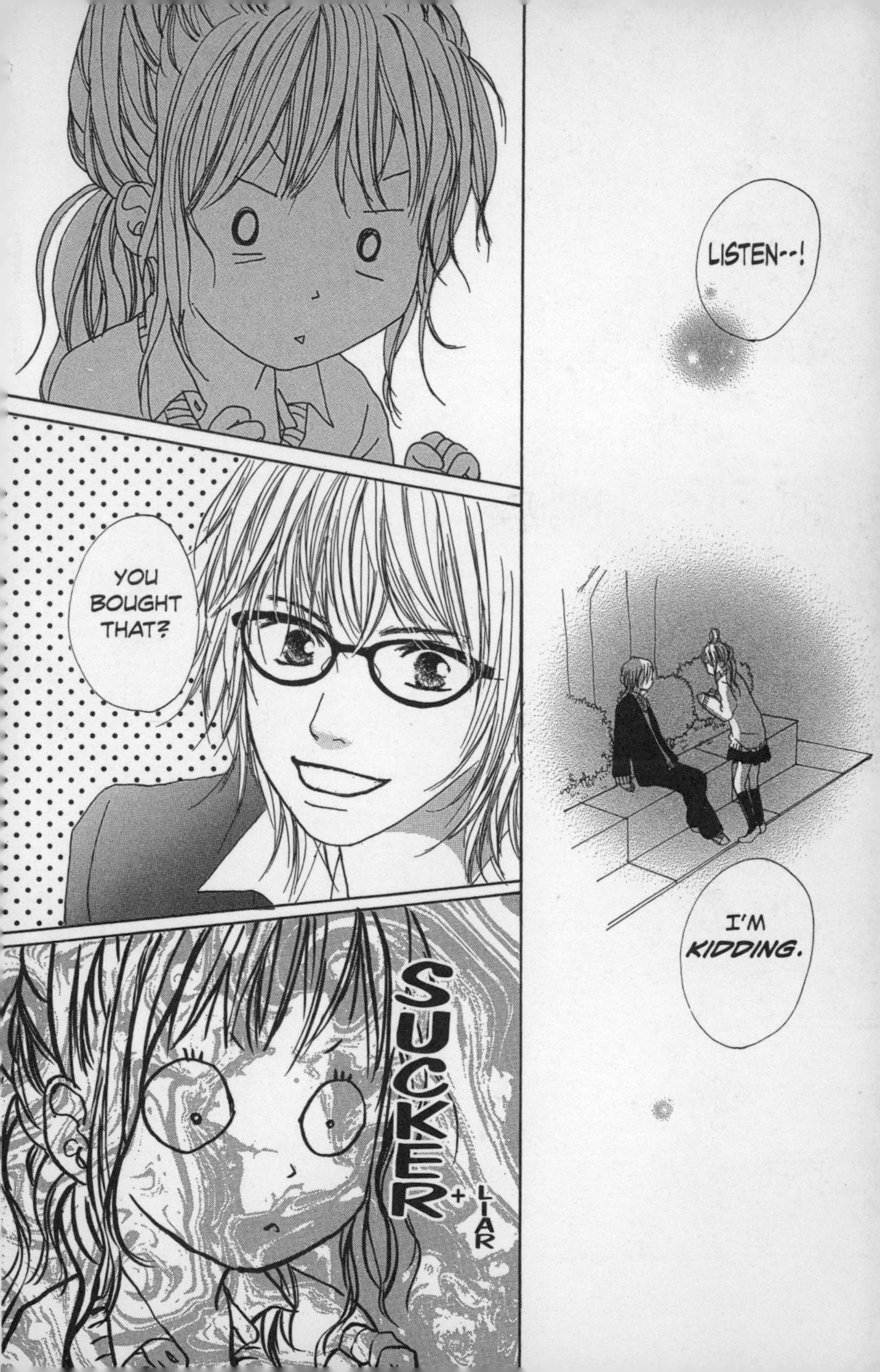
LISTEN--!
I'M KIDDING.
YOU BOUGHT THAT?
SUCKER + LIAR

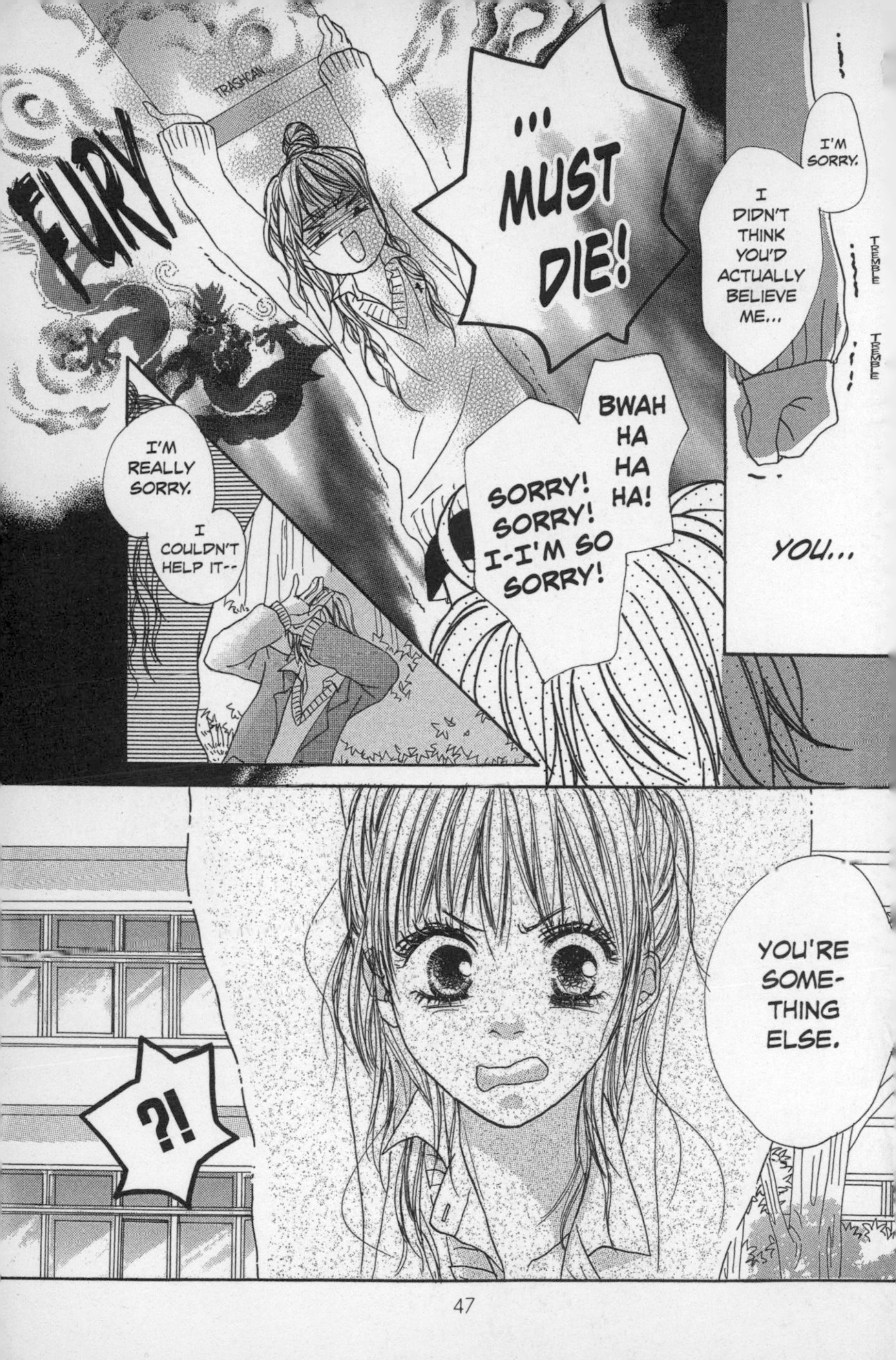
I'M SORRY.
I DIDN'T THINK YOU'D ACTUALLY BELIEVE ME...
TREMBLE
TREMBLE
YOU...
TRASHCAN
... MUST DIE!
FURY
BWAH HA HA HA!
SORRY! SORRY! I-I'M SO SORRY!
I'M REALLY SORRY.
I COULDN'T HELP IT--
YOU'RE SOME-THING ELSE.
?!

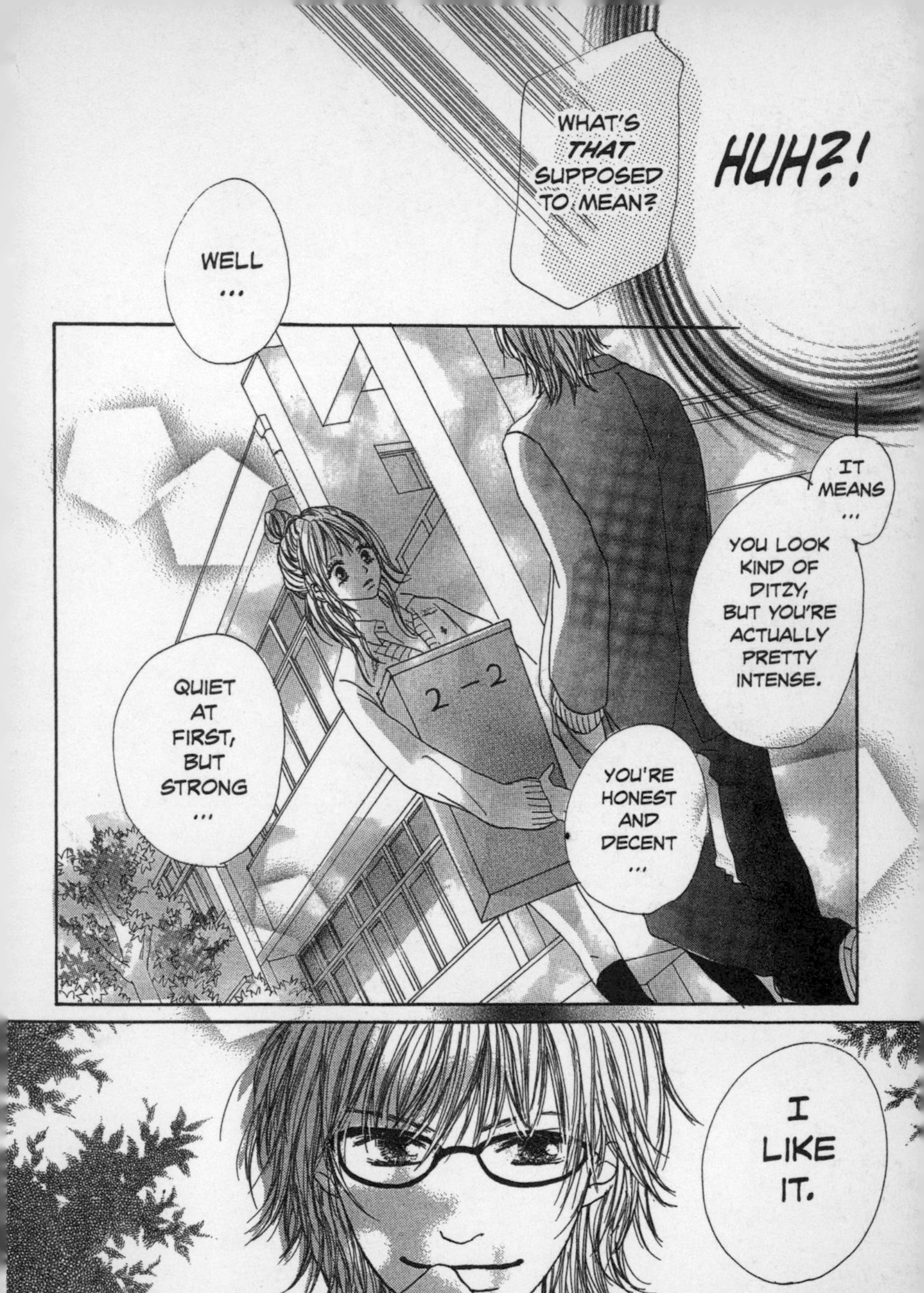
HUH?!
WHAT'S THAT SUPPOSED TO MEAN?
WELL ...
IT MEANS ...
YOU LOOK KIND OF DITZY, BUT YOU'RE ACTUALLY PRETTY INTENSE.
YOU'RE HONEST AND DECENT ...
2-2
QUIET AT FIRST, BUT STRONG ...
I LIKE IT.

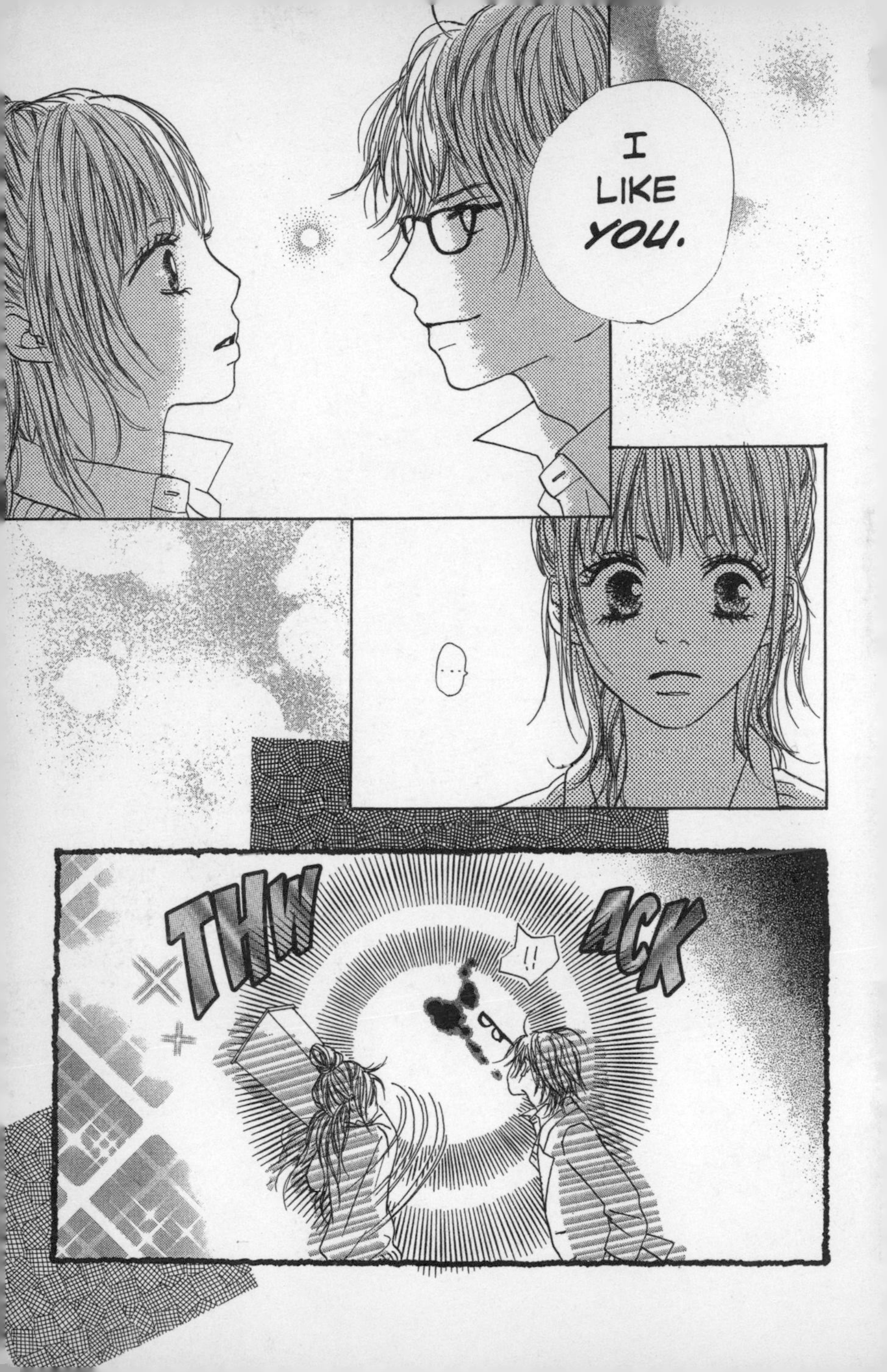
I LIKE YOU.
...
THWACK
!!

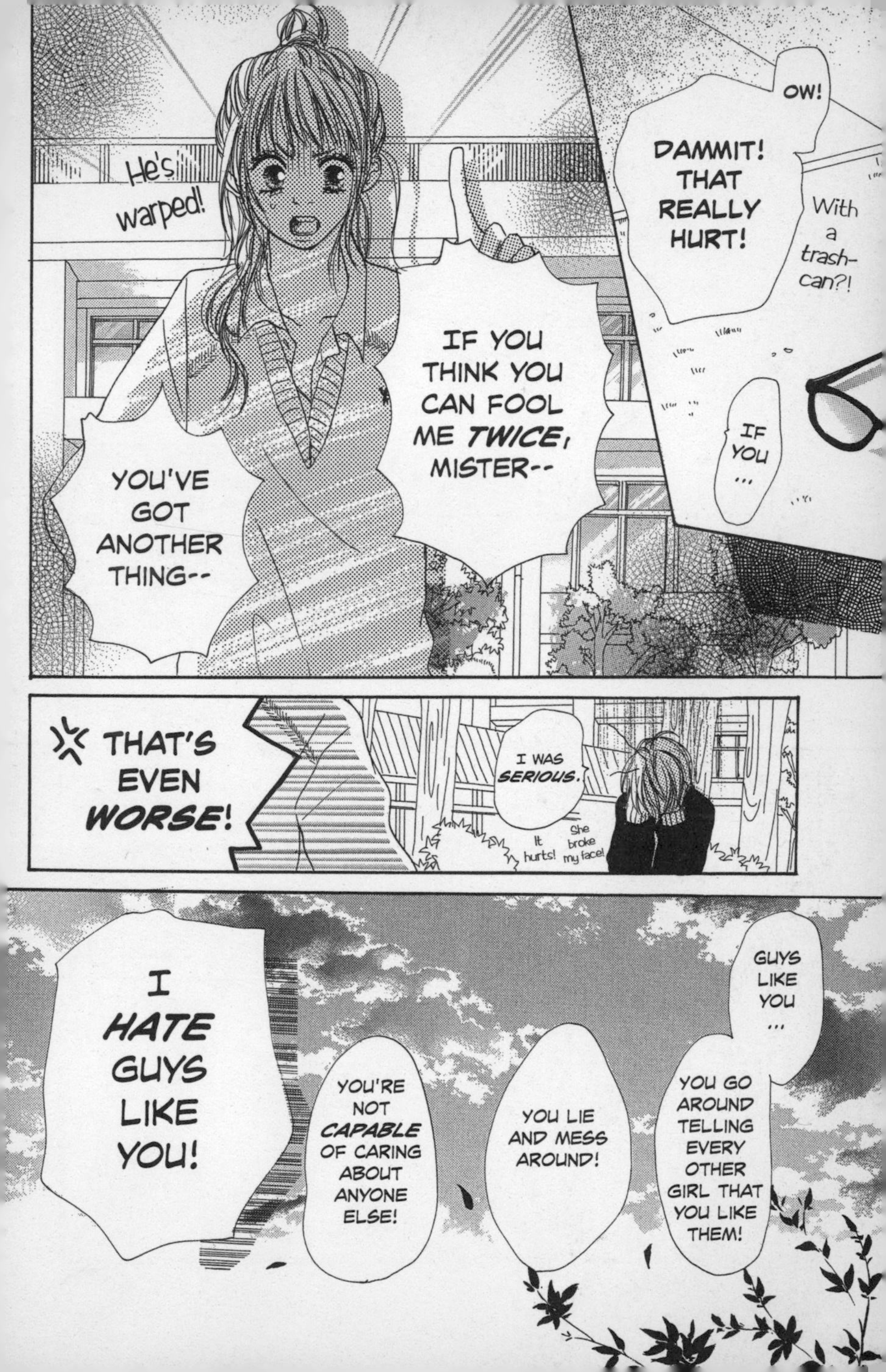
OW!
DAMMIT! THAT REALLY HURT!
With a trash-can?!
IF YOU ...
He's warped!
IF YOU THINK YOU CAN FOOL ME *TWICE*, MISTER--
YOU'VE GOT ANOTHER THING--
I WAS *SERIOUS*.
She broke my face!
It hurts!
THAT'S EVEN *WORSE*!
GUYS LIKE YOU ...
YOU GO AROUND TELLING EVERY OTHER GIRL THAT YOU LIKE THEM!
YOU LIE AND MESS AROUND!
YOU'RE NOT *CAPABLE* OF CARING ABOUT ANYONE ELSE!
I *HATE* GUYS LIKE YOU!

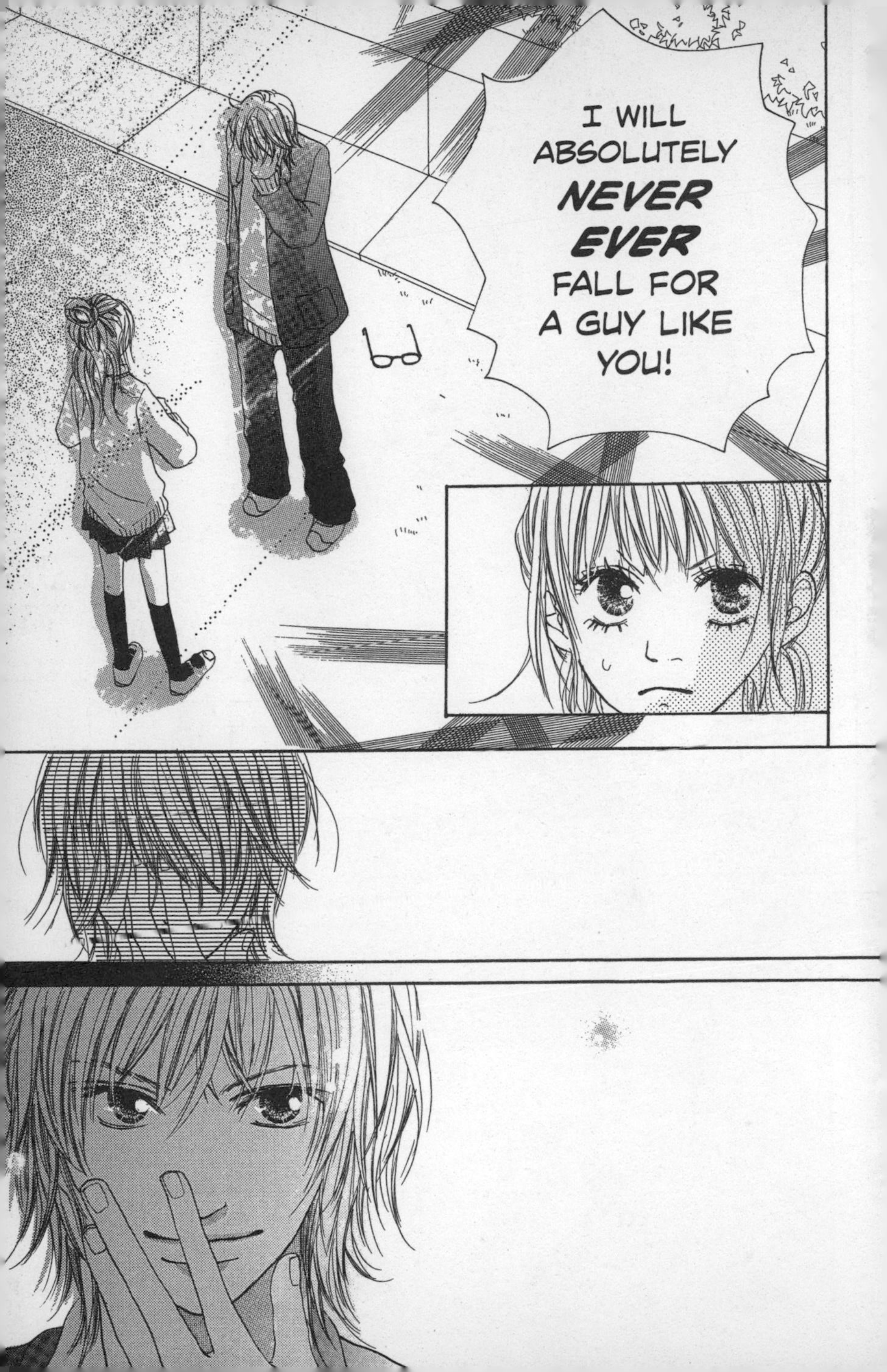
I WILL ABSOLUTELY ***NEVER EVER*** FALL FOR A GUY LIKE YOU!

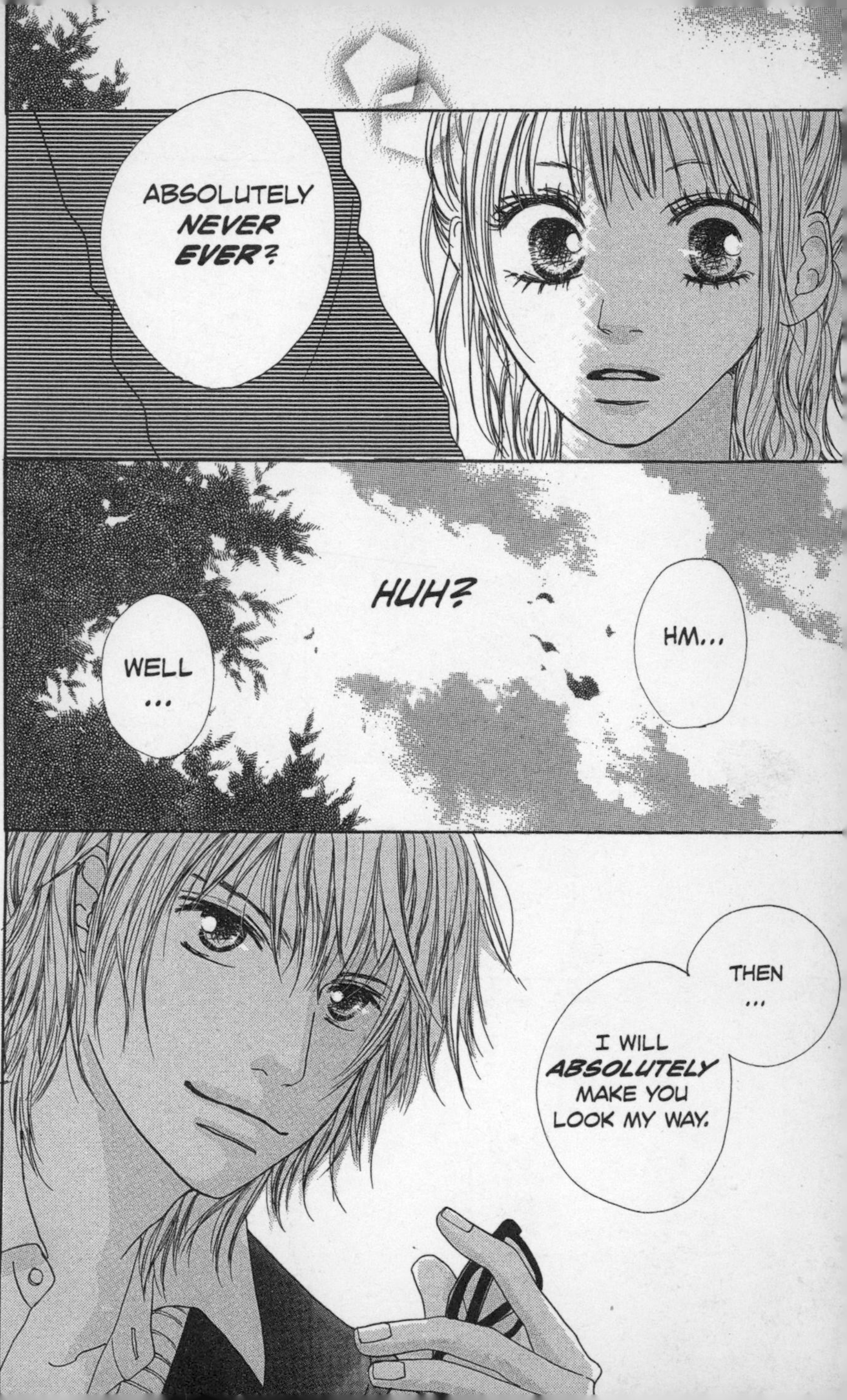
ABSOLUTELY NEVER EVER?
HM...
HUH?
WELL ...
THEN ...
I WILL ABSOLUTELY MAKE YOU LOOK MY WAY.

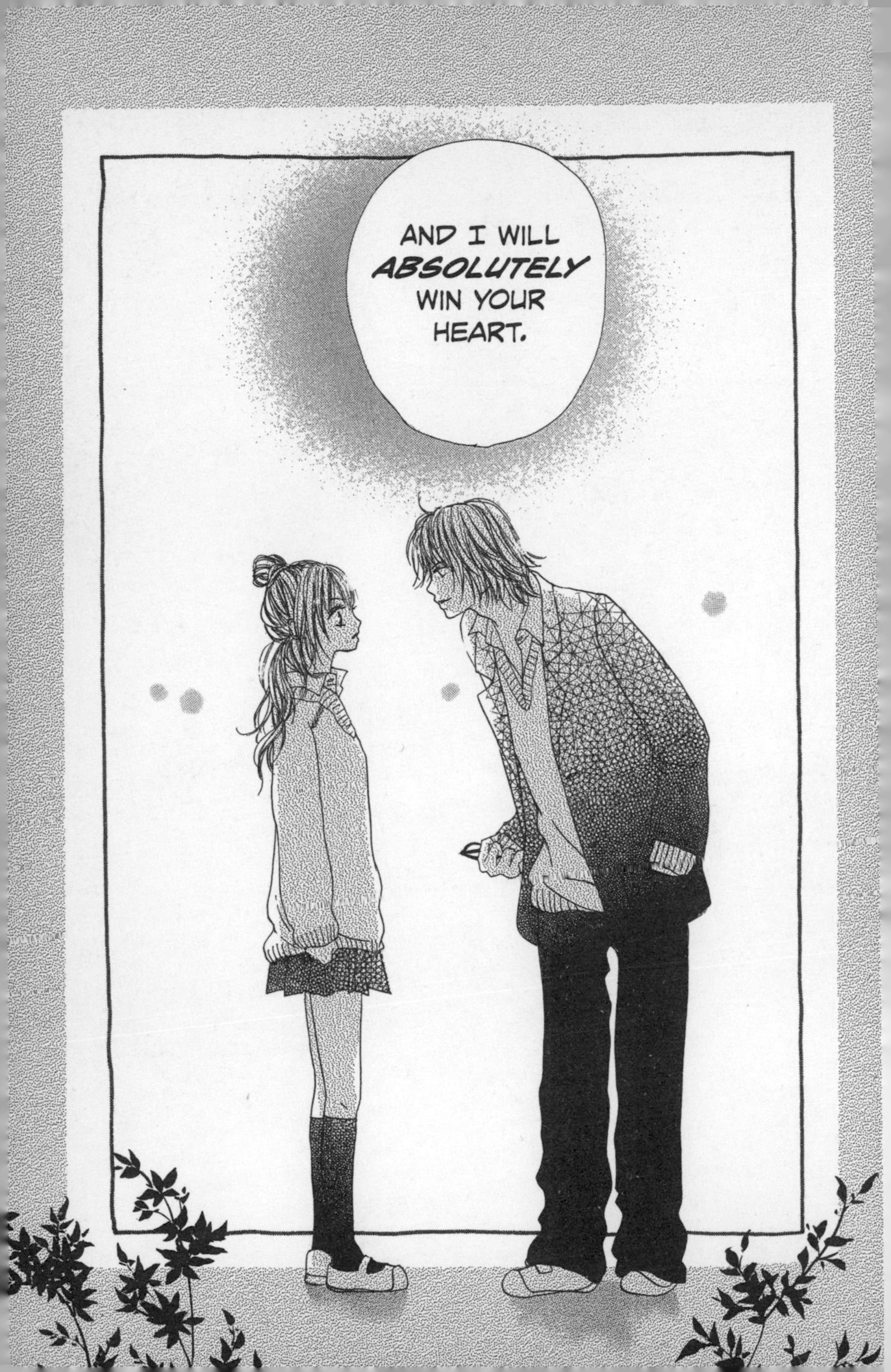
AND I WILL ABSOLUTELY WIN YOUR HEART.

Once upon a time at a bookstore...

Whenever I come across a bookstore, I run in and check to see if they have my books. Usually they don't. AH HA HA HA...

Dark clouds!

This is the story of something that happened after I left a bookstore in Odaiba feeling blue.

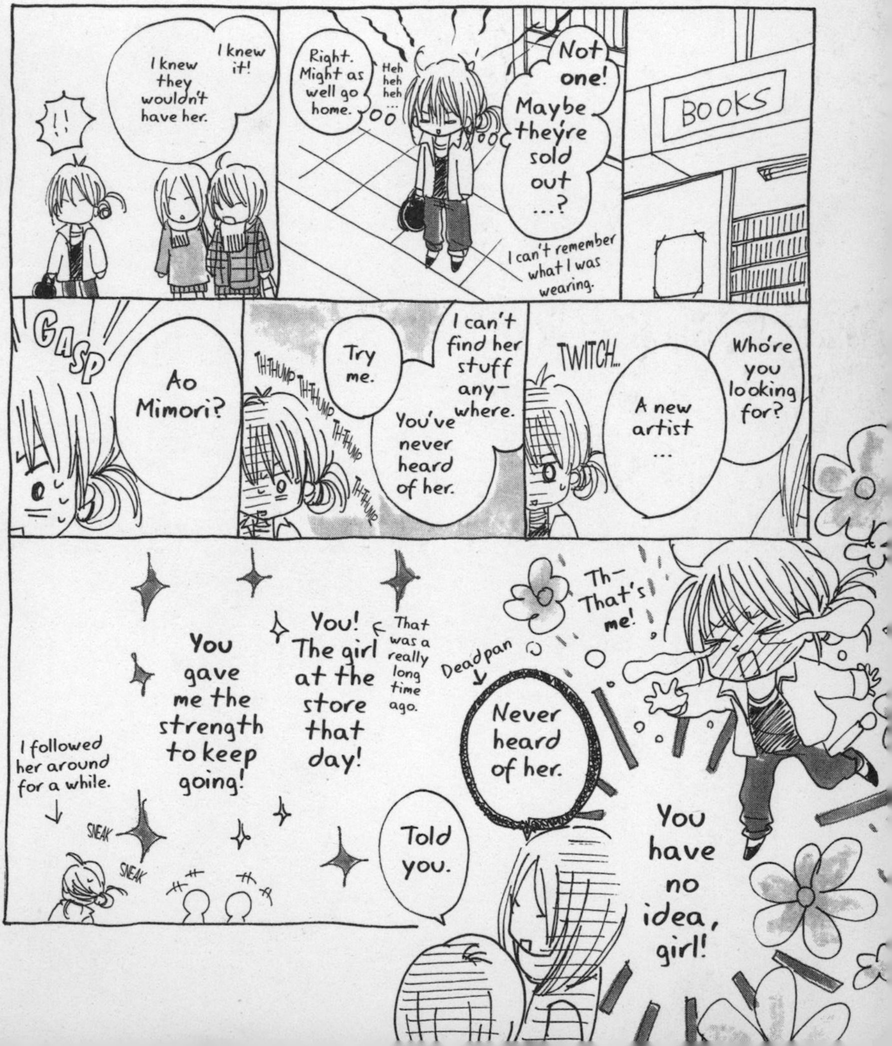
BOOKS
Not one! Maybe they're sold out ...?
I can't remember what I was wearing.
Heh heh heh ...
Right. Might as well go home.
!!
I knew it!
I knew they wouldn't have her.
TWITCH...
Who're you looking for?
A new artist ...
I can't find her stuff anywhere.
Try me.
You've never heard of her.
TH-THUMP TH-THUMP TH-THUMP TH-THUMP
GASP
Ao Mimori?
Th- That's me!
You have no idea, girl!
Deadpan
Never heard of her.
Told you.
You! The girl at the store that day!
That was a really long time ago.
You gave me the strength to keep going!
I followed her around for a while.
SNEAK
SNEAK

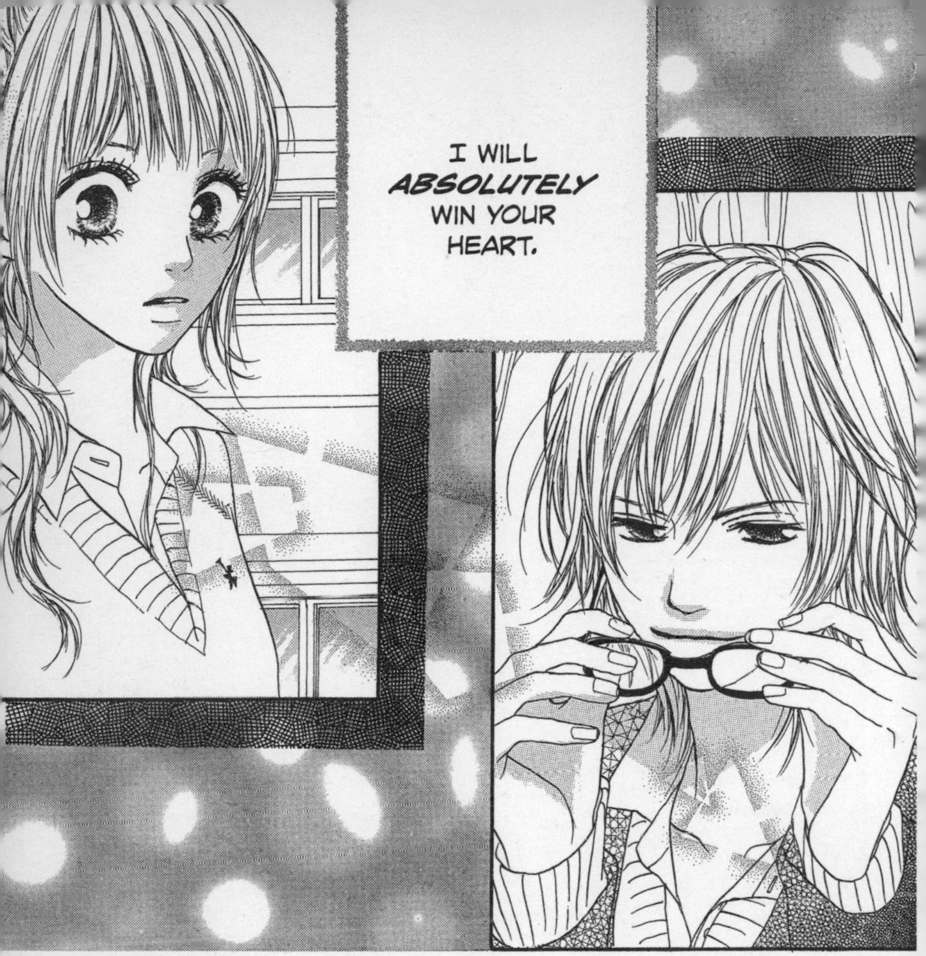
I WILL *ABSOLUTELY* WIN YOUR HEART.

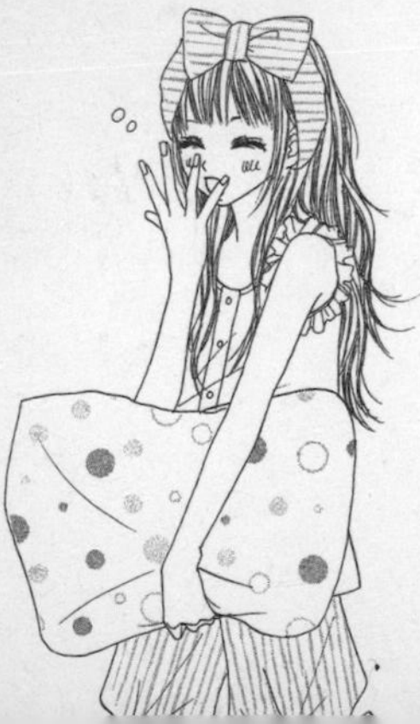

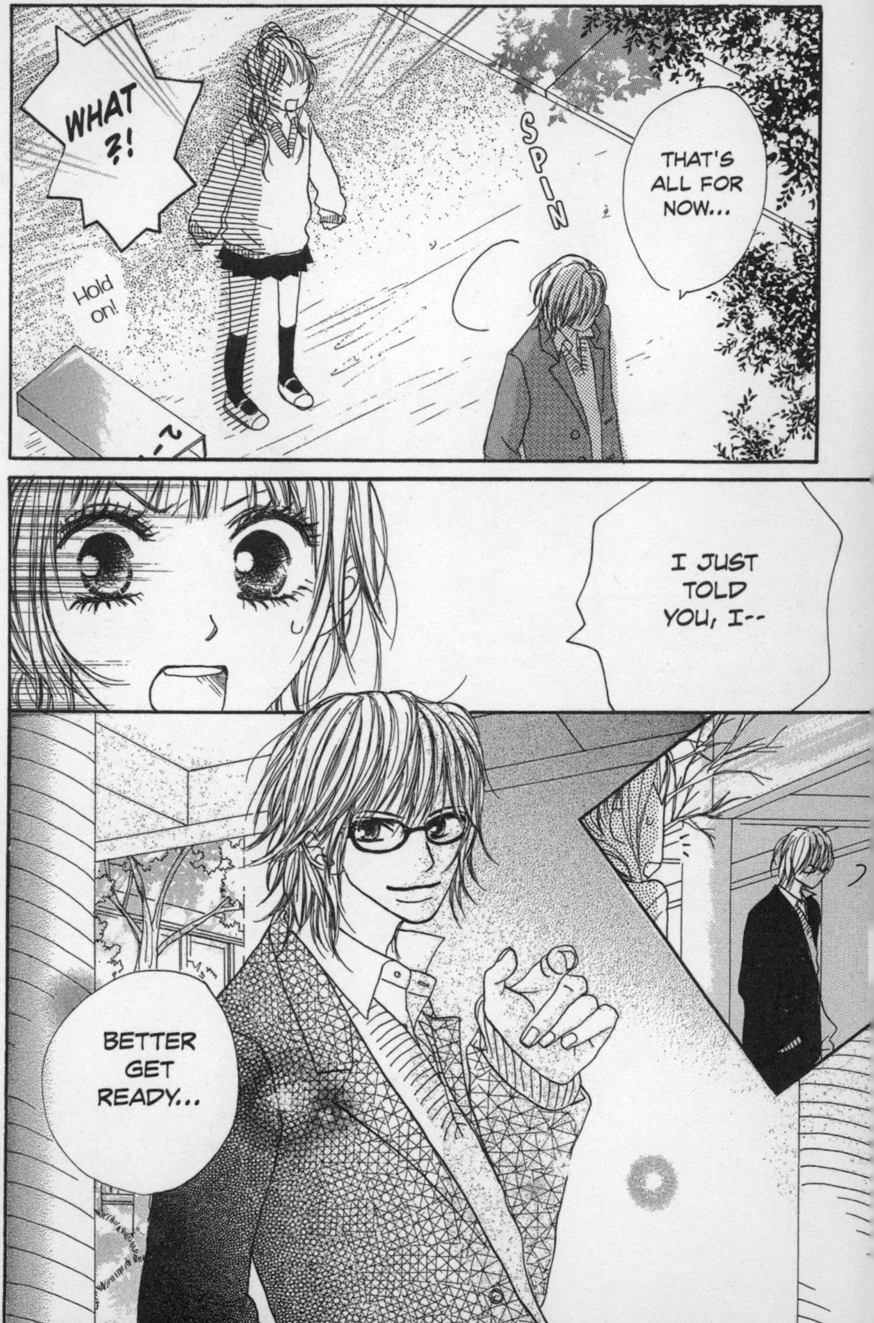
THAT'S ALL FOR NOW...
SPIN
WHAT?!
Hold on!
I JUST TOLD YOU, I--
BETTER GET READY...

Random Meaningless Musings

I was on the phone with Natsume Hirose the other day, when out of nowhere and for no reason at all, I started talking in a strange voice. It was such an unconscious thing that I didn't even realize I was doing an impersonation! Natsume was like, "Who's that supposed to be?"

"I don't know," I said, "but it sounds familiar, doesn't it?"

It took us a while, but we finally figured out it was the actor Ichiro Zaitsu. What exactly does an unconscious impersonation of Ichiro Zaitsu say about a woman, hm? What do you think? Am I all right? The line was "Do something about it, Mom!" Oh well, I guess you had to be there...

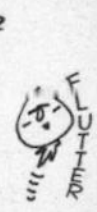
FLUTTER

I love writing funny e-mails, and almost 100% of them go to Natsume. She saves the good ones and sends them back to me after I've forgotten about them. Then I read my own e-mails and crack myself up! BWAH HA HA! I'm an idiot...

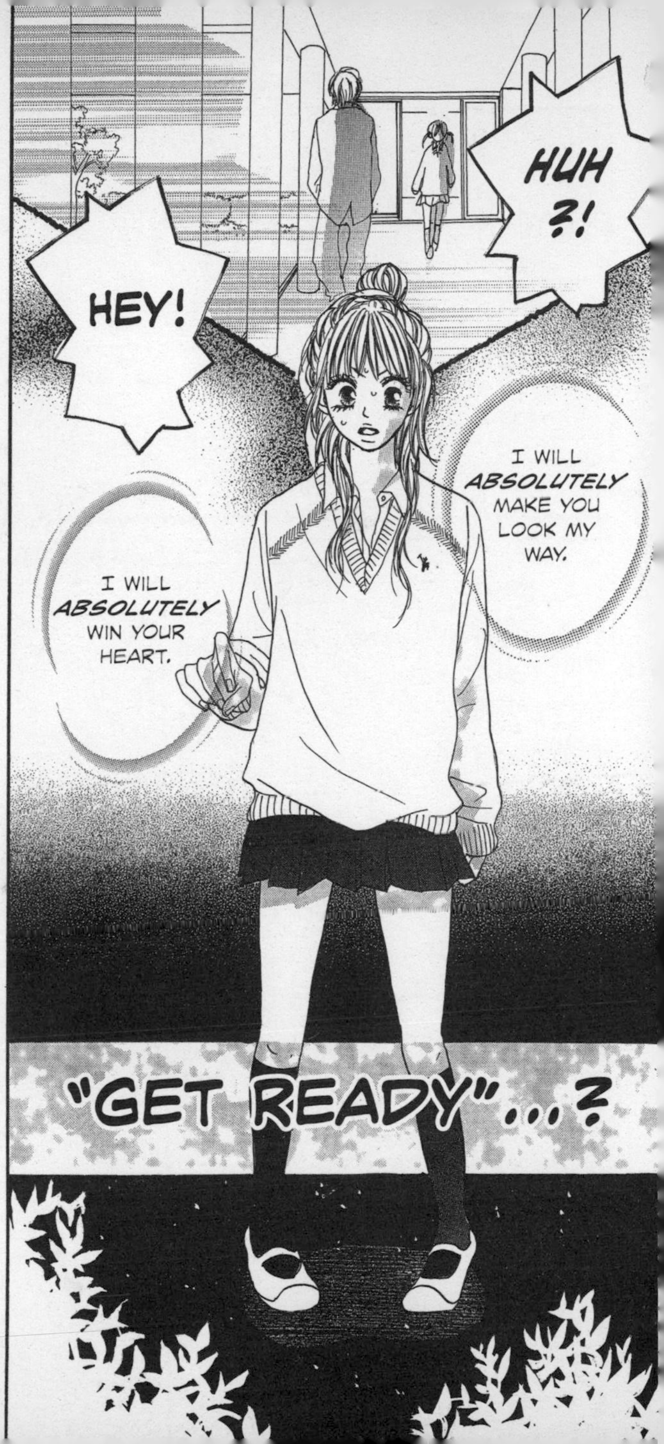
HUH ?!
HEY!
I WILL ABSOLUTELY MAKE YOU LOOK MY WAY.
I WILL ABSOLUTELY WIN YOUR HEART.
"GET READY"...?

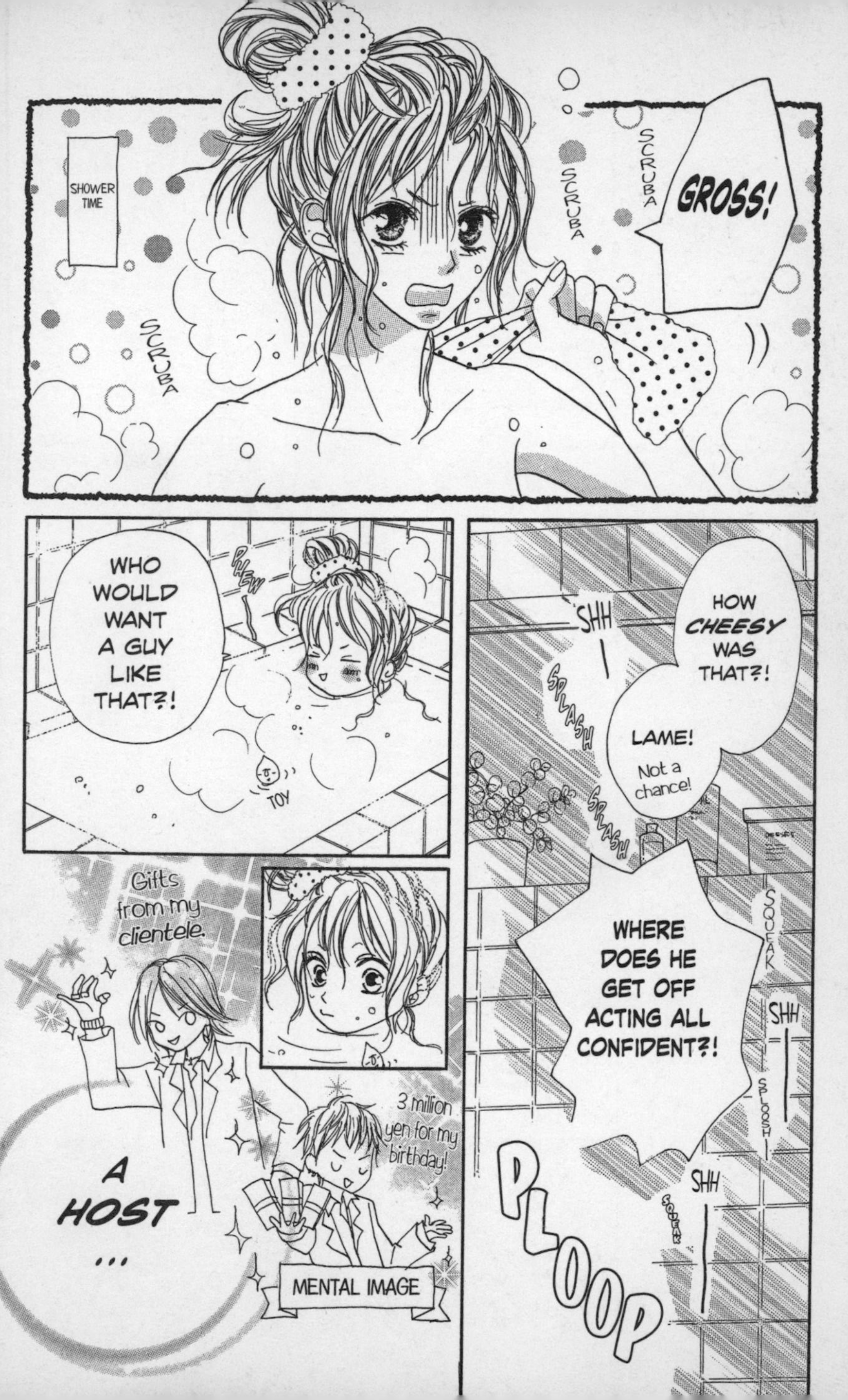
GROSS!
SCRUBA SCRUBA
SHOWER TIME
SCRUBA
HOW CHEESY WAS THAT?!
SHH
SPLASH
LAME!
Not a chance!
SPLASH
WHERE DOES HE GET OFF ACTING ALL CONFIDENT?!
SQUEAK
SHH
SPLOOSH
SHH
SQUEAK
PLOOP
PHEW
WHO WOULD WANT A GUY LIKE THAT?!
TOY
Gifts from my clientele.
3 million yen for my birthday!
A HOST ...
MENTAL IMAGE

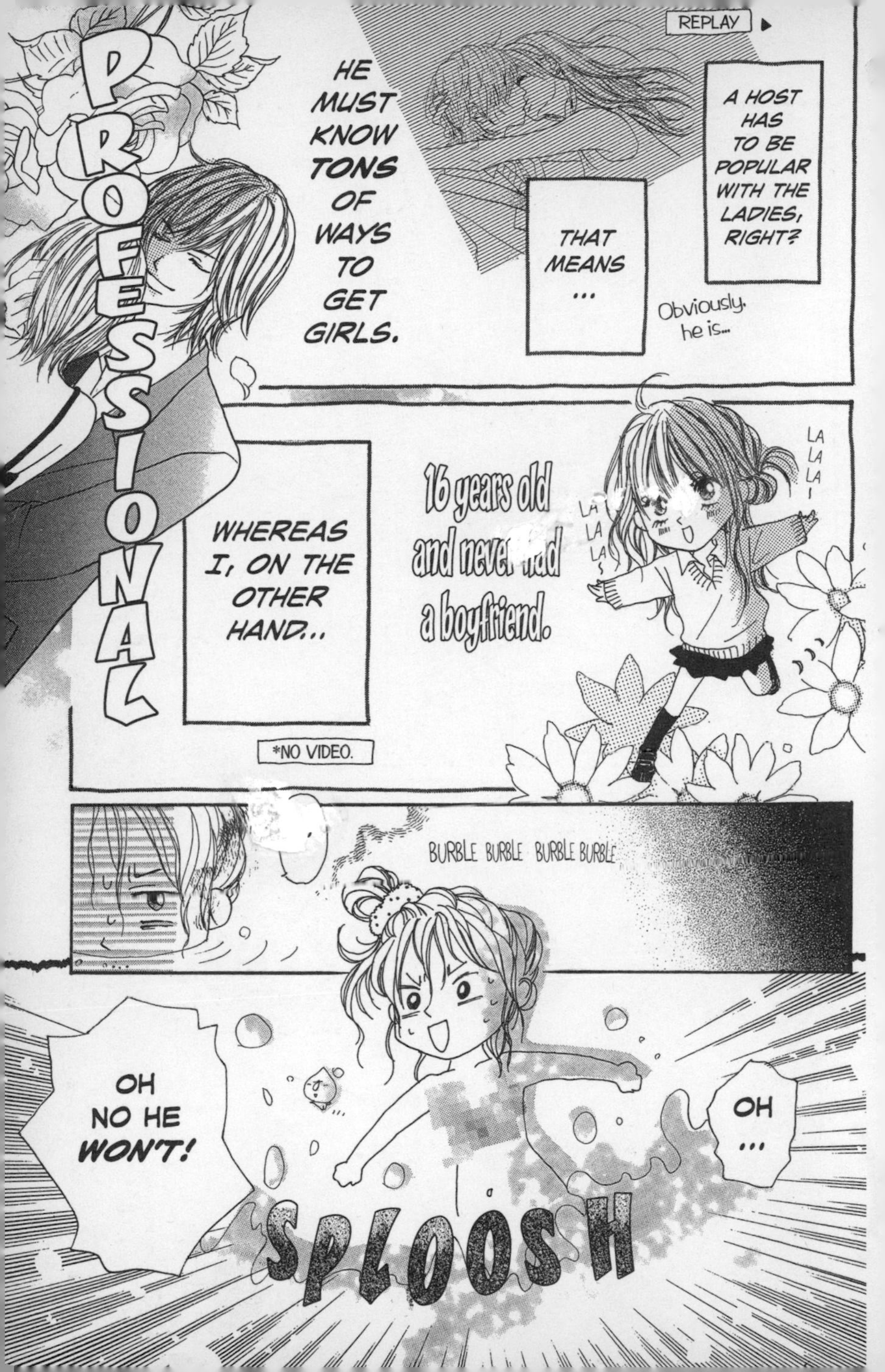
REPLAY ▶
A HOST HAS TO BE POPULAR WITH THE LADIES, RIGHT?
Obviously, he is...
THAT MEANS...
HE MUST KNOW TONS OF WAYS TO GET GIRLS.
PROFESSIONAL
LA LA LA!
LA LA LA
16 years old and never had a boyfriend.
WHEREAS I, ON THE OTHER HAND...
*NO VIDEO.
BURBLE BURBLE BURBLE BURBLE
OH...
SPLOOSH
OH NO HE WON'T!

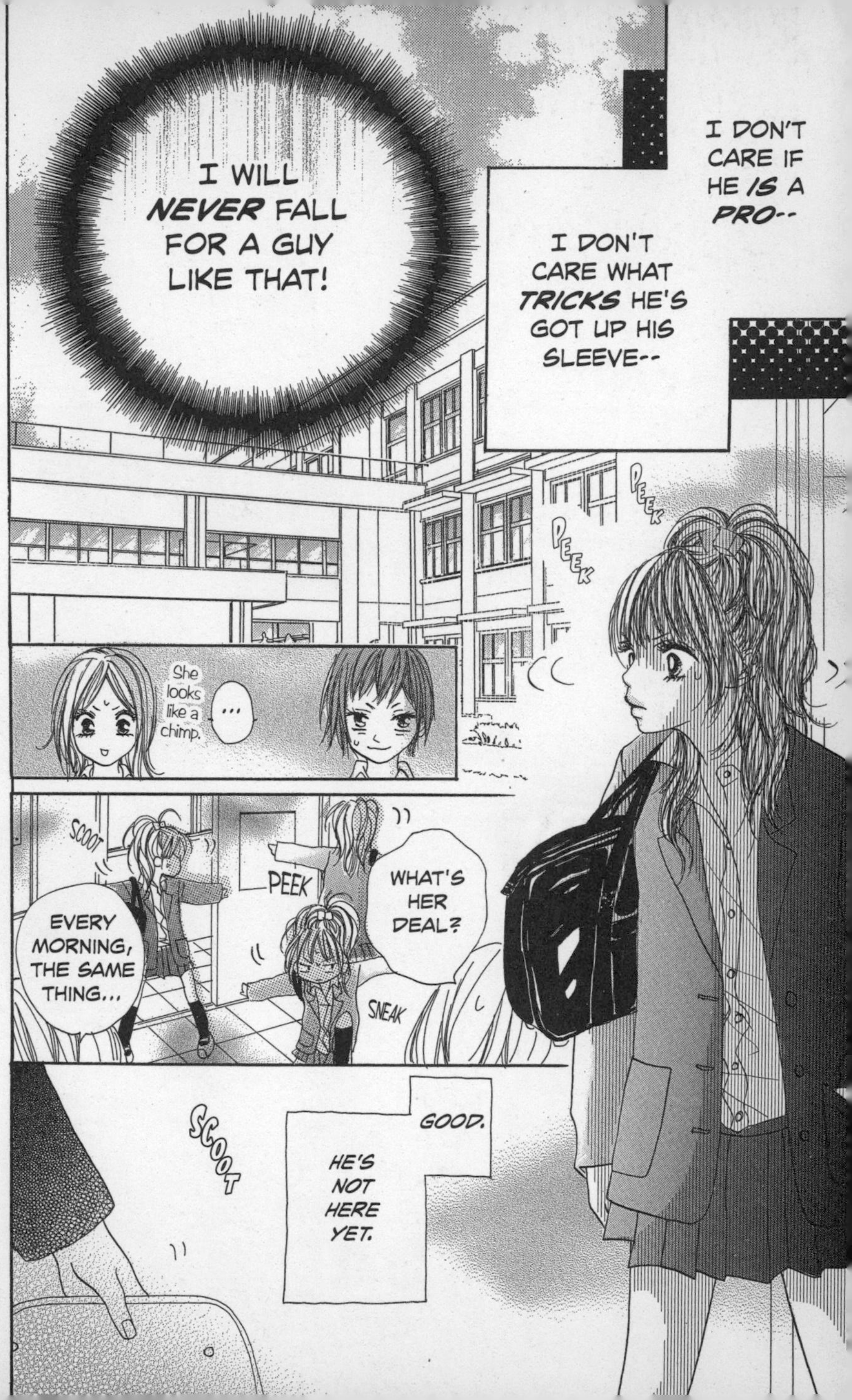
I DON'T CARE IF HE *IS* A *PRO*--
I DON'T CARE WHAT *TRICKS* HE'S GOT UP HIS SLEEVE--
I WILL *NEVER* FALL FOR A GUY LIKE THAT!
PEEK
PEEK
She looks like a chimp.
...
WHAT'S HER DEAL?
PEEK
SCOOT
EVERY MORNING, THE SAME THING...
SNEAK
GOOD.
HE'S NOT HERE YET.
SCOOT

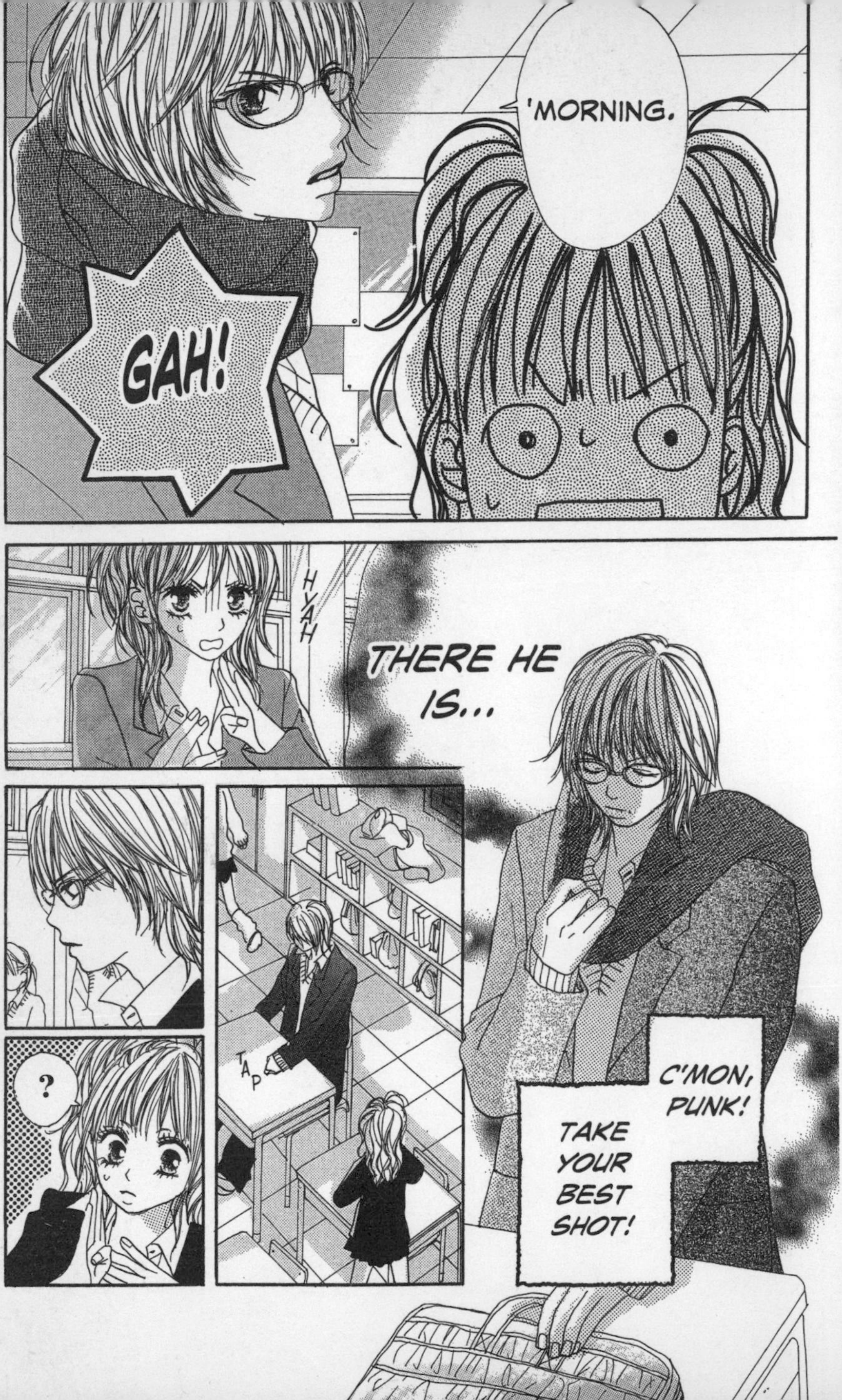
'MORNING.
GAH!
THERE HE IS...
C'MON, PUNK!
TAKE YOUR BEST SHOT!
HYAH
TAP
?

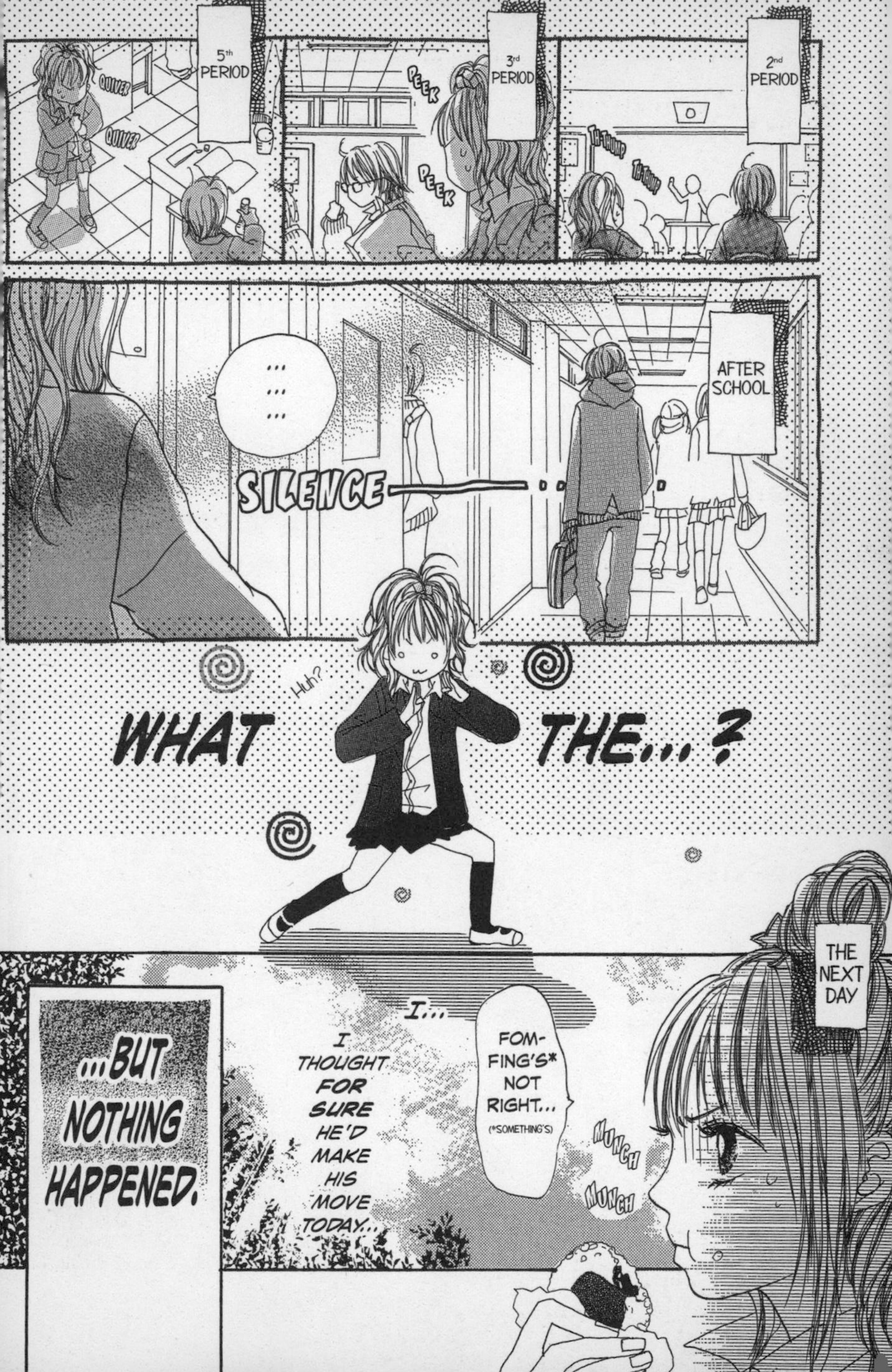
2nd PERIOD
TH-THUMP
TH-THUMP
3rd PERIOD
PEEK
PEEK
5th PERIOD
QUIVER
QUIVER
AFTER SCHOOL
SILENCE
...
...
...
WHAT THE...?
Huh?
THE NEXT DAY
FOM-FING'S* NOT RIGHT...
(*SOMETHING'S)
MUNCH
MUNCH
I...
I THOUGHT FOR SURE HE'D MAKE HIS MOVE TODAY...
...BUT NOTHING HAPPENED.

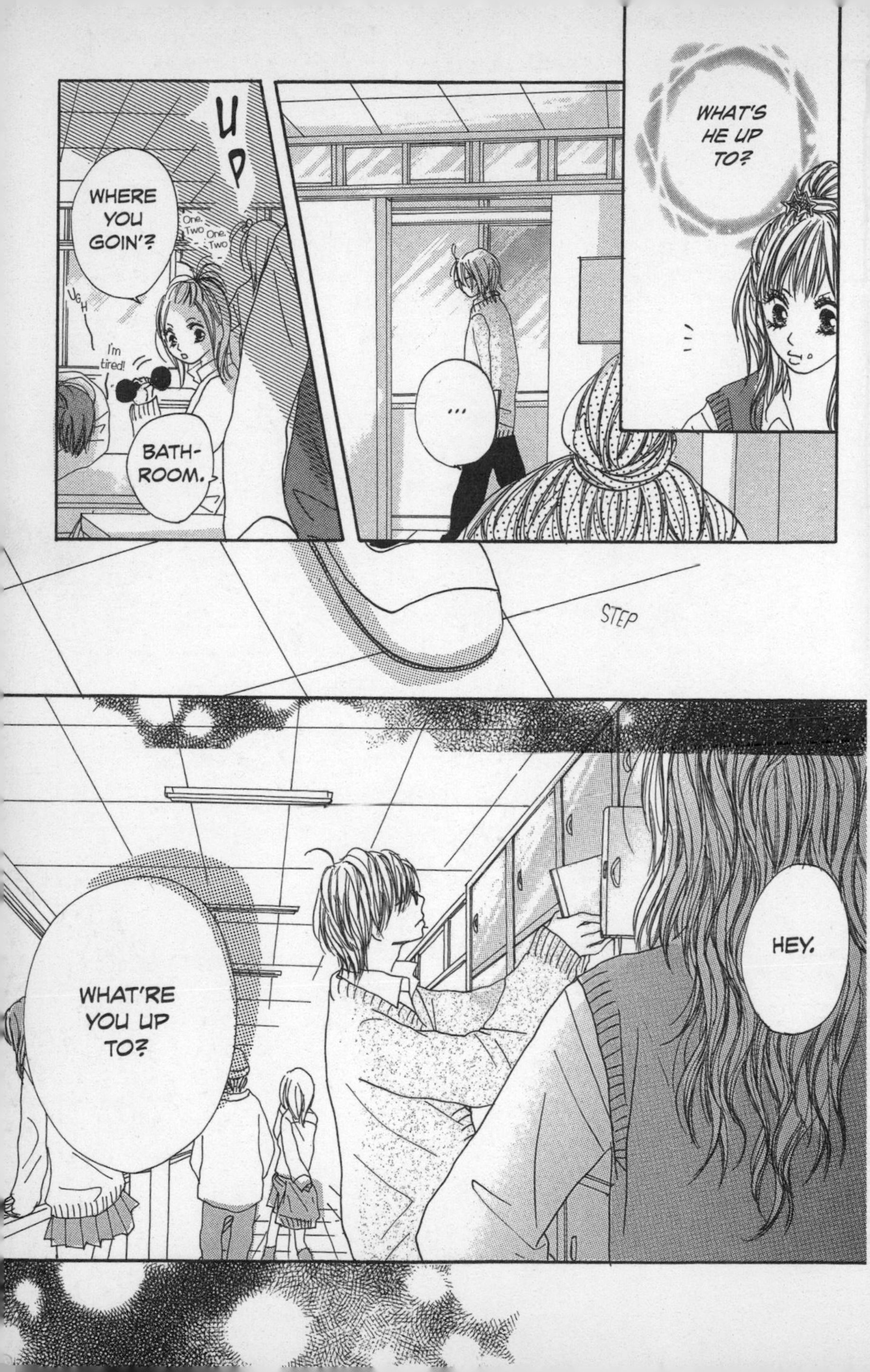
WHAT'S HE UP TO?
...
UP UP
WHERE YOU GOIN'?
One. Two One. Two
UGH
I'm tired!
BATHROOM.
STEP
HEY.
WHAT'RE YOU UP TO?

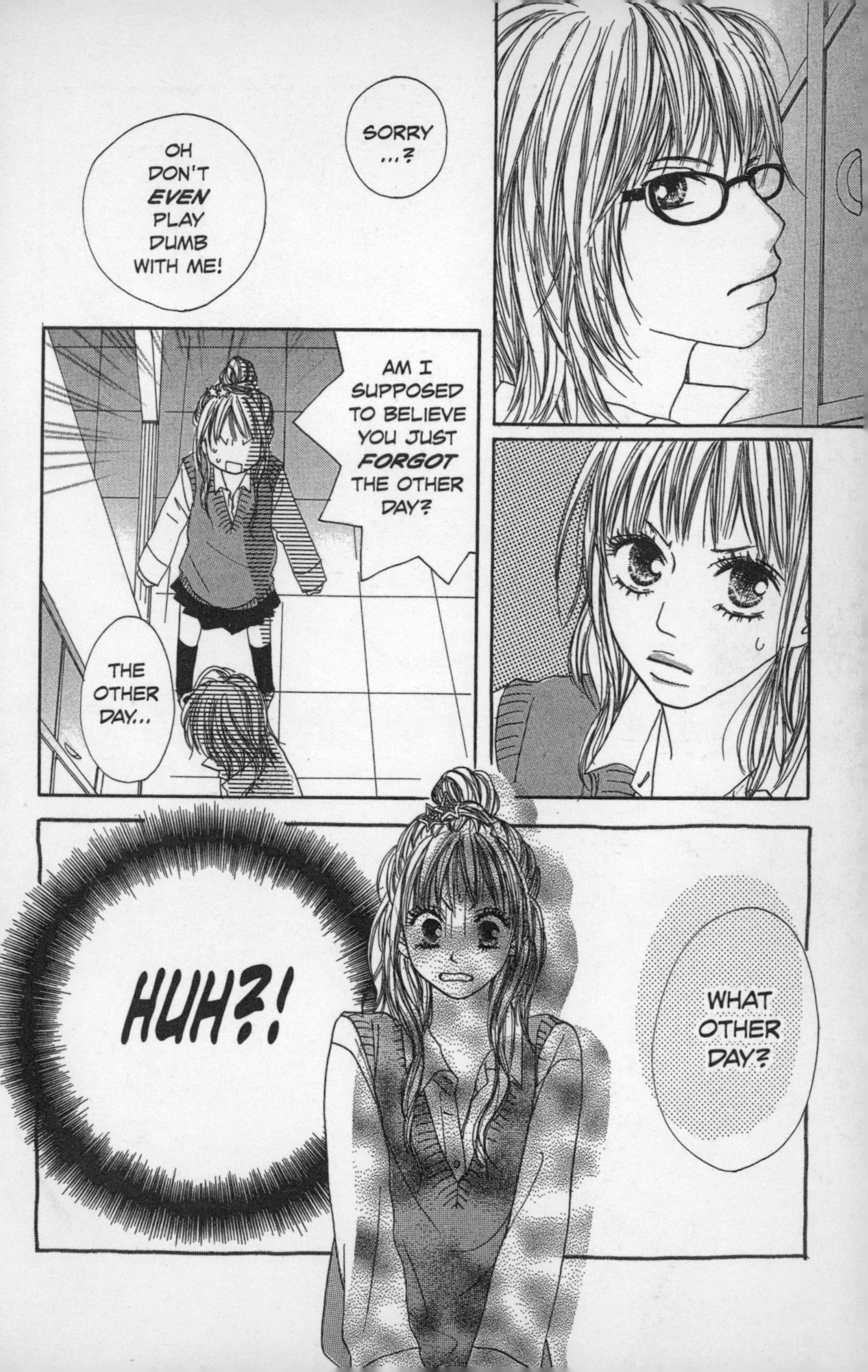
SORRY ...?
OH DON'T *EVEN* PLAY DUMB WITH ME!
AM I SUPPOSED TO BELIEVE YOU JUST *FORGOT* THE OTHER DAY?
THE OTHER DAY...
WHAT OTHER DAY?
HUH?!

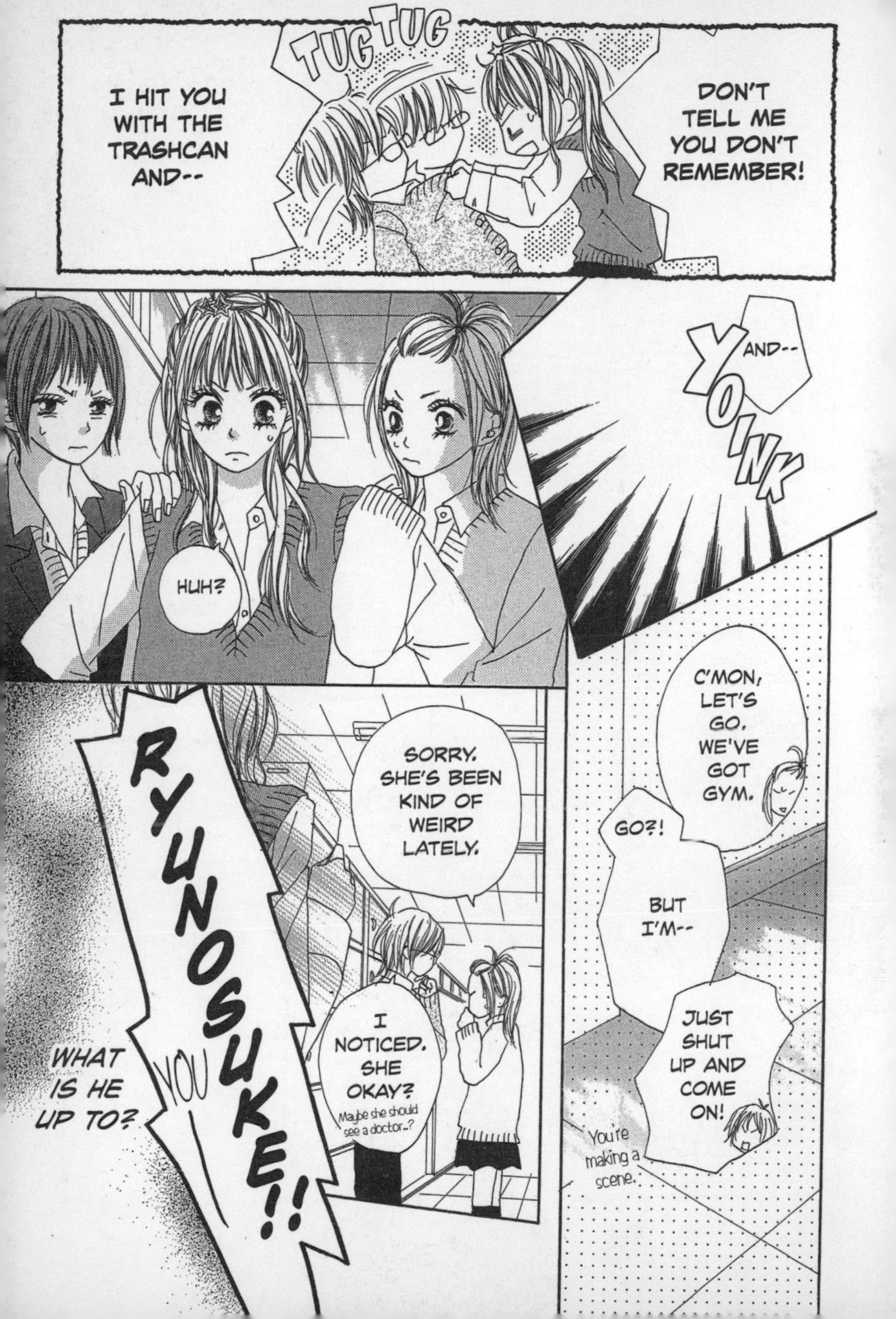
TUG TUG
DON'T TELL ME YOU DON'T REMEMBER!
I HIT YOU WITH THE TRASHCAN AND--
AND--
YOINK
HUH?
C'MON, LET'S GO. WE'VE GOT GYM.
GO?!
BUT I'M--
JUST SHUT UP AND COME ON!
You're making a scene.
SORRY. SHE'S BEEN KIND OF WEIRD LATELY.
I NOTICED. SHE OKAY?
Maybe she should see a doctor..?
YOU
RYUNOSUKE!!
WHAT IS HE UP TO?

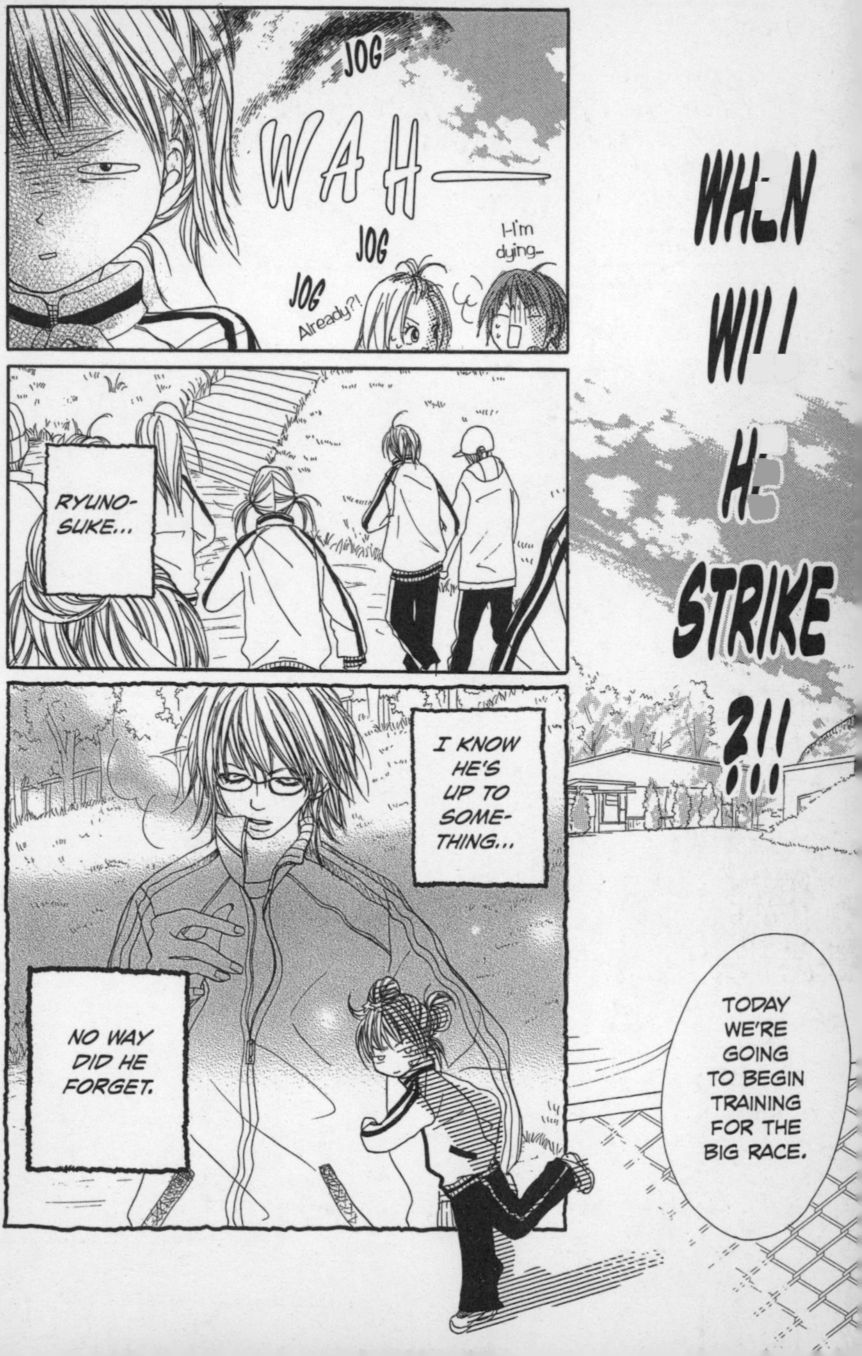
WHEN WILL HE STRIKE?!!
TODAY WE'RE GOING TO BEGIN TRAINING FOR THE BIG RACE.
JOG
I-I'm dying...
WAH—
JOG
JOG
Already?!
RYUNO-SUKE...
I KNOW HE'S UP TO SOME-THING...
NO WAY DID HE FORGET.

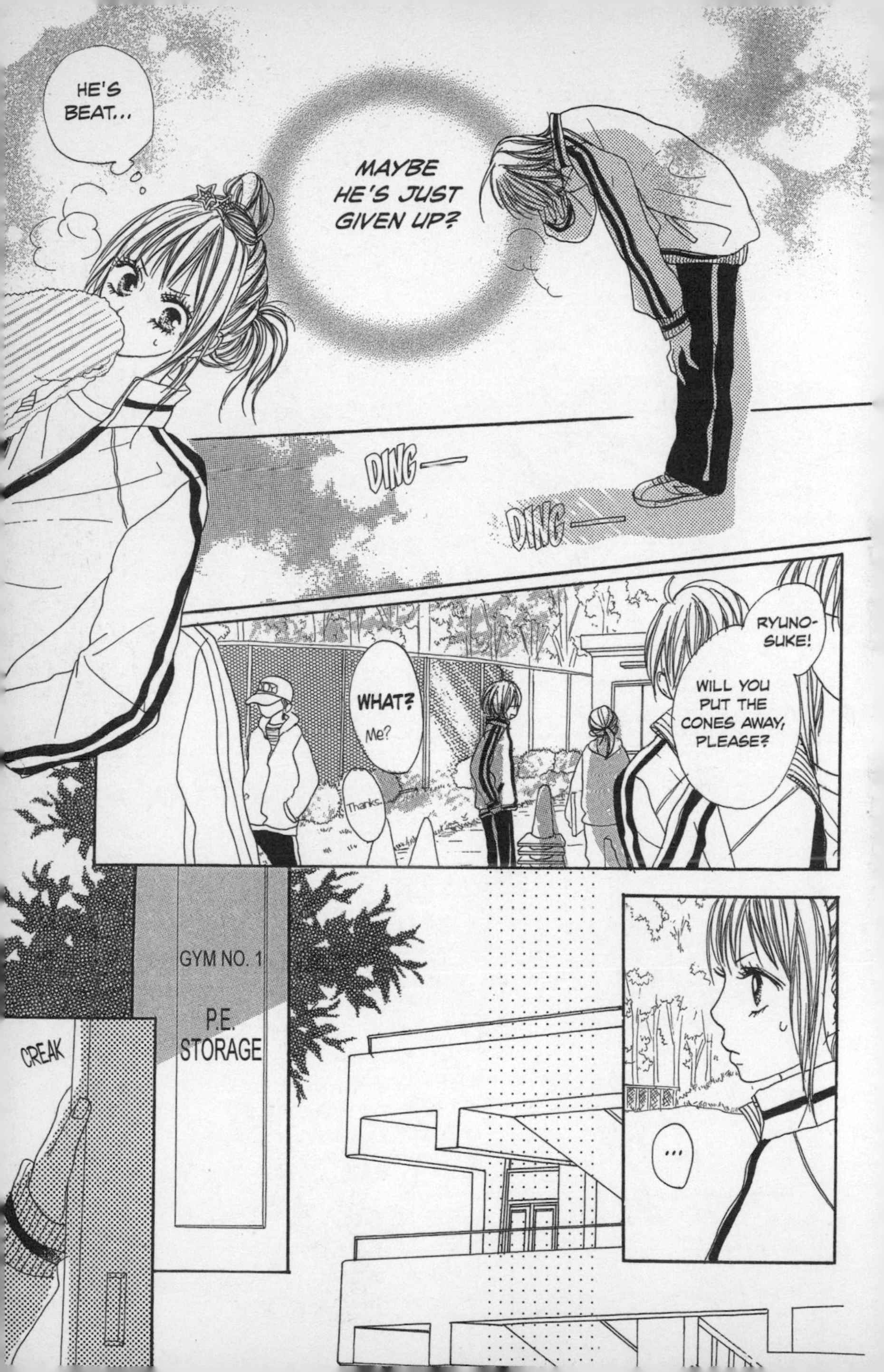
HE'S BEAT...
MAYBE HE'S JUST GIVEN UP?
DING—
DING—
RYUNO-SUKE!
WILL YOU PUT THE CONES AWAY, PLEASE?
WHAT?
Me?
Thanks.
...
GYM NO. 1
P.E. STORAGE
CREAK

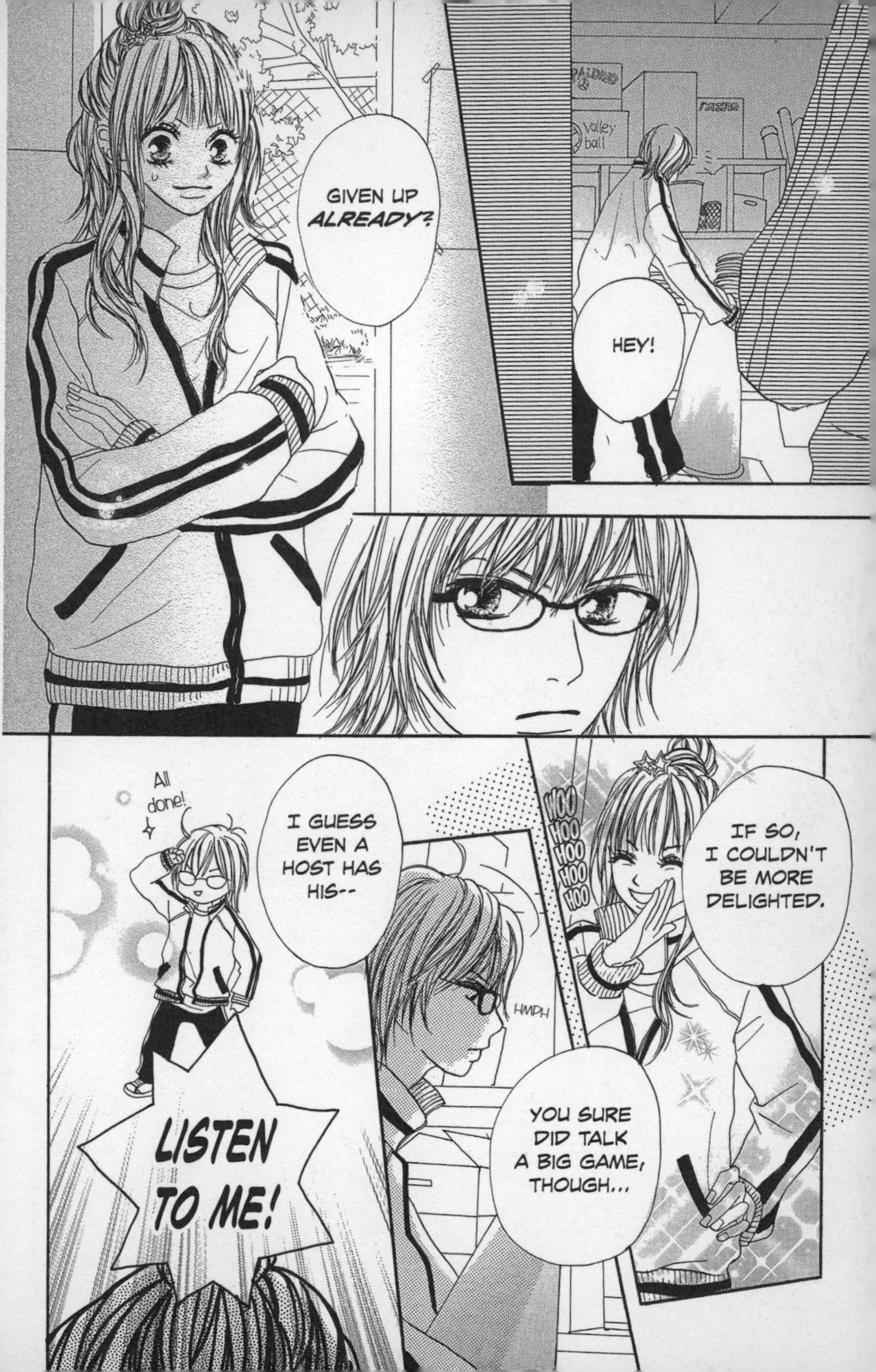
HEY!
GIVEN UP ALREADY?
WOO HOO HOO HOO HOO
I GUESS EVEN A HOST HAS HIS--
IF SO, I COULDN'T BE MORE DELIGHTED.
YOU SURE DID TALK A BIG GAME, THOUGH...
HMPH
All done!
LISTEN TO ME!

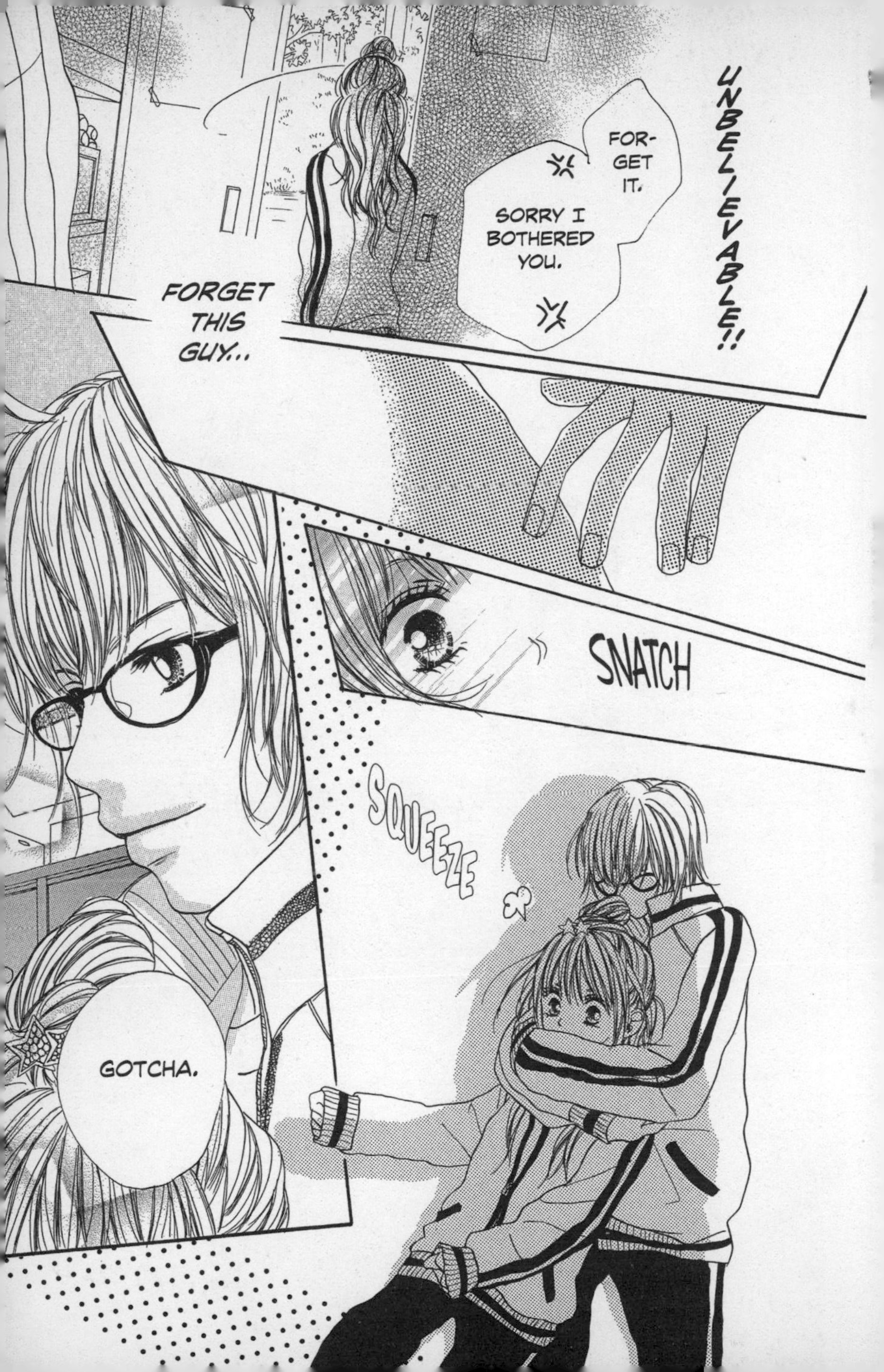
UNBELIEVABLE!!
FOR-GET IT.
SORRY I BOTHERED YOU.
FORGET THIS GUY...
SNATCH
SQUEEZE
GOTCHA.

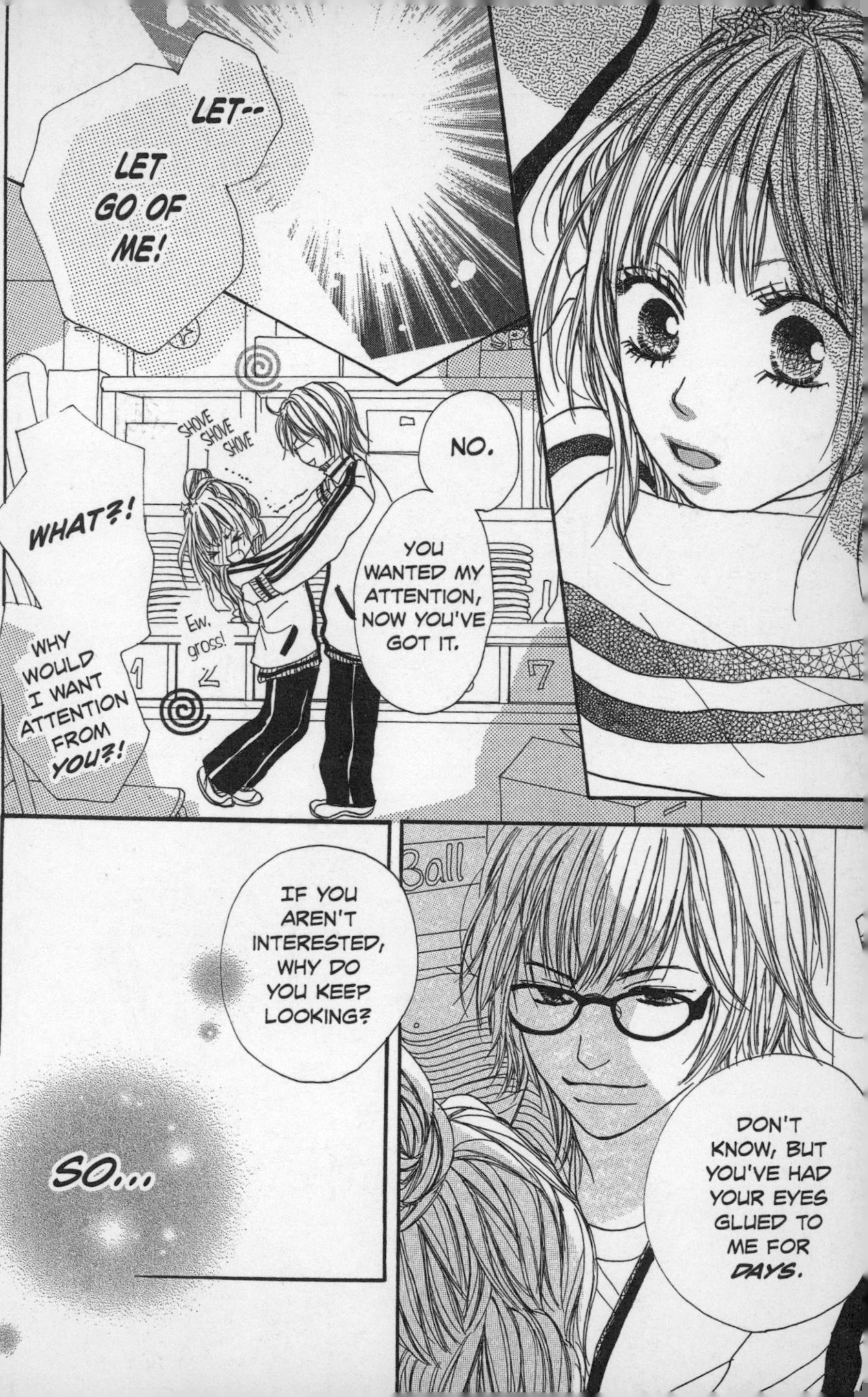
LET--
LET GO OF ME!
NO.
YOU WANTED MY ATTENTION, NOW YOU'VE GOT IT.
SHOVE SHOVE SHOVE
WHAT?!
WHY WOULD I WANT ATTENTION FROM YOU?!
Ew. gross!
IF YOU AREN'T INTERESTED, WHY DO YOU KEEP LOOKING?
DON'T KNOW, BUT YOU'VE HAD YOUR EYES GLUED TO ME FOR DAYS.
SO...

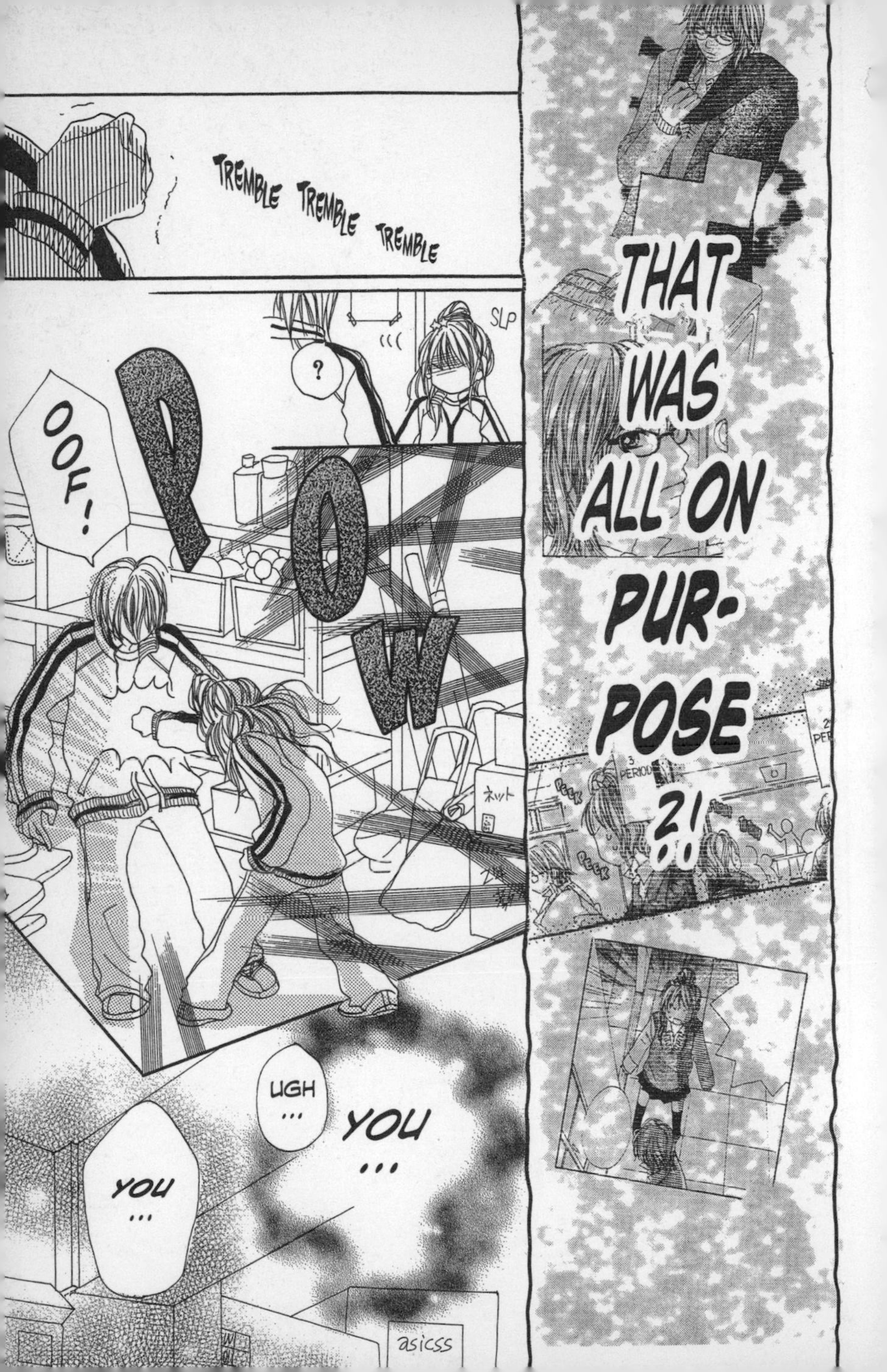
THAT WAS ALL ON PUR-POSE ?!
3 PERIOD
PEEK
PEEK
TREMBLE TREMBLE TREMBLE
SLP
?
POW
OOF!
ネット
UGH...
YOU...
YOU...
asicss

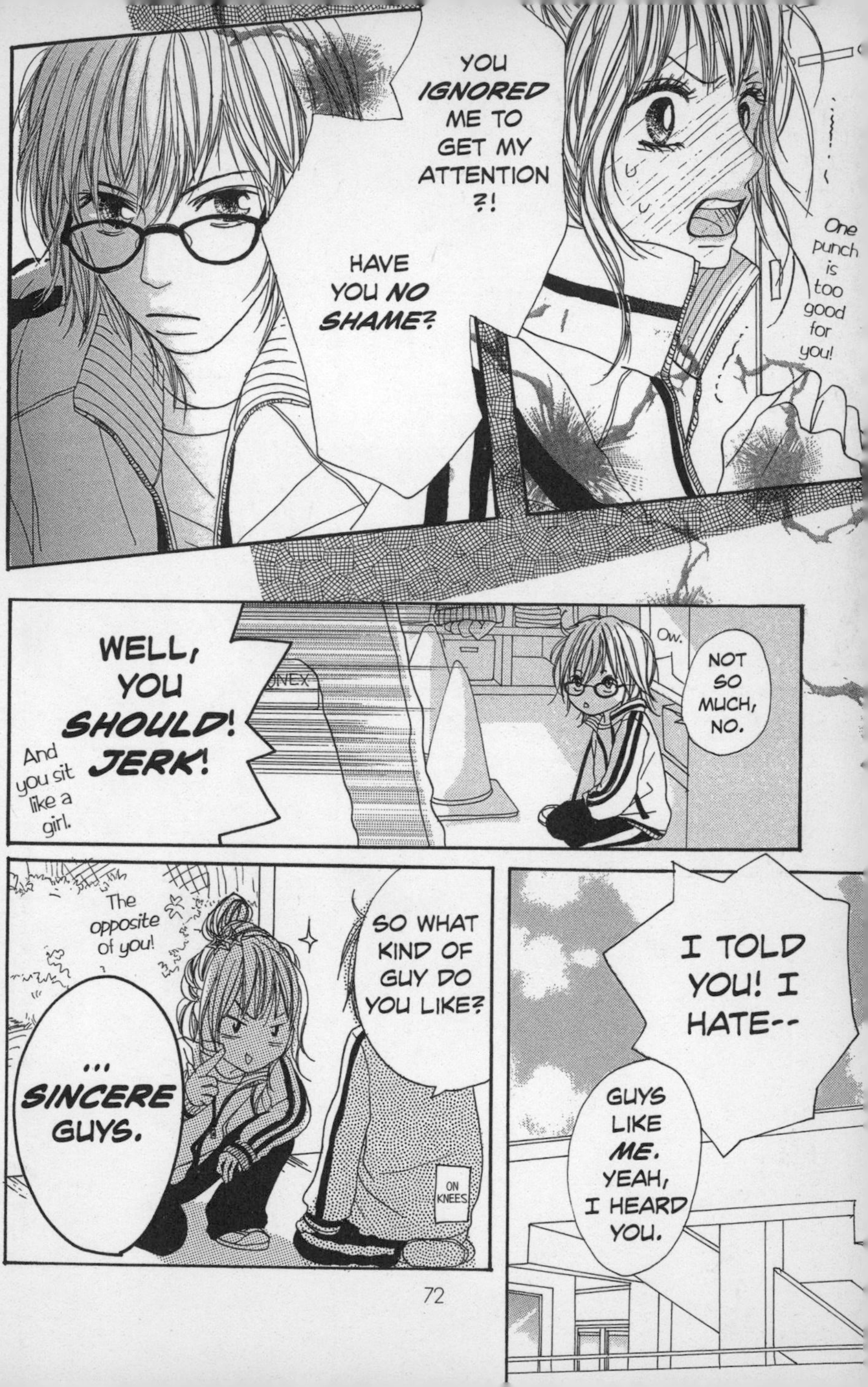
YOU IGNORED ME TO GET MY ATTENTION?!
HAVE YOU NO SHAME?
One punch is too good for you!
Ow.
NOT SO MUCH, NO.
WELL, YOU SHOULD! JERK!
And you sit like a girl.
I TOLD YOU! I HATE--
GUYS LIKE ME. YEAH, I HEARD YOU.
SO WHAT KIND OF GUY DO YOU LIKE?
ON KNEES
The opposite of you!
... SINCERE GUYS.

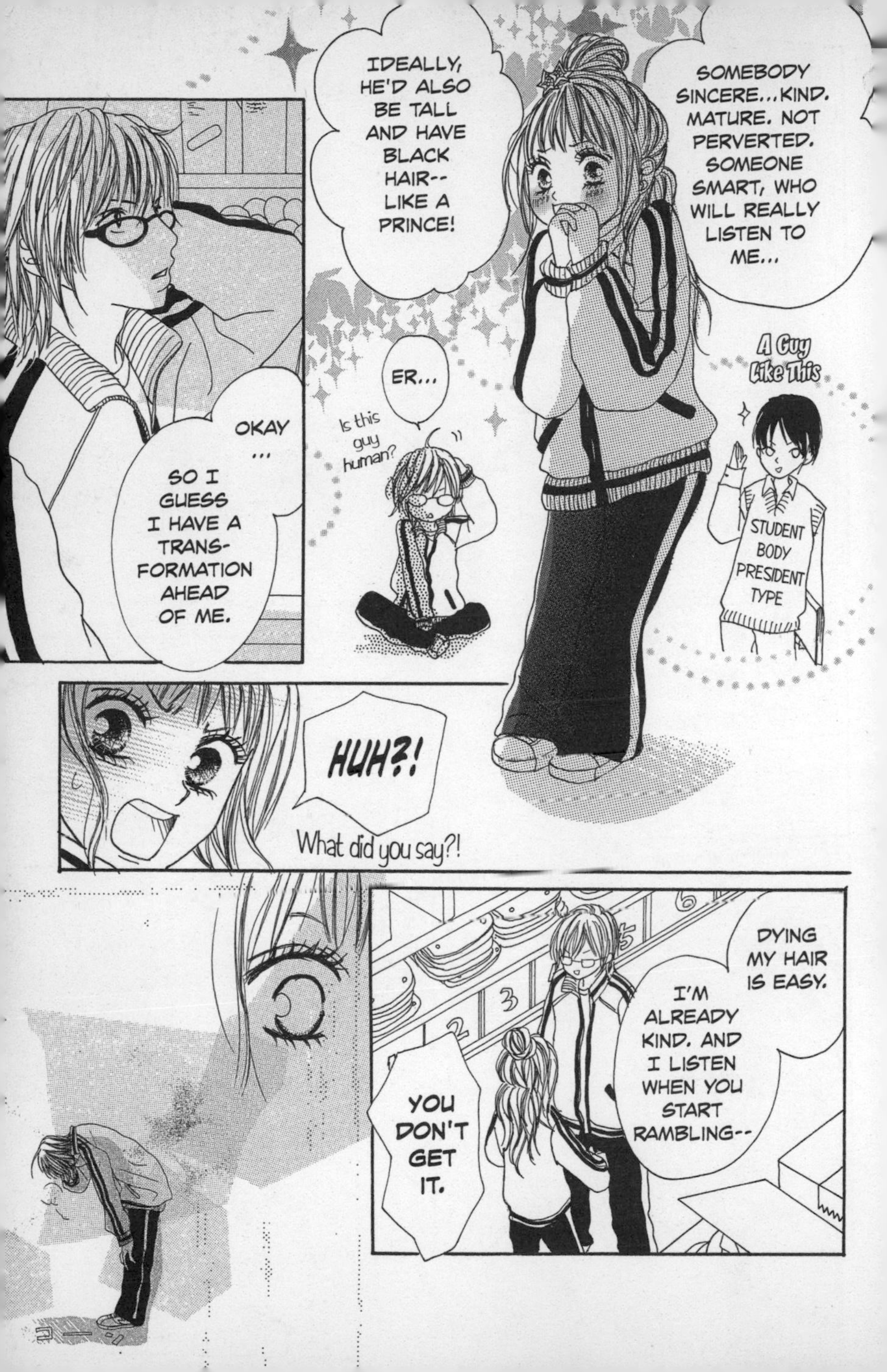
SOMEBODY SINCERE...KIND. MATURE. NOT PERVERTED. SOMEONE SMART, WHO WILL REALLY LISTEN TO ME...
IDEALLY, HE'D ALSO BE TALL AND HAVE BLACK HAIR--LIKE A PRINCE!
A Guy Like This
STUDENT BODY PRESIDENT TYPE
ER...
Is this guy human?
OKAY ... SO I GUESS I HAVE A TRANS-FORMATION AHEAD OF ME.
HUH?!
What did you say?!
DYING MY HAIR IS EASY.
I'M ALREADY KIND. AND I LISTEN WHEN YOU START RAMBLING--
YOU DON'T GET IT.

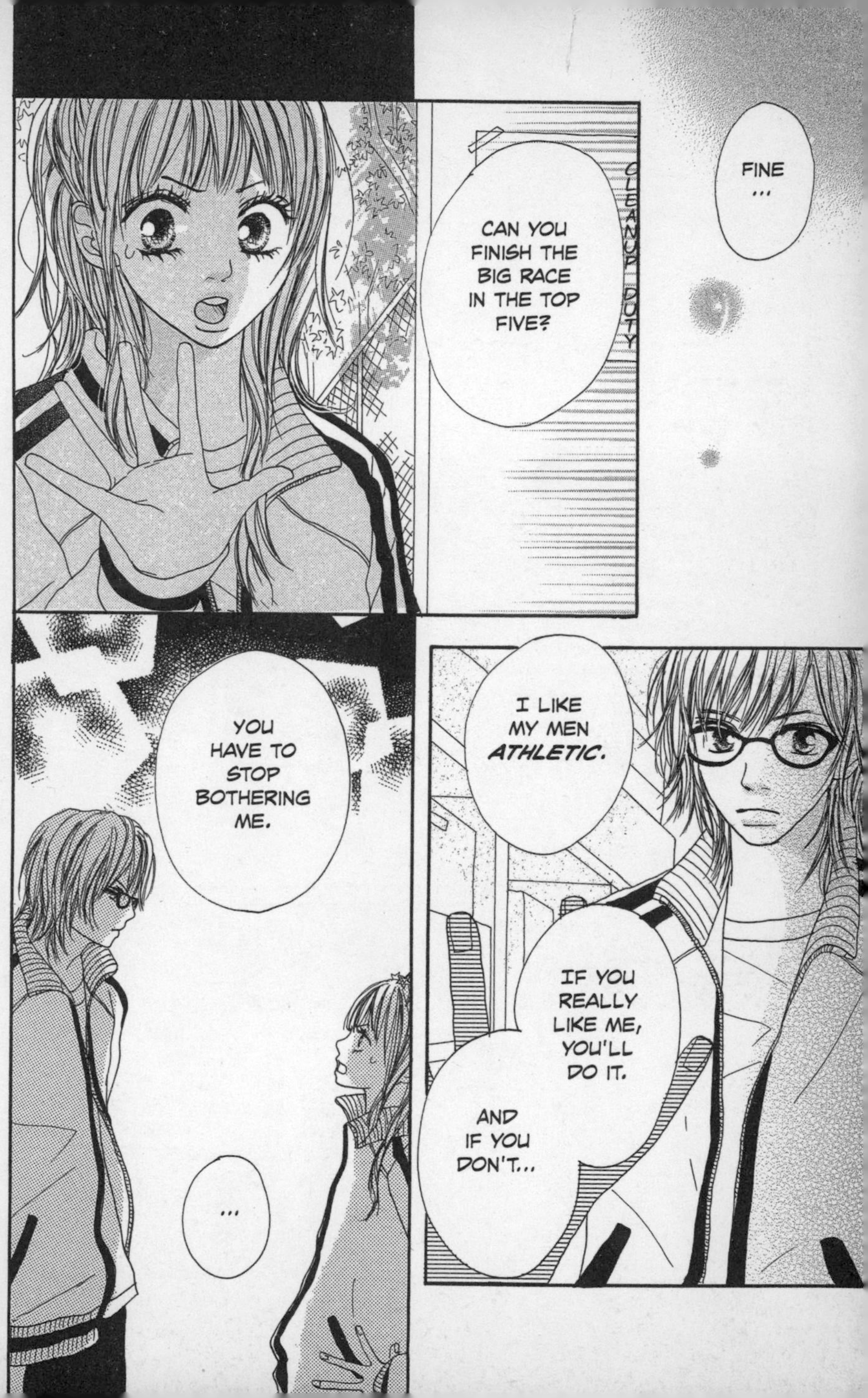
FINE ...
CAN YOU FINISH THE BIG RACE IN THE TOP FIVE?
CLEANUP DUTY
I LIKE MY MEN ATHLETIC.
IF YOU REALLY LIKE ME, YOU'LL DO IT.
AND IF YOU DON'T...
YOU HAVE TO STOP BOTHERING ME.
...

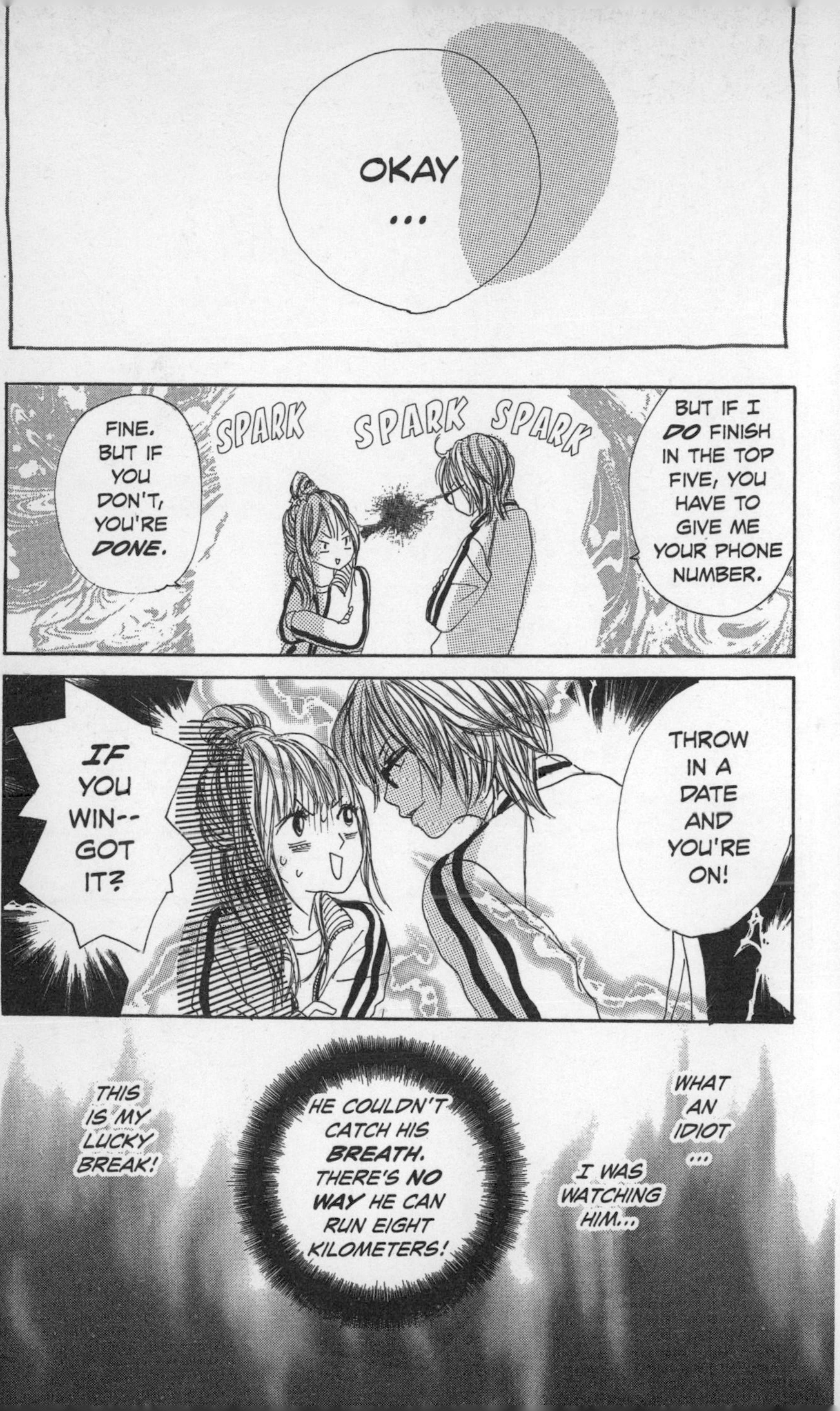
OKAY ...
BUT IF I DO FINISH IN THE TOP FIVE, YOU HAVE TO GIVE ME YOUR PHONE NUMBER.
SPARK SPARK SPARK
FINE. BUT IF YOU DON'T, YOU'RE DONE.
THROW IN A DATE AND YOU'RE ON!
IF YOU WIN--GOT IT?
WHAT AN IDIOT ...
I WAS WATCHING HIM...
HE COULDN'T CATCH HIS BREATH. THERE'S NO WAY HE CAN RUN EIGHT KILOMETERS!
THIS IS MY LUCKY BREAK!

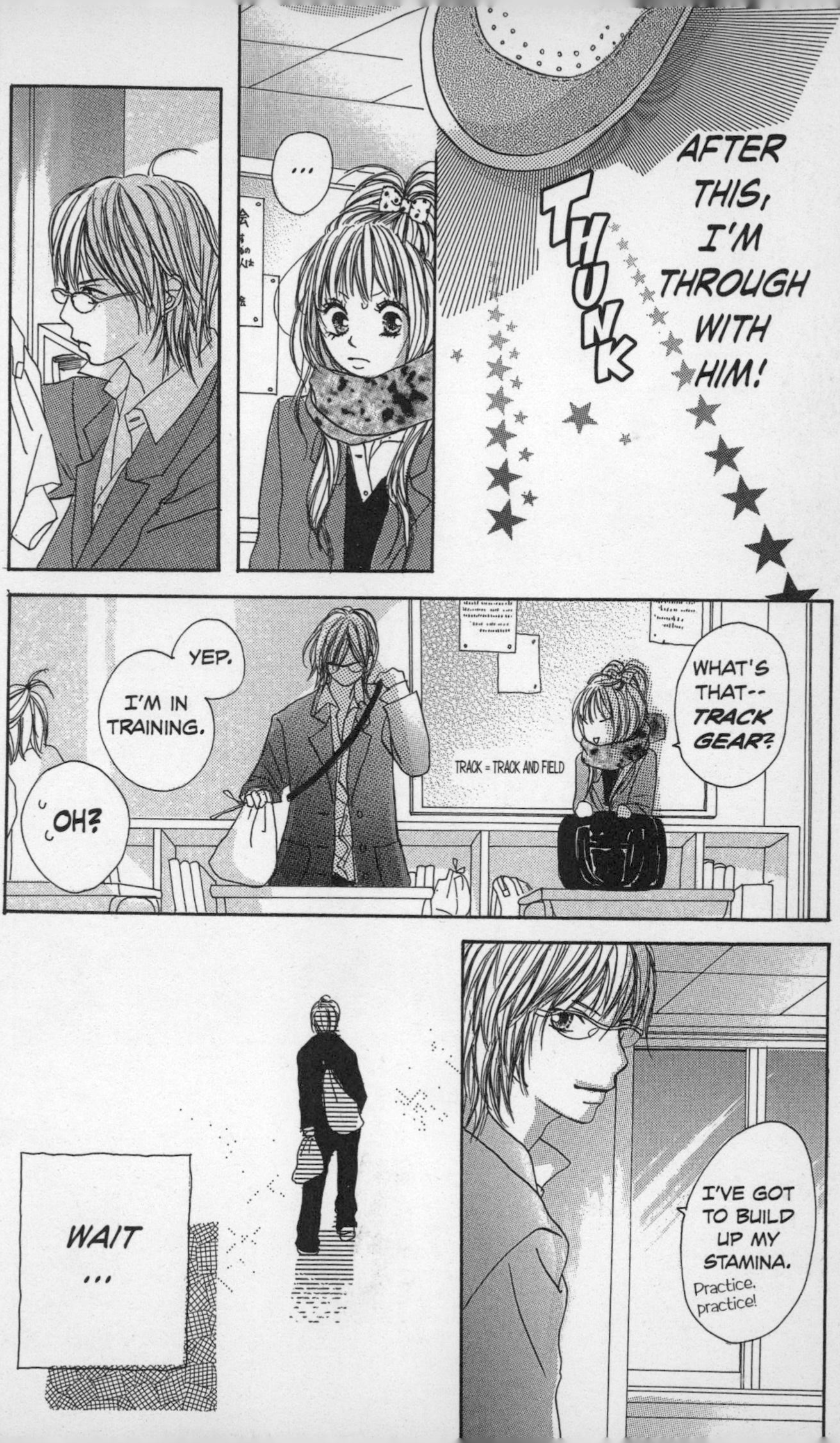
AFTER THIS, I'M THROUGH WITH HIM!
THUNK
...
WHAT'S THAT-- TRACK GEAR?
TRACK = TRACK AND FIELD
YEP. I'M IN TRAINING.
OH?
I'VE GOT TO BUILD UP MY STAMINA.
Practice, practice!
WAIT ...

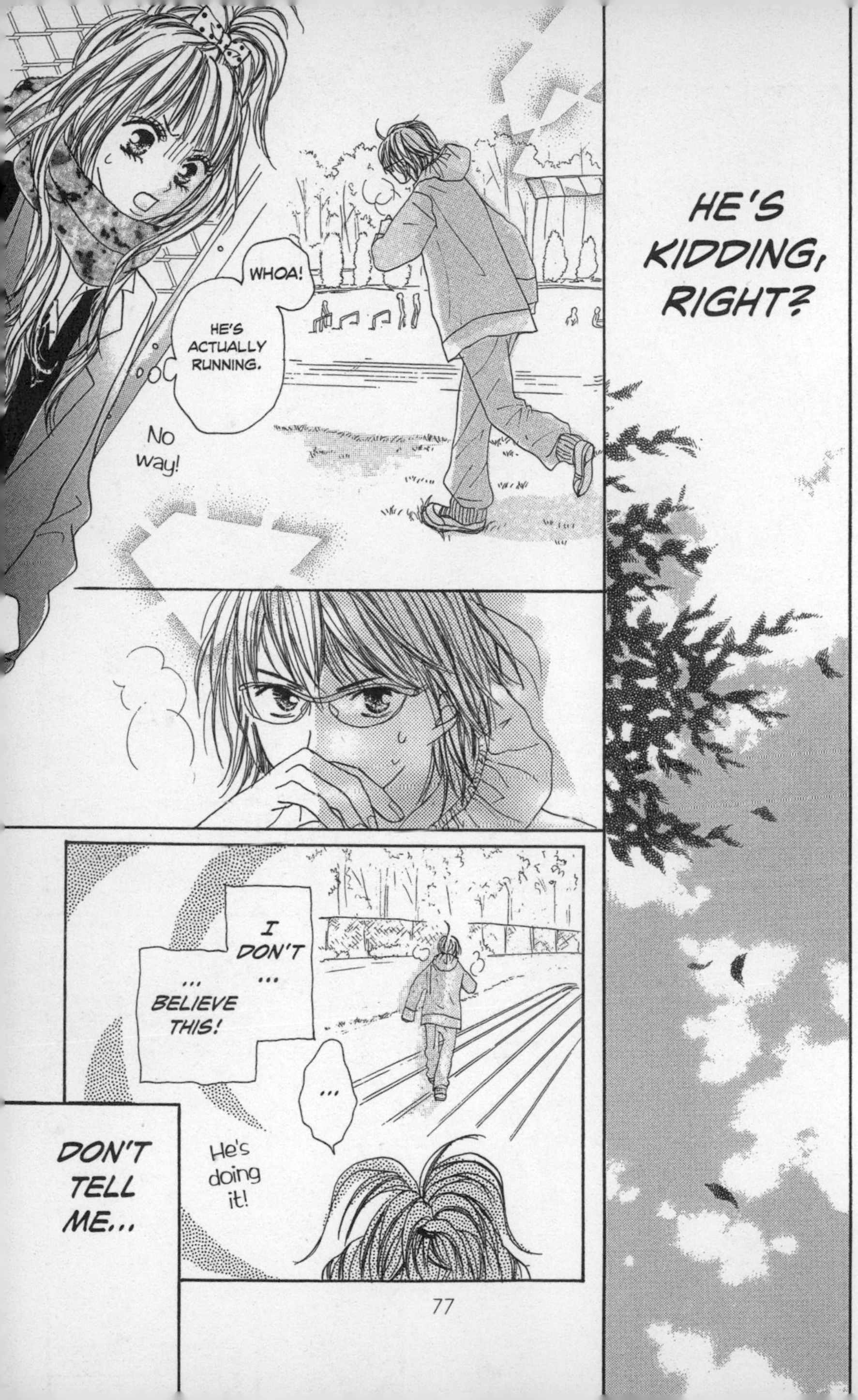
HE'S KIDDING, RIGHT?
WHOA!
HE'S ACTUALLY RUNNING.
No way!
I DON'T ...
... BELIEVE THIS!
...
He's doing it!
DON'T TELL ME...

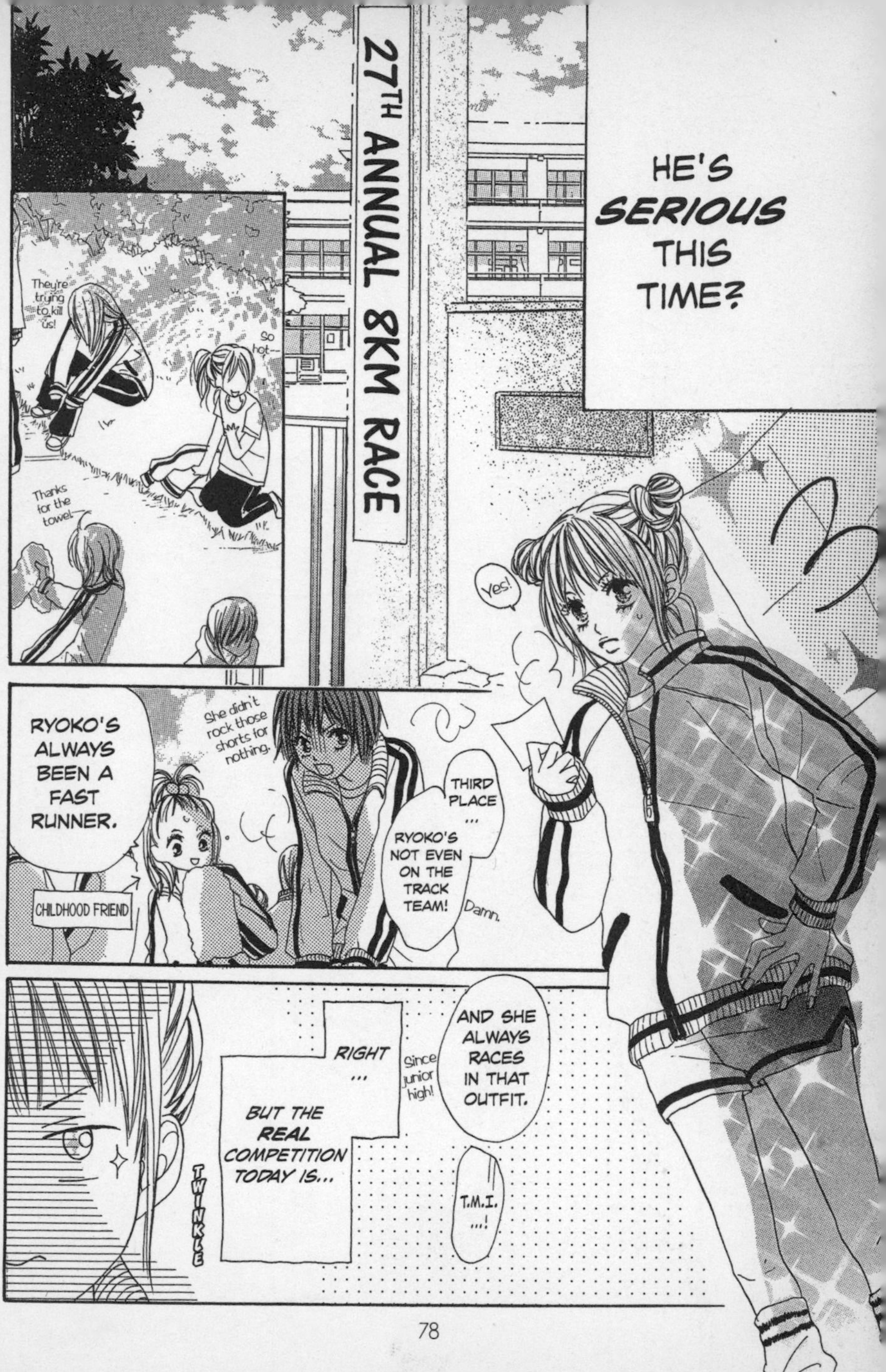
HE'S *SERIOUS* THIS TIME?
27TH ANNUAL 8KM RACE
They're trying to kill us!
So hot...
Thanks for the towel.
Yes!
THIRD PLACE...
RYOKO'S NOT EVEN ON THE TRACK TEAM!
Damn.
She didn't rock those shorts for nothing.
RYOKO'S ALWAYS BEEN A FAST RUNNER.
CHILDHOOD FRIEND
AND SHE ALWAYS RACES IN THAT OUTFIT.
T.M.I. ...!
Since junior high!
RIGHT...
BUT THE REAL COMPETITION TODAY IS...
TWINKLE

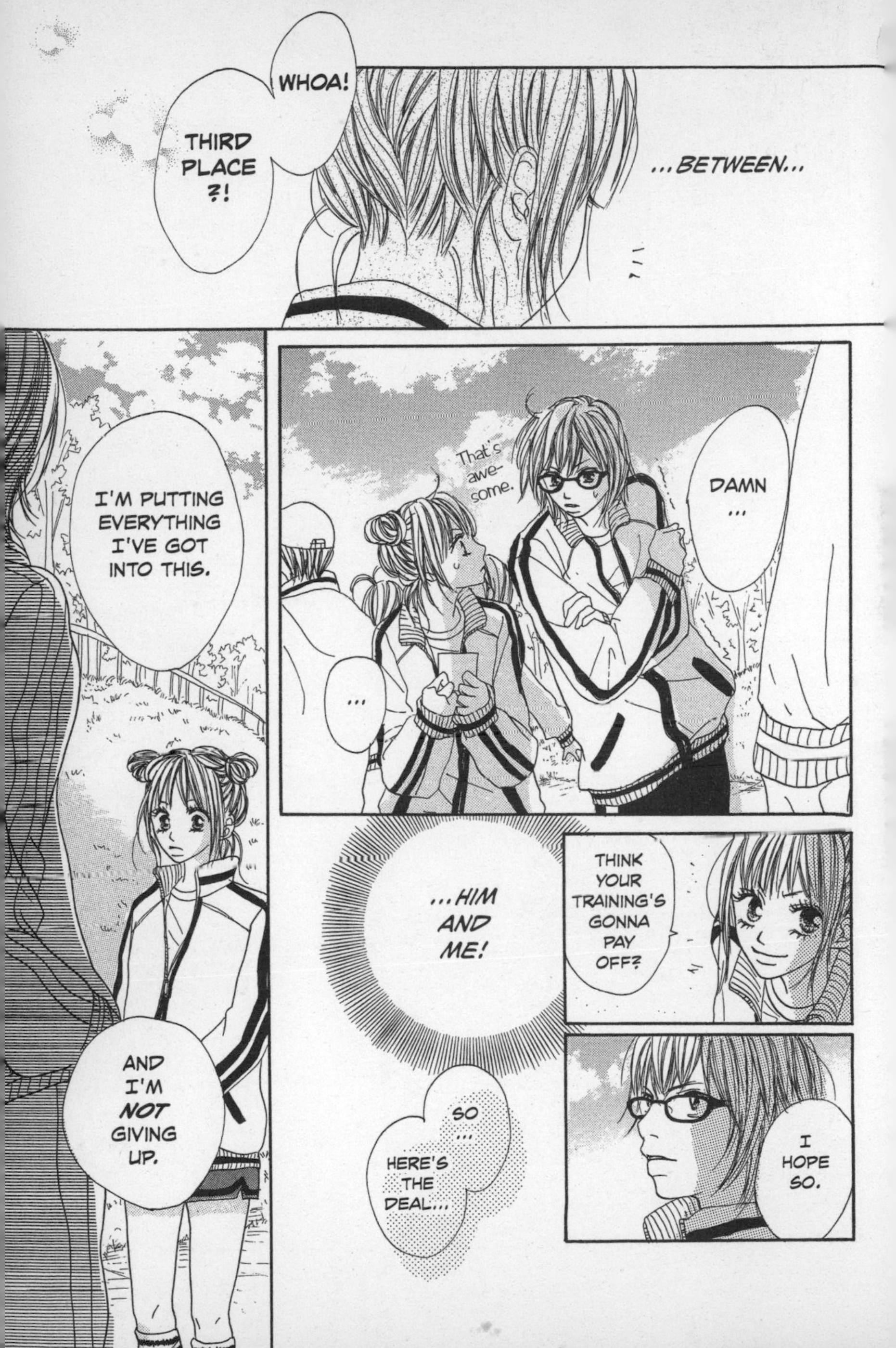

WHOA!
THIRD PLACE ?!
...BETWEEN...
DAMN ...
That's awe-some.
...
THINK YOUR TRAINING'S GONNA PAY OFF?
...HIM AND ME!
I HOPE SO.
SO ... HERE'S THE DEAL...
I'M PUTTING EVERYTHING I'VE GOT INTO THIS.
AND I'M NOT GIVING UP.

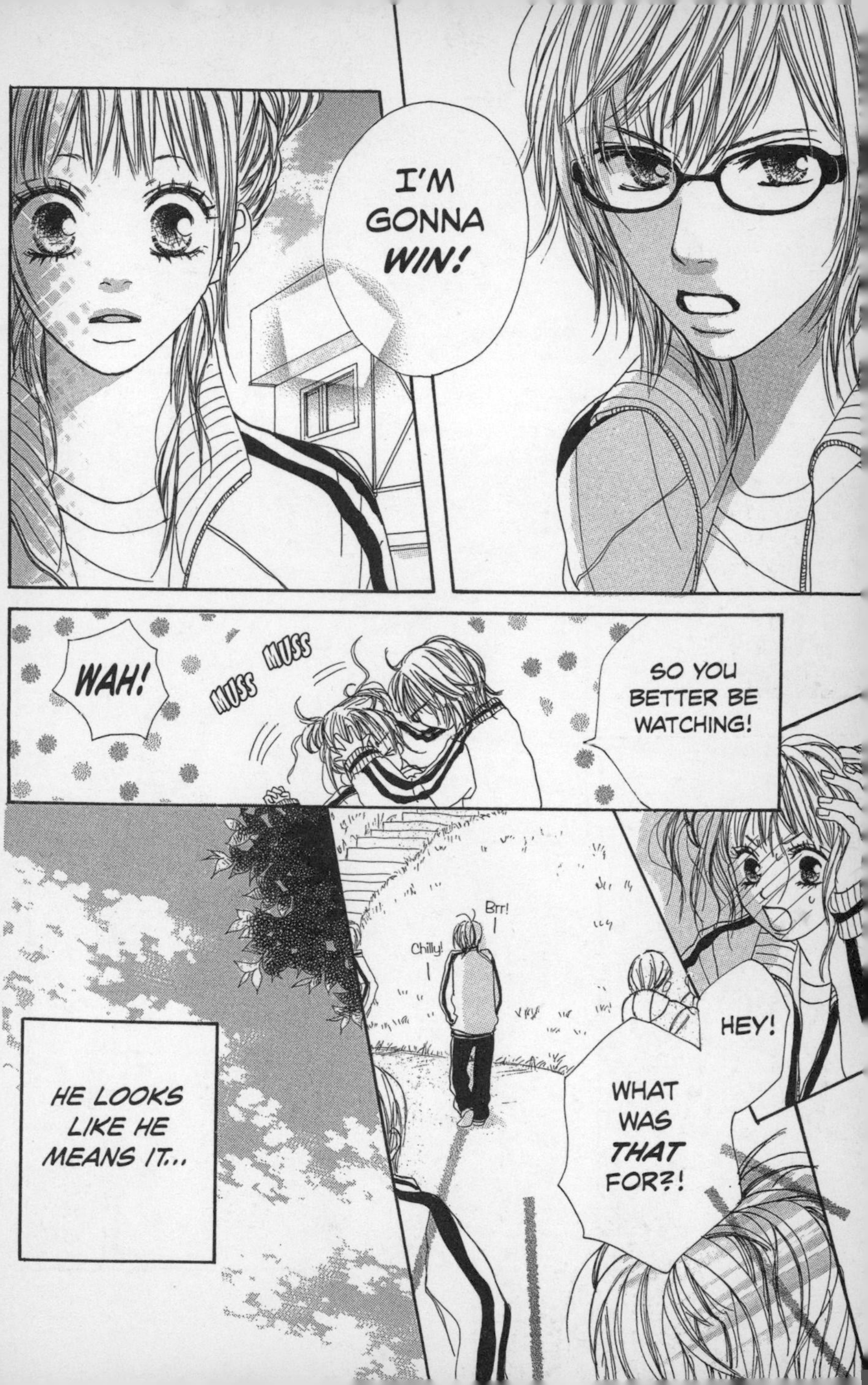
I'M GONNA WIN!
SO YOU BETTER BE WATCHING!
MUSS
MUSS
WAH!
HEY!
WHAT WAS THAT FOR?!
Brr!
Chilly!
HE LOOKS LIKE HE MEANS IT...

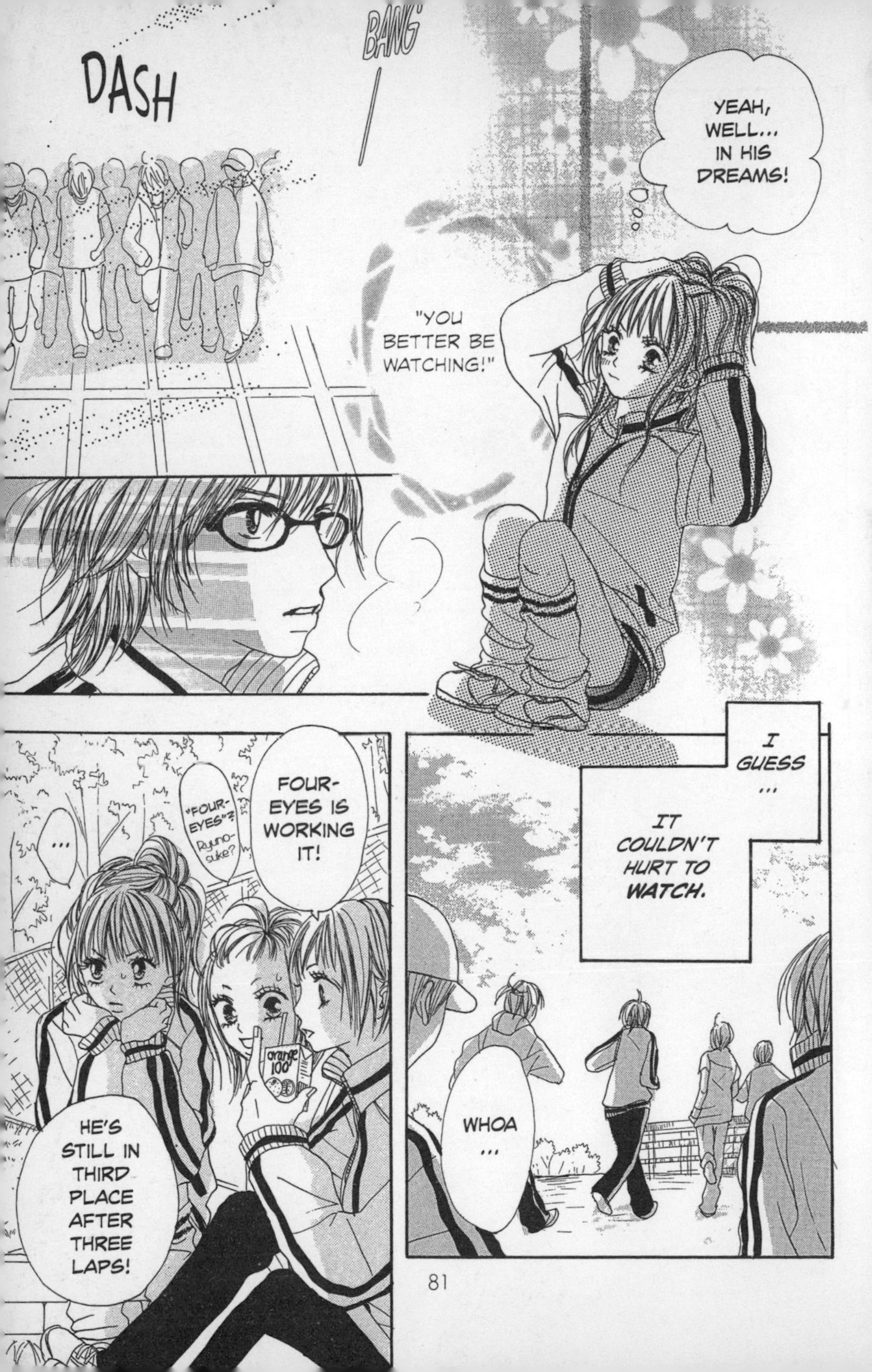
YEAH, WELL... IN HIS DREAMS!
"YOU BETTER BE WATCHING!"
BANG
DASH
I GUESS...
IT COULDN'T HURT TO WATCH.
WHOA...
FOUR-EYES IS WORKING IT!
"FOUR-EYES"? Ryunosuke?
...
HE'S STILL IN THIRD PLACE AFTER THREE LAPS!

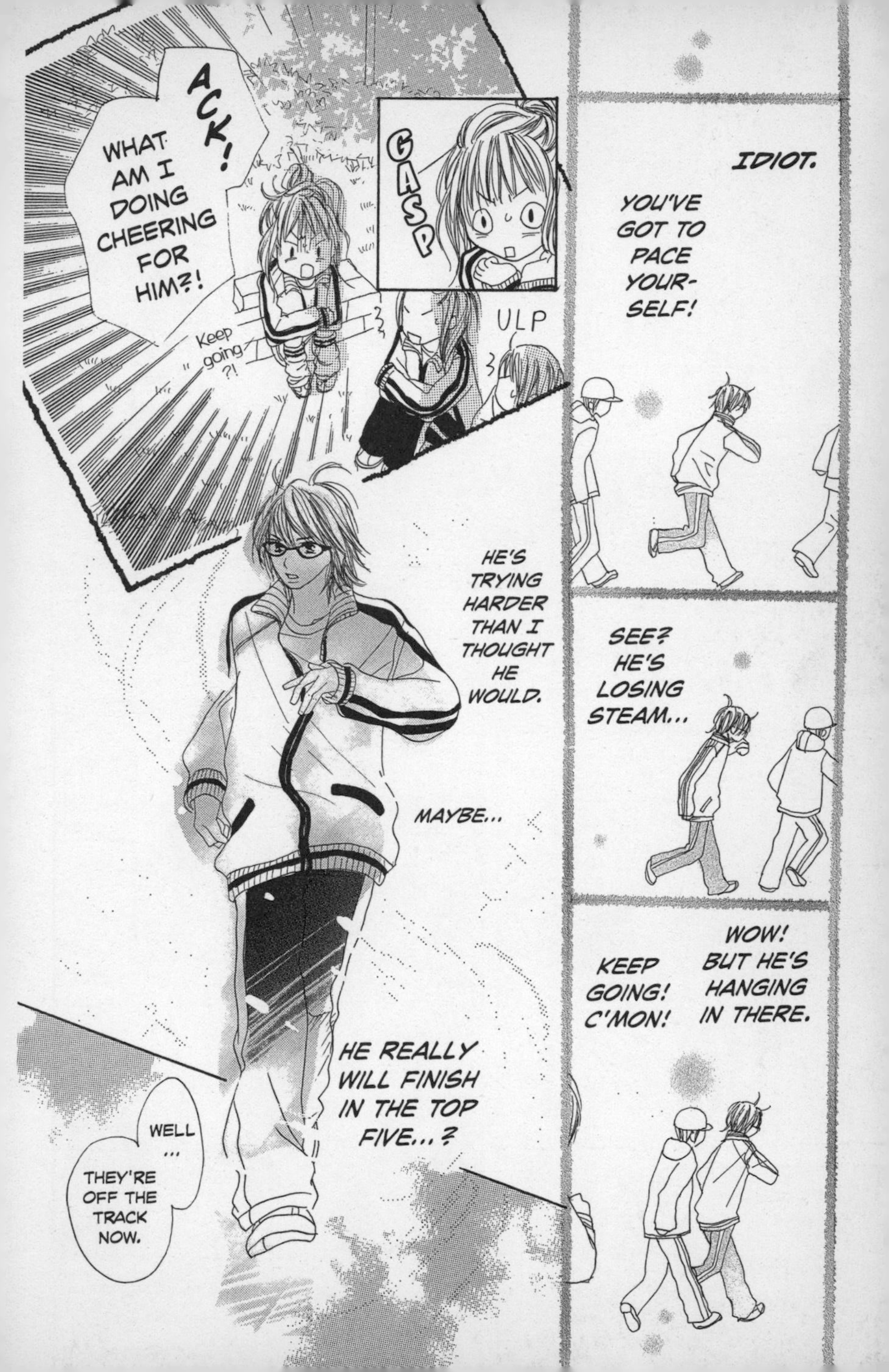
IDIOT.
YOU'VE GOT TO PACE YOURSELF!
SEE? HE'S LOSING STEAM...
WOW! BUT HE'S HANGING IN THERE.
KEEP GOING! C'MON!
GASP
ACK!
WHAT AM I DOING CHEERING FOR HIM?!
ULP
Keep going?!
HE'S TRYING HARDER THAN I THOUGHT HE WOULD.
MAYBE...
HE REALLY WILL FINISH IN THE TOP FIVE...?
WELL... THEY'RE OFF THE TRACK NOW.

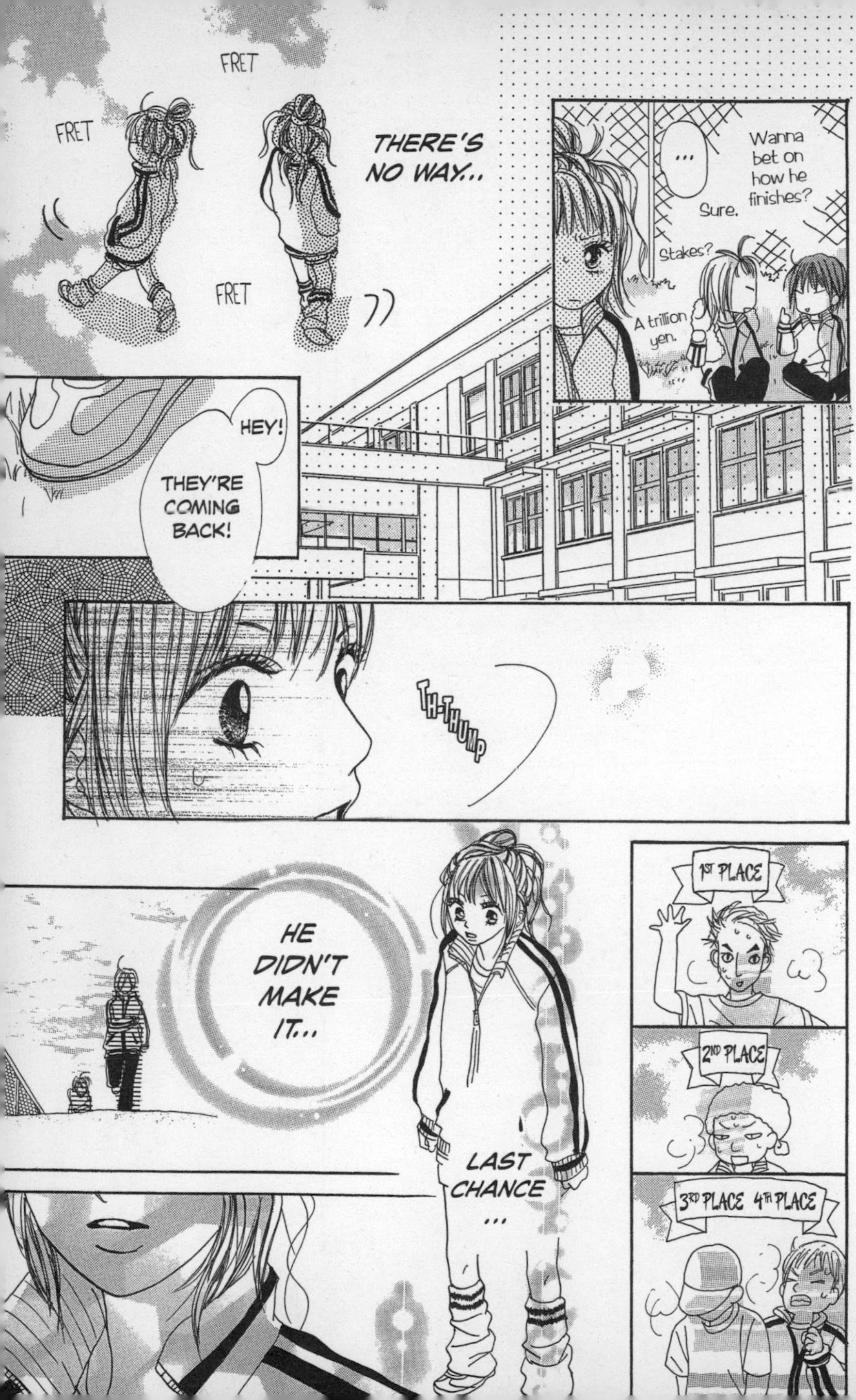

...
Wanna bet on how he finishes?
Sure.
Stakes?
A trillion yen.
FRET
FRET
FRET
THERE'S NO WAY...
HEY!
THEY'RE COMING BACK!
TH-THUMP
1ST PLACE
2ND PLACE
3RD PLACE 4TH PLACE
HE DIDN'T MAKE IT...
LAST CHANCE ...

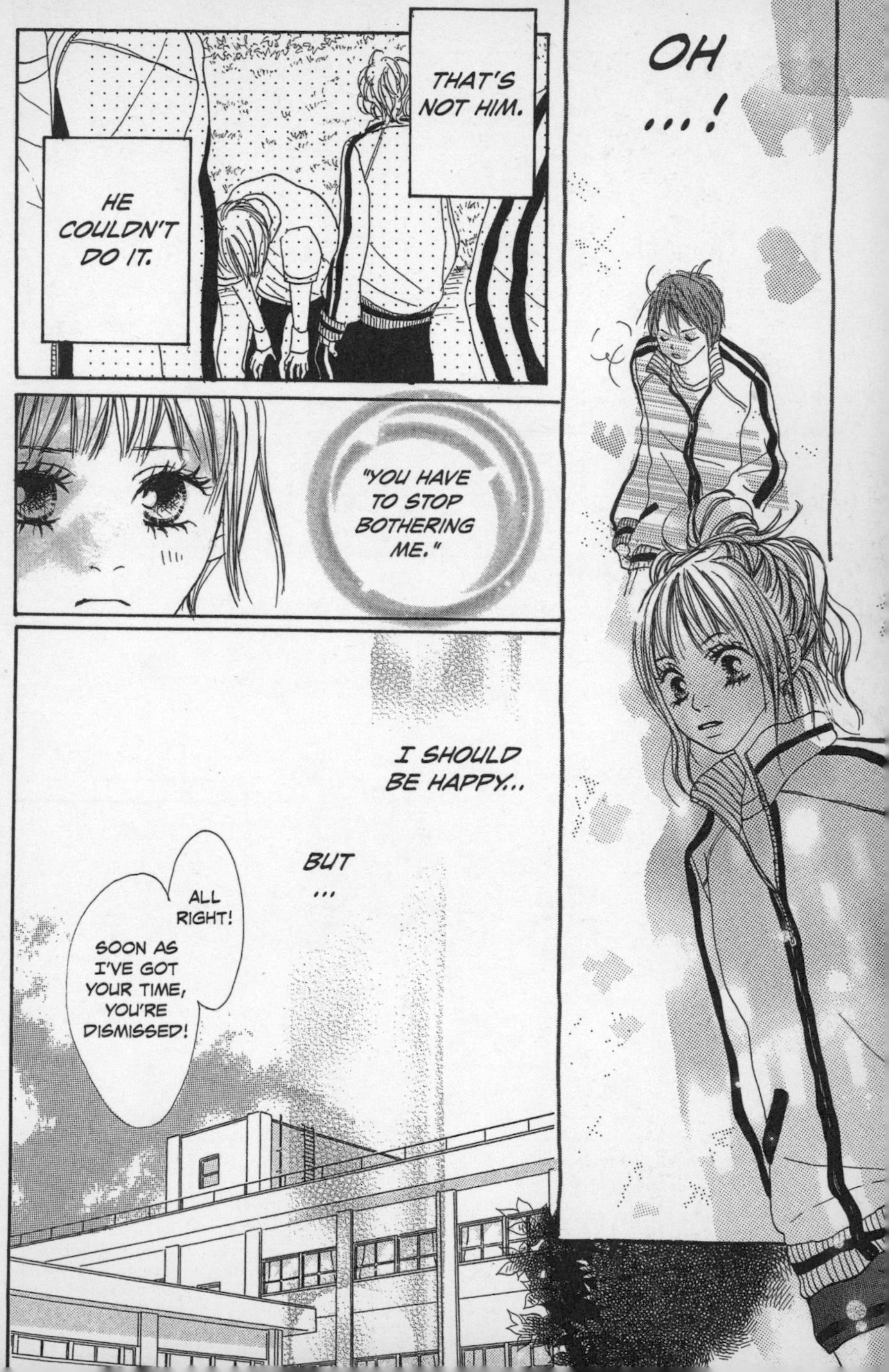
OH ...!
THAT'S NOT HIM.
HE COULDN'T DO IT.
"YOU HAVE TO STOP BOTHERING ME."
I SHOULD BE HAPPY...
BUT ...
ALL RIGHT! SOON AS I'VE GOT YOUR TIME, YOU'RE DISMISSED!

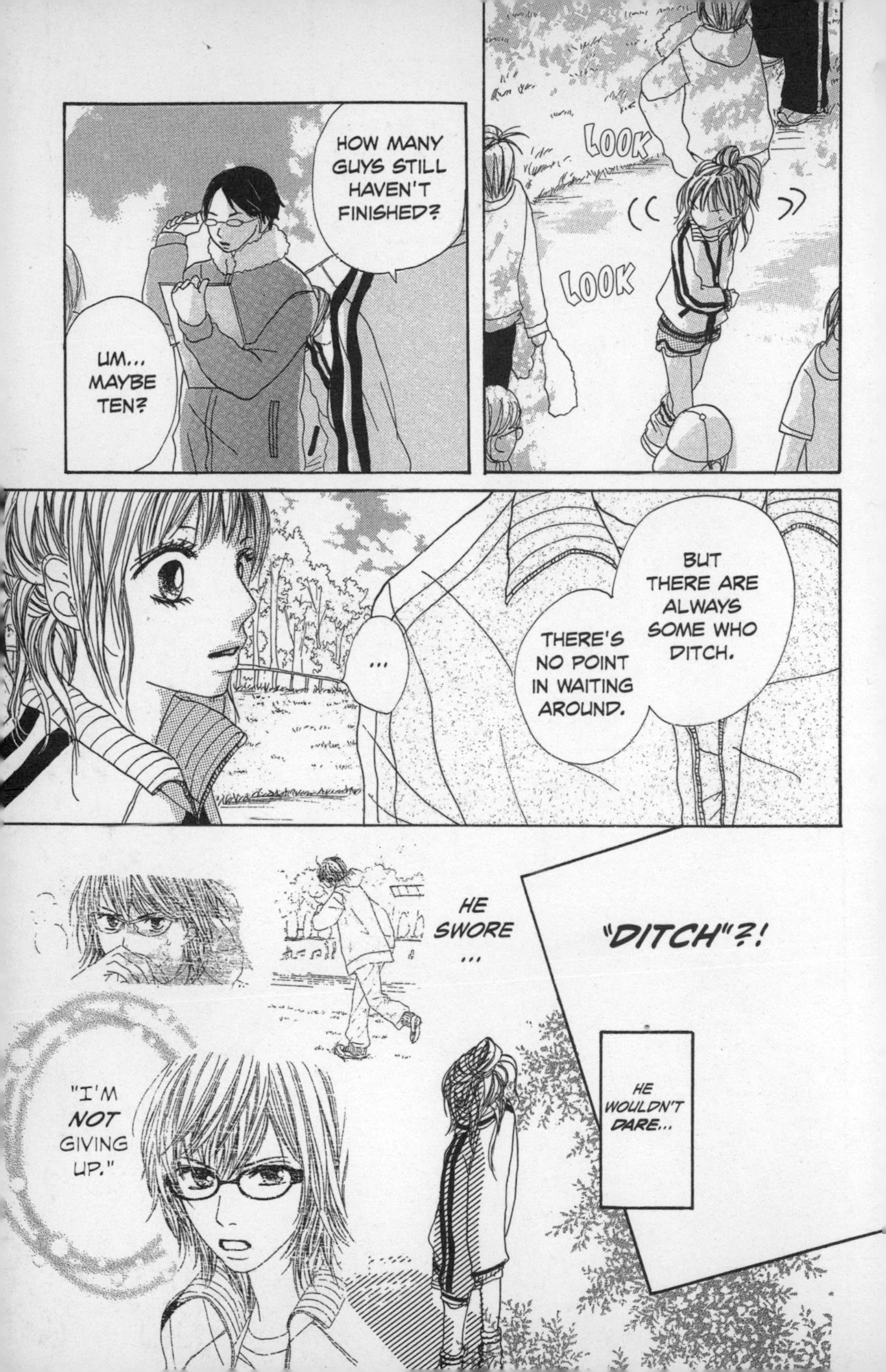
LOOK
LOOK
HOW MANY GUYS STILL HAVEN'T FINISHED?
UM... MAYBE TEN?
BUT THERE ARE ALWAYS SOME WHO DITCH.
THERE'S NO POINT IN WAITING AROUND.
...
"DITCH"?!
HE WOULDN'T DARE...
HE SWORE ...
"I'M *NOT* GIVING UP."

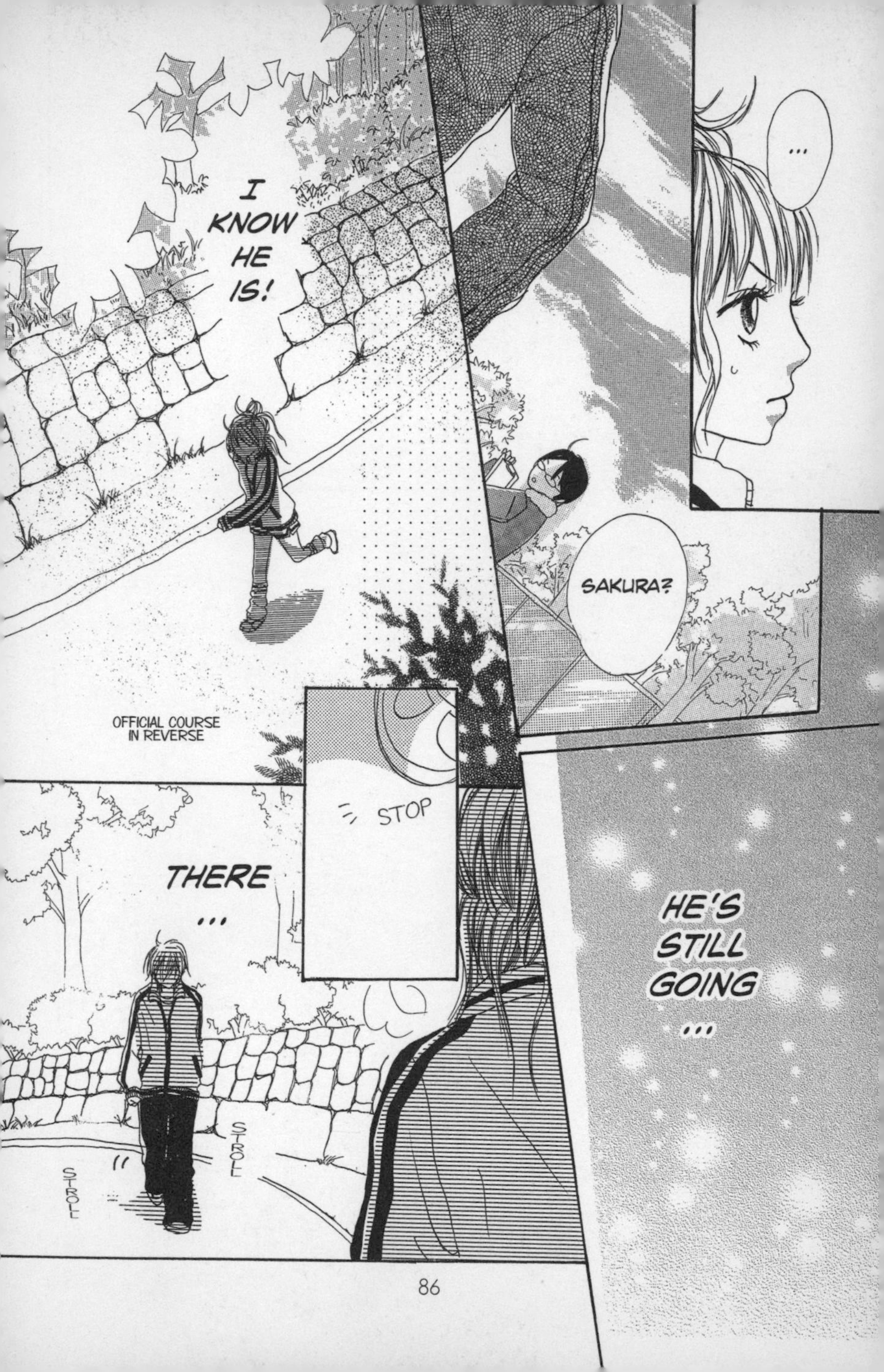
...
SAKURA?
I KNOW HE IS!
OFFICIAL COURSE IN REVERSE
HE'S STILL GOING ...
STOP
THERE ...
STROLL
STROLL

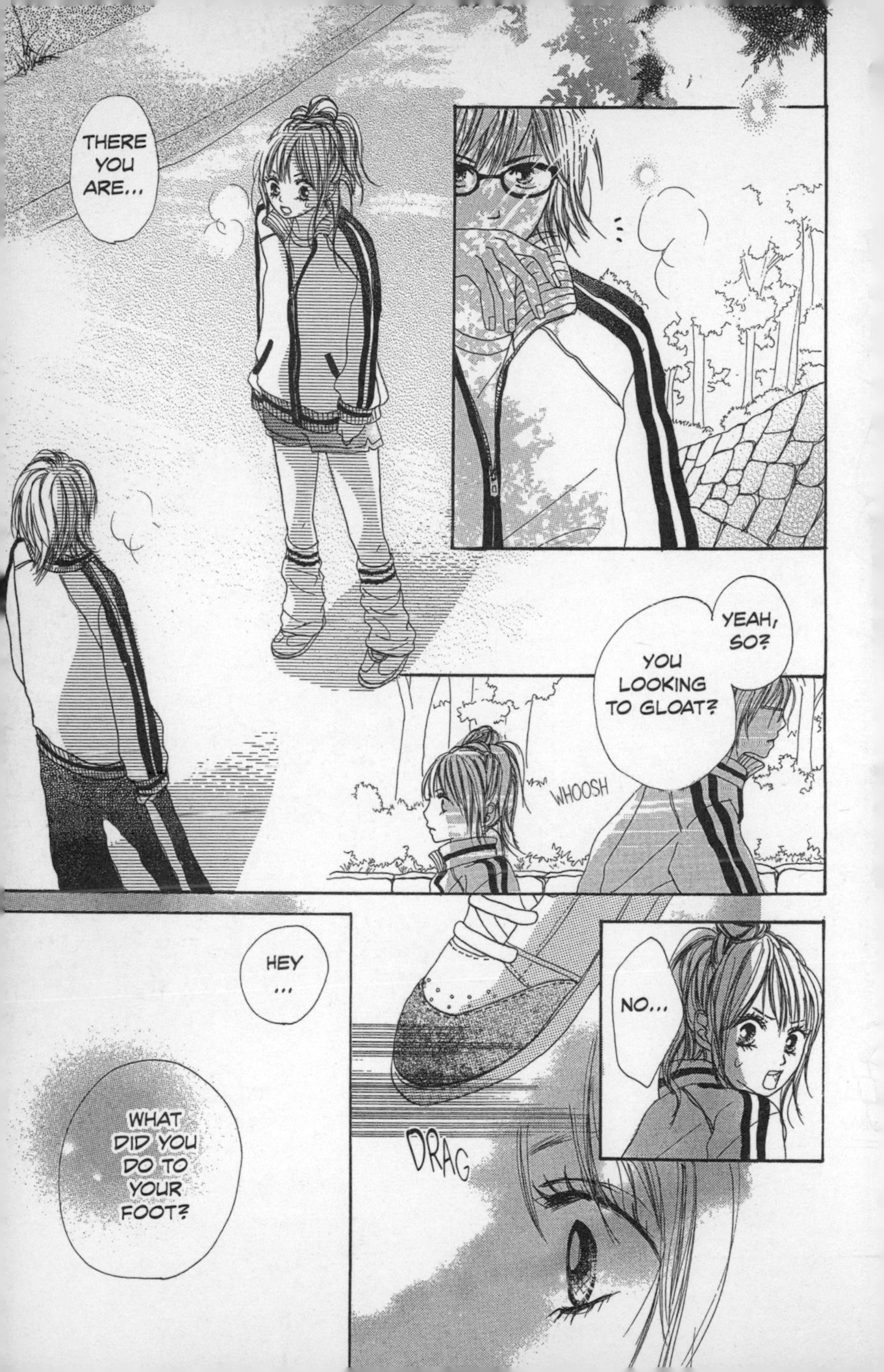
THERE YOU ARE...
YEAH, SO? YOU LOOKING TO GLOAT?
WHOOSH
NO...
HEY ...
DRAG
WHAT DID YOU DO TO YOUR FOOT?

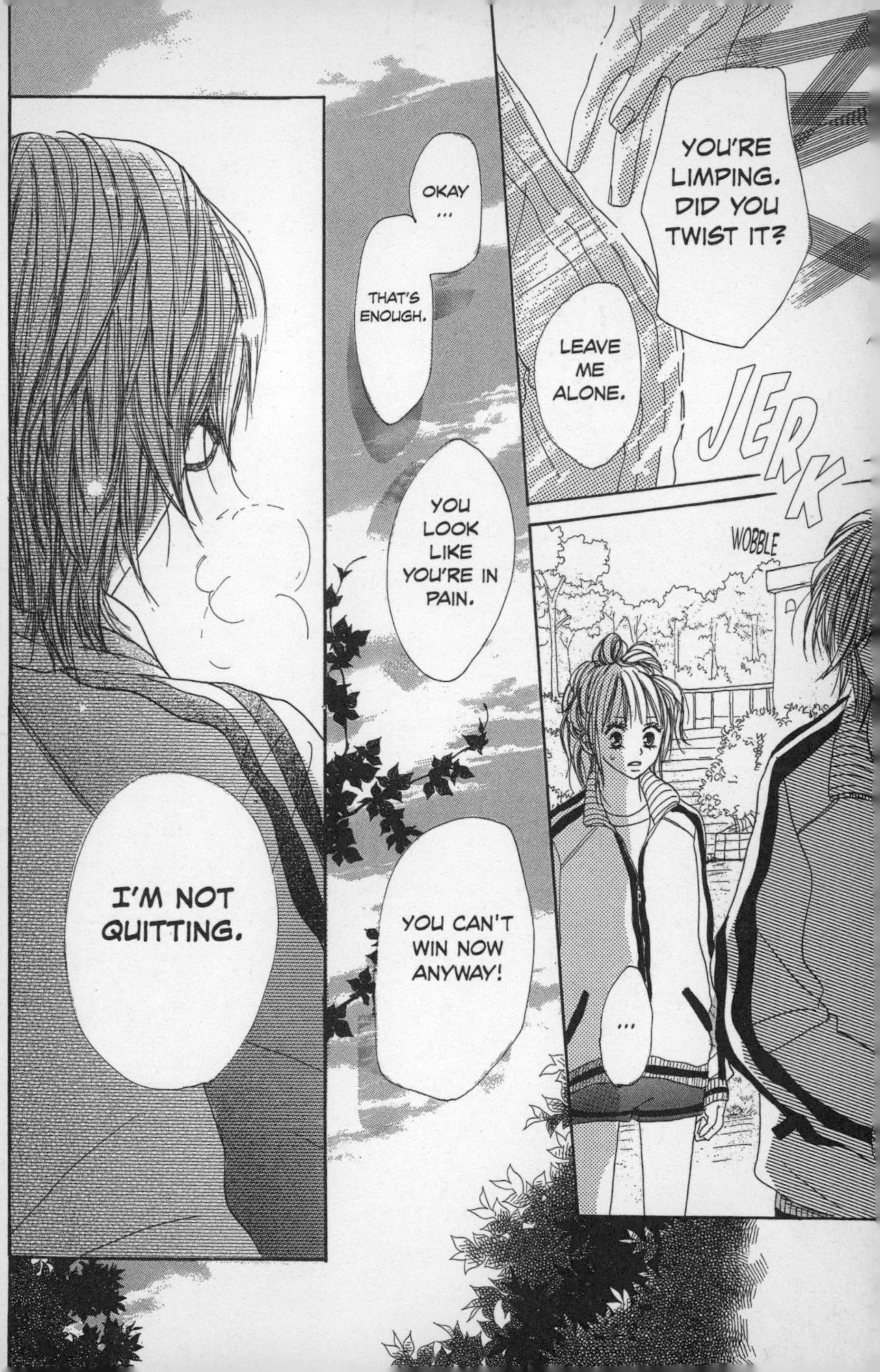
YOU'RE LIMPING. DID YOU TWIST IT?
LEAVE ME ALONE.
JERK
WOBBLE
...
OKAY ...
THAT'S ENOUGH.
YOU LOOK LIKE YOU'RE IN PAIN.
YOU CAN'T WIN NOW ANYWAY!
I'M NOT QUITTING.

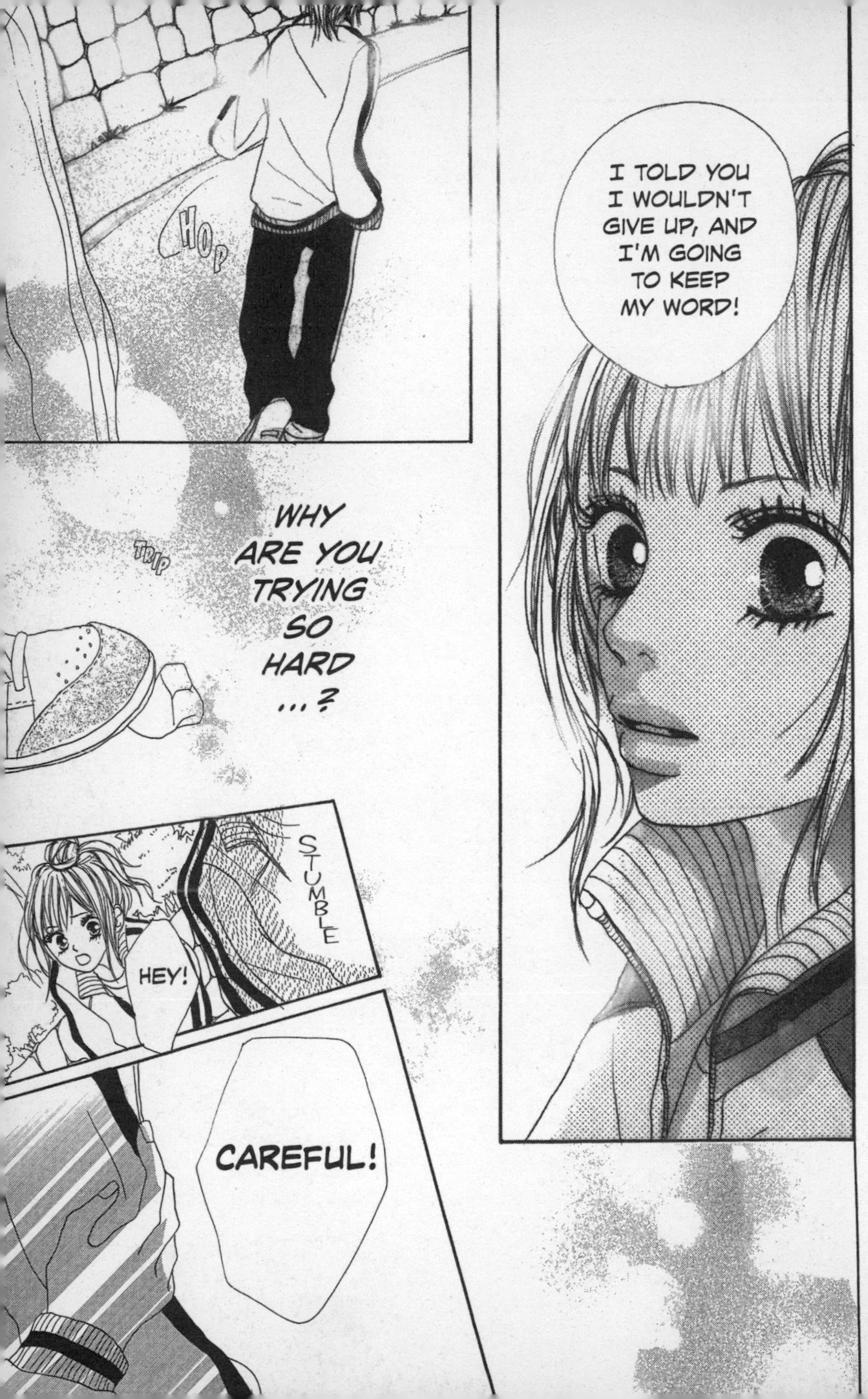
I TOLD YOU I WOULDN'T GIVE UP, AND I'M GOING TO KEEP MY WORD!
HOP
WHY ARE YOU TRYING SO HARD ...?
TRIP
STUMBLE
HEY!
CAREFUL!

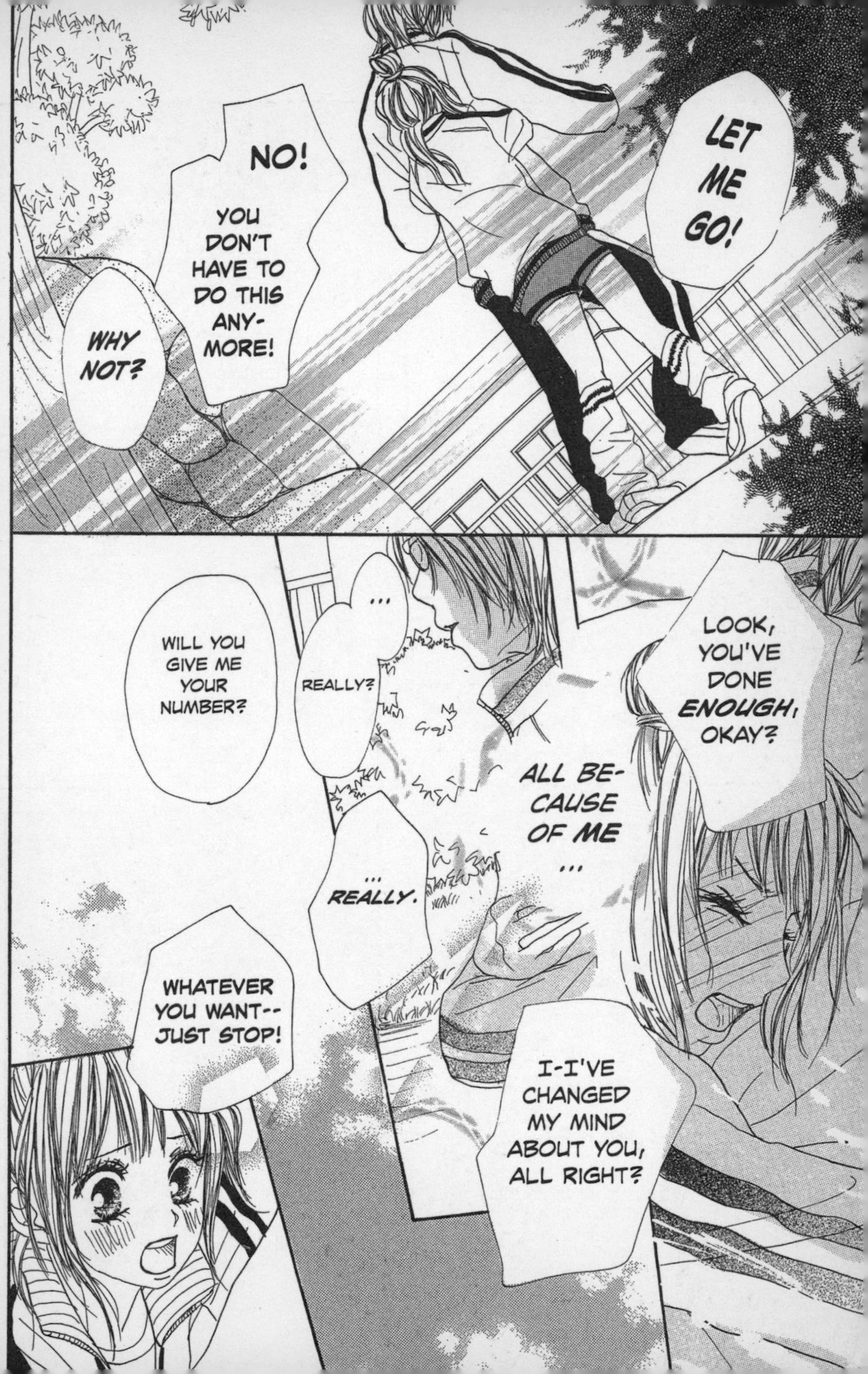
LET ME GO!
NO!
YOU DON'T HAVE TO DO THIS ANY-MORE!
WHY NOT?
LOOK, YOU'VE DONE ENOUGH, OKAY?
...
REALLY?
WILL YOU GIVE ME YOUR NUMBER?
ALL BE-CAUSE OF ME ...
... REALLY.
I-I'VE CHANGED MY MIND ABOUT YOU, ALL RIGHT?
WHATEVER YOU WANT-- JUST STOP!

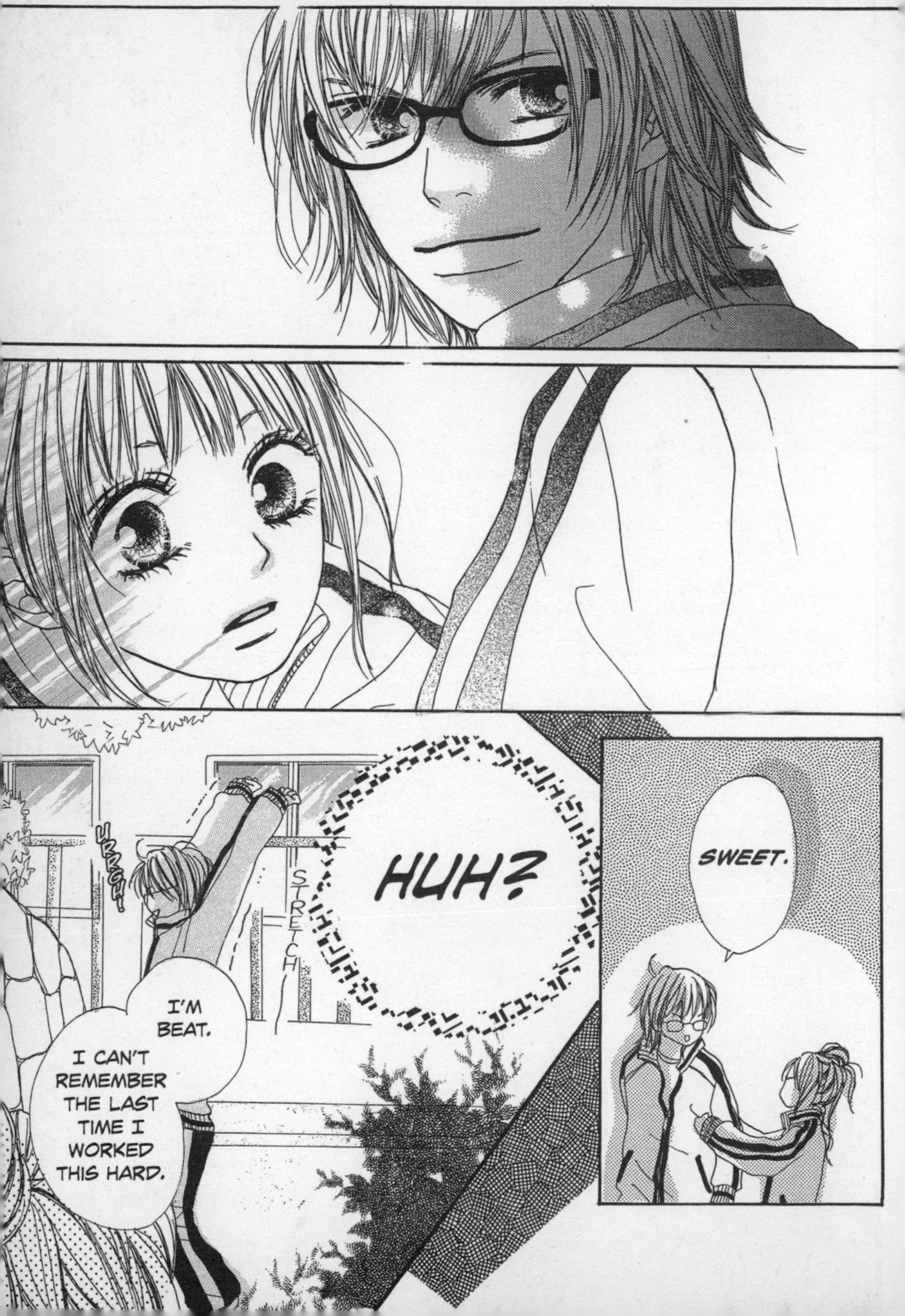
SWEET.
HUH?
URRGH!
STRETCH
I'M BEAT.
I CAN'T REMEMBER THE LAST TIME I WORKED THIS HARD.

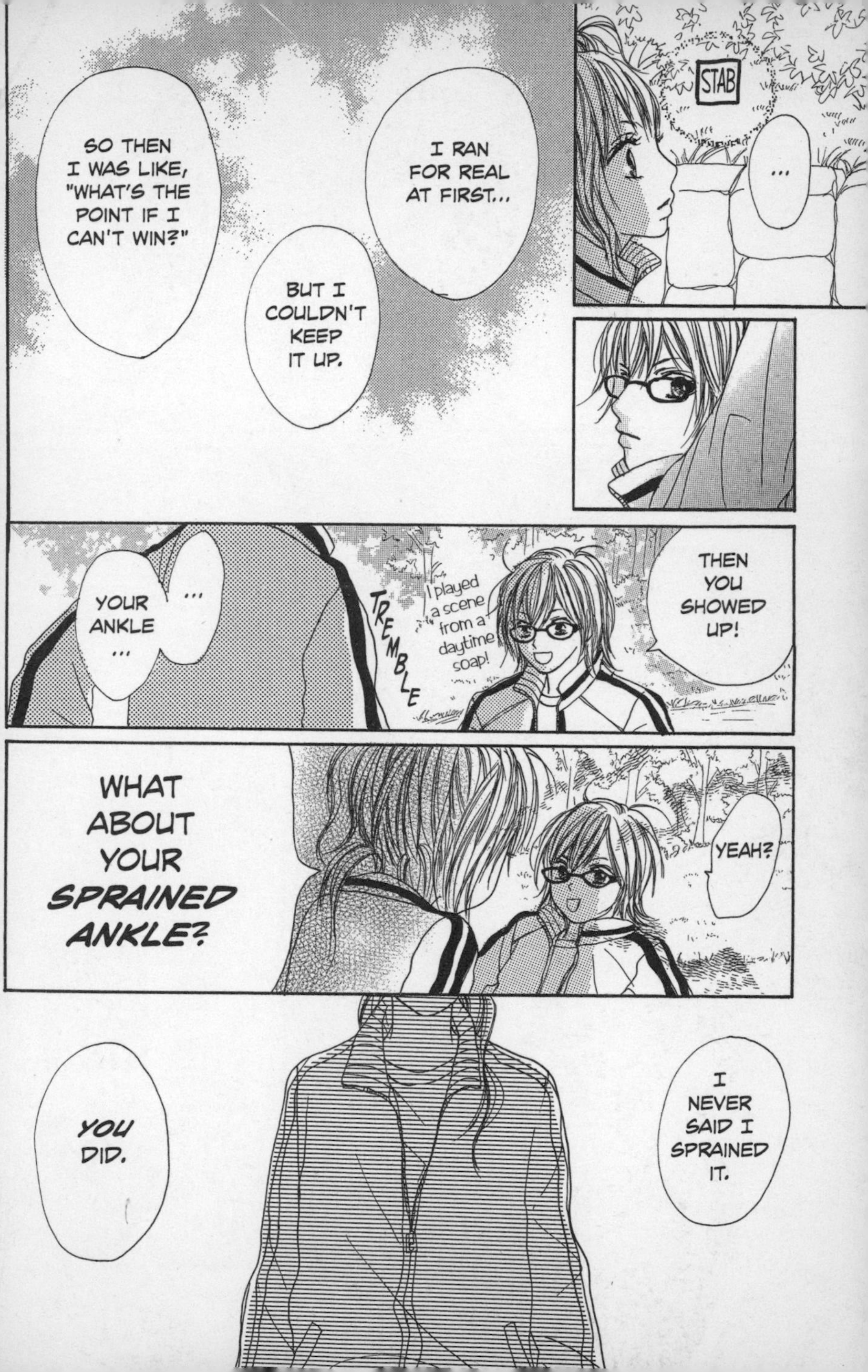
STAB
...
I RAN FOR REAL AT FIRST...
BUT I COULDN'T KEEP IT UP.
SO THEN I WAS LIKE, "WHAT'S THE POINT IF I CAN'T WIN?"
THEN YOU SHOWED UP!
I played a scene from a daytime soap!
TREMBLE
...
YOUR ANKLE ...
YEAH?
WHAT ABOUT YOUR *SPRAINED ANKLE?*
I NEVER SAID I SPRAINED IT.
YOU DID.

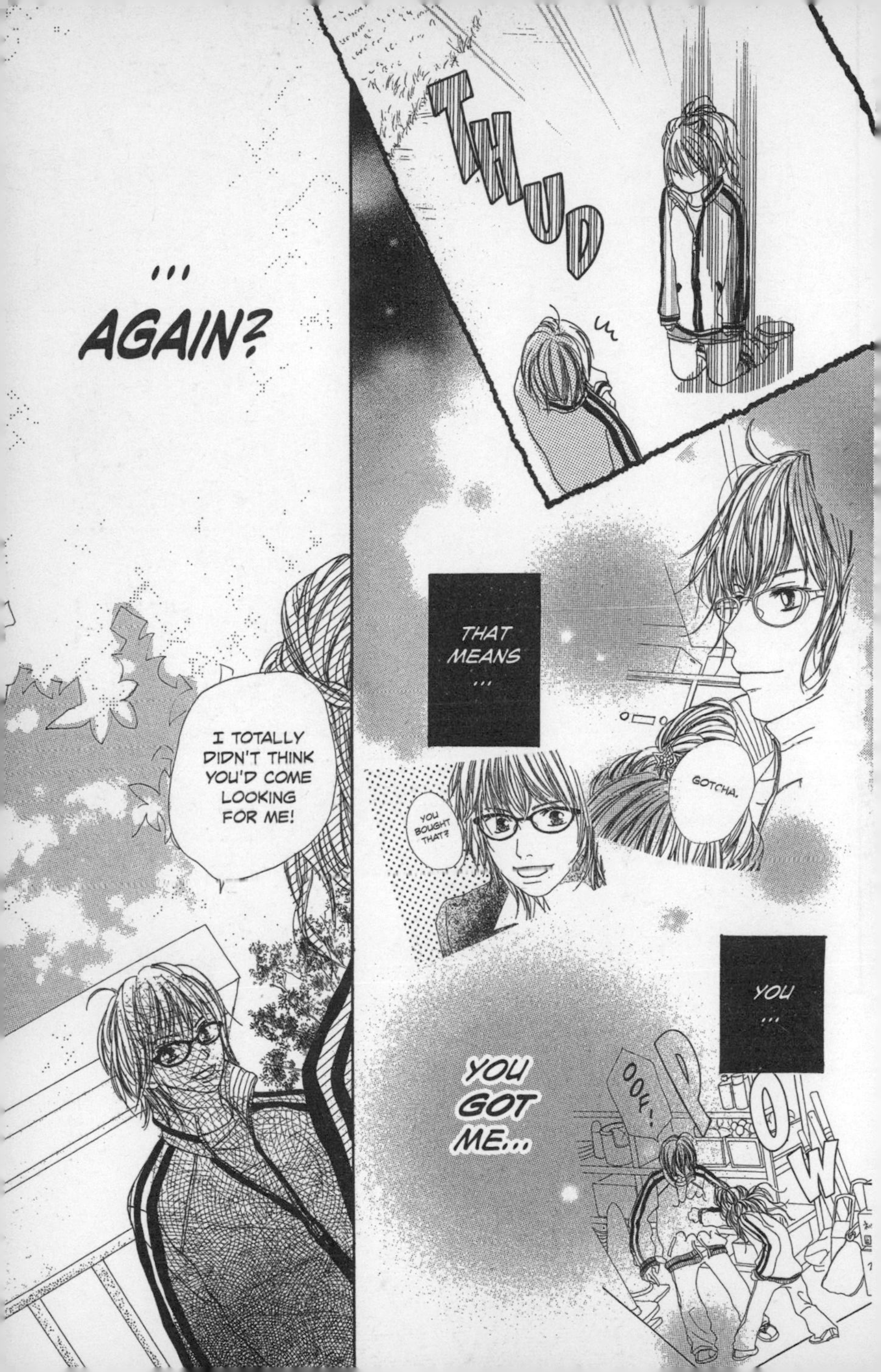
THUD
THAT MEANS ...
GOTCHA.
YOU BOUGHT THAT?
YOU ...
YOU GOT ME...
OOF!
POW
... AGAIN?
I TOTALLY DIDN'T THINK YOU'D COME LOOKING FOR ME!

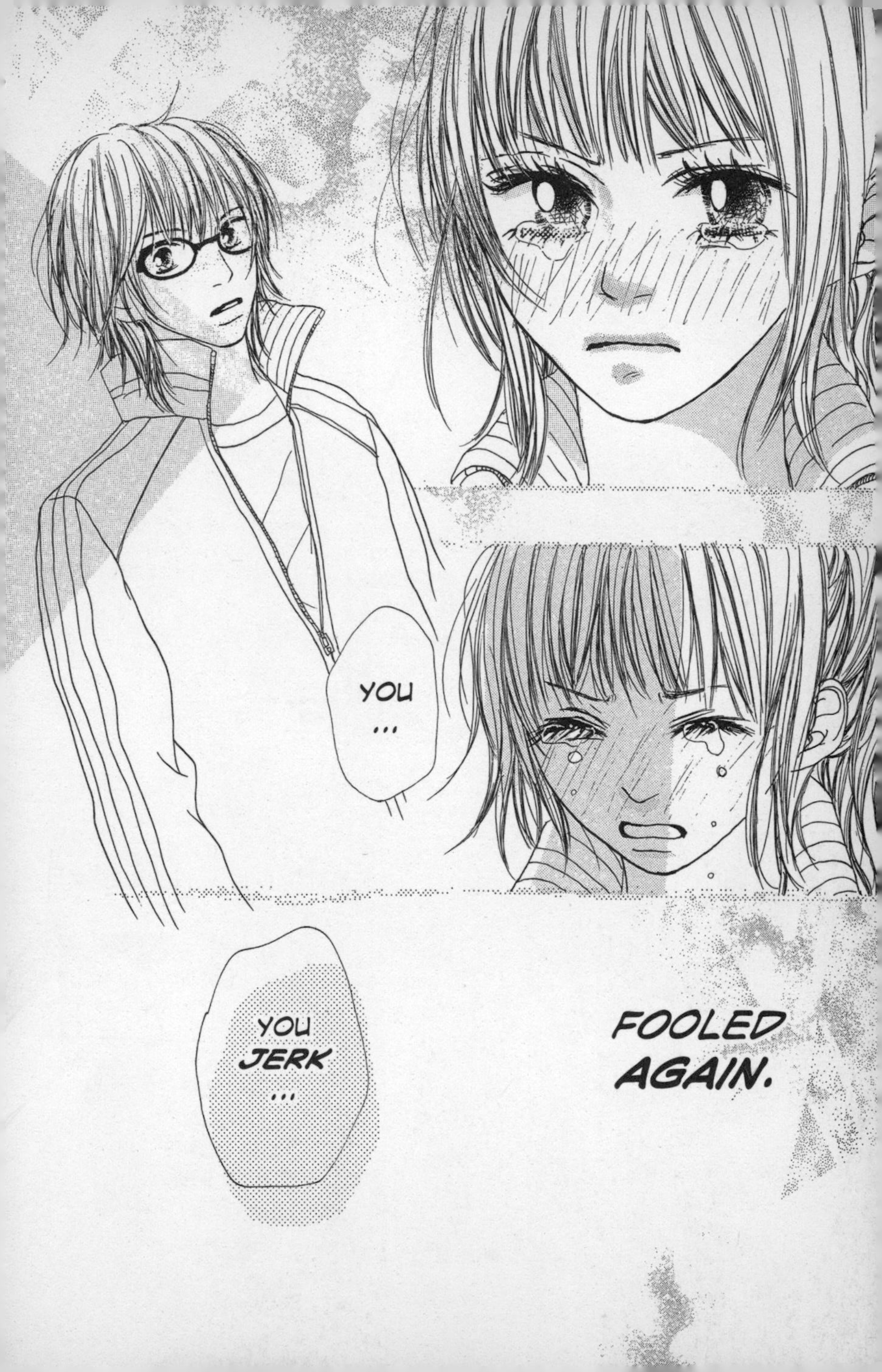
YOU ...
YOU JERK ...
FOOLED AGAIN.

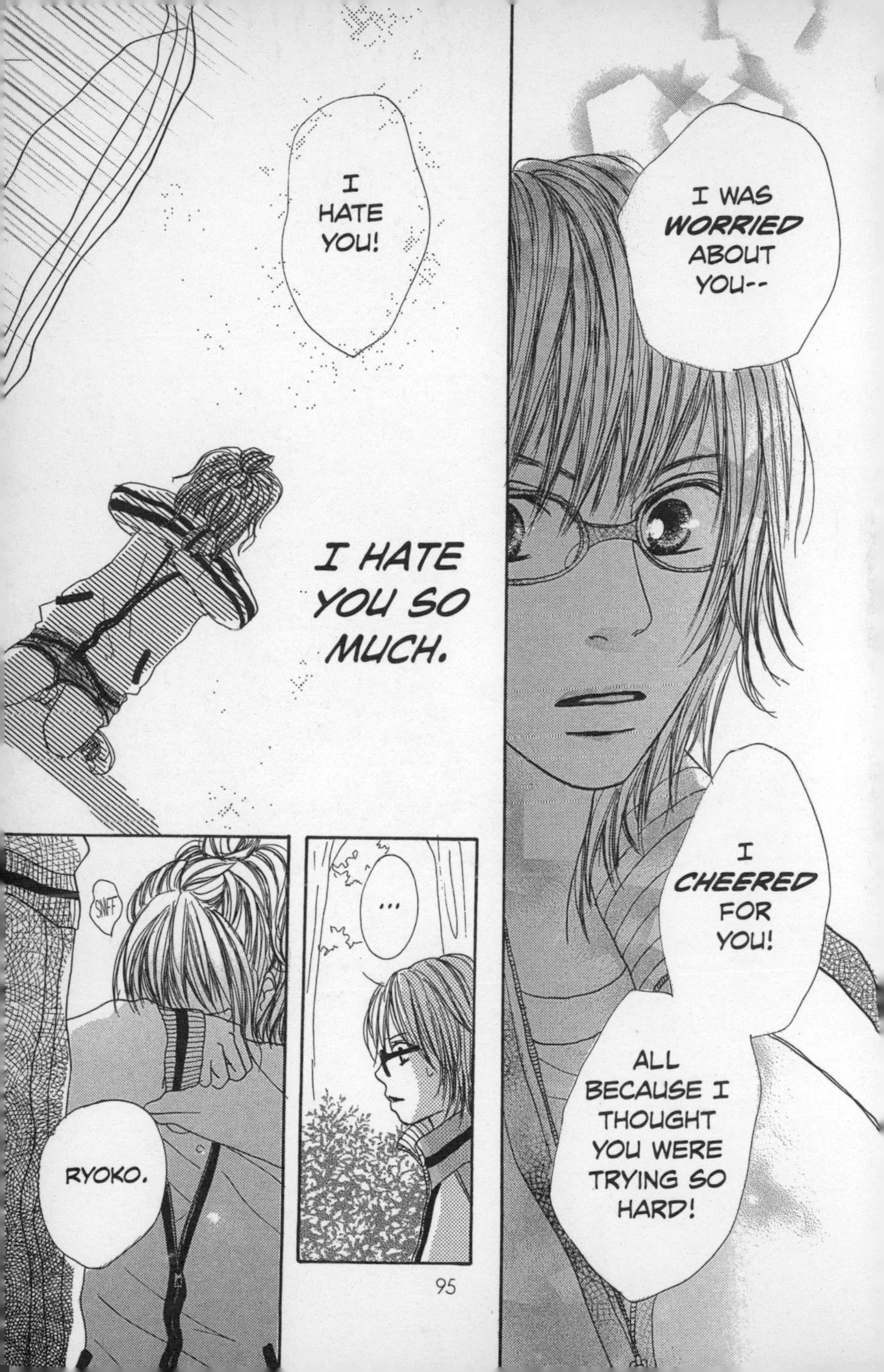
I WAS WORRIED ABOUT YOU--
I CHEERED FOR YOU!
ALL BECAUSE I THOUGHT YOU WERE TRYING SO HARD!
I HATE YOU!
I HATE YOU SO MUCH.
...
SNIFF
RYOKO.

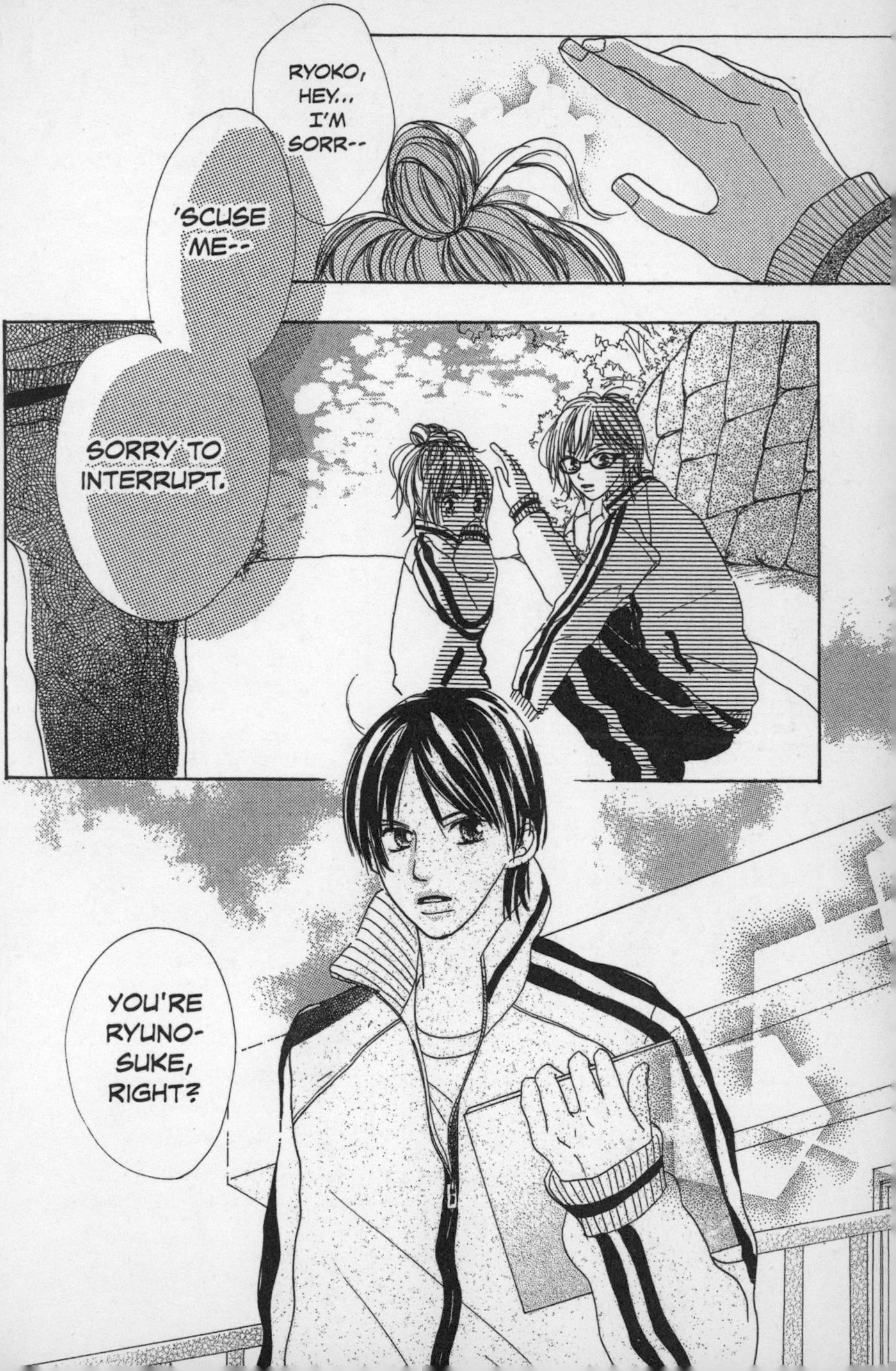
RYOKO, HEY... I'M SORR--
'SCUSE ME--
SORRY TO INTERRUPT.
YOU'RE RYUNO-SUKE, RIGHT?

About Making Manga

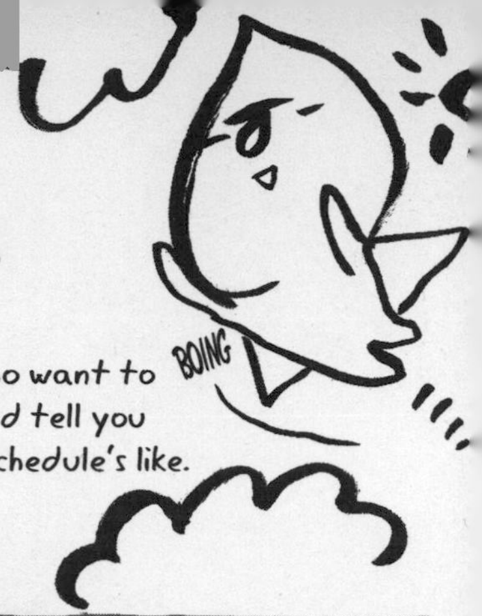
BOING

I keep getting letters from people who want to become manga artists, so I thought I'd tell you about the tools I use and what my schedule's like. Maybe it'll be helpful to someone...

Ugh! So messy...

Manuscript Paper	I.C. brand, the heavy kind
Ink	Kaimei Drawing Sol K
Tone	Mostly mail-order these days. I.C., Maxon, J-Tone, Design Tone, Letraset, etc.... I'll use anything
White [white ink]	Dr. Martin Pen White Regular correction pen
Mechanical Pencil	Dr. Grip, B lead
Pen Tip	Zebra G Pen: Outlines, Hair Nikko Maru Pen: Eyes only
Back-grounds	Rotring 0.1, 0.2 Milipen (Maxon, Staedtler)
Eraser	Air-In, Soft
Other Necessities	Copier, Reference photos, Ruler, Tracer, Tone knife, Kneaded eraser (handy)

The breakdown period varies, but when I'm working my fastest, it takes me 4-5 days.

Penciling 3-4 Days	Inking 1 Day	Finishing Touches 4 Days
My least favorite part of the process...I get bored.	Easy compared to penciling.	Takes me a long time to decide on tones, so 15 pages is the most I can do in a day.

I can do the whole thing in 10 days if I have to, but if I hope to take a bath and get some sleep at some point, it takes me two weeks. On this schedule, I only average five hours of sleep a night... What? You say that's enough...? Well, I'm an old lady and I feel heavy if I don't get enough sleep. Toward the end of every month I'm cooped up at home.

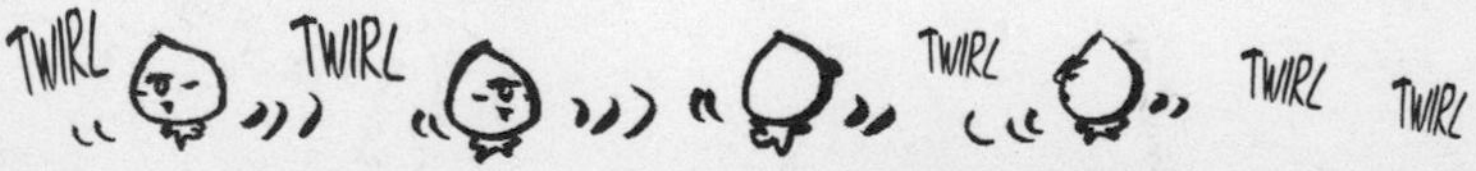
TWIRL
TWIRL
TWIRL
TWIRL
TWIRL

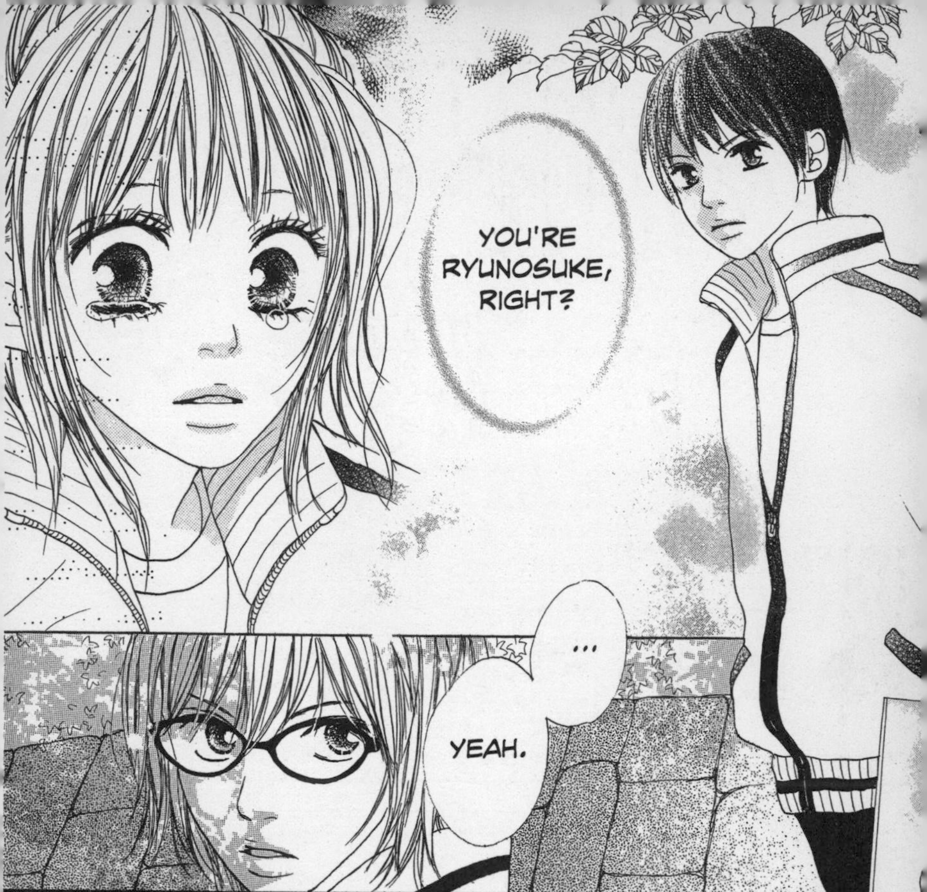
YOU'RE RYUNOSUKE, RIGHT?
...
YEAH.

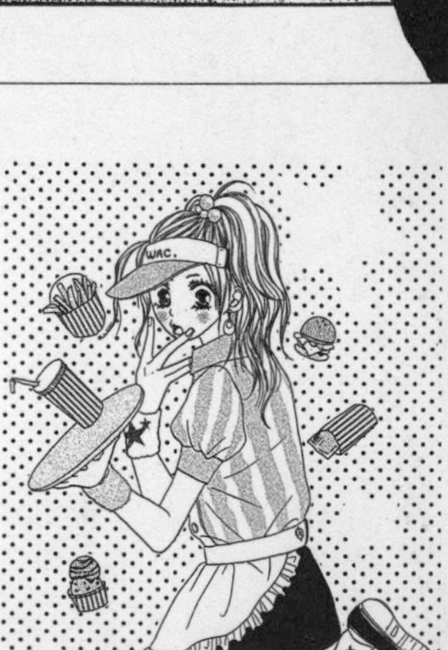

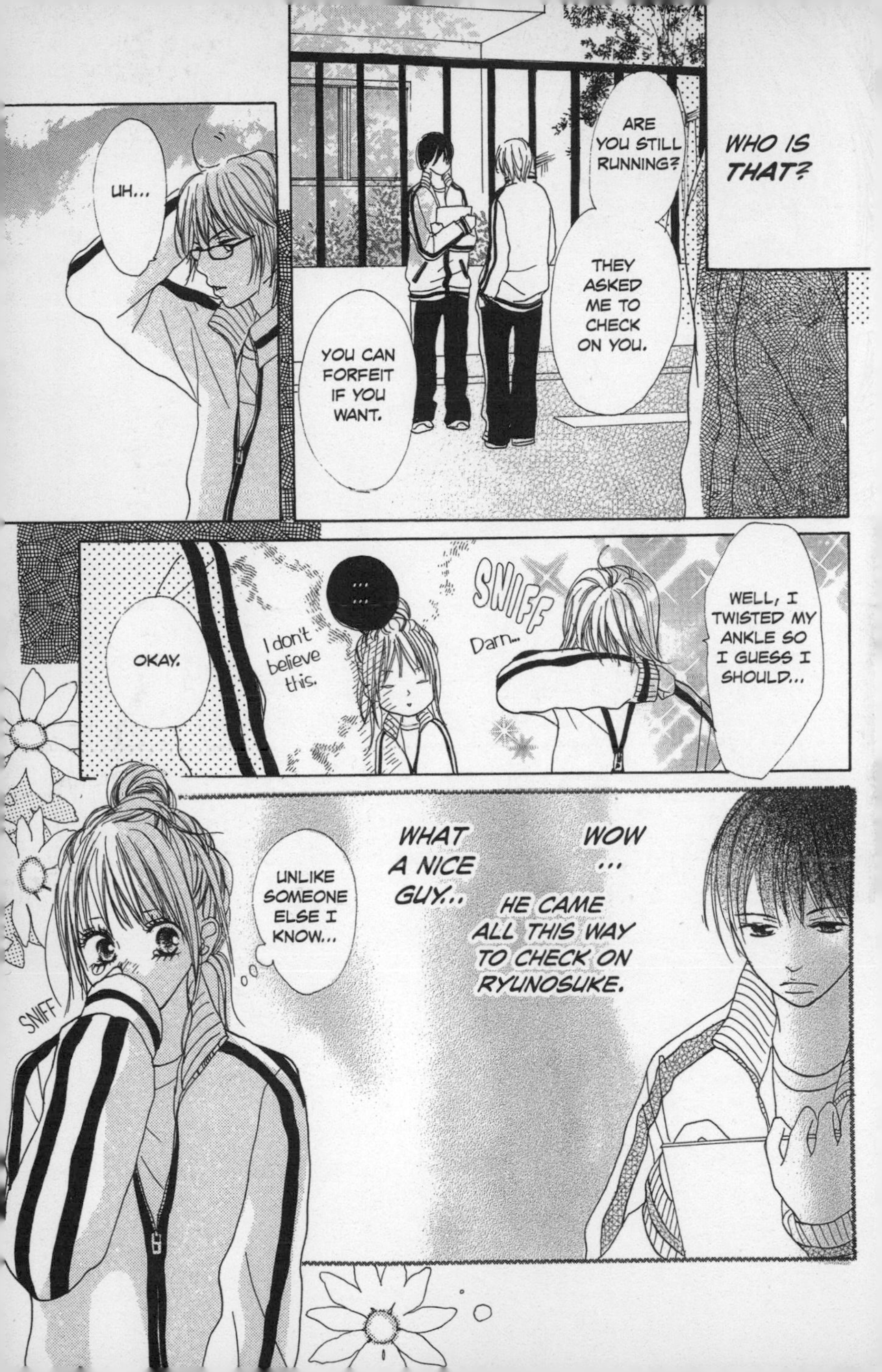
WHO IS THAT?
ARE YOU STILL RUNNING?
THEY ASKED ME TO CHECK ON YOU.
YOU CAN FORFEIT IF YOU WANT.
UH...
WELL, I TWISTED MY ANKLE SO I GUESS I SHOULD...
SNIFF
Darn...
...
I don't believe this.
OKAY.
WOW ...
HE CAME ALL THIS WAY TO CHECK ON RYUNOSUKE.
WHAT A NICE GUY...
UNLIKE SOMEONE ELSE I KNOW...
SNIFF

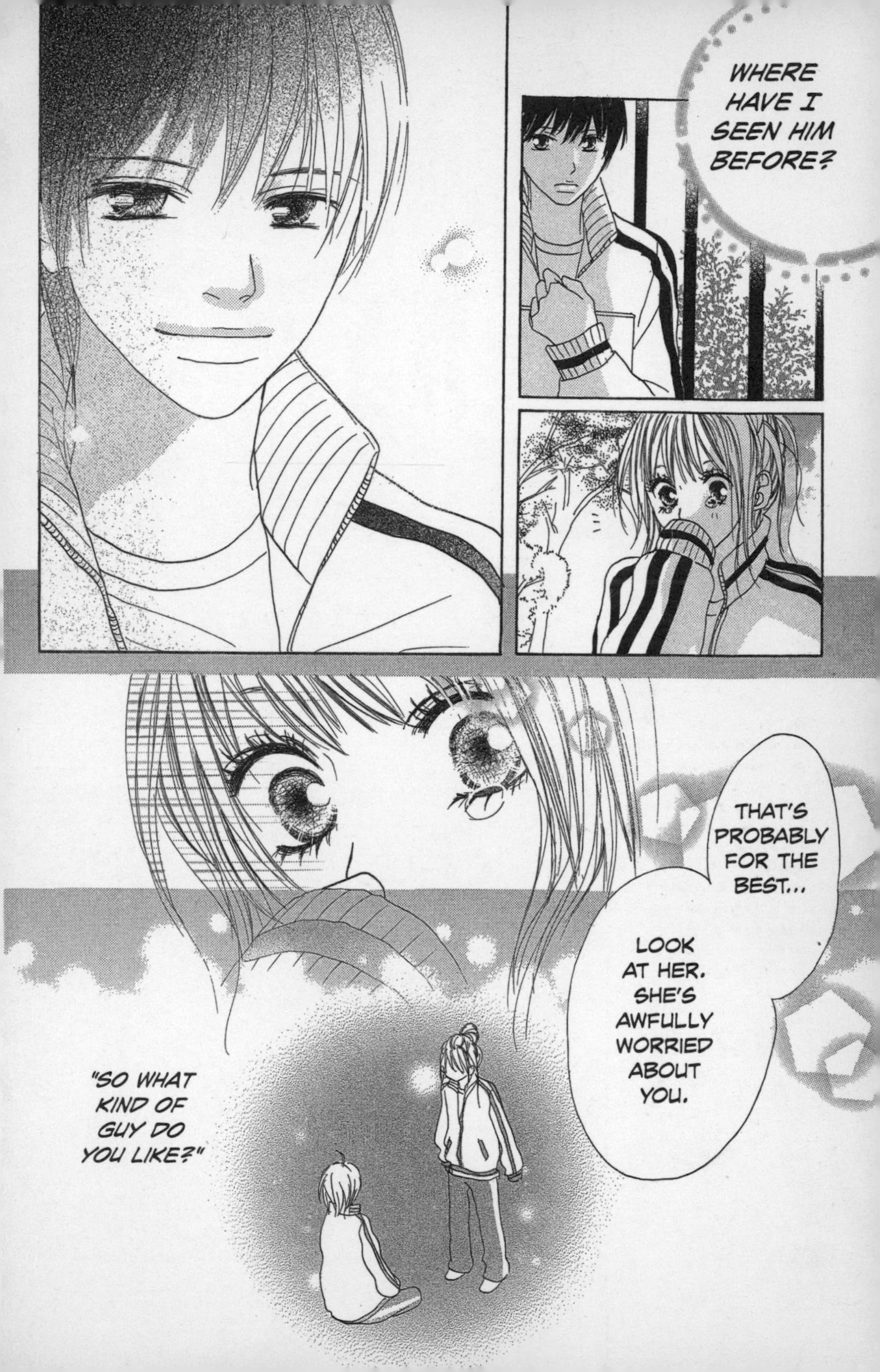
WHERE HAVE I SEEN HIM BEFORE?
THAT'S PROBABLY FOR THE BEST...
LOOK AT HER. SHE'S AWFULLY WORRIED ABOUT YOU.
"SO WHAT KIND OF GUY DO YOU LIKE?"

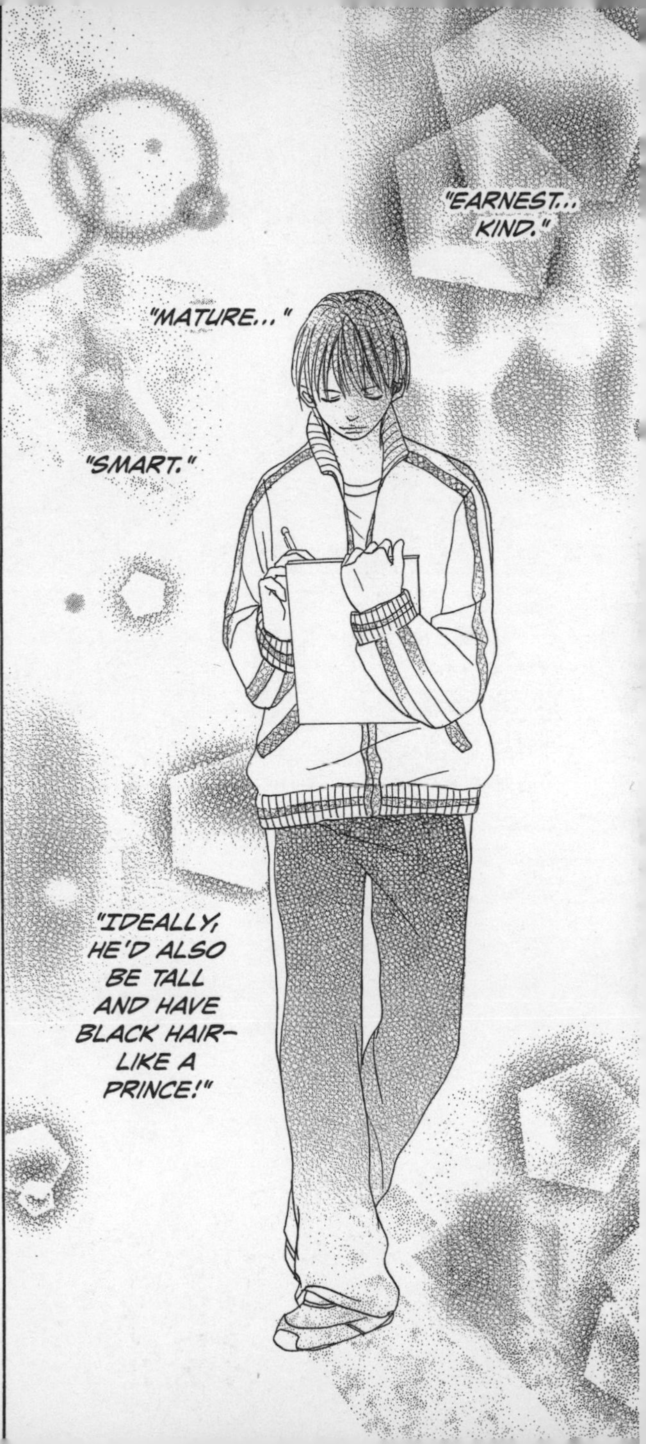
"EARNEST... KIND."
"MATURE..."
"SMART."
"IDEALLY, HE'D ALSO BE TALL AND HAVE BLACK HAIR–LIKE A PRINCE!"

A Story About Work

I've noticed that I can't work with any background noise. Maybe it's because I don't concentrate as well as the average person. I don't know, but I can't outline, pencil, ink or do anything well if there's sound around me. So I work in complete silence.

It's grueling. Plus, I often work by myself so the only people I talk to are my family.

Talking to myself. Depressing...

One exception: when I draw a love scene I do play music. It's always Chara's *Yasashii Kimochi*. It makes me feel sweet so I play it when drawing a sweet scene. Oddly enough, I didn't play it at all during my last series. Maybe because there wasn't much of a love angle? I've been playing it a lot for B.O.D.Y.

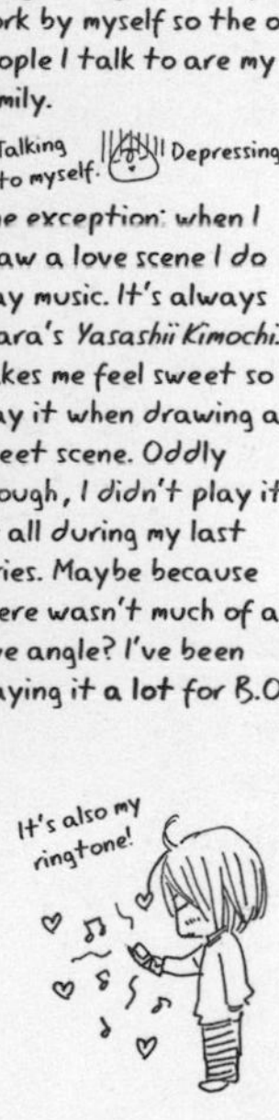
It's also my ringtone!

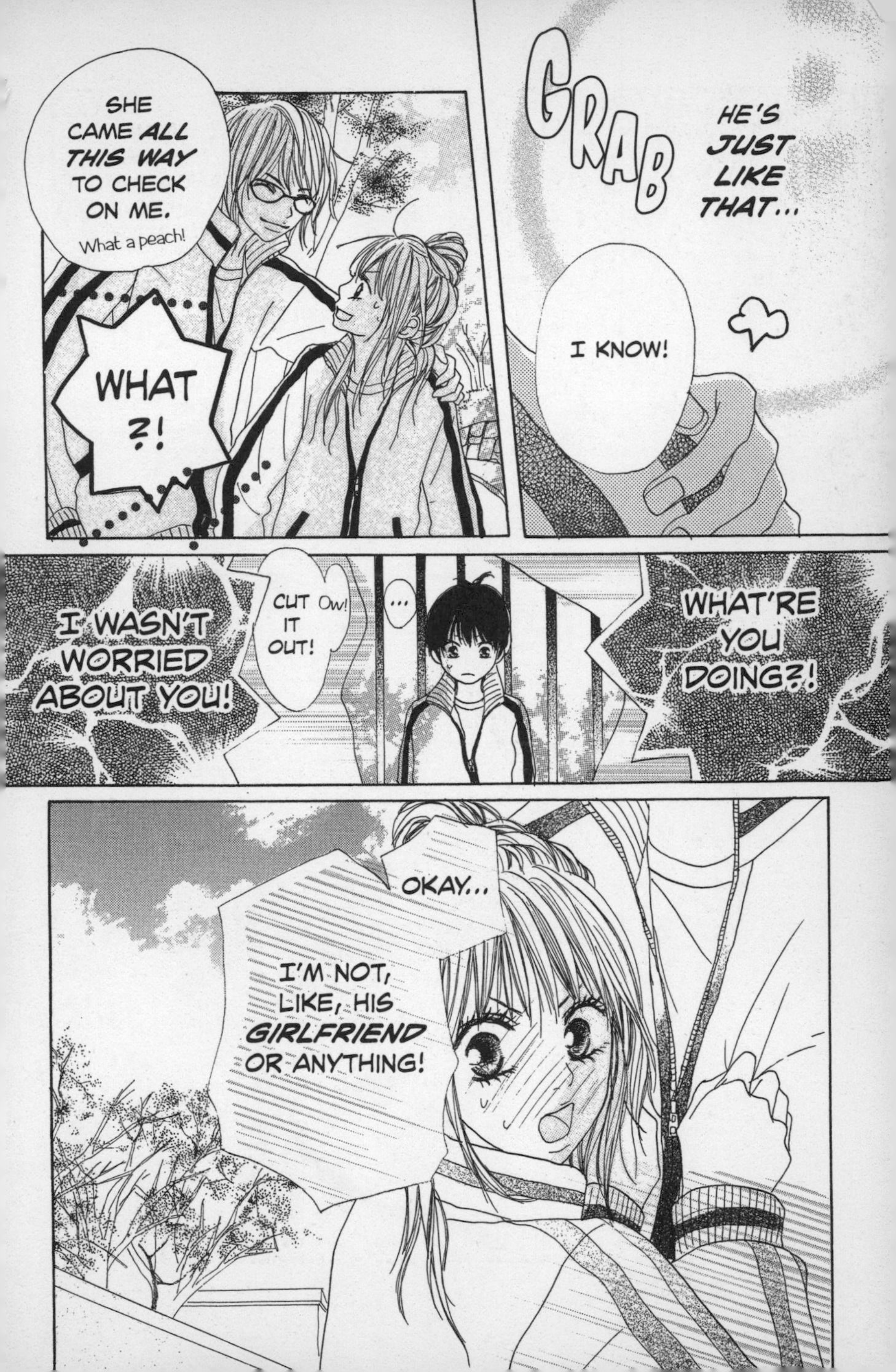
GRAB
HE'S JUST LIKE THAT...
I KNOW!
SHE CAME ALL THIS WAY TO CHECK ON ME.
What a peach!
WHAT?!
WHAT'RE YOU DOING?!
...
CUT IT OUT!
Ow!
I WASN'T WORRIED ABOUT YOU!
OKAY...
I'M NOT, LIKE, HIS GIRLFRIEND OR ANYTHING!

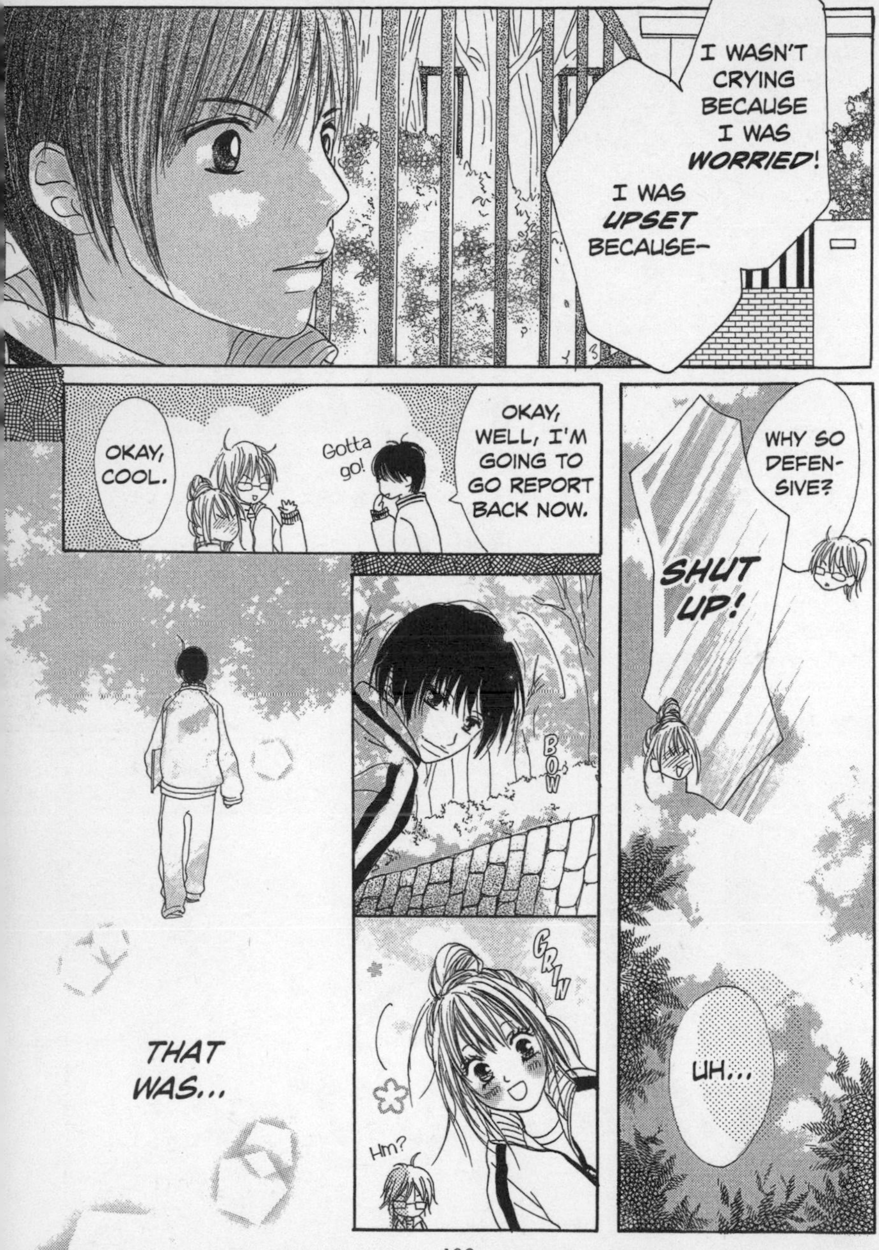

I WASN'T CRYING BECAUSE I WAS WORRIED!
I WAS UPSET BECAUSE-
WHY SO DEFEN-SIVE?
SHUT UP!
UH...
OKAY, WELL, I'M GOING TO GO REPORT BACK NOW.
Gotta go!
OKAY, COOL.
BOW
GRIN
Hm?
THAT WAS...

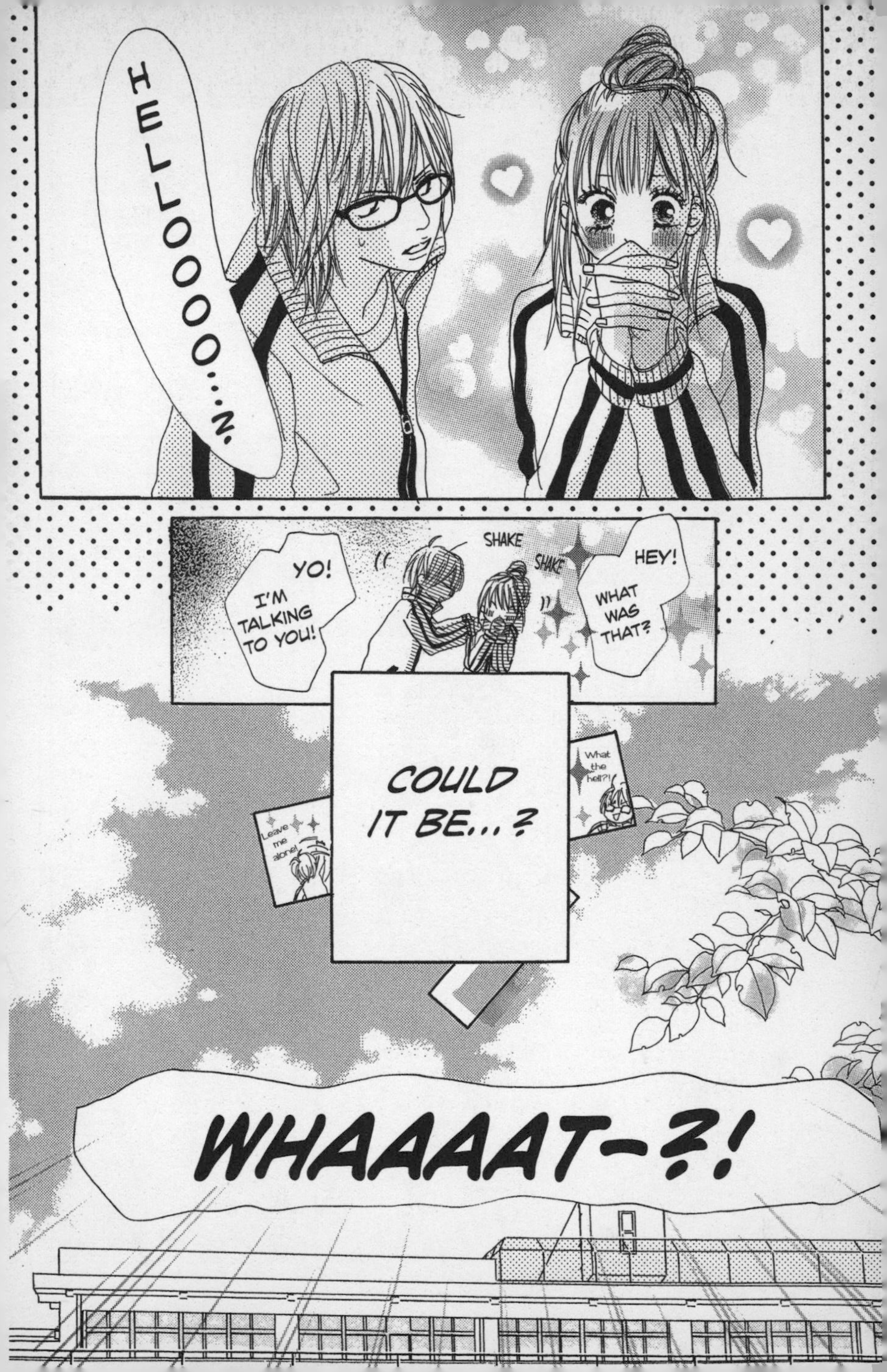
HELLOOOO...?
HEY! WHAT WAS THAT?
SHAKE SHAKE
YO! I'M TALKING TO YOU!
What the hell?!
COULD IT BE...?
Leave me alone!
WHAAAAT-?!

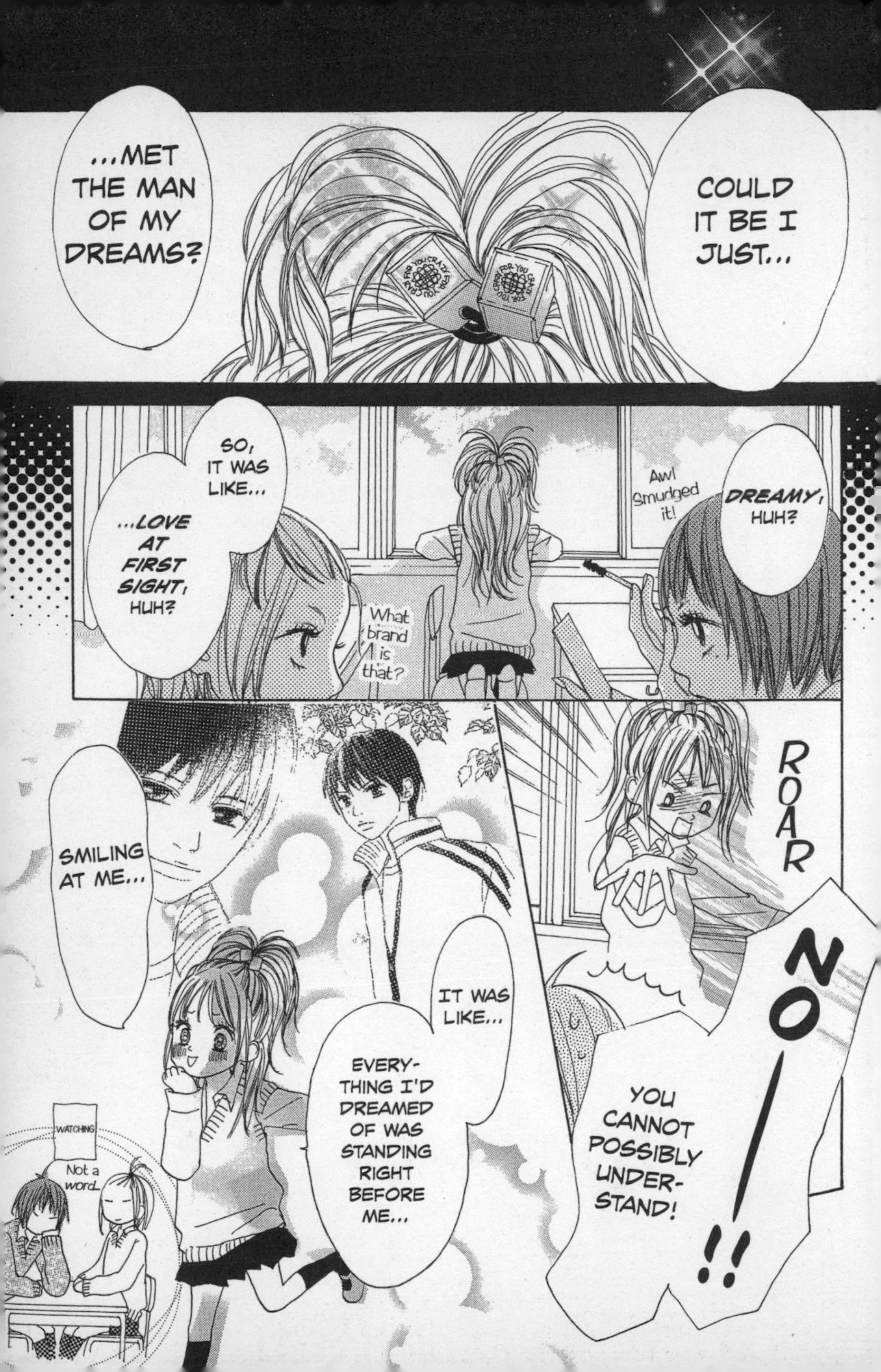
COULD IT BE I JUST...
...MET THE MAN OF MY DREAMS?
DREAMY, HUH?
Aw! Smudged it!
SO, IT WAS LIKE...
...LOVE AT FIRST SIGHT, HUH?
What brand is that?
ROAR
NO—!!
YOU CANNOT POSSIBLY UNDER-STAND!
SMILING AT ME...
IT WAS LIKE...
EVERY-THING I'D DREAMED OF WAS STANDING RIGHT BEFORE ME...
WATCHING
Not a word.

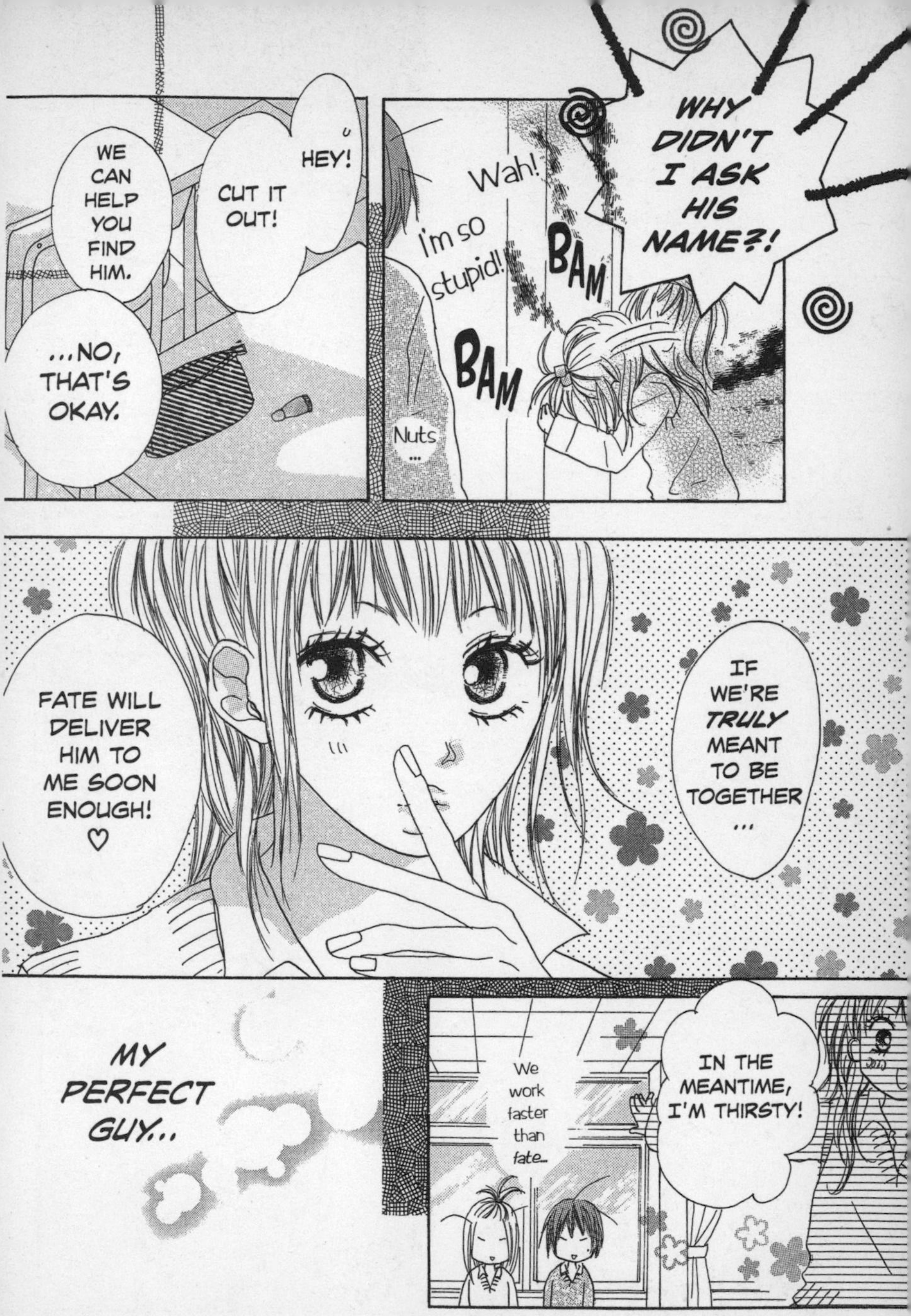
WHY DIDN'T I ASK HIS NAME?!
BAM
BAM
Wah!
I'm so stupid!
Nuts...
HEY!
CUT IT OUT!
WE CAN HELP YOU FIND HIM.
...NO, THAT'S OKAY.
IF WE'RE *TRULY* MEANT TO BE TOGETHER...
FATE WILL DELIVER HIM TO ME SOON ENOUGH! ♡
IN THE MEANTIME, I'M THIRSTY!
We work faster than *fate*...
MY PERFECT GUY...

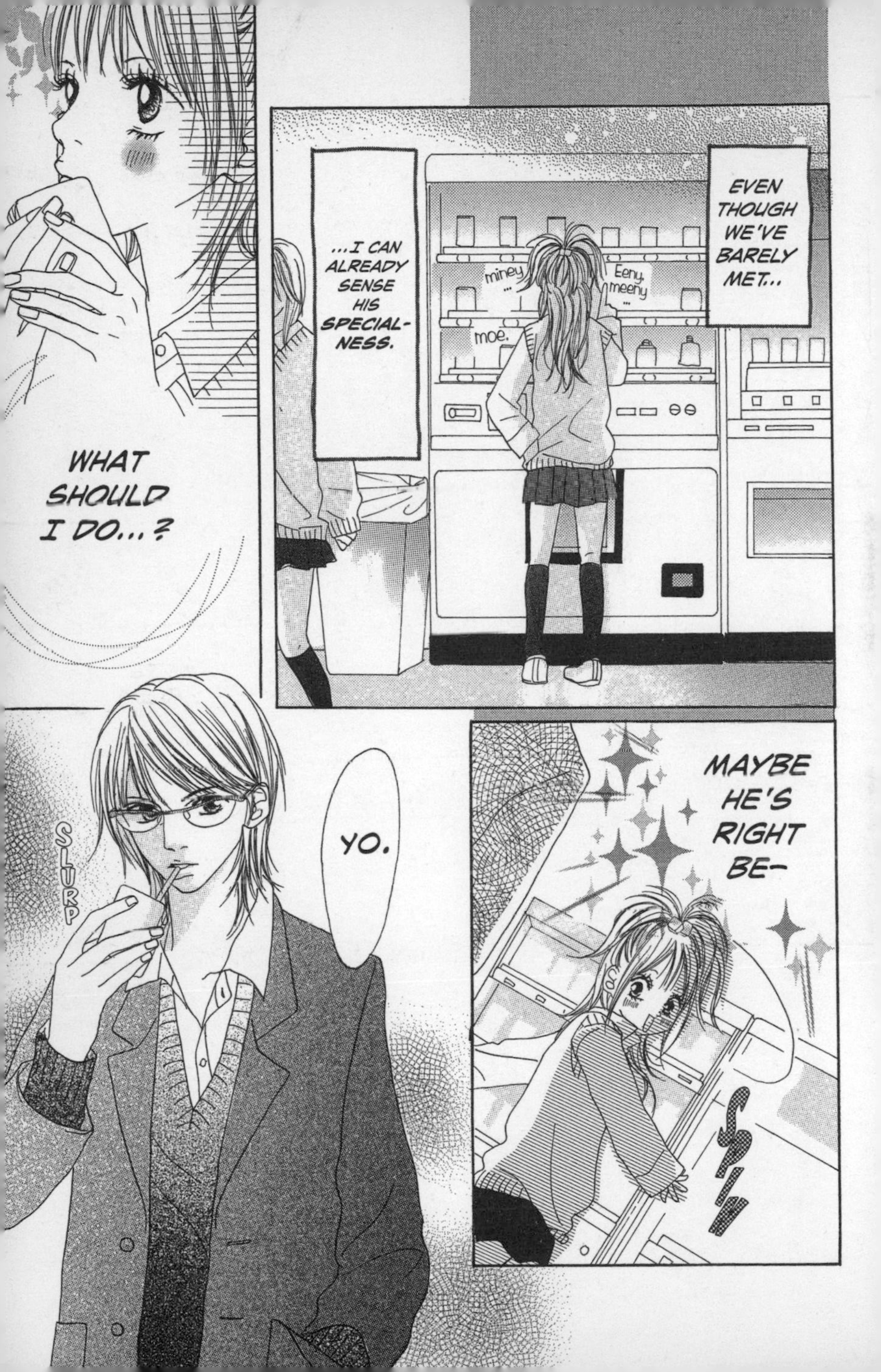
EVEN THOUGH WE'VE BARELY MET...
Eeny, meeny ...
miney ...
moe.
...I CAN ALREADY SENSE HIS SPECIAL-NESS.
WHAT SHOULD I DO...?
MAYBE HE'S RIGHT BE-
YO.
SLURP

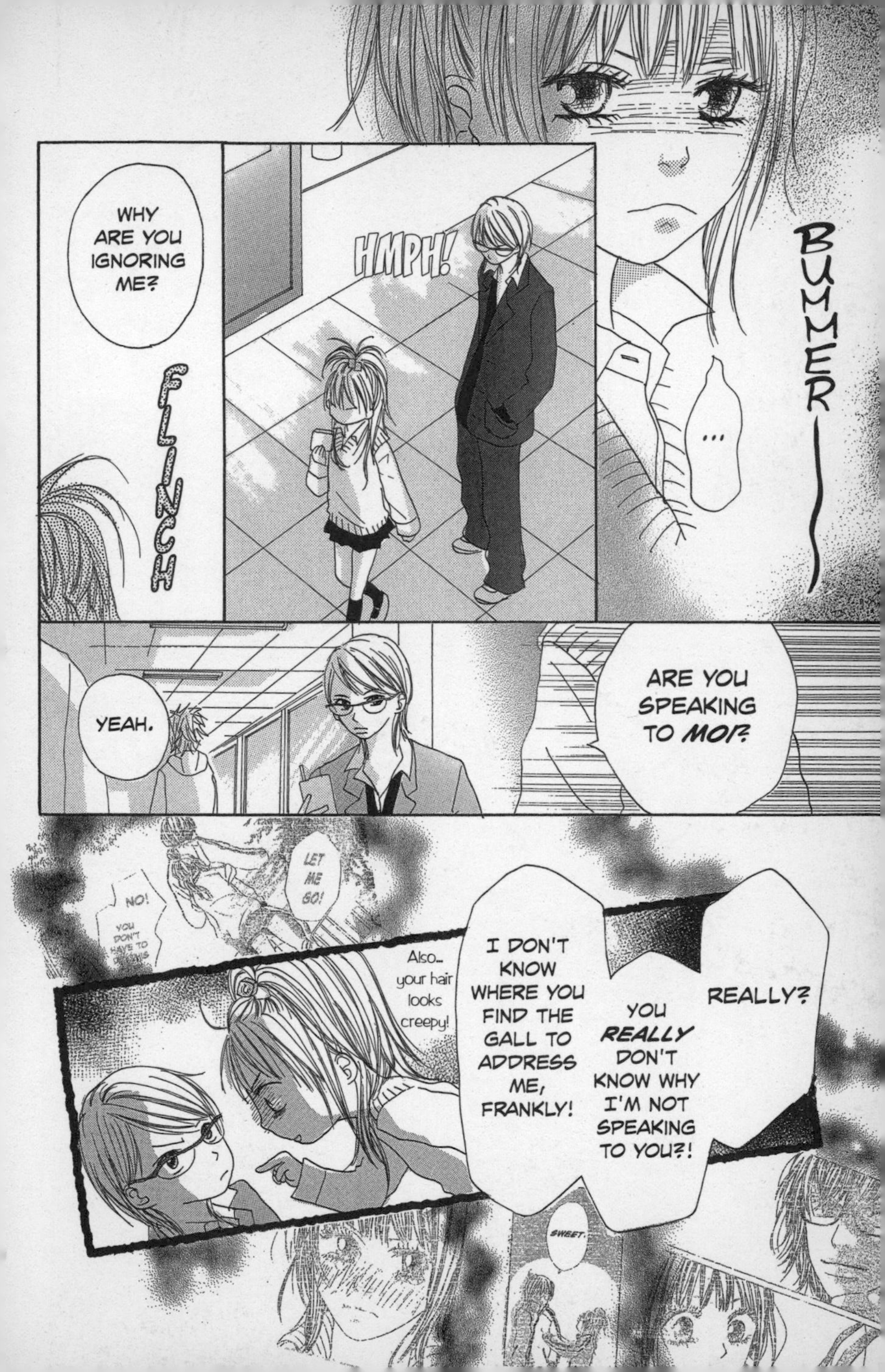
BUMMER
...
HMPH!
WHY ARE YOU IGNORING ME?
FLINCH
ARE YOU SPEAKING TO *MOI*?
YEAH.
REALLY? YOU *REALLY* DON'T KNOW WHY I'M NOT SPEAKING TO YOU?!
I DON'T KNOW WHERE YOU FIND THE GALL TO ADDRESS ME, FRANKLY!
Also... your hair looks creepy!
LET ME GO!
NO!
YOU DON'T HAVE TO

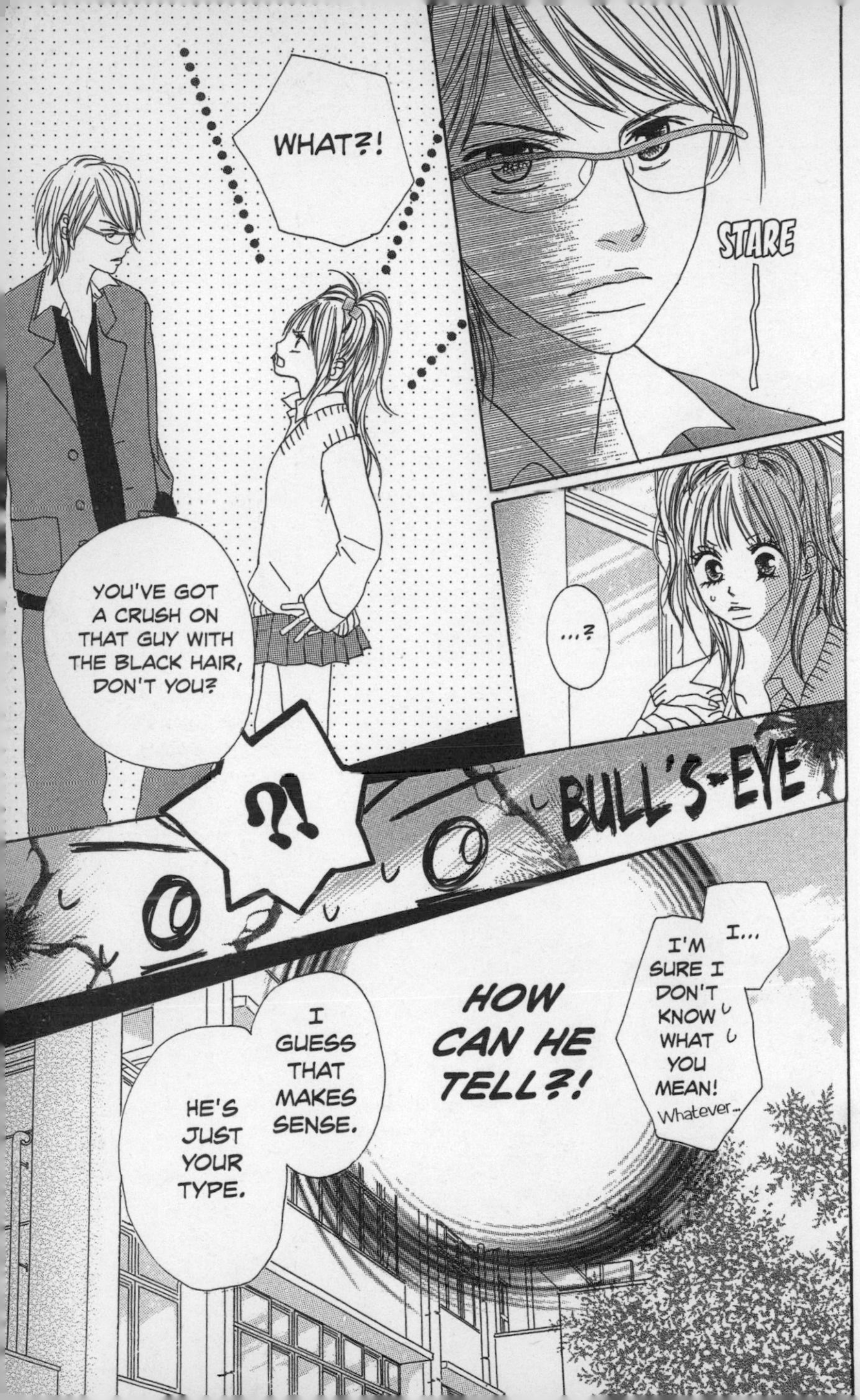
STARE
...?
WHAT?!
YOU'VE GOT A CRUSH ON THAT GUY WITH THE BLACK HAIR, DON'T YOU?
BULL'S-EYE
?!
I...
I'M SURE I DON'T KNOW WHAT YOU MEAN!
Whatever...
HOW CAN HE TELL?!
I GUESS THAT MAKES SENSE.
HE'S JUST YOUR TYPE.

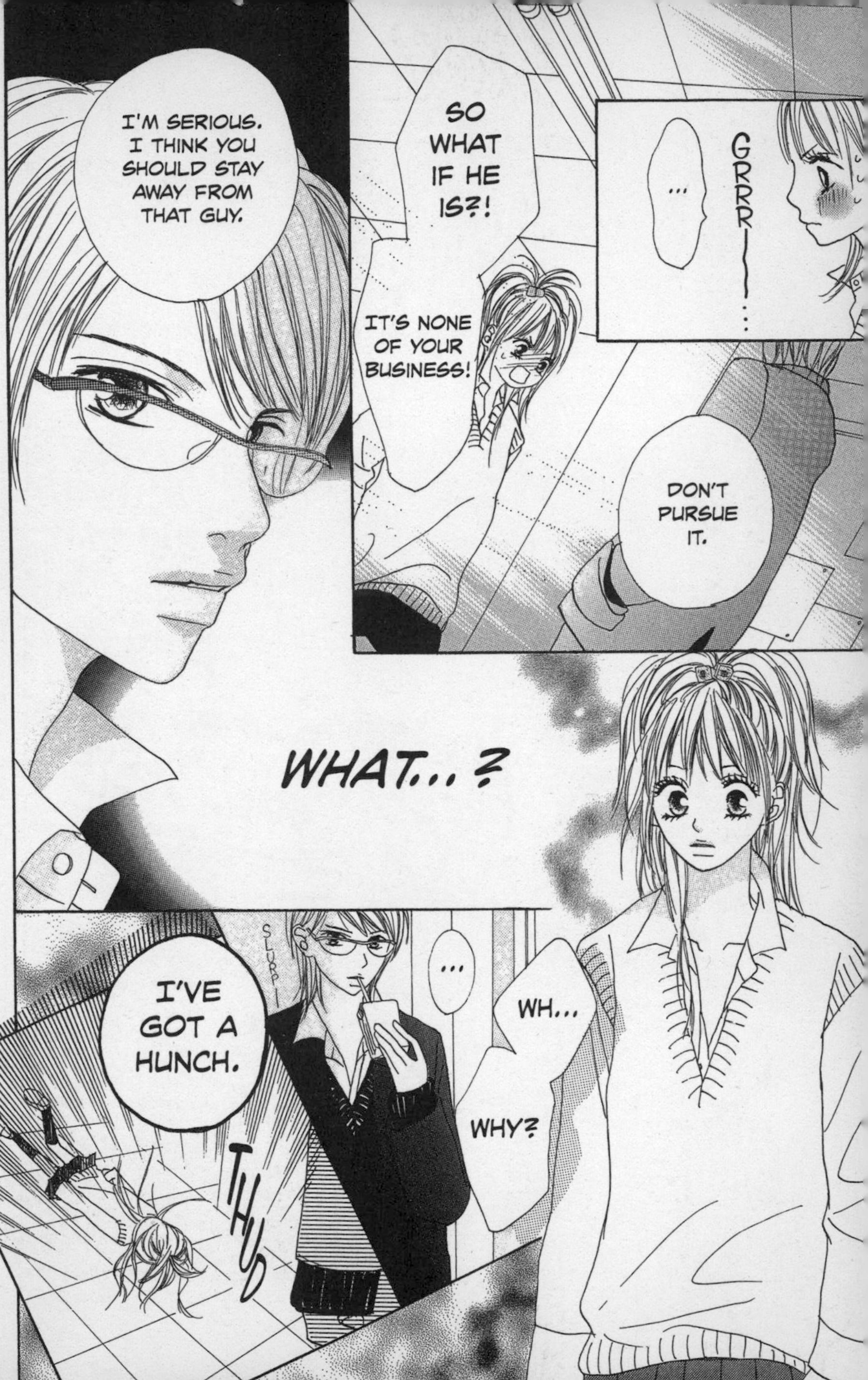
SO WHAT IF HE IS?!
IT'S NONE OF YOUR BUSINESS!
...
GRRRR...
DON'T PURSUE IT.
I'M SERIOUS. I THINK YOU SHOULD STAY AWAY FROM THAT GUY.
WHAT...?
WH...
WHY?
...
SLURP
I'VE GOT A HUNCH.
THUD

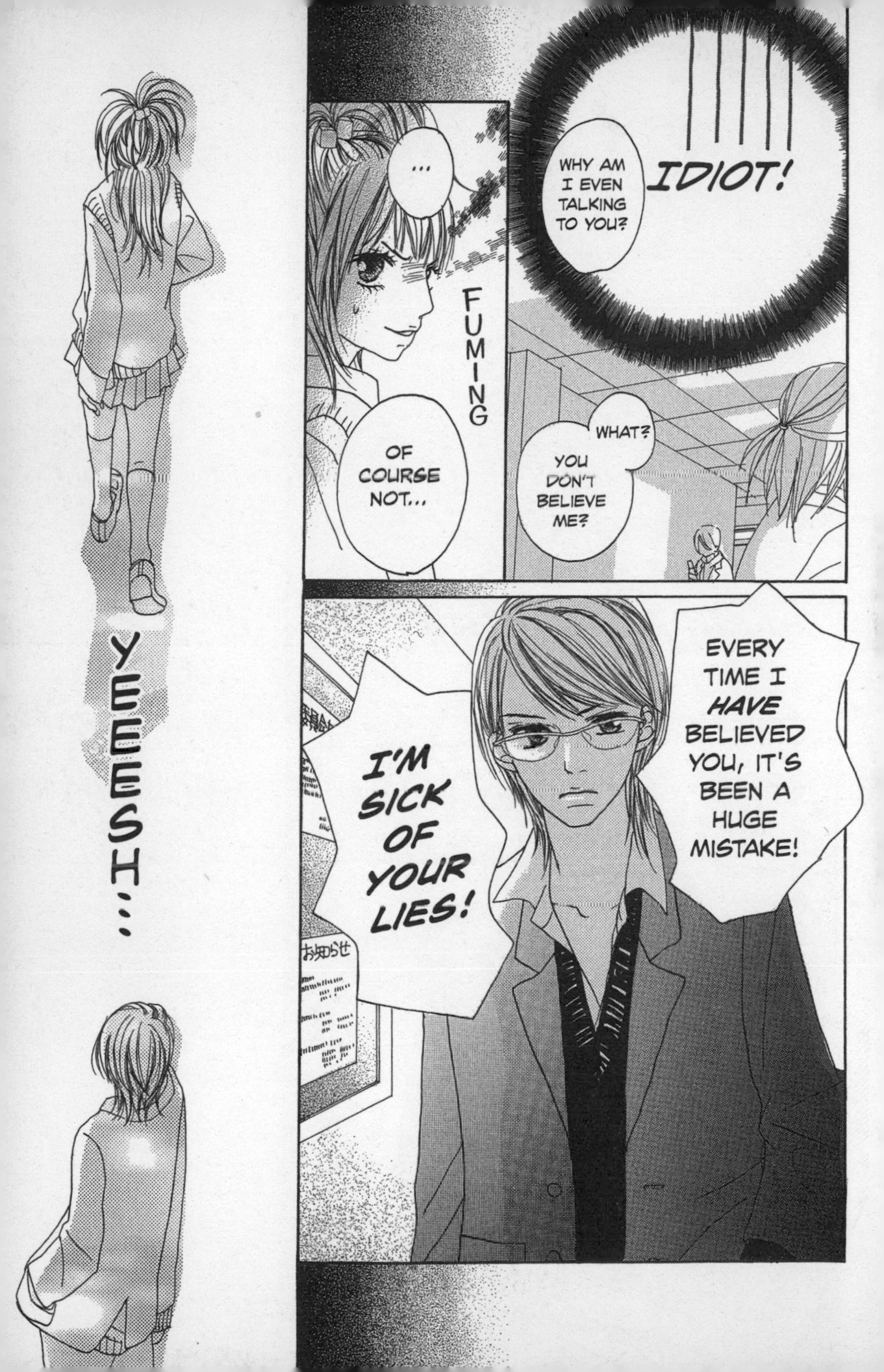
IDIOT!
WHY AM I EVEN TALKING TO YOU?
WHAT?
YOU DON'T BELIEVE ME?
...
FUMING
OF COURSE NOT...
EVERY TIME I *HAVE* BELIEVED YOU, IT'S BEEN A HUGE MISTAKE!
I'M SICK OF YOUR LIES!
お知らせ
YEEESH..

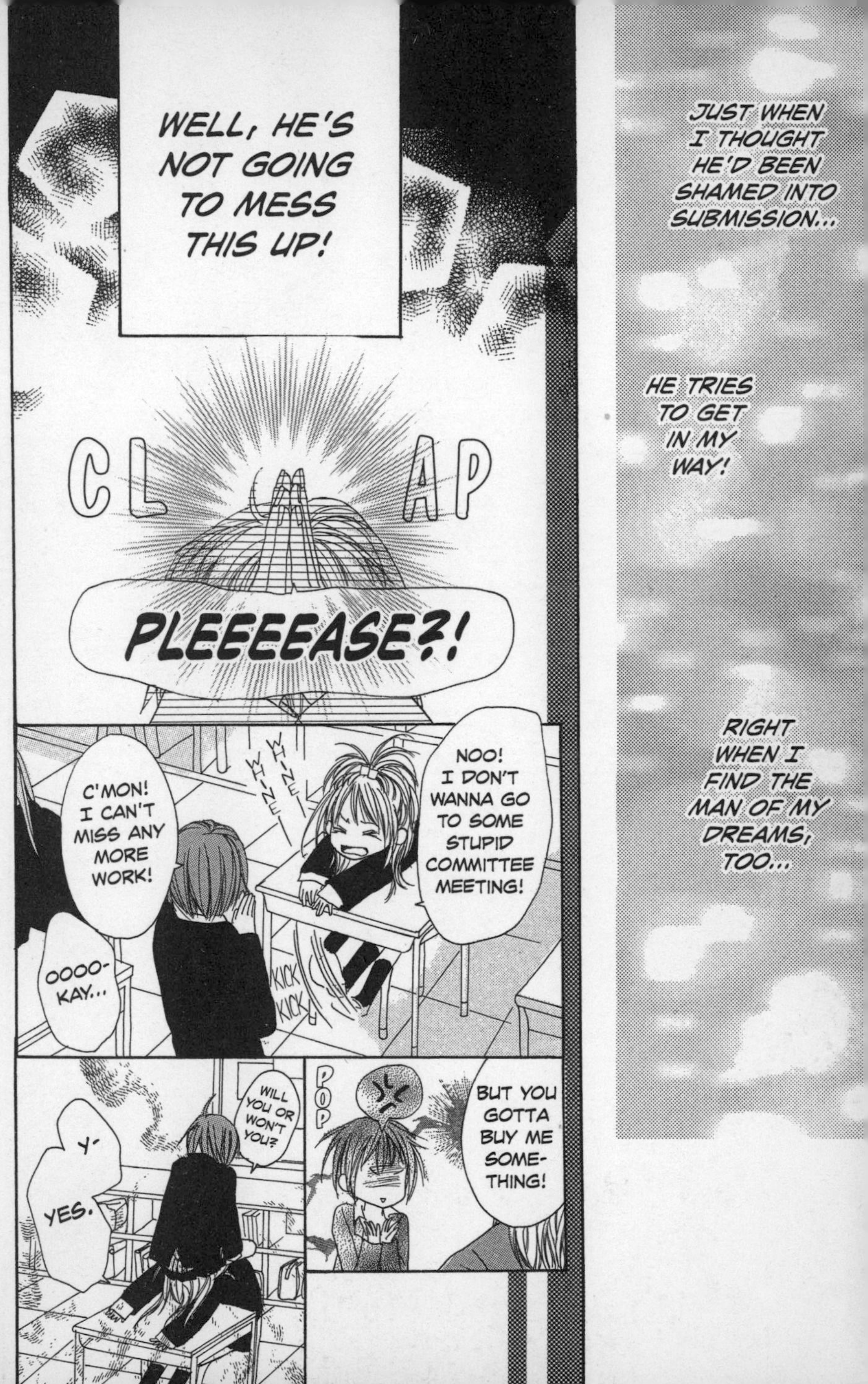
JUST WHEN I THOUGHT HE'D BEEN SHAMED INTO SUBMISSION...
HE TRIES TO GET IN MY WAY!
RIGHT WHEN I FIND THE MAN OF MY DREAMS, TOO...
WELL, HE'S NOT GOING TO MESS THIS UP!
CLAP
PLEEEEASE?!
NOO! I DON'T WANNA GO TO SOME STUPID COMMITTEE MEETING!
WHINE
WHINE
C'MON! I CAN'T MISS ANY MORE WORK!
KICK
KICK
OOOO-KAY...
BUT YOU GOTTA BUY ME SOME-THING!
POP
WILL YOU OR WON'T YOU?
Y-
YES.

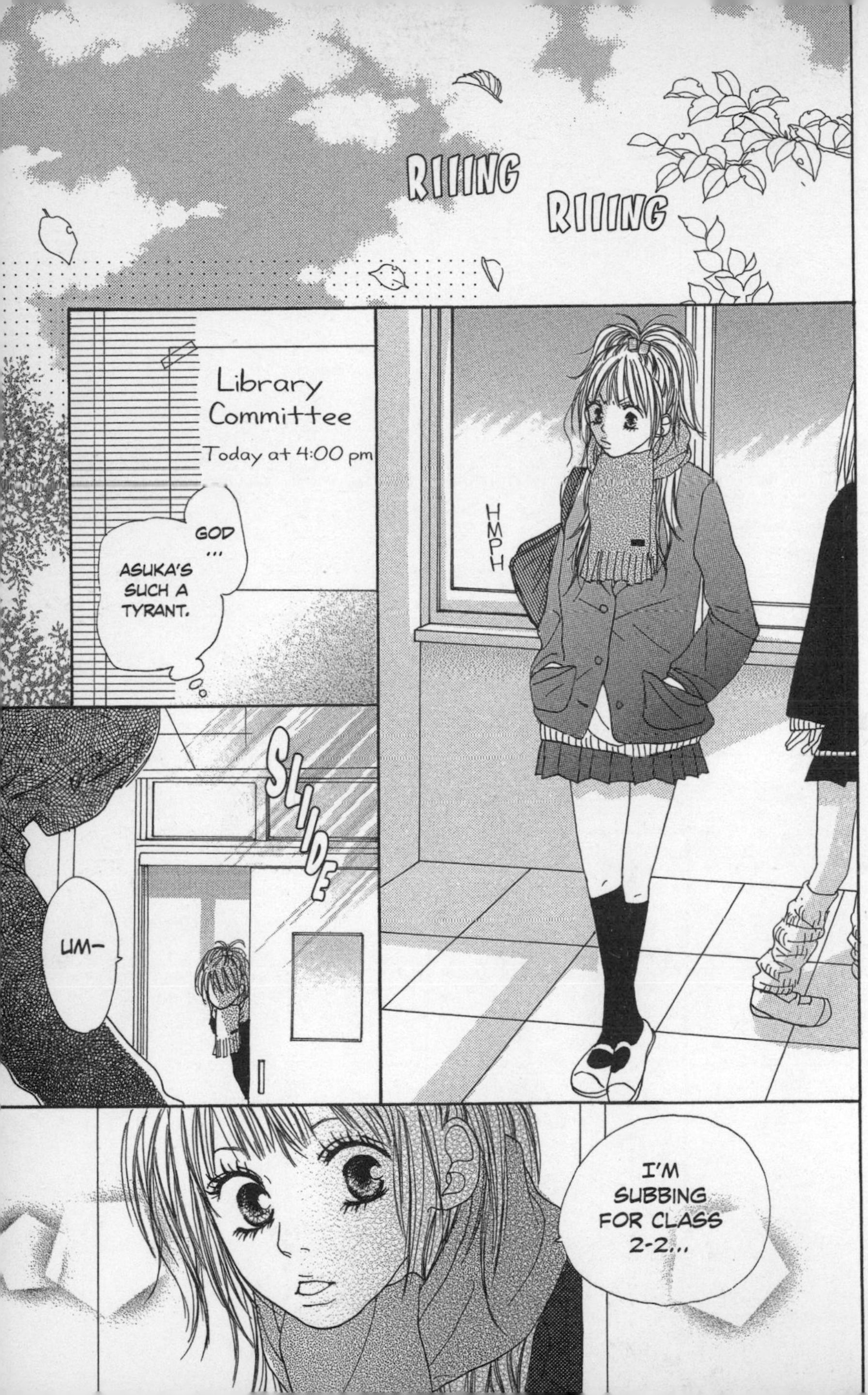
RIIING
RIIING
HMPH
Library Committee
Today at 4:00 pm
GOD ... ASUKA'S SUCH A TYRANT.
SLIDE
UM-
I'M SUBBING FOR CLASS 2-2...

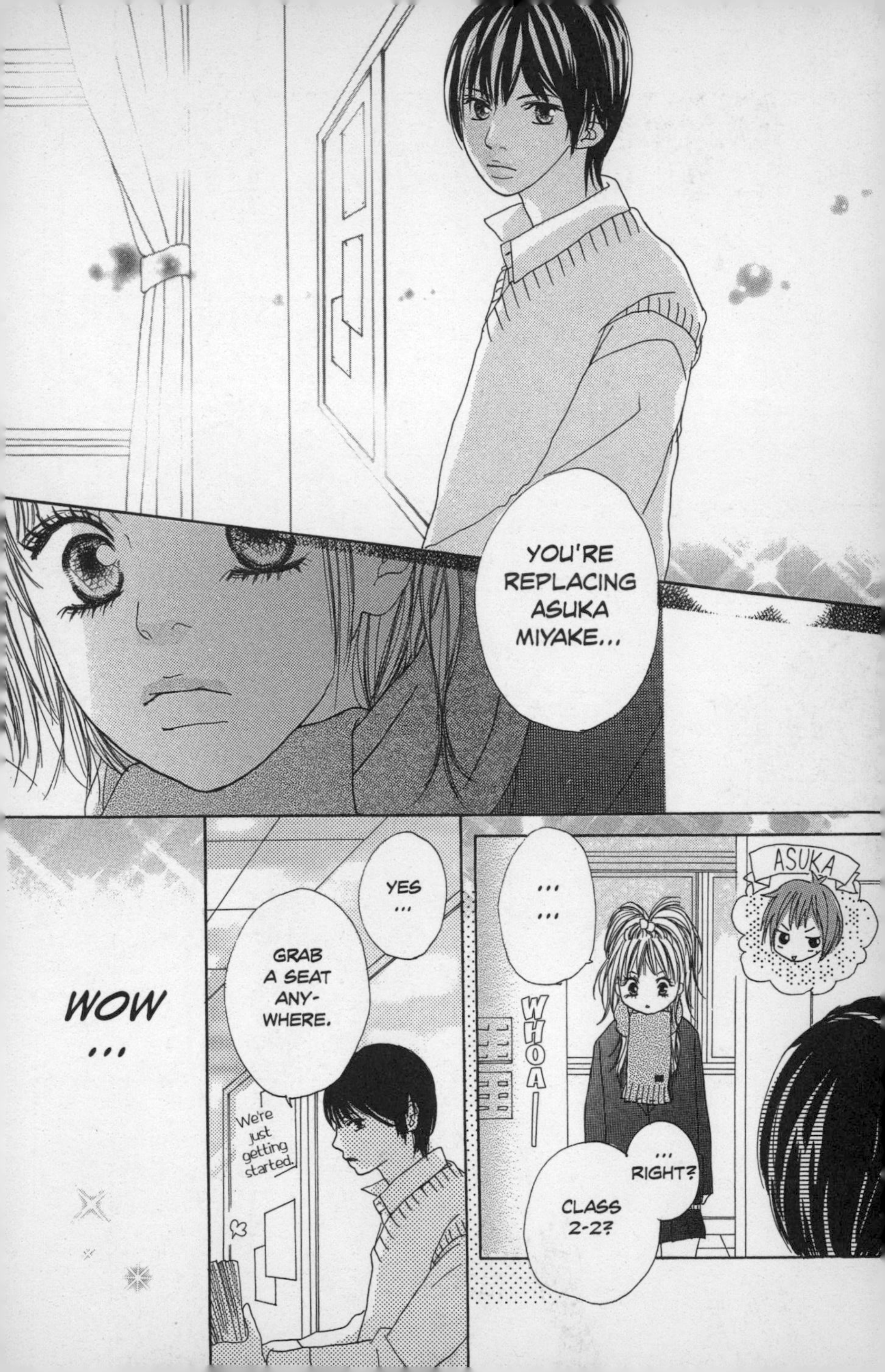
YOU'RE REPLACING ASUKA MIYAKE...
ASUKA
... ...
WHOA
CLASS 2-2?
...RIGHT?
YES ...
GRAB A SEAT ANY-WHERE.
We're just getting started.
WOW ...

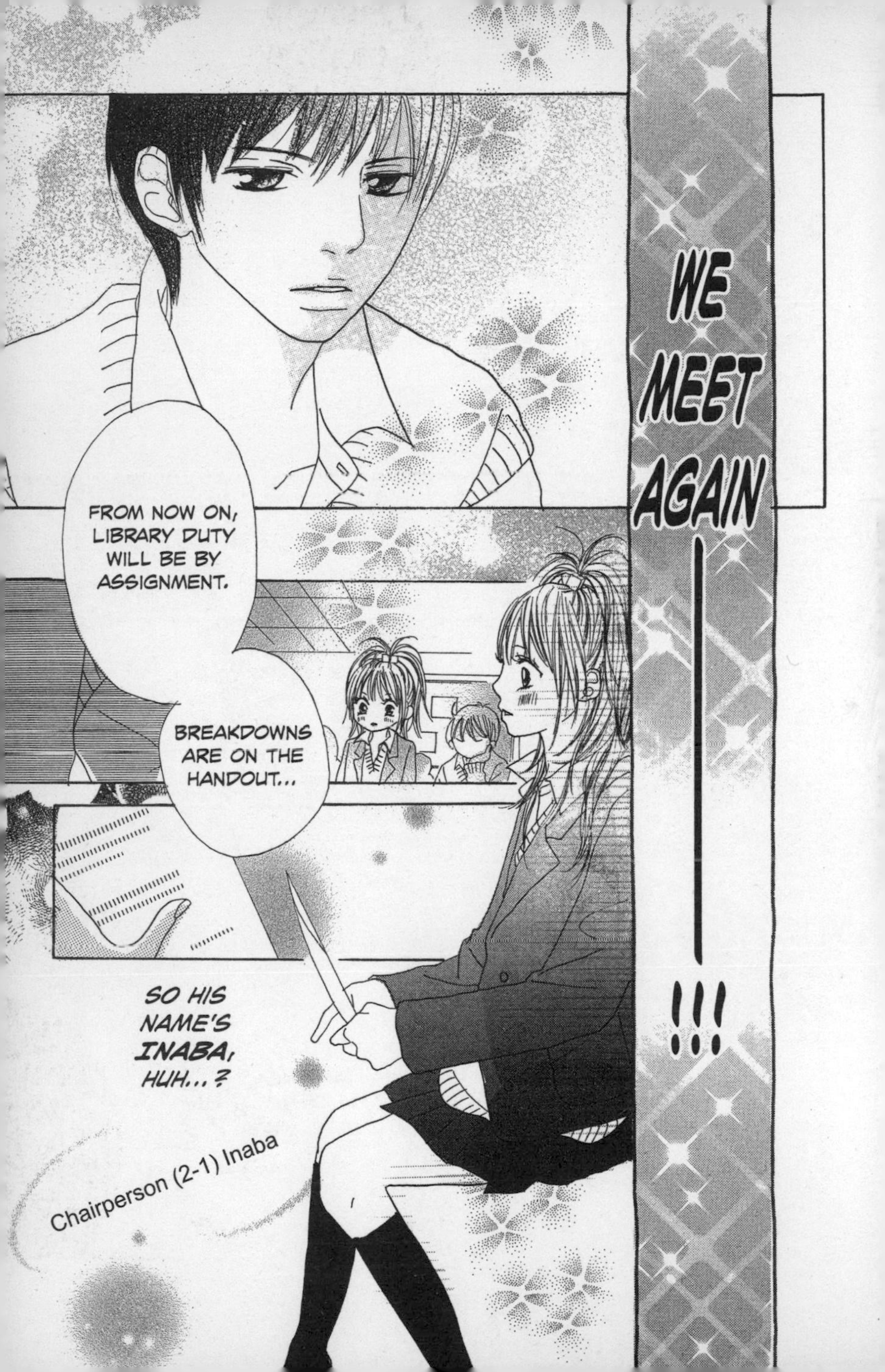
WE MEET AGAIN—!!!
FROM NOW ON, LIBRARY DUTY WILL BE BY ASSIGNMENT.
BREAKDOWNS ARE ON THE HANDOUT...
SO HIS NAME'S INABA, HUH...?
Chairperson (2-1) Inaba

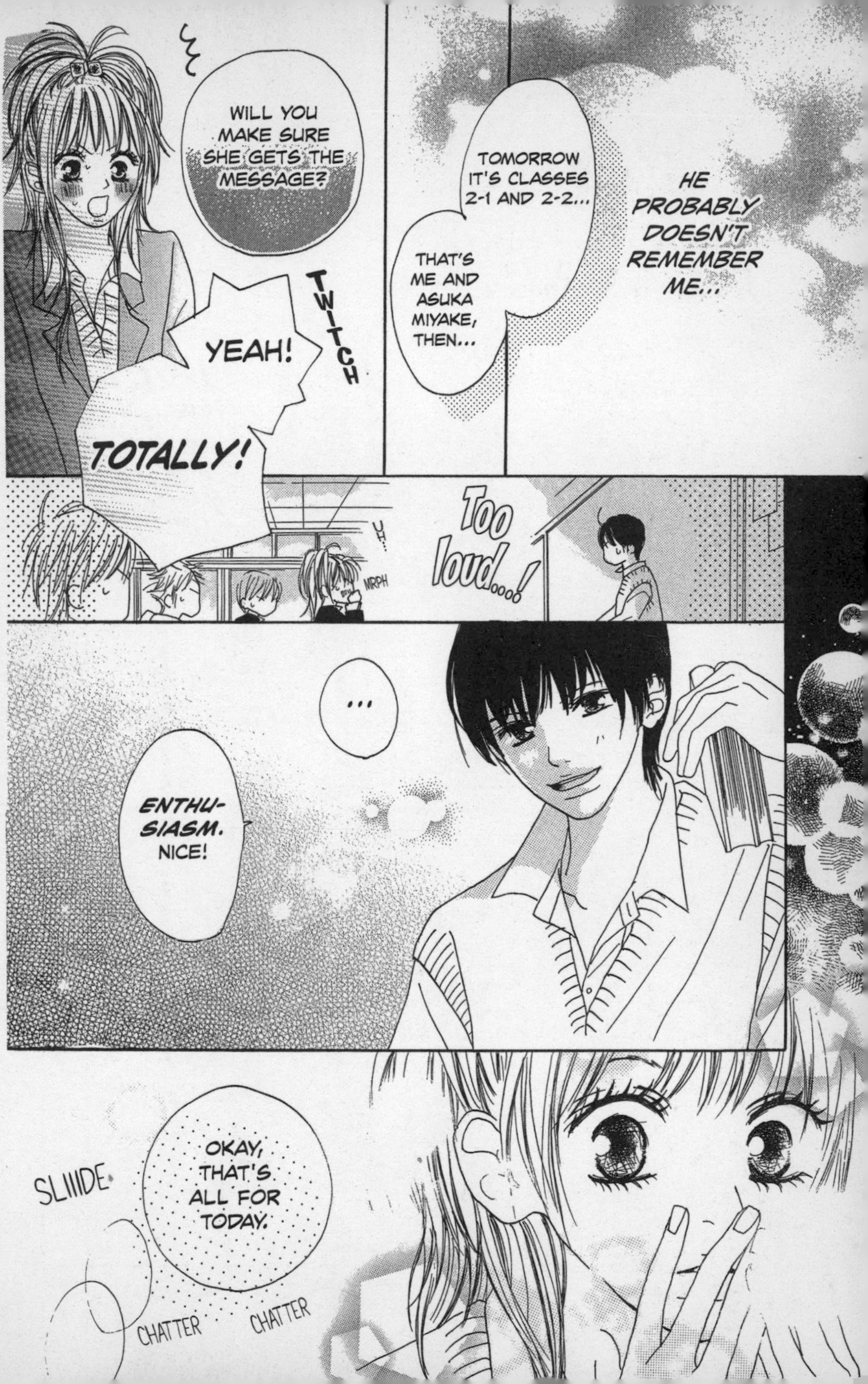
TOMORROW IT'S CLASSES 2-1 AND 2-2...
THAT'S ME AND ASUKA MIYAKE, THEN...
HE PROBABLY DOESN'T REMEMBER ME...
WILL YOU MAKE SURE SHE GETS THE MESSAGE?
TWITCH
YEAH!
TOTALLY!
Too loud...!
UH...
MRPH
...
ENTHU-SIASM. NICE!
OKAY, THAT'S ALL FOR TODAY.
SLIIDE
CHATTER
CHATTER

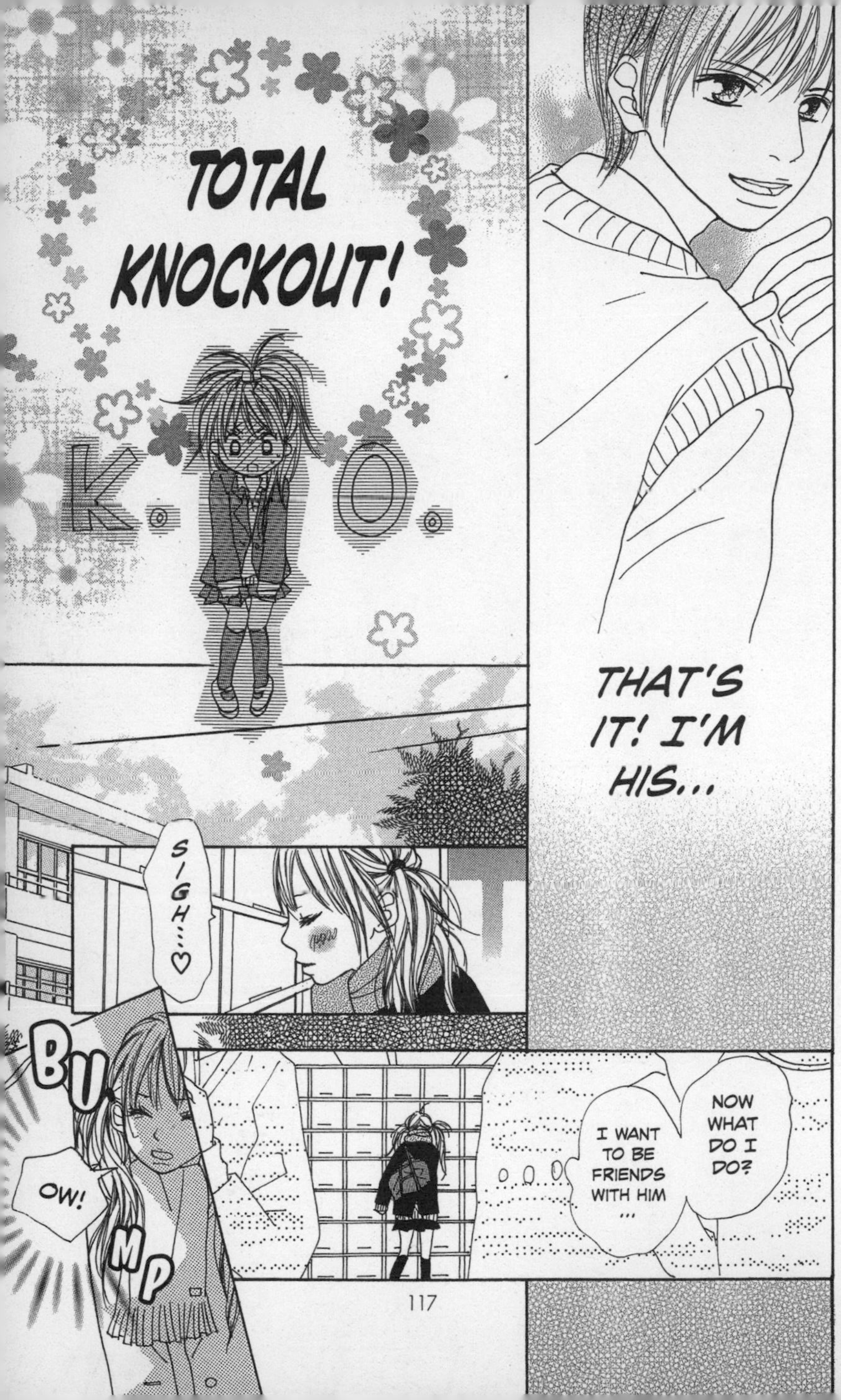
THAT'S IT! I'M HIS...
TOTAL KNOCKOUT!
K.O.
SIGH...♡
NOW WHAT DO I DO?
I WANT TO BE FRIENDS WITH HIM ...
BUMP
OW!

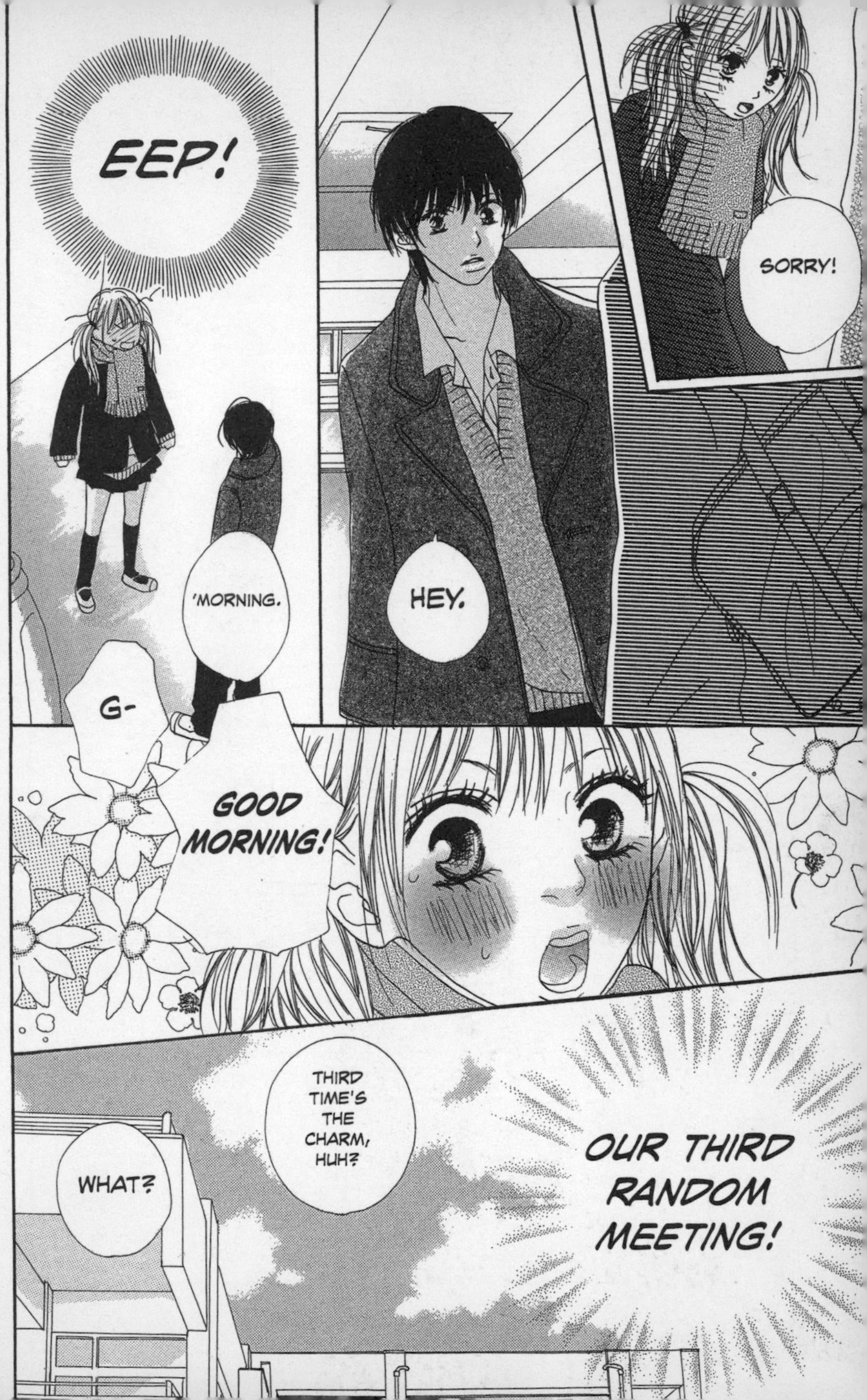
SORRY!
HEY.
EEP!
'MORNING.
G-
GOOD MORNING!
OUR THIRD RANDOM MEETING!
THIRD TIME'S THE CHARM, HUH?
WHAT?

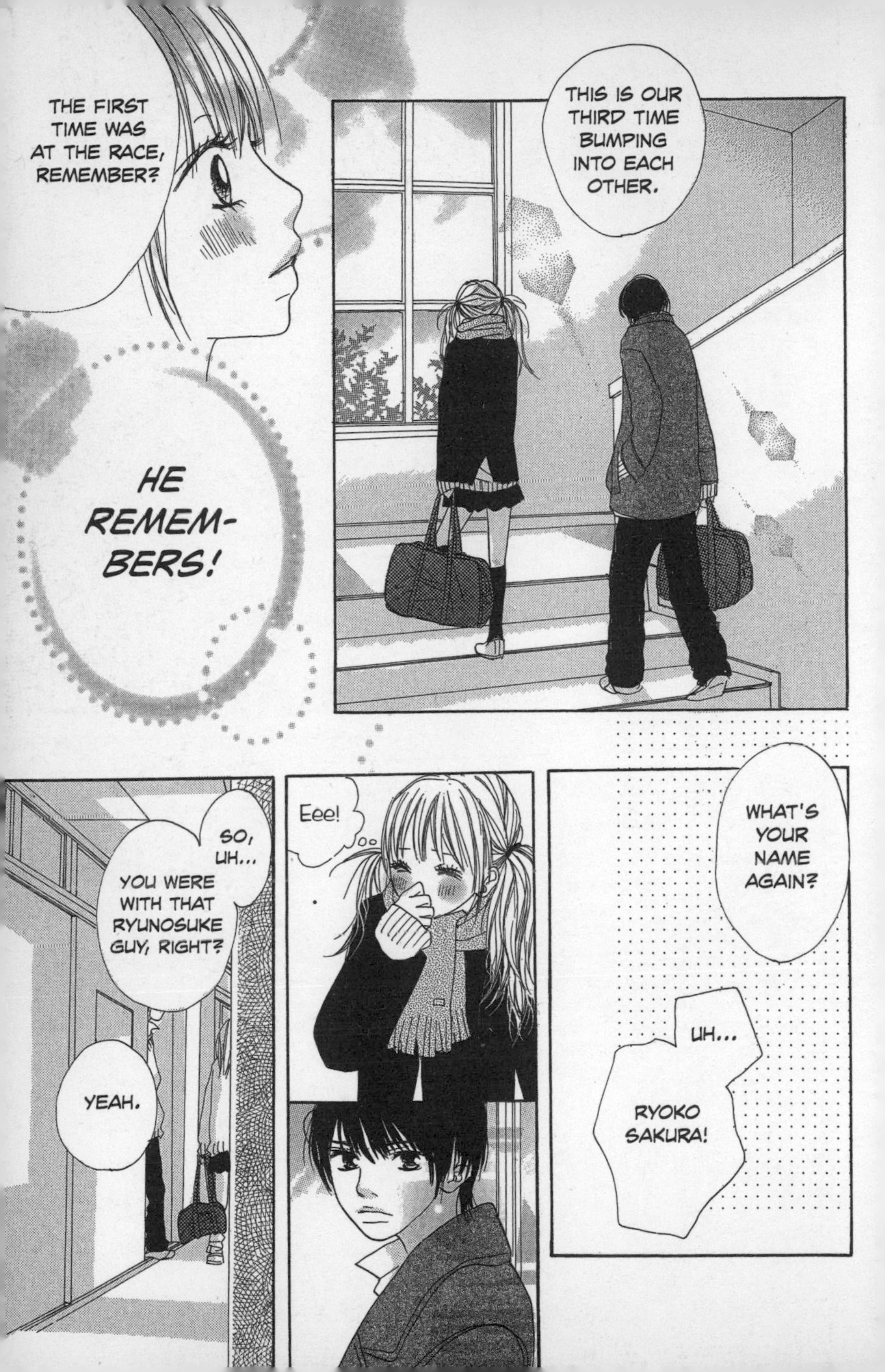
THIS IS OUR THIRD TIME BUMPING INTO EACH OTHER.
THE FIRST TIME WAS AT THE RACE, REMEMBER?
HE REMEMBERS!
WHAT'S YOUR NAME AGAIN?
UH...
RYOKO SAKURA!
Eee!
SO, UH...
YOU WERE WITH THAT RYUNOSUKE GUY, RIGHT?
YEAH.

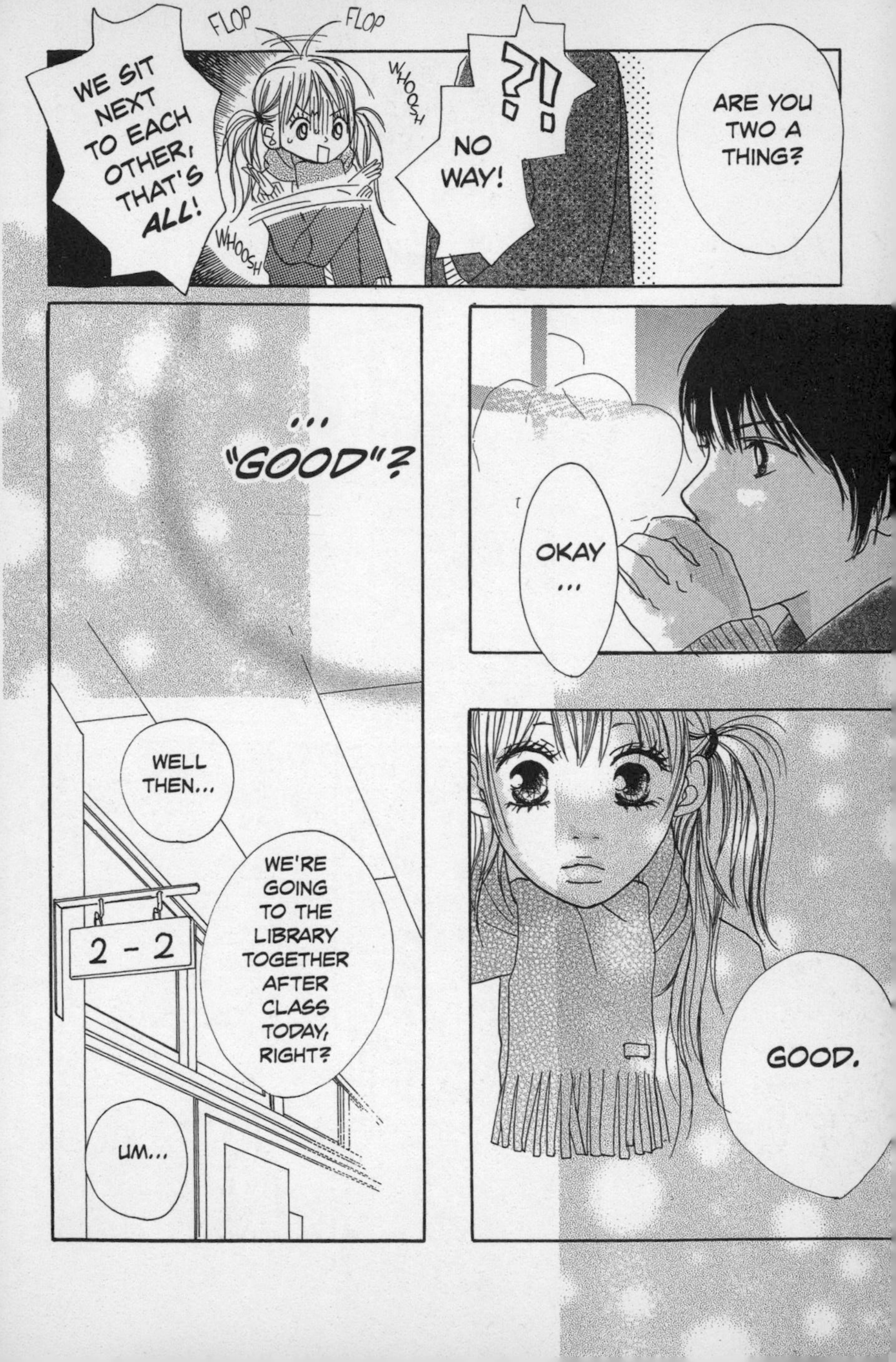

ARE YOU TWO A THING?
?!
NO WAY!
WHOOSH
FLOP
FLOP
WE SIT NEXT TO EACH OTHER, THAT'S ALL!
WHOOSH
OKAY ...
GOOD.
... "GOOD"?
WELL THEN...
WE'RE GOING TO THE LIBRARY TOGETHER AFTER CLASS TODAY, RIGHT?
2 - 2
UM...

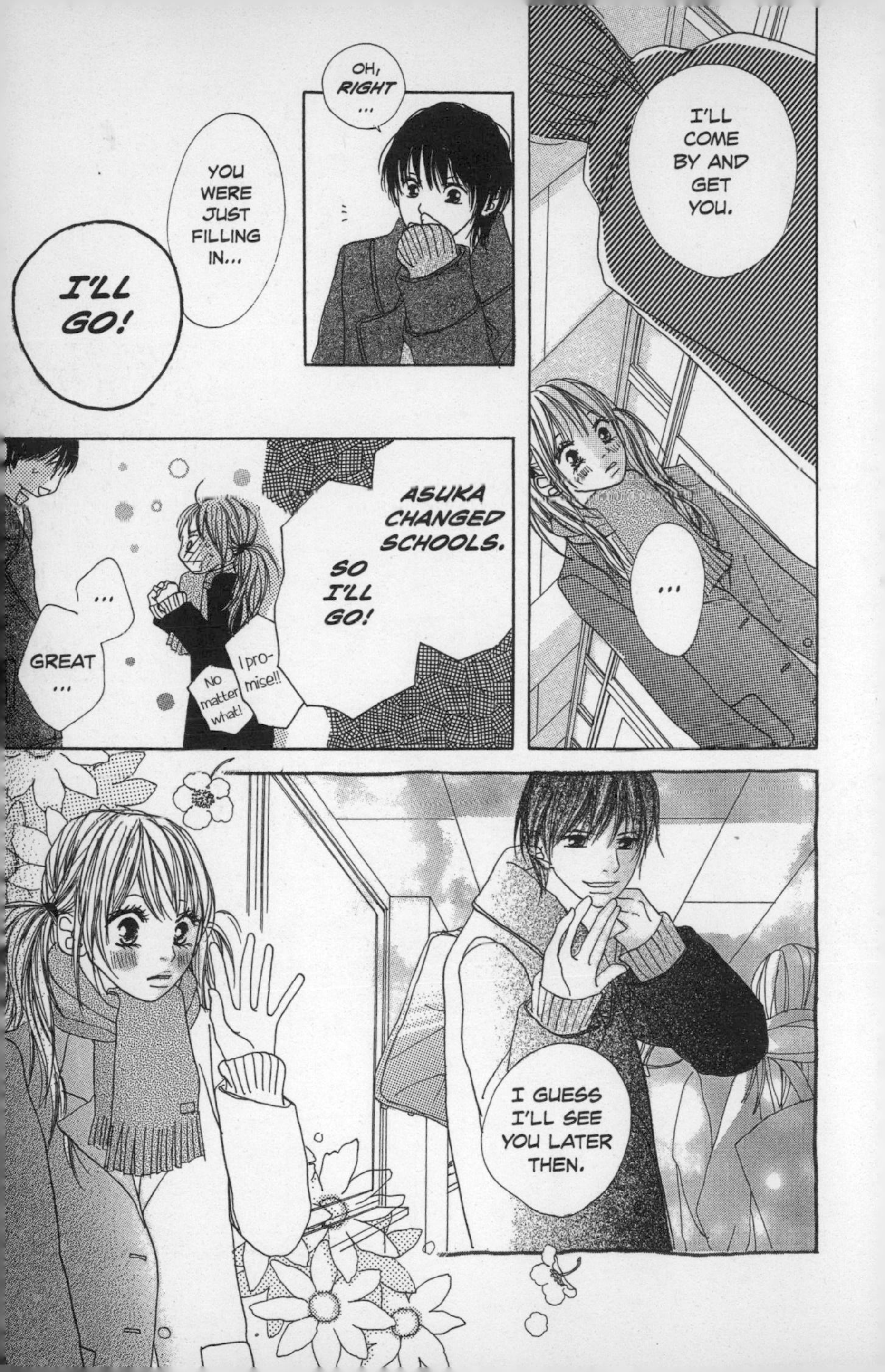
I'LL COME BY AND GET YOU.
...
OH, RIGHT ...
YOU WERE JUST FILLING IN...
I'LL GO!
ASUKA CHANGED SCHOOLS.
SO I'LL GO!
I promise!!
No matter what!
...
GREAT ...
I GUESS I'LL SEE YOU LATER THEN.

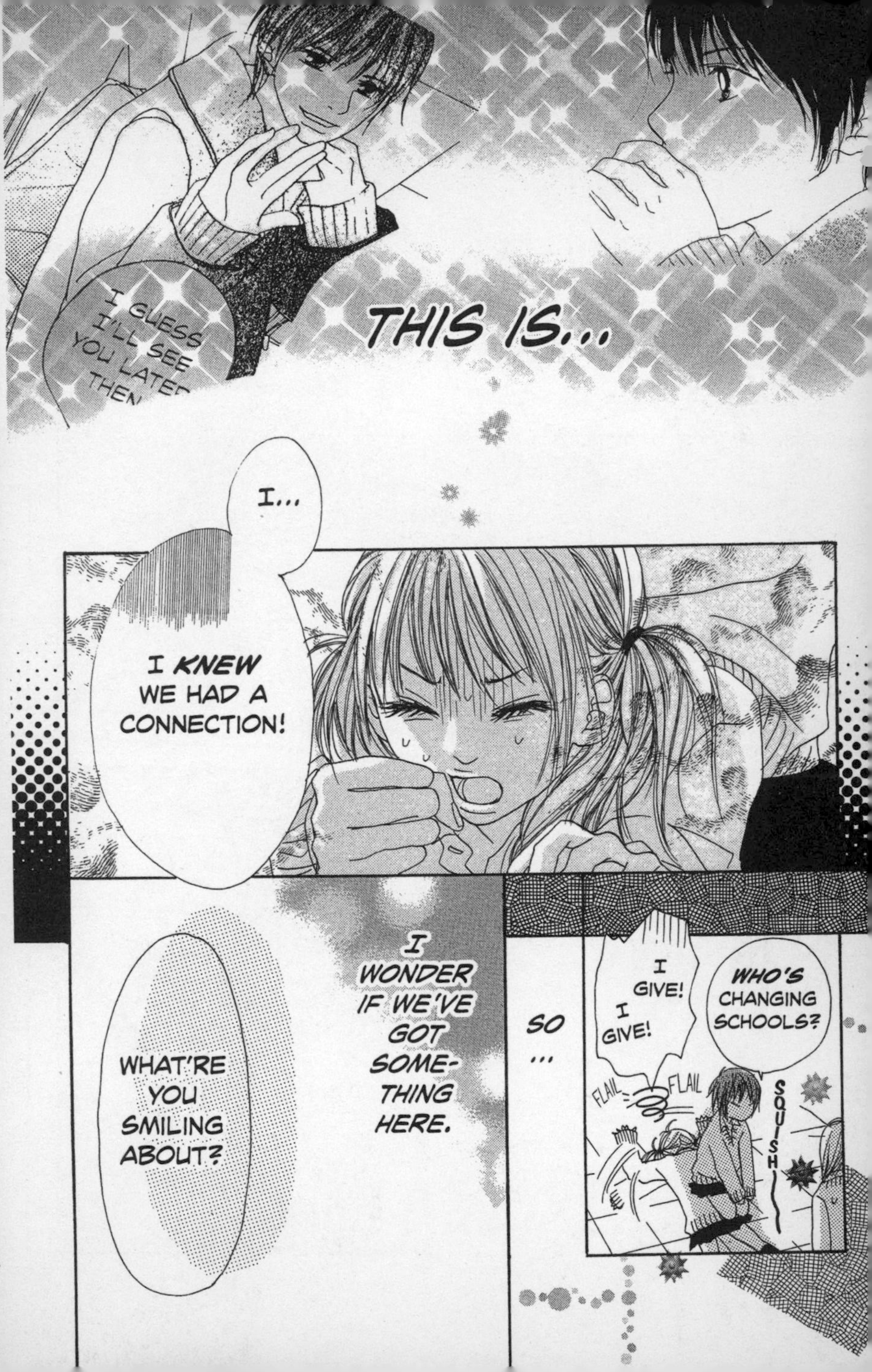
I GUESS I'LL SEE YOU LATER THEN
THIS IS...
I...
I KNEW WE HAD A CONNECTION!
WHO'S CHANGING SCHOOLS?
SQUISH
I GIVE! I GIVE!
FLAIL FLAIL
SO ...
I WONDER IF WE'VE GOT SOMETHING HERE.
WHAT'RE YOU SMILING ABOUT?

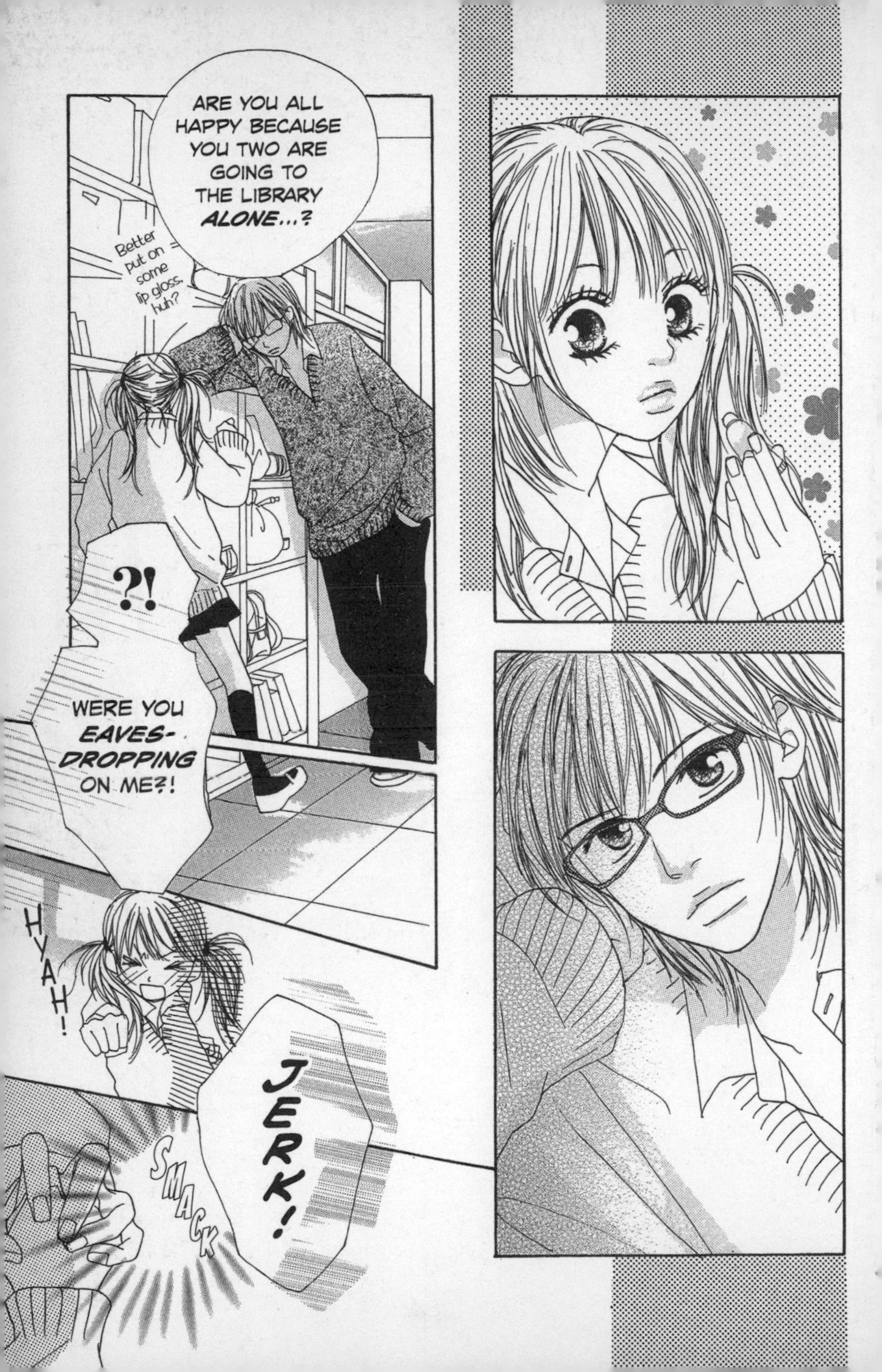
ARE YOU ALL HAPPY BECAUSE YOU TWO ARE GOING TO THE LIBRARY ALONE...?
Better put on some lip gloss, huh?
?!
WERE YOU EAVES-DROPPING ON ME?!
HYAH!
JERK!
SMACK

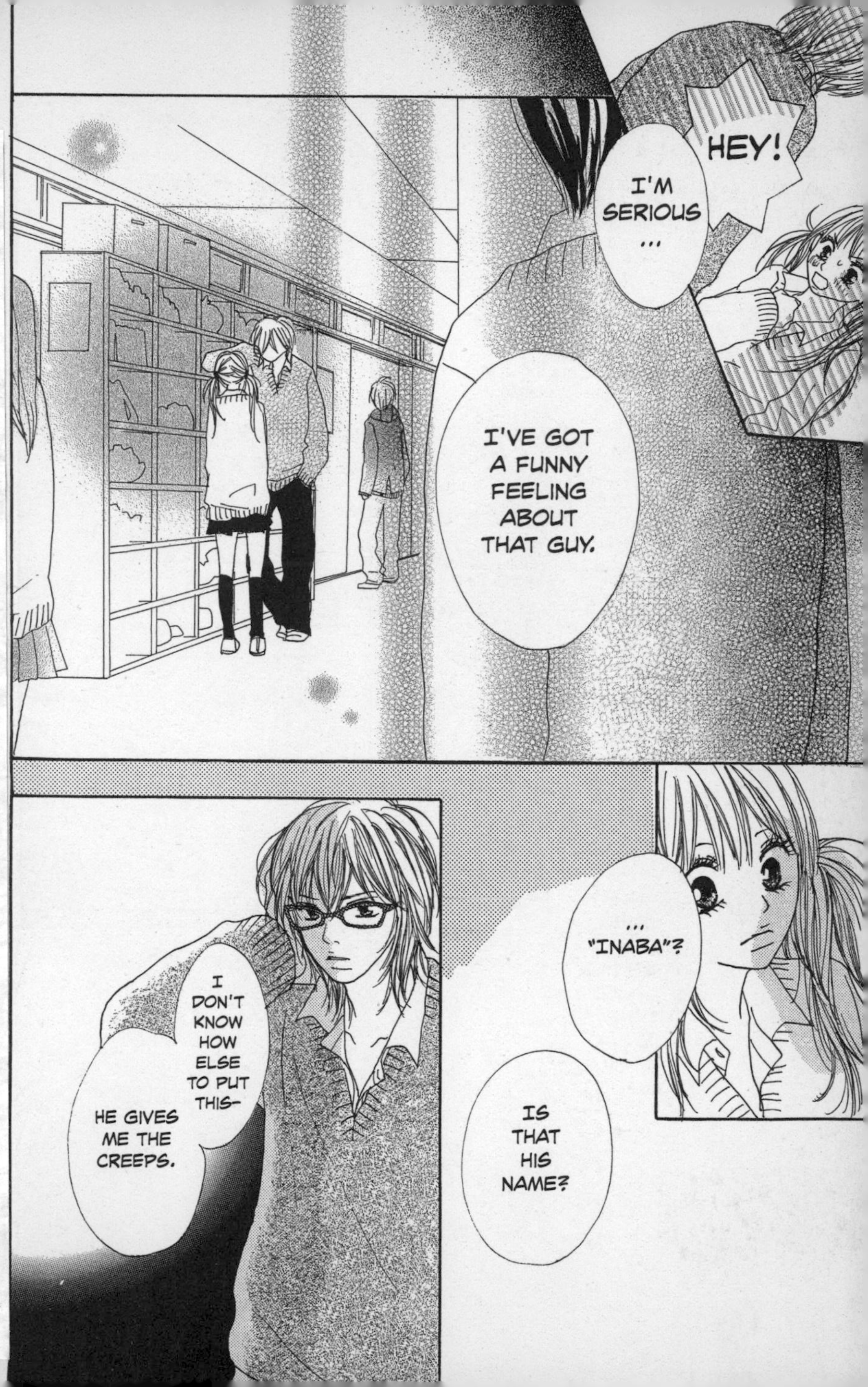
HEY!
I'M SERIOUS ...
I'VE GOT A FUNNY FEELING ABOUT THAT GUY.
... "INABA"?
IS THAT HIS NAME?
I DON'T KNOW HOW ELSE TO PUT THIS-
HE GIVES ME THE CREEPS.

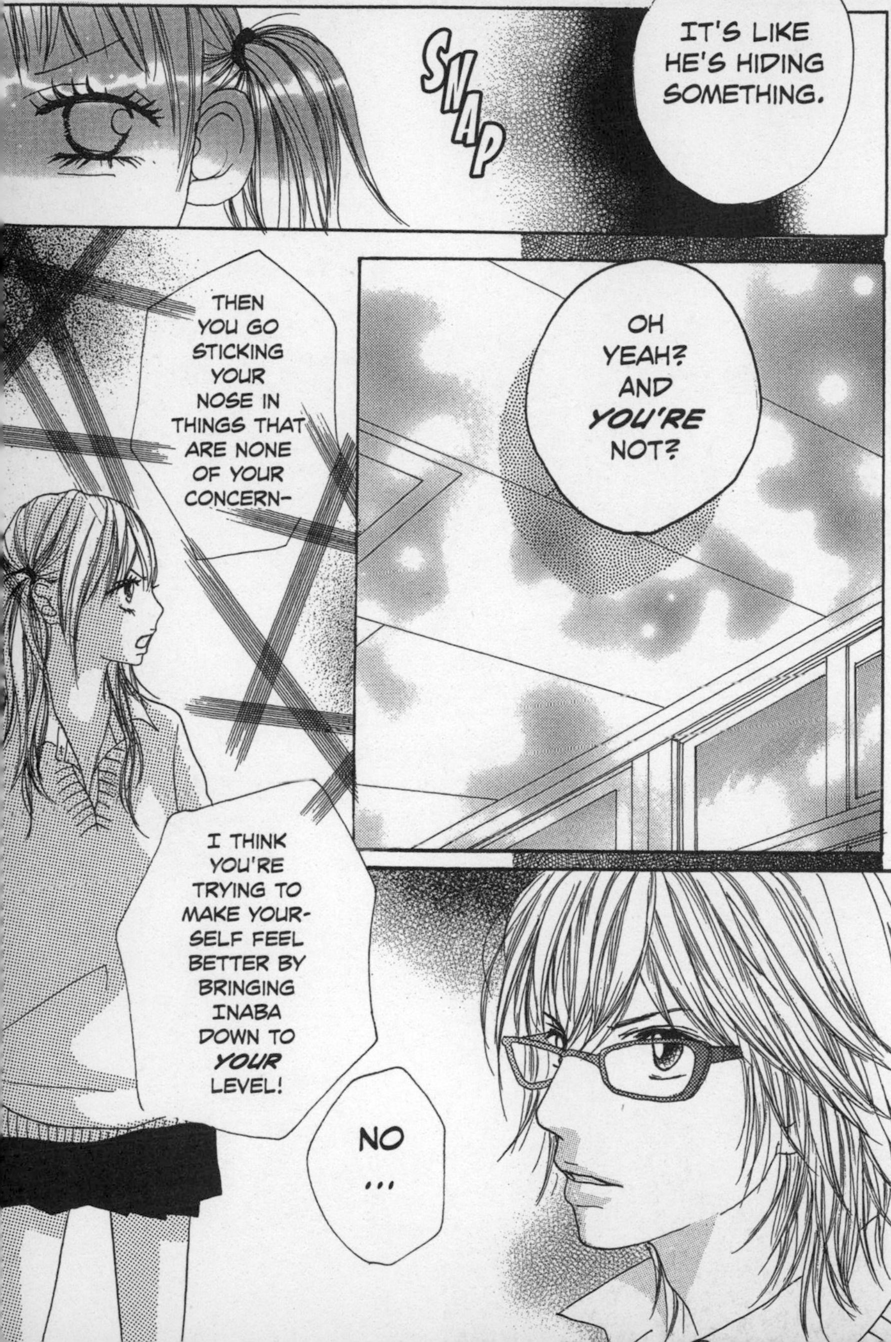
IT'S LIKE HE'S HIDING SOMETHING.
SNAP
THEN YOU GO STICKING YOUR NOSE IN THINGS THAT ARE NONE OF YOUR CONCERN-
OH YEAH? AND *YOU'RE* NOT?
I THINK YOU'RE TRYING TO MAKE YOUR-SELF FEEL BETTER BY BRINGING INABA DOWN TO *YOUR* LEVEL!
NO ...

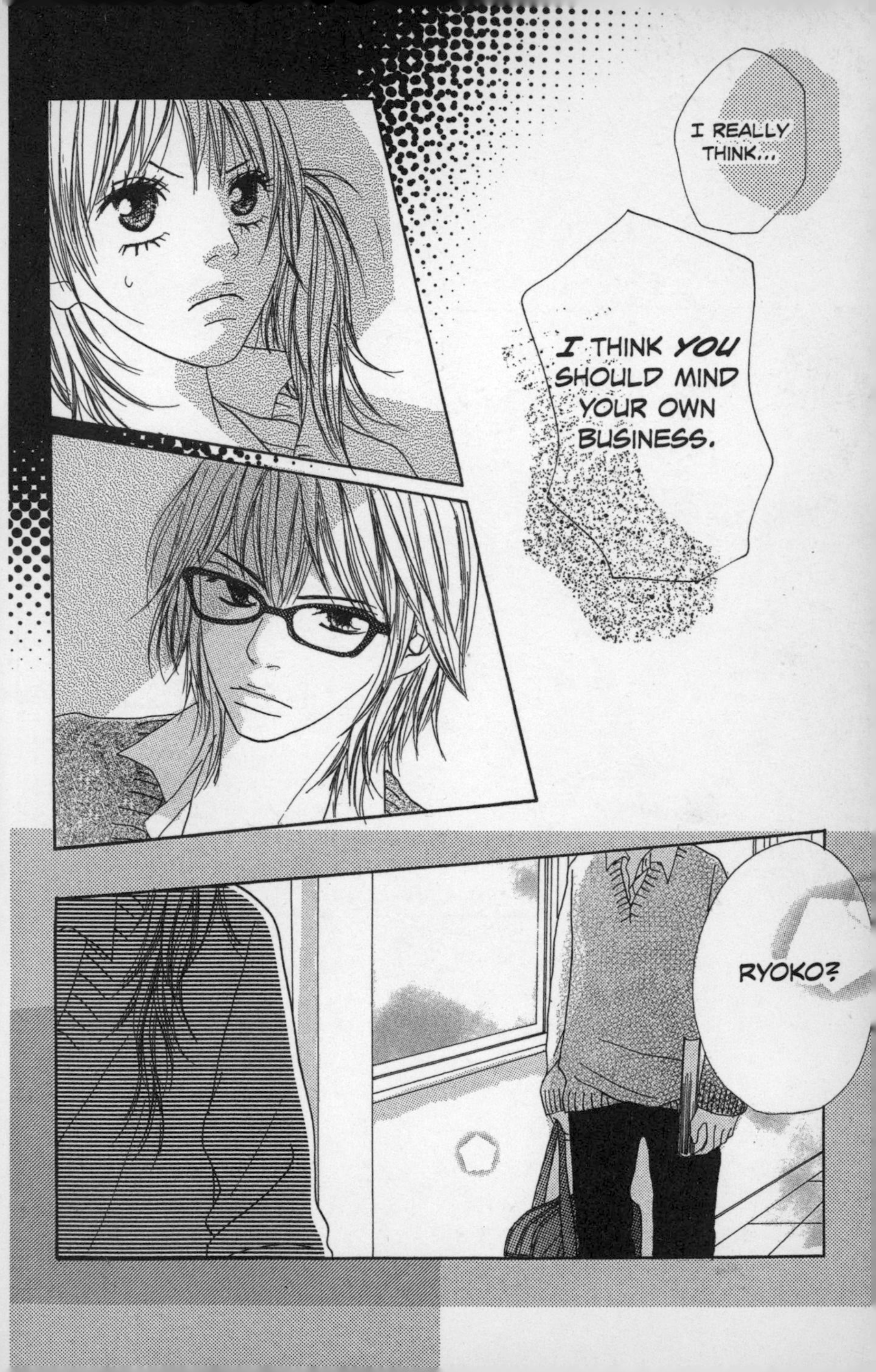
I REALLY THINK...
I THINK YOU SHOULD MIND YOUR OWN BUSINESS.
RYOKO?

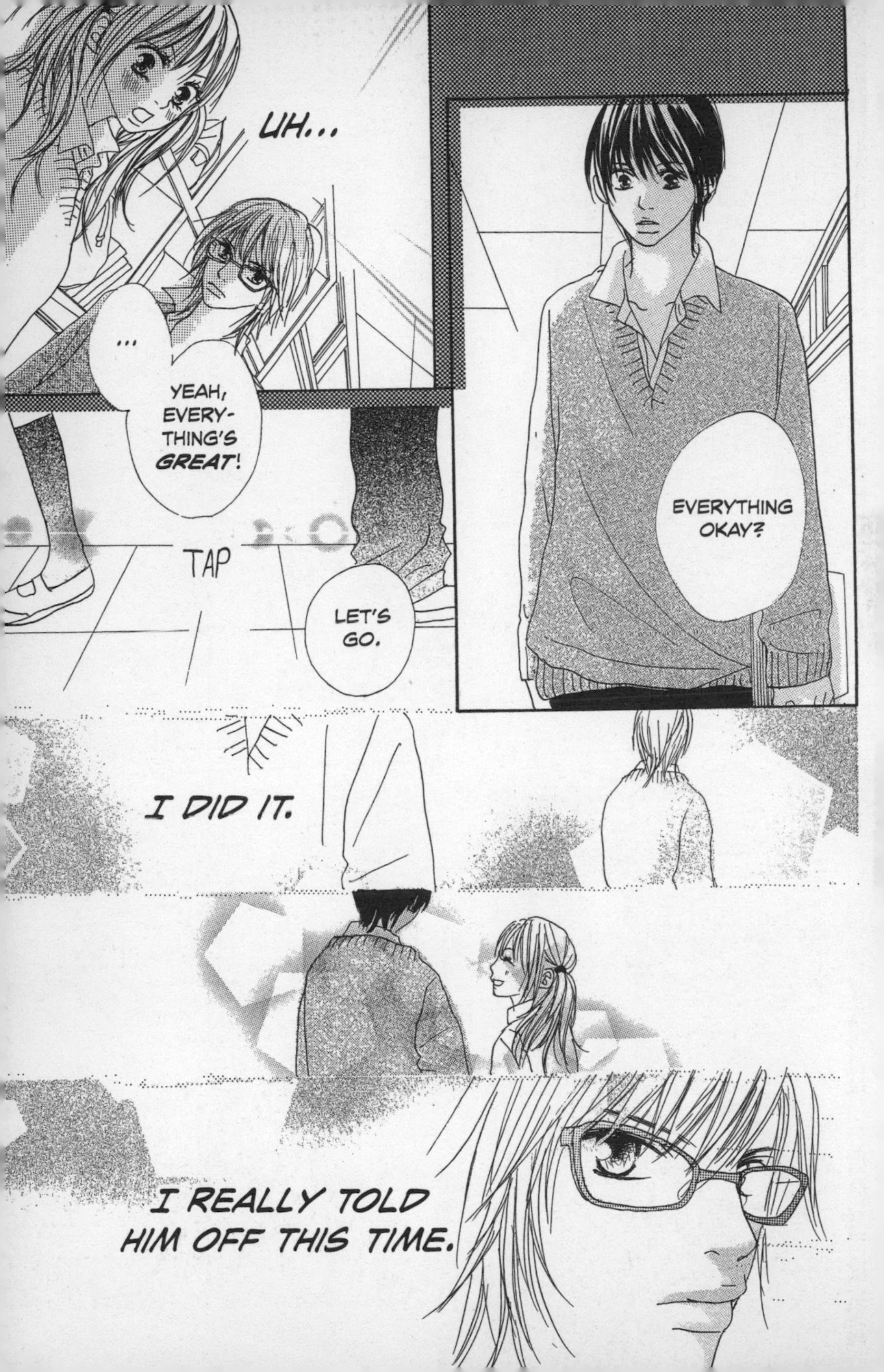
EVERYTHING OKAY?
UH...
...
YEAH, EVERYTHING'S *GREAT*!
TAP
LET'S GO.
I DID IT.
I REALLY TOLD HIM OFF THIS TIME.

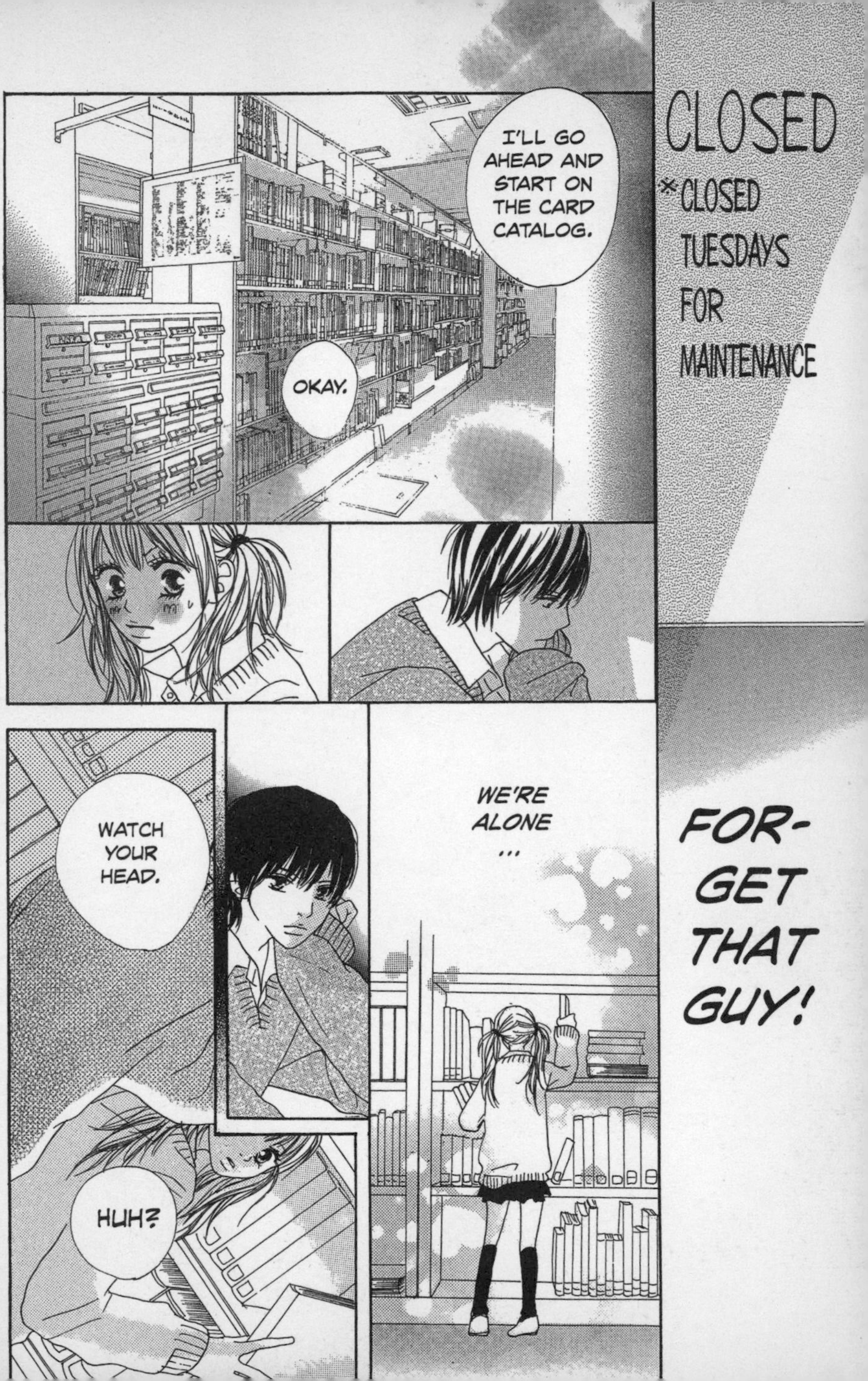
CLOSED
*CLOSED TUESDAYS FOR MAINTENANCE
I'LL GO AHEAD AND START ON THE CARD CATALOG.
OKAY.
FOR-GET THAT GUY!
WE'RE ALONE...
WATCH YOUR HEAD.
HUH?

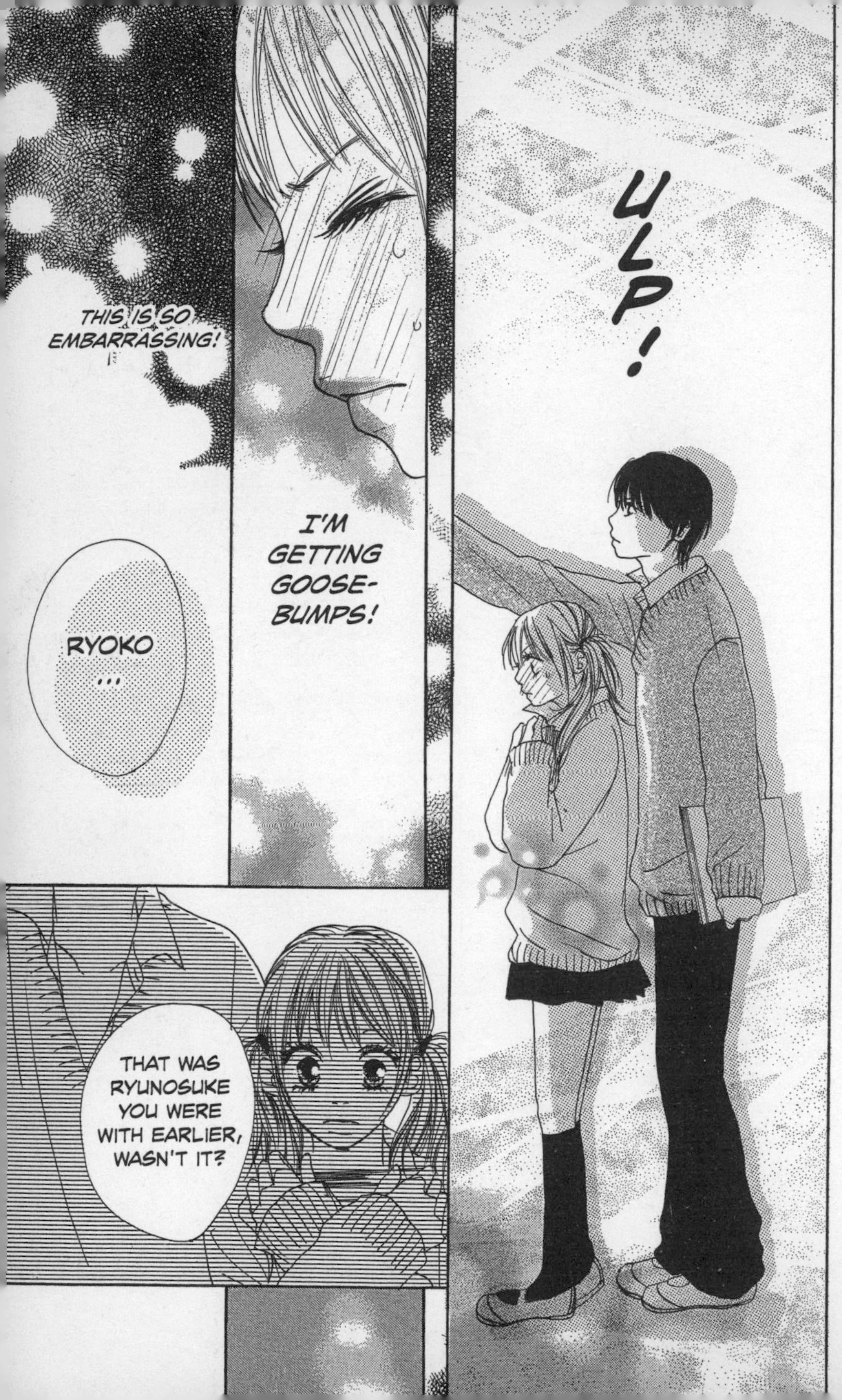
ULP!
I'M GETTING GOOSE-BUMPS!
THIS IS SO EMBARRASSING!
RYOKO ...
THAT WAS RYUNOSUKE YOU WERE WITH EARLIER, WASN'T IT?

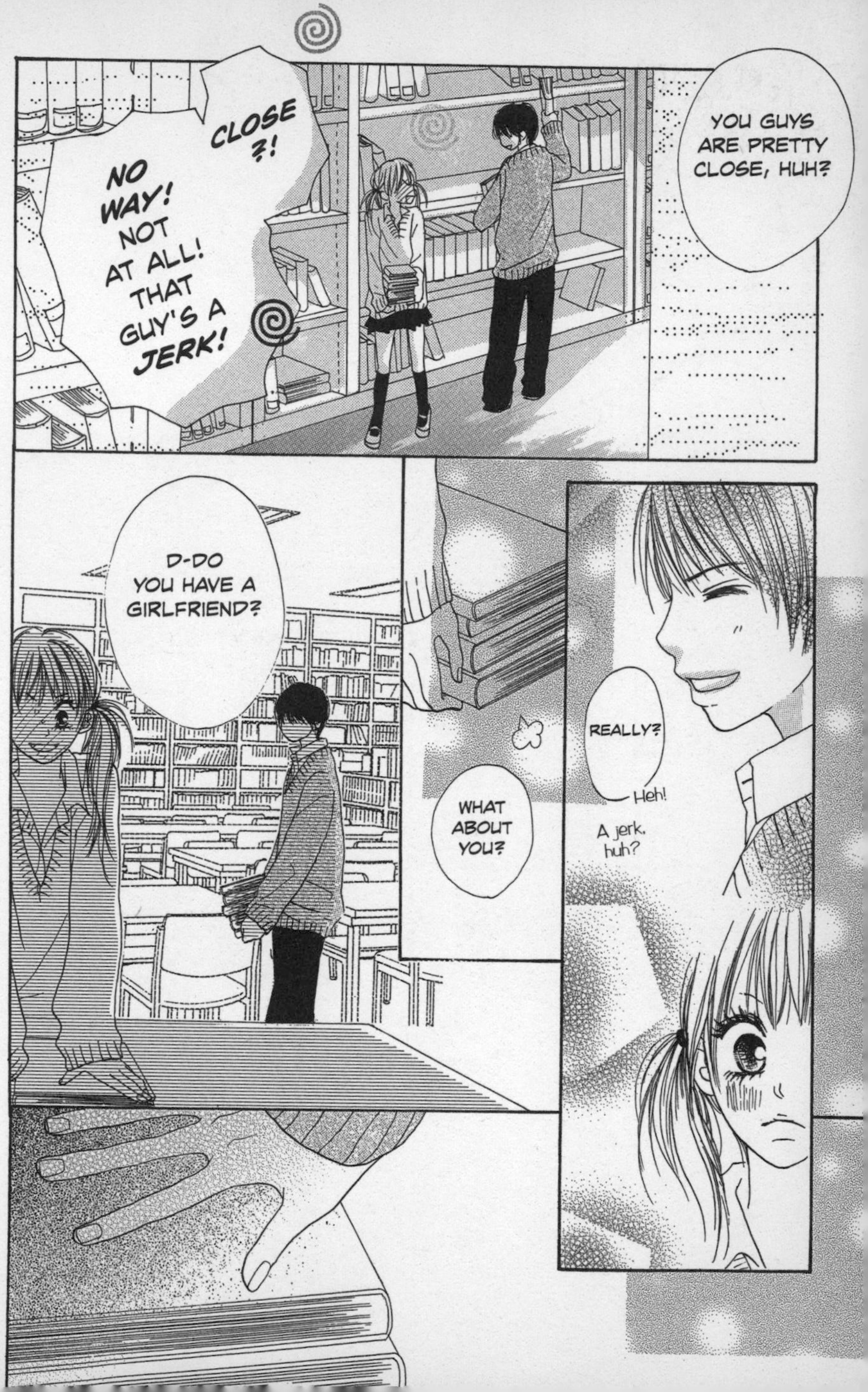
YOU GUYS ARE PRETTY CLOSE, HUH?
CLOSE?!
NO WAY! NOT AT ALL! THAT GUY'S A JERK!
REALLY?
Heh!
A jerk, huh?
WHAT ABOUT YOU?
D-DO YOU HAVE A GIRLFRIEND?

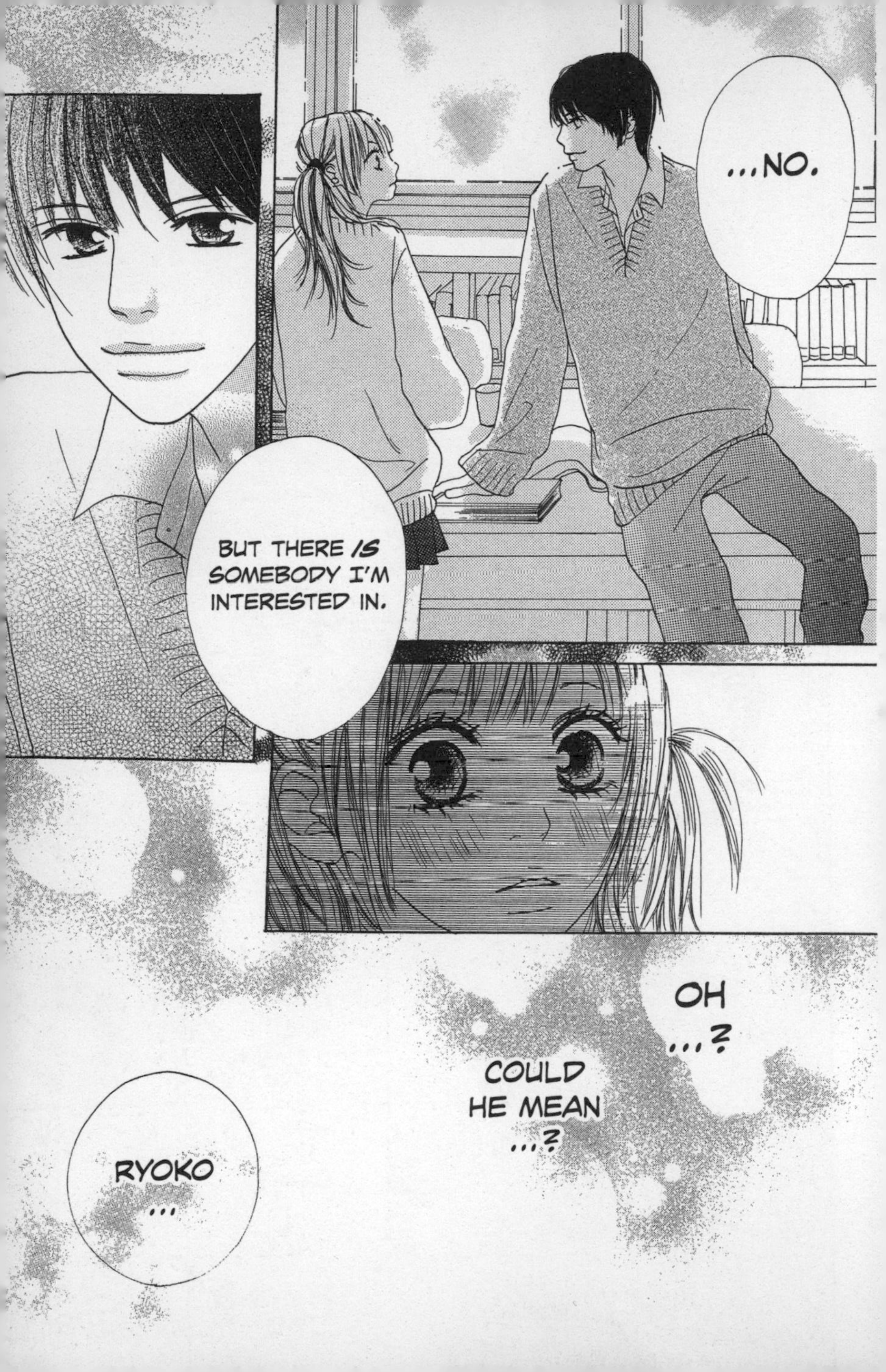
...NO.
BUT THERE IS SOMEBODY I'M INTERESTED IN.
OH ...?
COULD HE MEAN ...?
RYOKO ...

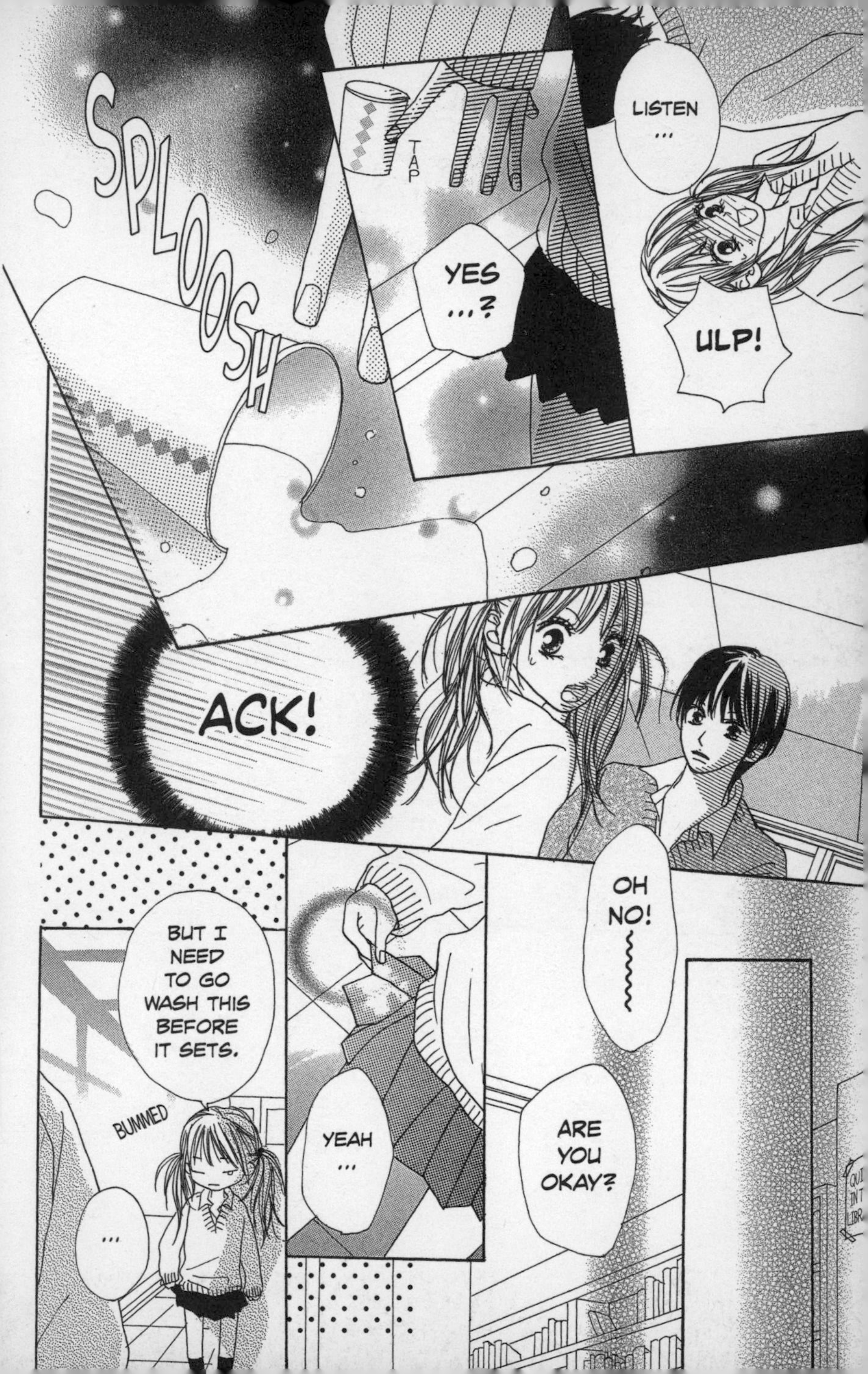
LISTEN ...
ULP!
TAP
YES ...?
SPLOOSH
ACK!
OH NO! ~~~
ARE YOU OKAY?
YEAH ...
BUT I NEED TO GO WASH THIS BEFORE IT SETS.
BUMMED
...

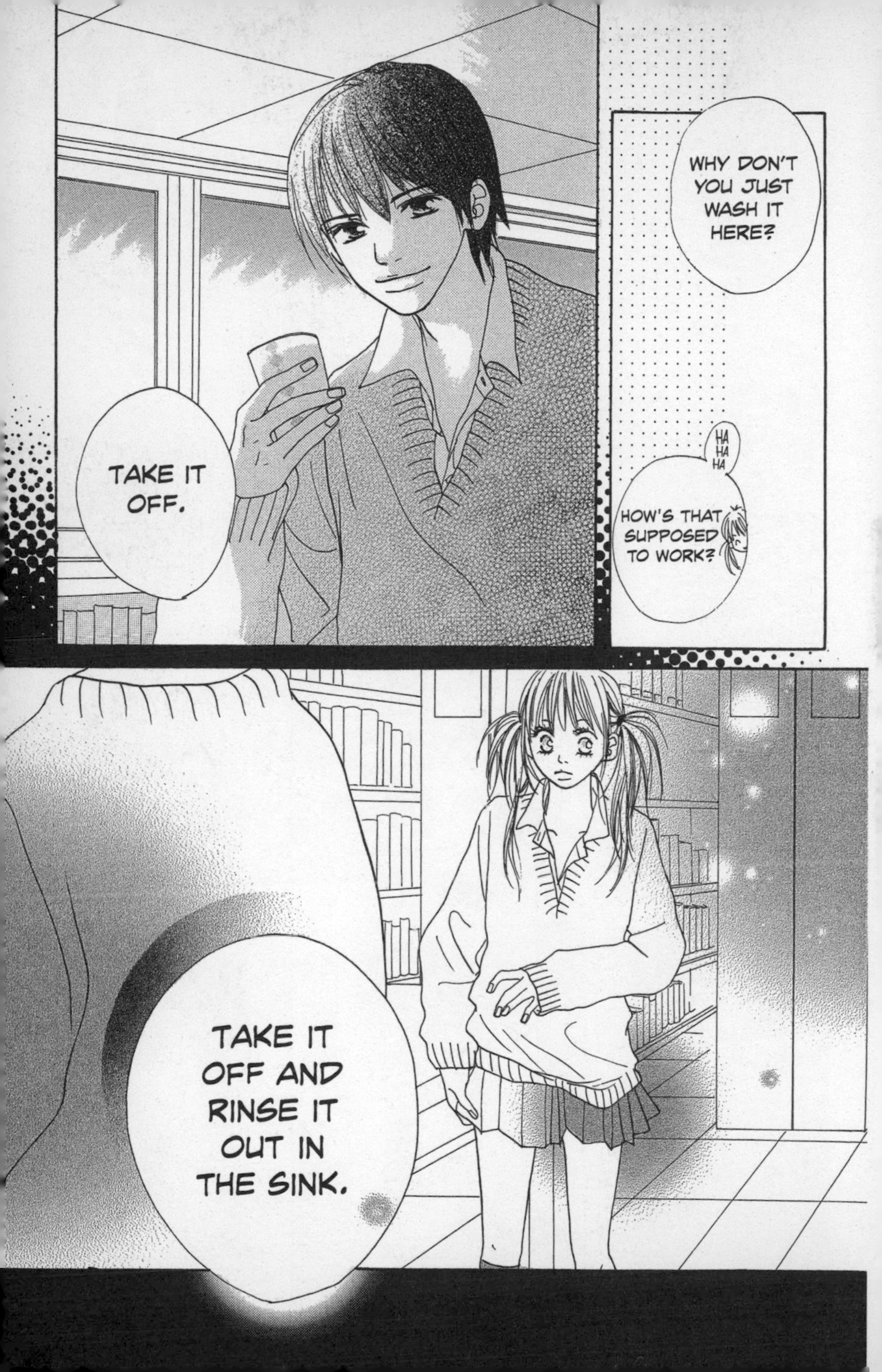
WHY DON'T YOU JUST WASH IT HERE?
HA HA HA
HOW'S THAT SUPPOSED TO WORK?
TAKE IT OFF.
TAKE IT OFF AND RINSE IT OUT IN THE SINK.

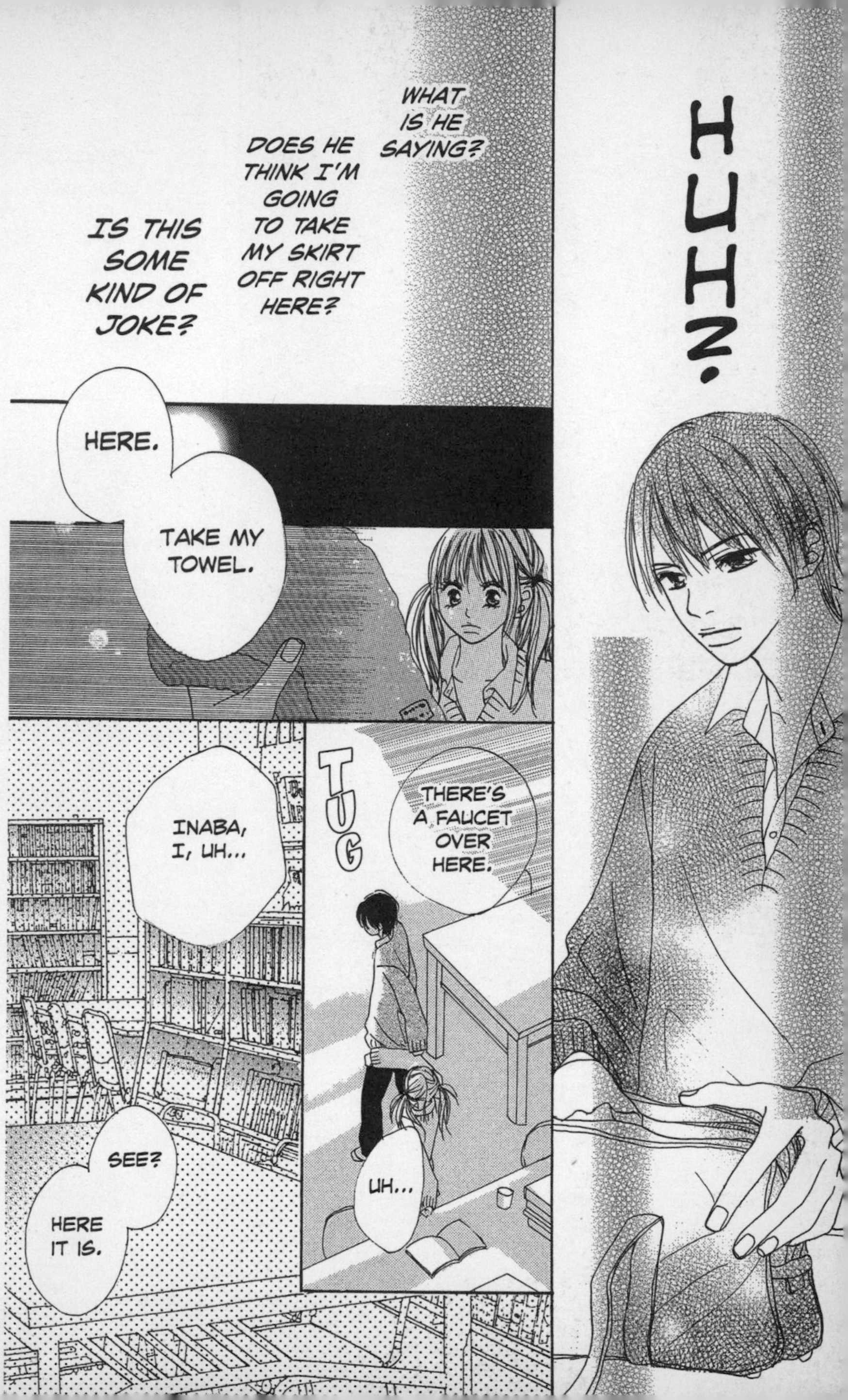
HUH?
WHAT IS HE SAYING?
DOES HE THINK I'M GOING TO TAKE MY SKIRT OFF RIGHT HERE?
IS THIS SOME KIND OF JOKE?
HERE.
TAKE MY TOWEL.
TUG
THERE'S A FAUCET OVER HERE.
UH...
INABA, I, UH...
SEE?
HERE IT IS.

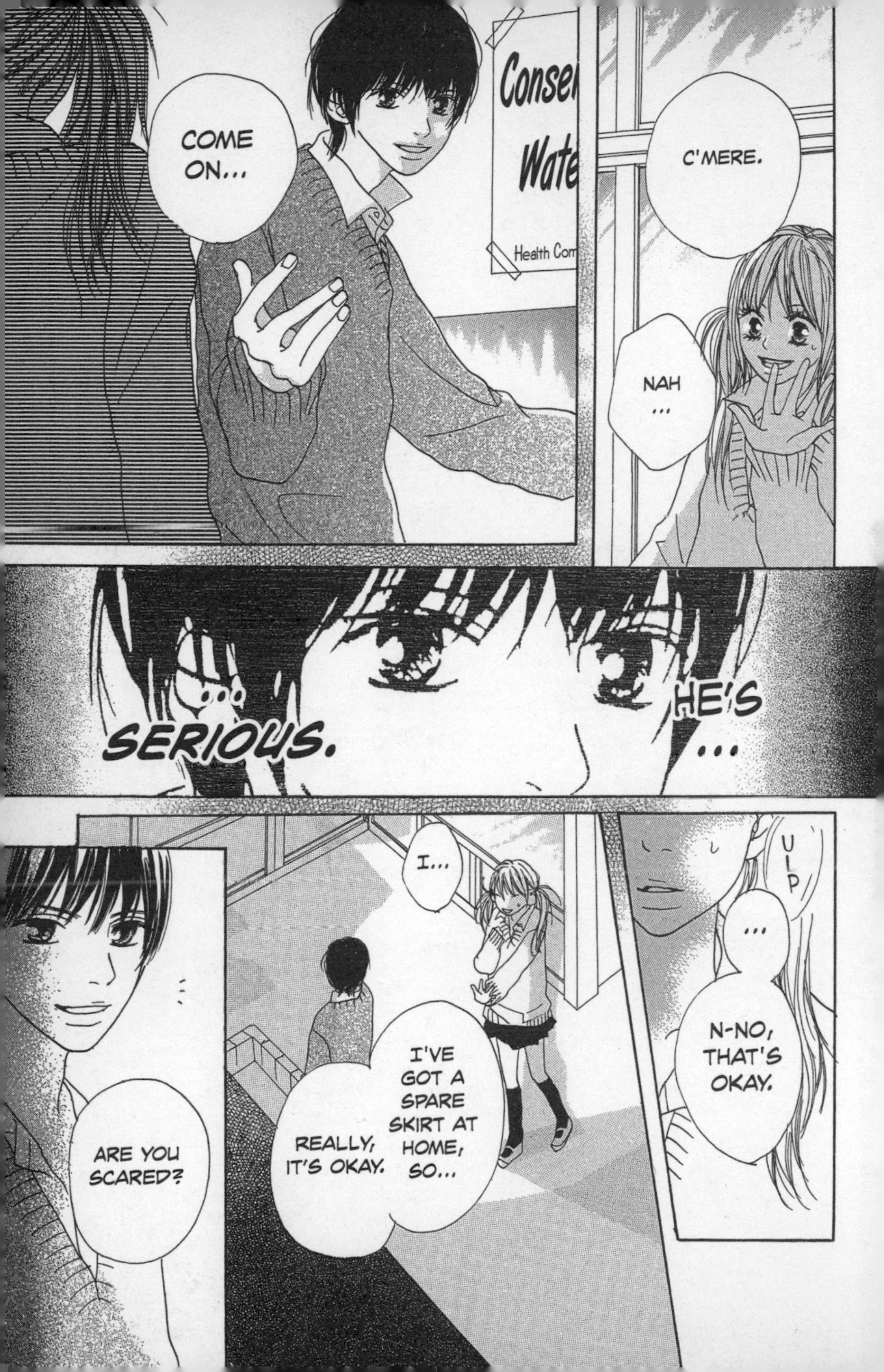
C'MERE.
NAH ...
COME ON...
HE'S ...
... SERIOUS.
ULP
...
N-NO, THAT'S OKAY.
I...
I'VE GOT A SPARE SKIRT AT HOME, SO...
REALLY, IT'S OKAY.
ARE YOU SCARED?

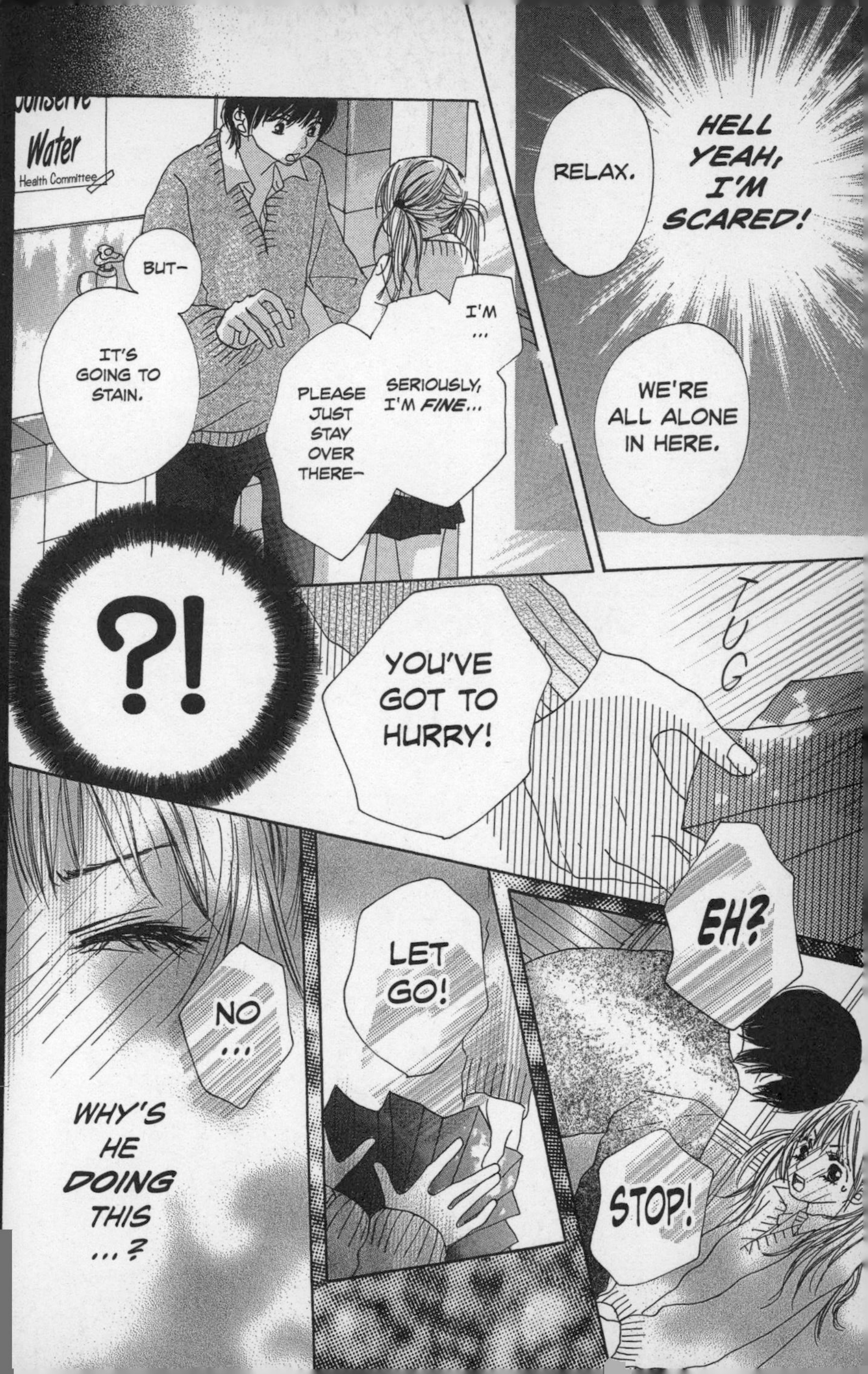
HELL YEAH, I'M SCARED!
RELAX.
WE'RE ALL ALONE IN HERE.
I'M ...
SERIOUSLY, I'M *FINE*...
PLEASE JUST STAY OVER THERE-
BUT-
IT'S GOING TO STAIN.
Water
Health Committee
TUG
YOU'VE GOT TO HURRY!
?!
EH?
STOP!
LET GO!
NO ...
WHY'S HE DOING THIS ...?

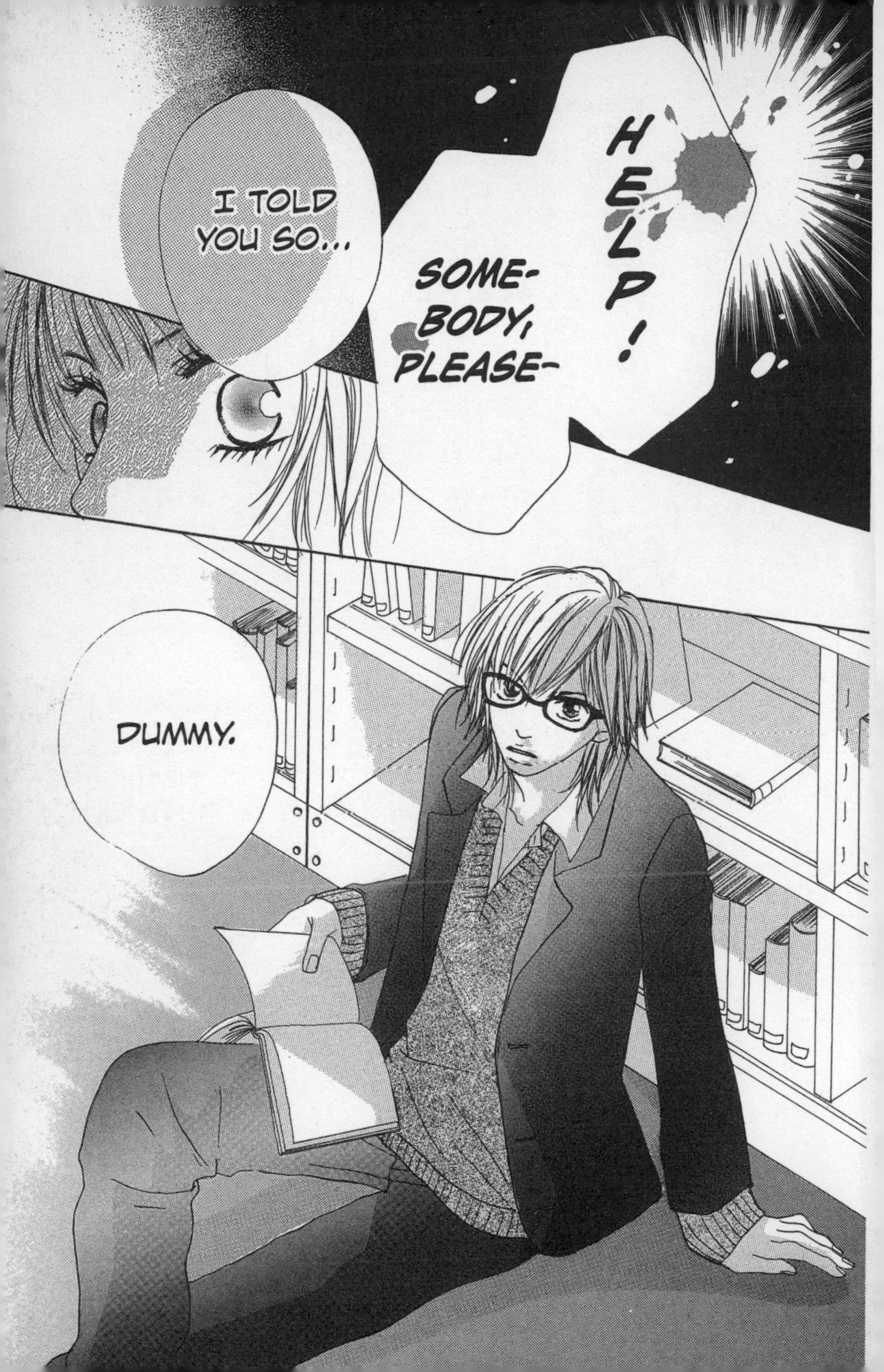
SOME-BODY, PLEASE-
HELP!
I TOLD YOU SO...
DUMMY.

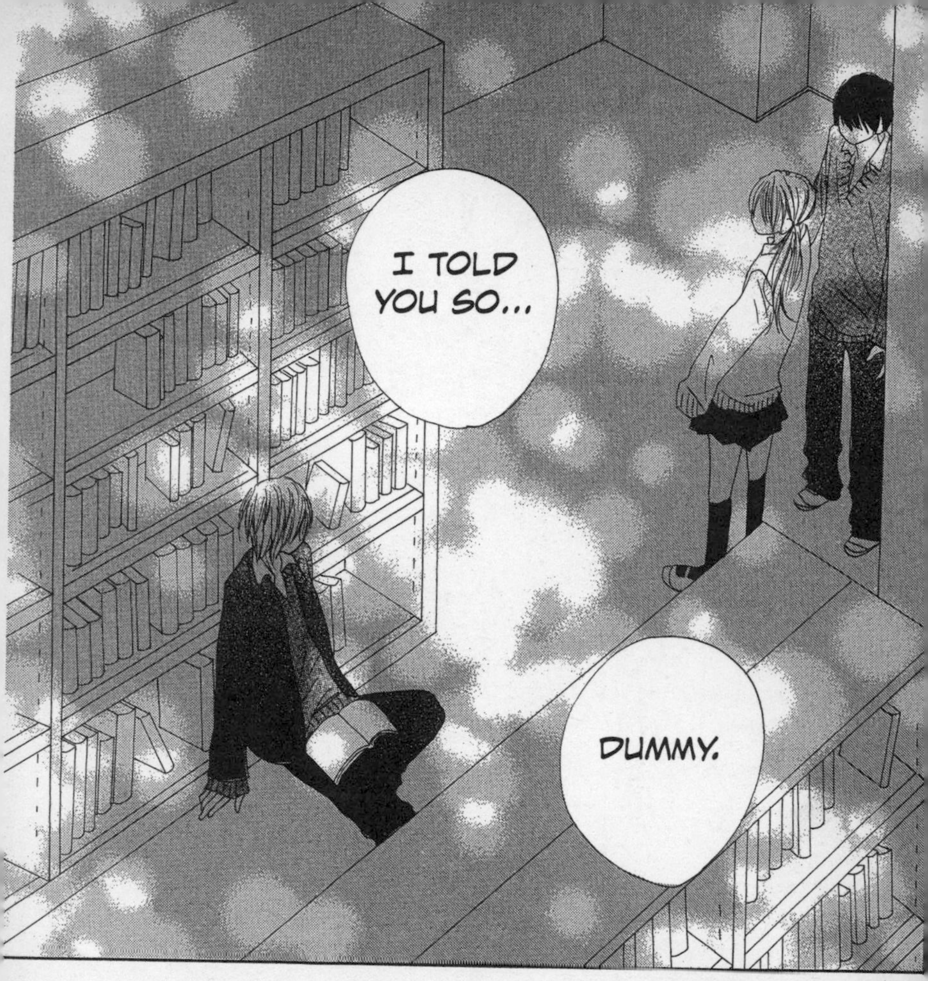
I TOLD YOU SO...
DUMMY.
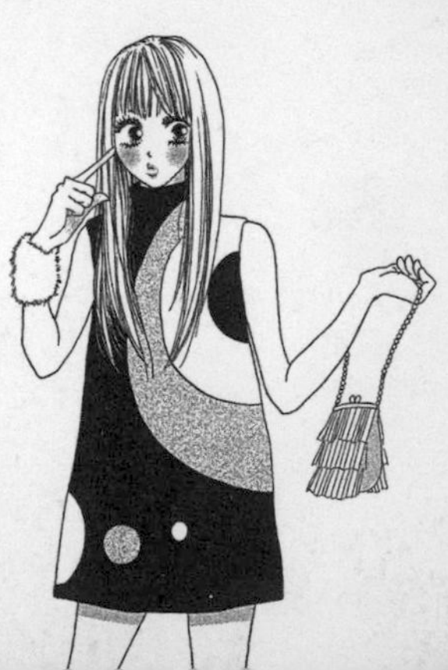

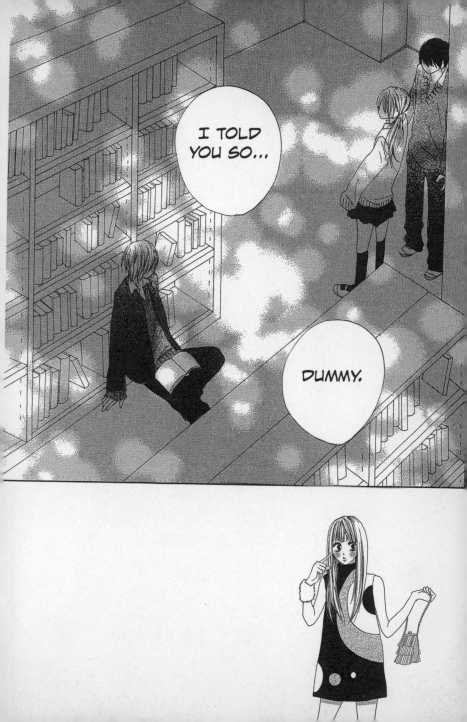

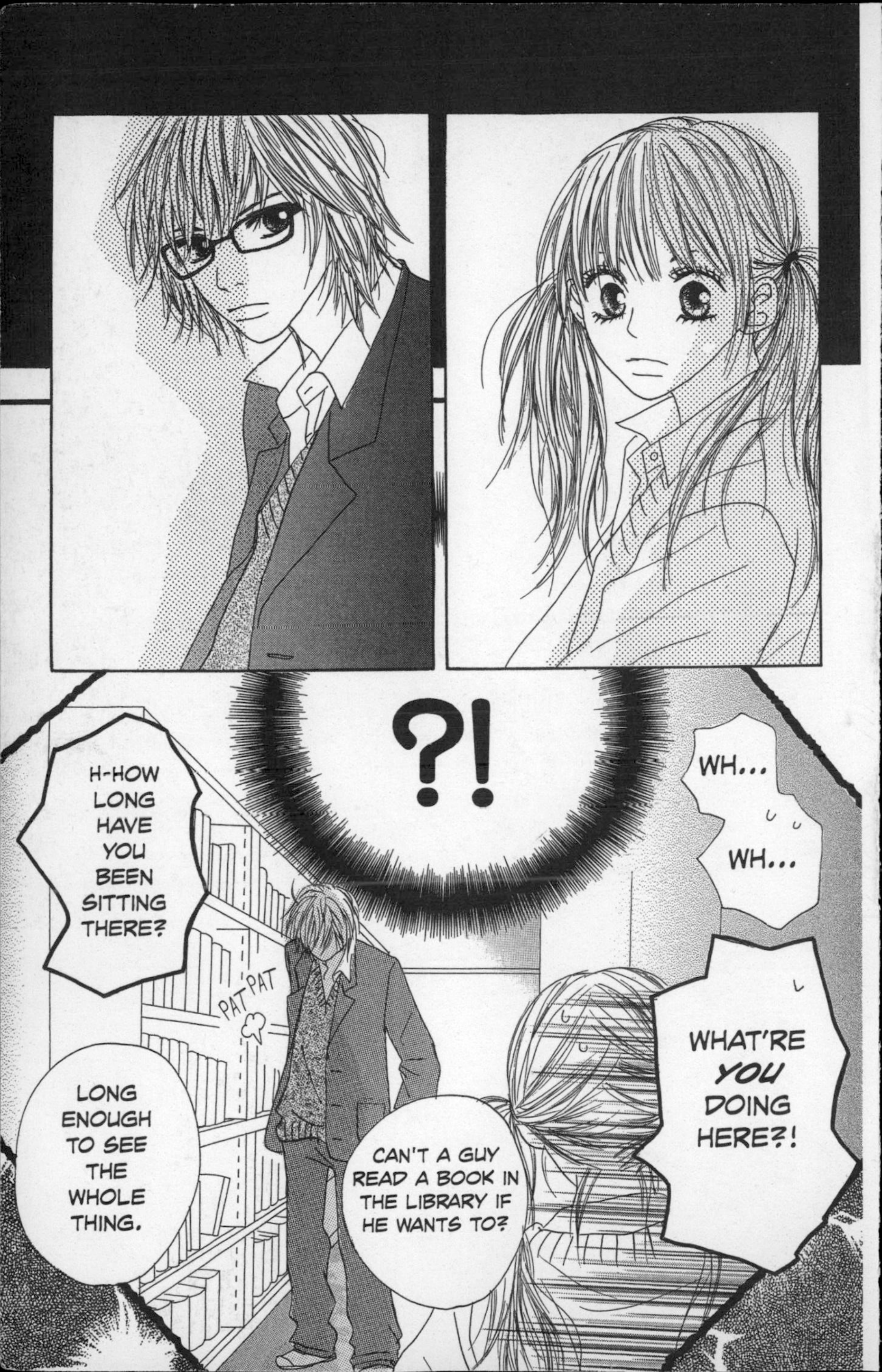
?!
WH...
WH...
WHAT'RE *YOU* DOING HERE?!
CAN'T A GUY READ A BOOK IN THE LIBRARY IF HE WANTS TO?
H-HOW LONG HAVE YOU BEEN SITTING THERE?
PAT PAT
LONG ENOUGH TO SEE THE WHOLE THING.

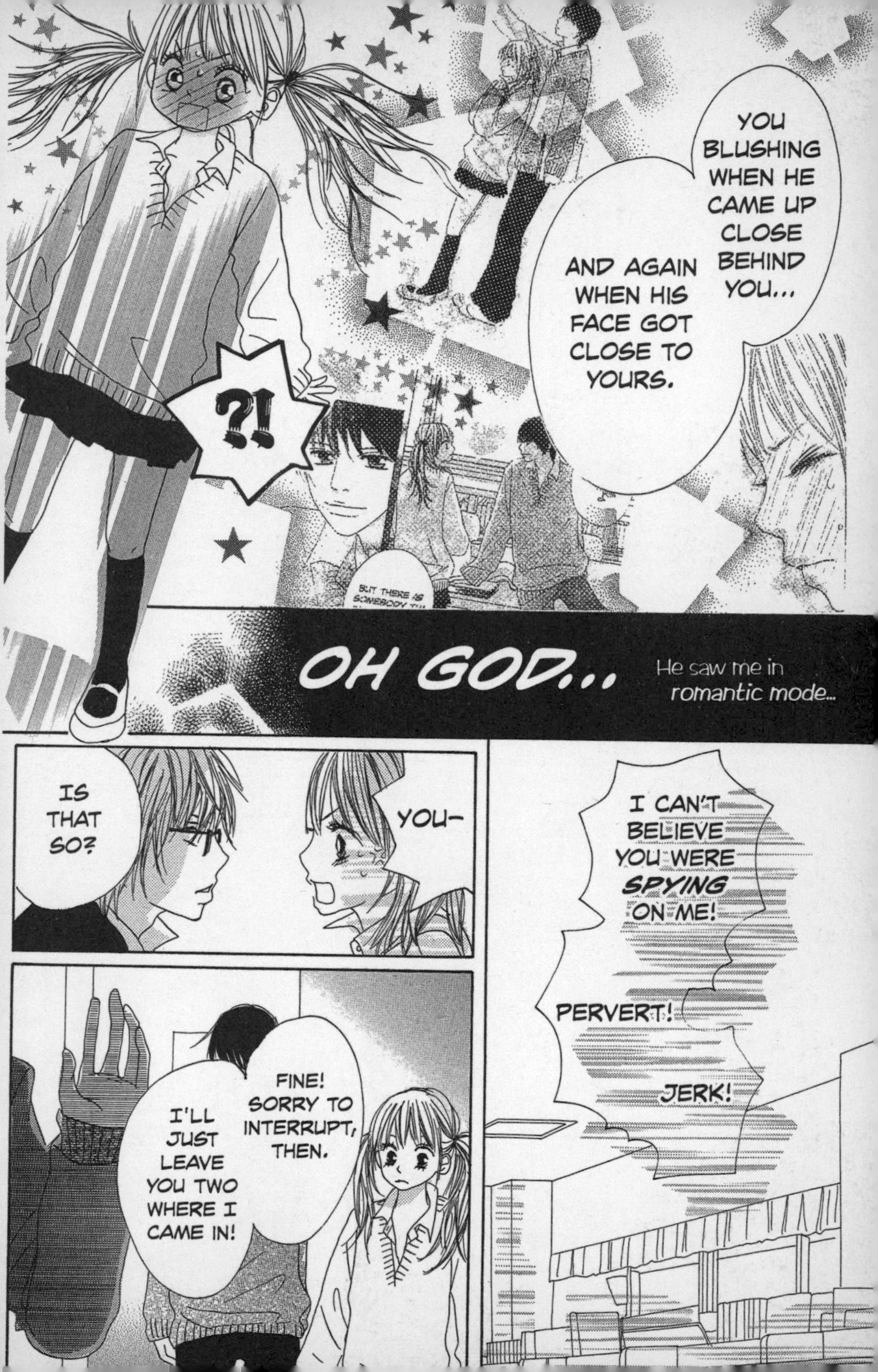
YOU BLUSHING WHEN HE CAME UP CLOSE BEHIND YOU...
AND AGAIN WHEN HIS FACE GOT CLOSE TO YOURS.
?!
OH GOD...
He saw me in romantic mode...
I CAN'T BELIEVE YOU WERE SPYING ON ME!
PERVERT!
JERK!
YOU-
IS THAT SO?
FINE! SORRY TO INTERRUPT, THEN.
I'LL JUST LEAVE YOU TWO WHERE I CAME IN!

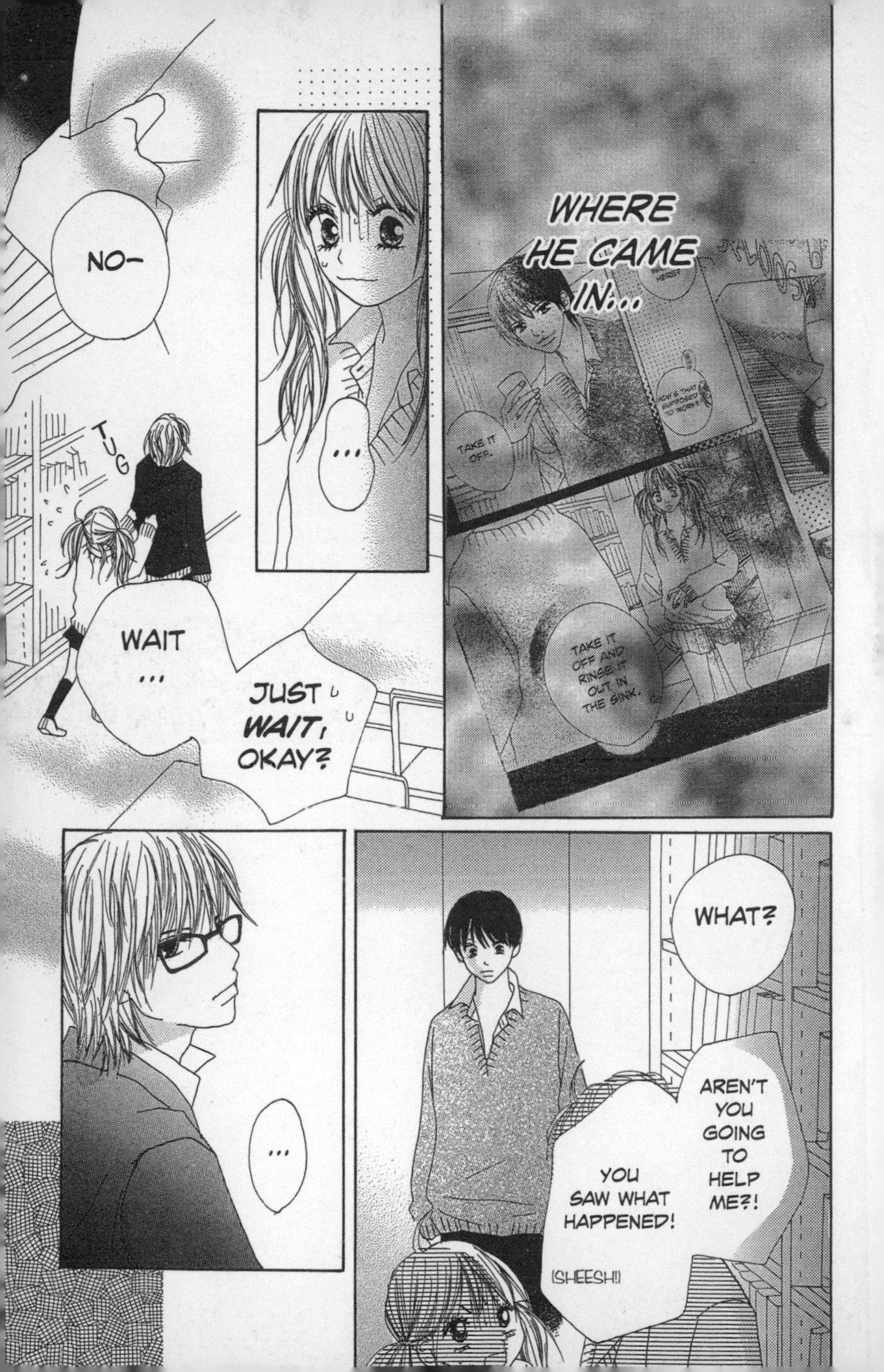
WHERE HE CAME IN...
TAKE IT OFF.
TAKE IT OFF AND RINSE IT OUT IN THE SINK.
...
NO–
TUG
WAIT ...
JUST WAIT, OKAY?
WHAT?
AREN'T YOU GOING TO HELP ME?!
YOU SAW WHAT HAPPENED!
(SHEESH!)
...

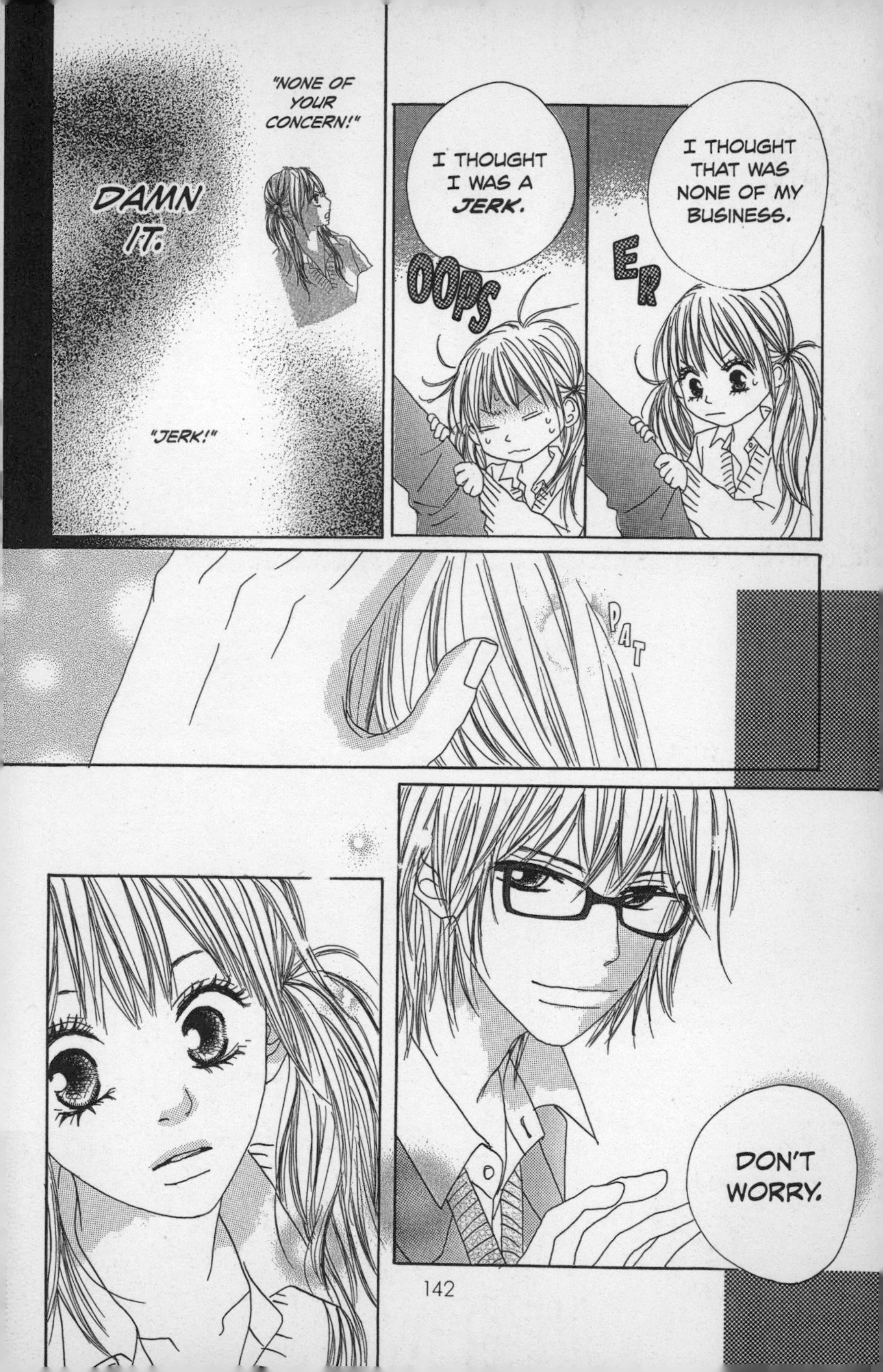
I THOUGHT THAT WAS NONE OF MY BUSINESS.
ER
I THOUGHT I WAS A JERK.
OOPS
"NONE OF YOUR CONCERN!"
DAMN IT.
"JERK!"
PAT
DON'T WORRY.

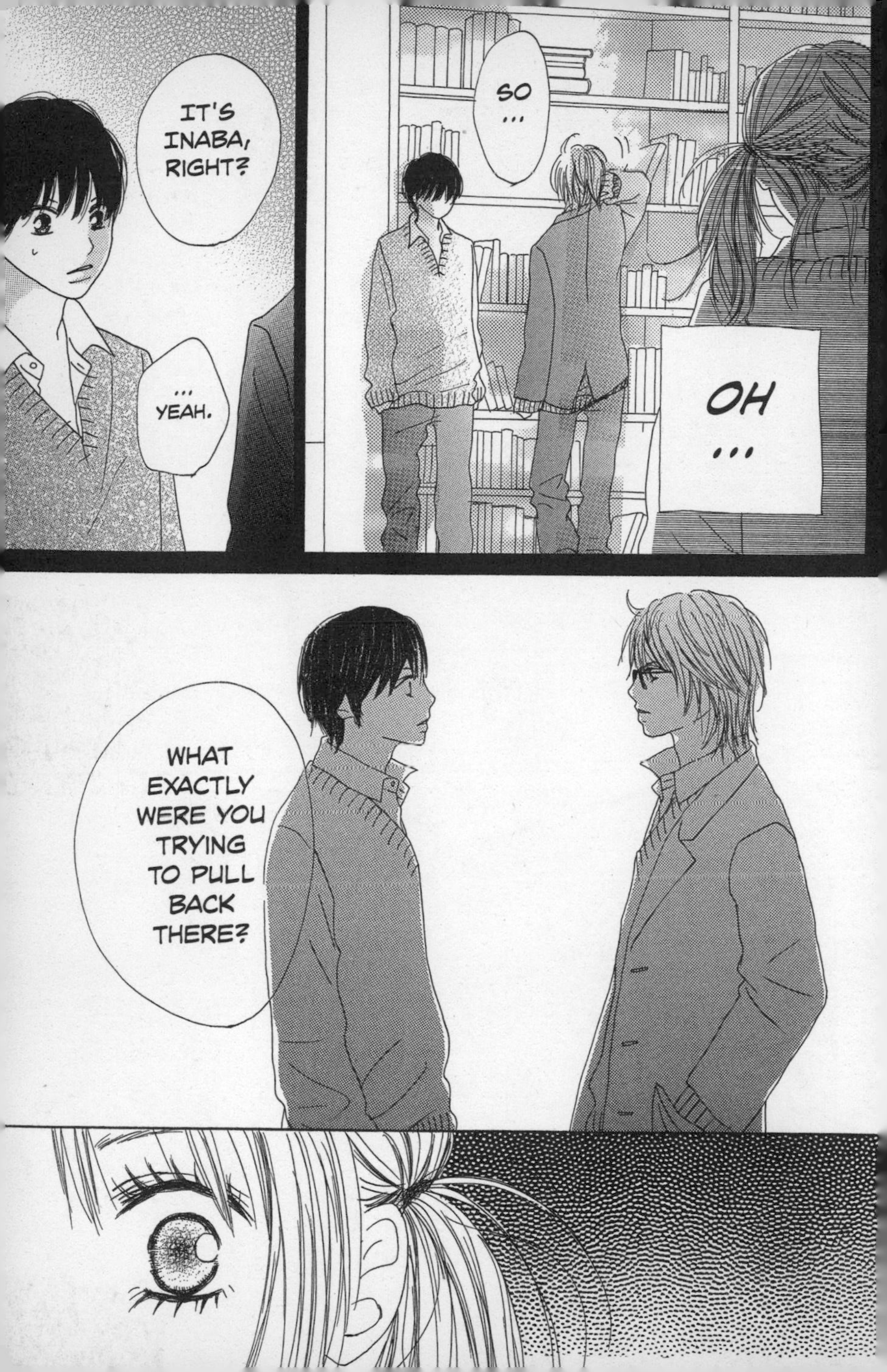

OH ...
SO ...
IT'S INABA, RIGHT?
... YEAH.
WHAT EXACTLY WERE YOU TRYING TO PULL BACK THERE?

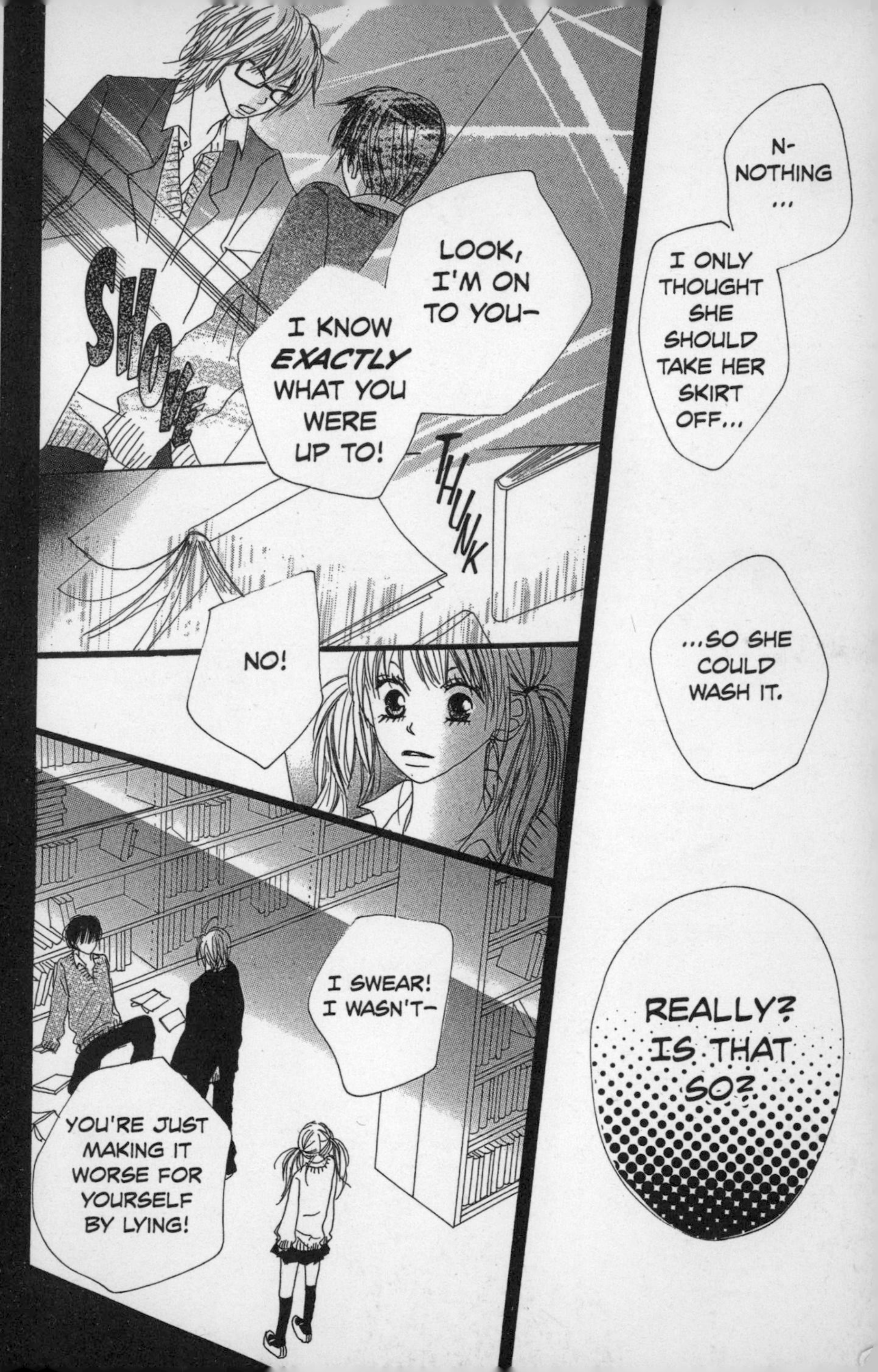
N-NOTHING...
I ONLY THOUGHT SHE SHOULD TAKE HER SKIRT OFF...
...SO SHE COULD WASH IT.
REALLY? IS THAT SO?
SHOVE
LOOK, I'M ON TO YOU-
I KNOW *EXACTLY* WHAT YOU WERE UP TO!
THUNK
NO!
I SWEAR! I WASN'T-
YOU'RE JUST MAKING IT WORSE FOR YOURSELF BY LYING!

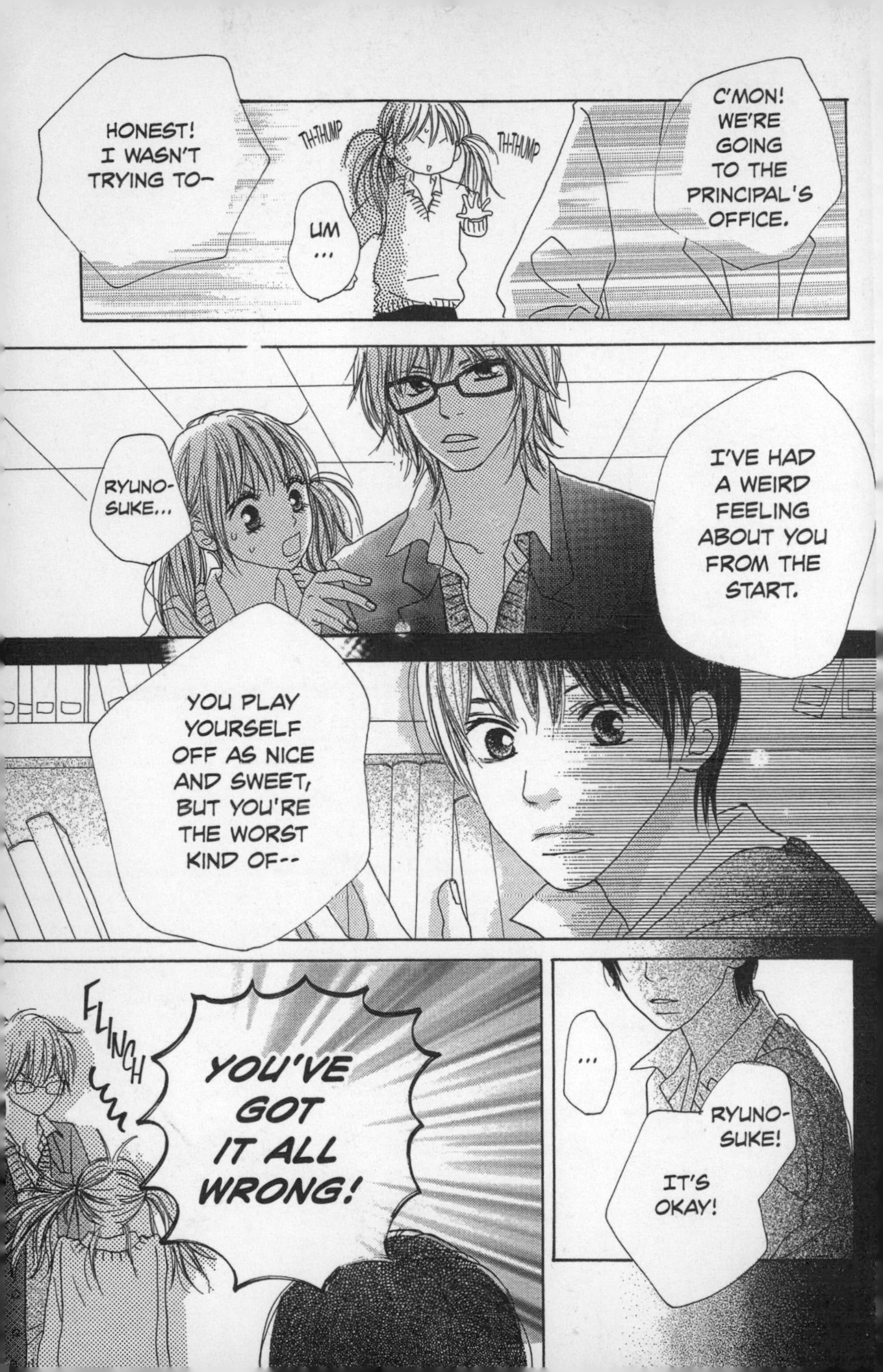
C'MON! WE'RE GOING TO THE PRINCIPAL'S OFFICE.
TH-THUMP
TH-THUMP
HONEST! I WASN'T TRYING TO—
UM ...
I'VE HAD A WEIRD FEELING ABOUT YOU FROM THE START.
RYUNO-SUKE...
YOU PLAY YOURSELF OFF AS NICE AND SWEET, BUT YOU'RE THE WORST KIND OF--
...
RYUNO-SUKE!
IT'S OKAY!
YOU'VE GOT IT ALL WRONG!
FLINCH

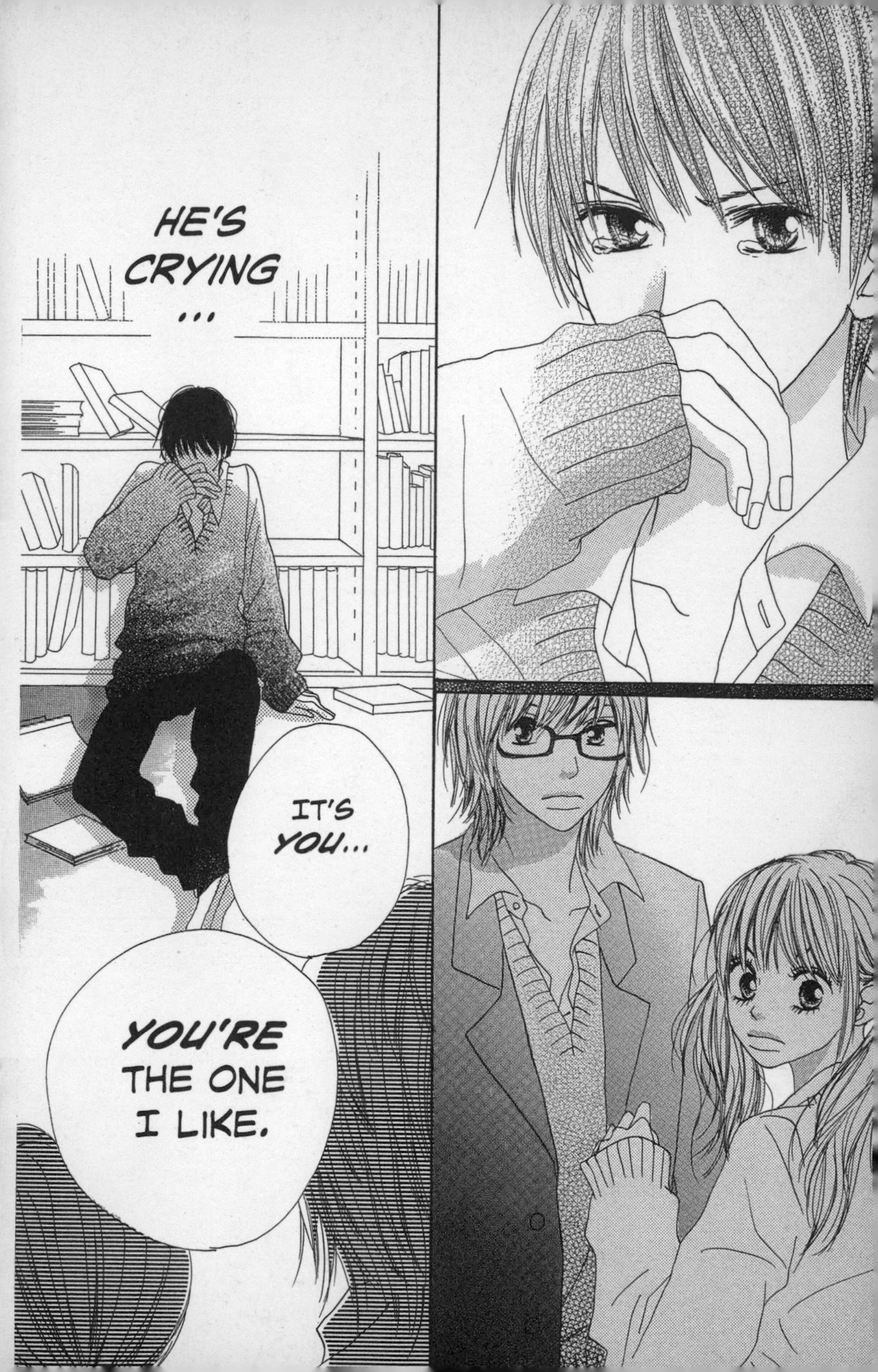
HE'S CRYING ...
IT'S YOU...
YOU'RE THE ONE I LIKE.

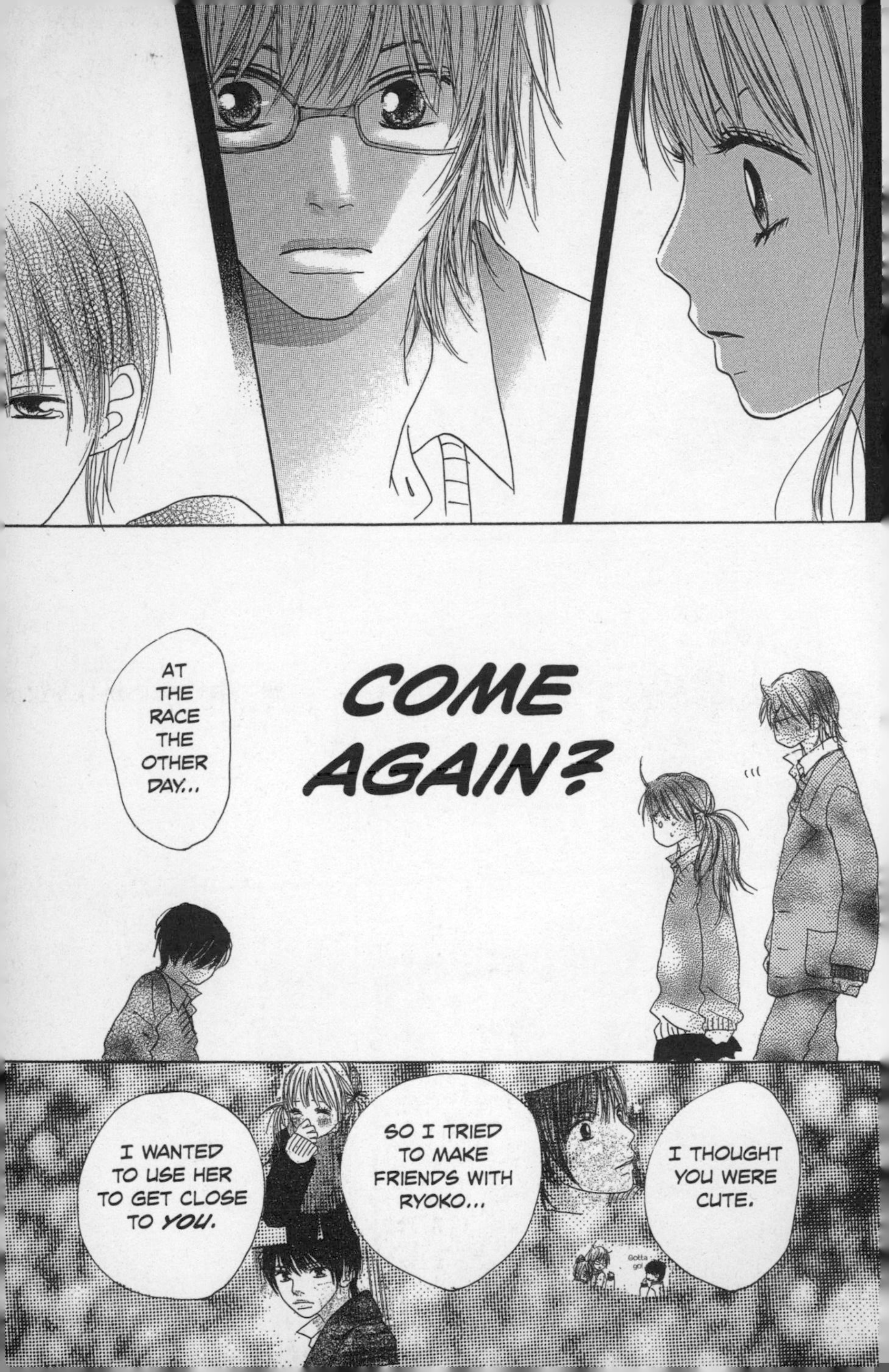
COME AGAIN?
AT THE RACE THE OTHER DAY...
I THOUGHT YOU WERE CUTE.
Gotta go!
SO I TRIED TO MAKE FRIENDS WITH RYOKO...
I WANTED TO USE HER TO GET CLOSE TO YOU.

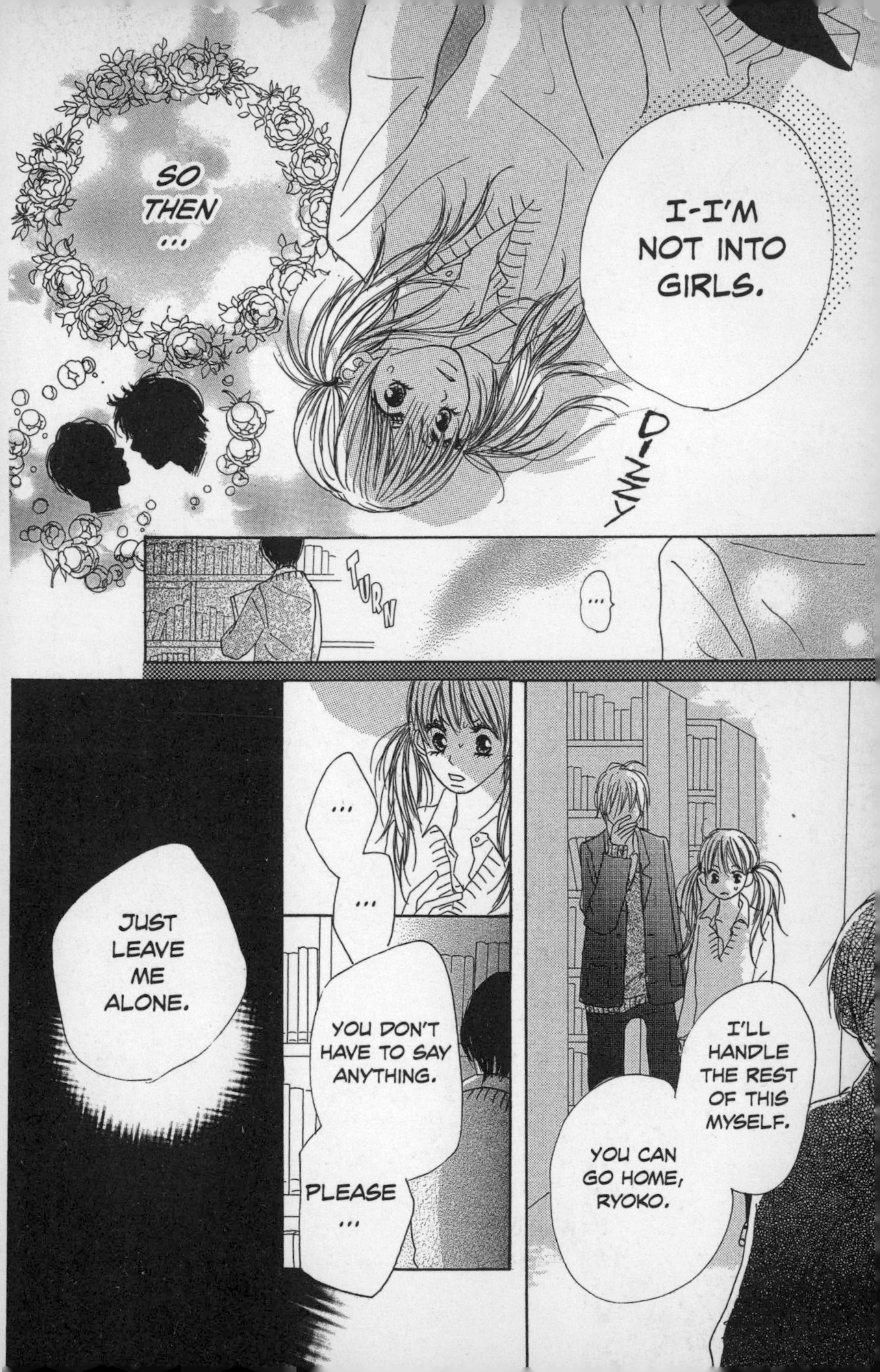
I-I'M NOT INTO GIRLS.
DIZZY
SO THEN ...
...
TURN
I'LL HANDLE THE REST OF THIS MYSELF.
YOU CAN GO HOME, RYOKO.
...
...
YOU DON'T HAVE TO SAY ANYTHING.
PLEASE ...
JUST LEAVE ME ALONE.

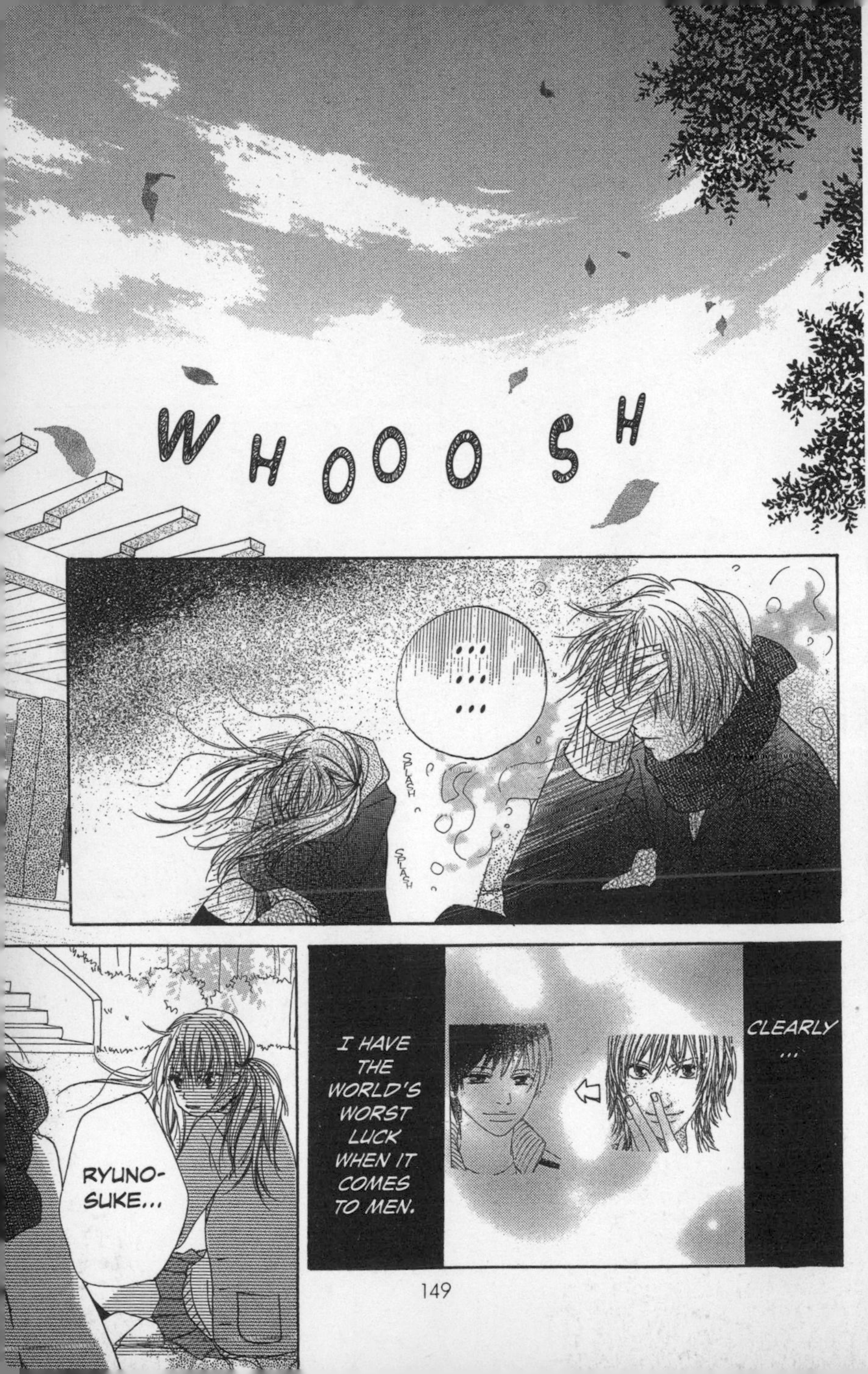
WHOOOSH
SPLASH
SPLASH
CLEARLY...
I HAVE THE WORLD'S WORST LUCK WHEN IT COMES TO MEN.
RYUNO-SUKE...

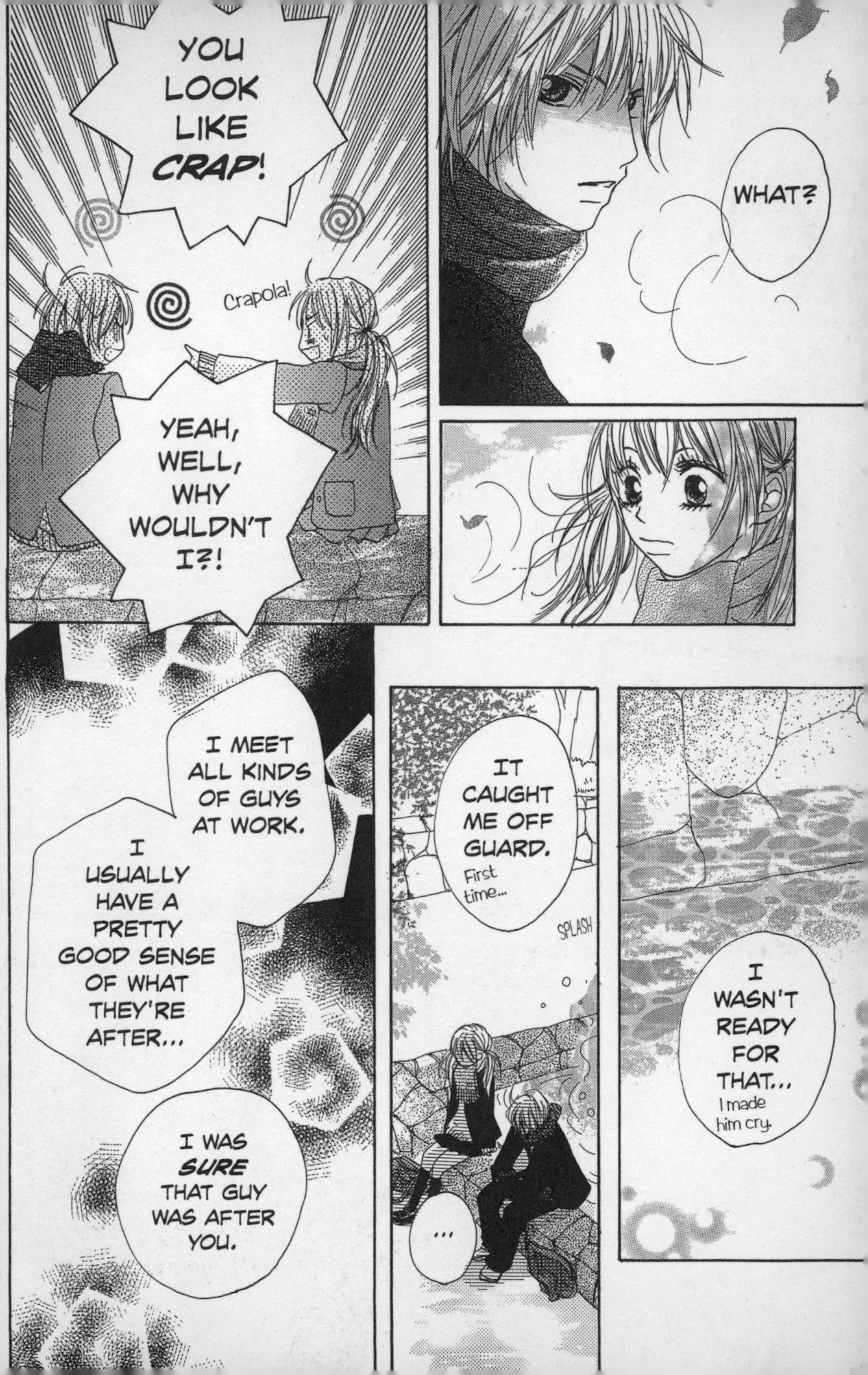
WHAT?
YOU LOOK LIKE CRAP!
Crapola!
YEAH, WELL, WHY WOULDN'T I?!
I WASN'T READY FOR THAT...
I made him cry.
IT CAUGHT ME OFF GUARD.
First time...
SPLASH
...
I MEET ALL KINDS OF GUYS AT WORK.
I USUALLY HAVE A PRETTY GOOD SENSE OF WHAT THEY'RE AFTER...
I WAS SURE THAT GUY WAS AFTER YOU.

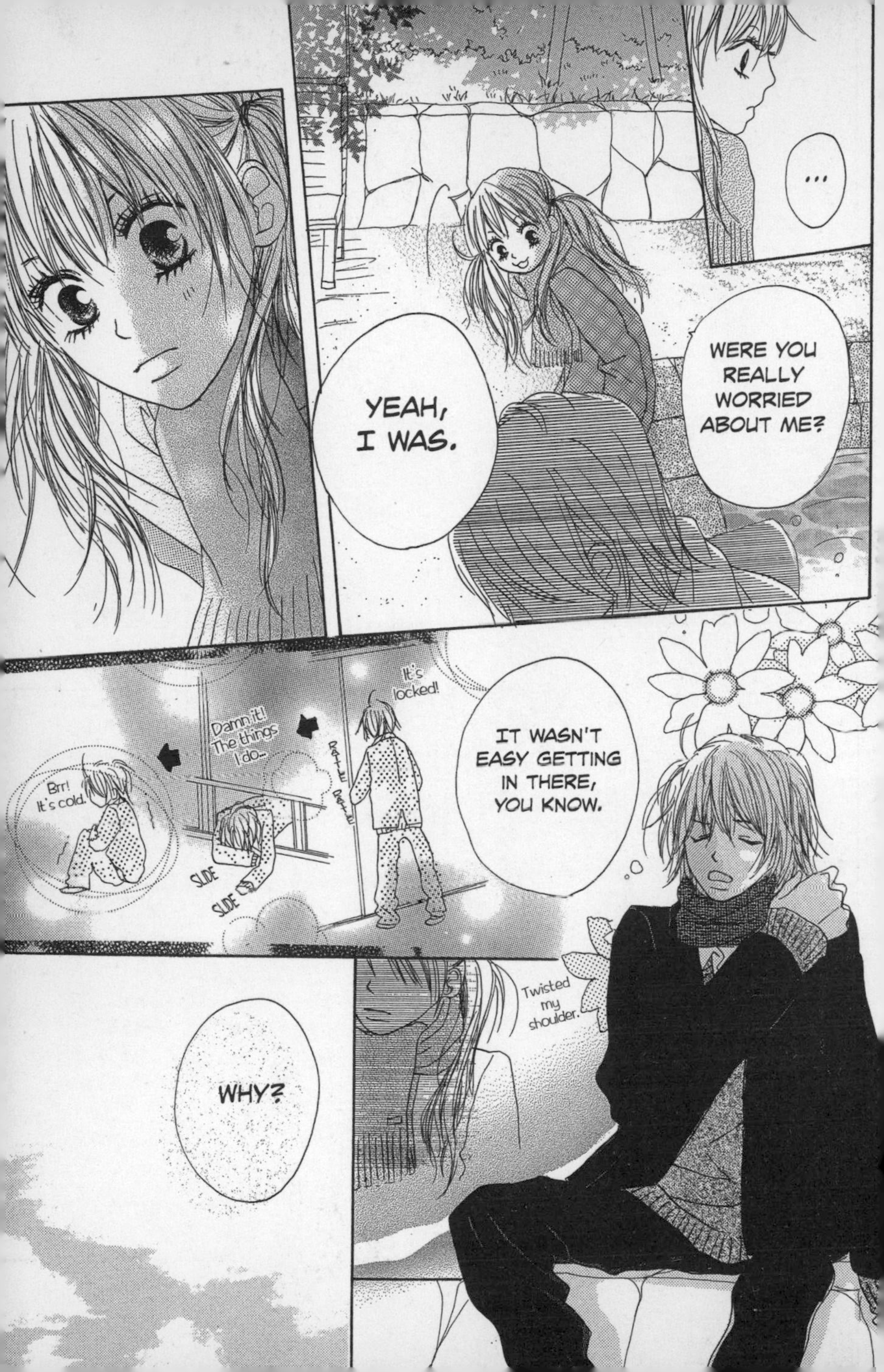
...
WERE YOU REALLY WORRIED ABOUT ME?
YEAH, I WAS.
IT WASN'T EASY GETTING IN THERE, YOU KNOW.
Twisted my shoulder.
It's locked!
RATTLE RATTLE
Damn it! The things I do..
SLIDE SLIDE
Brr! It's cold.
WHY?

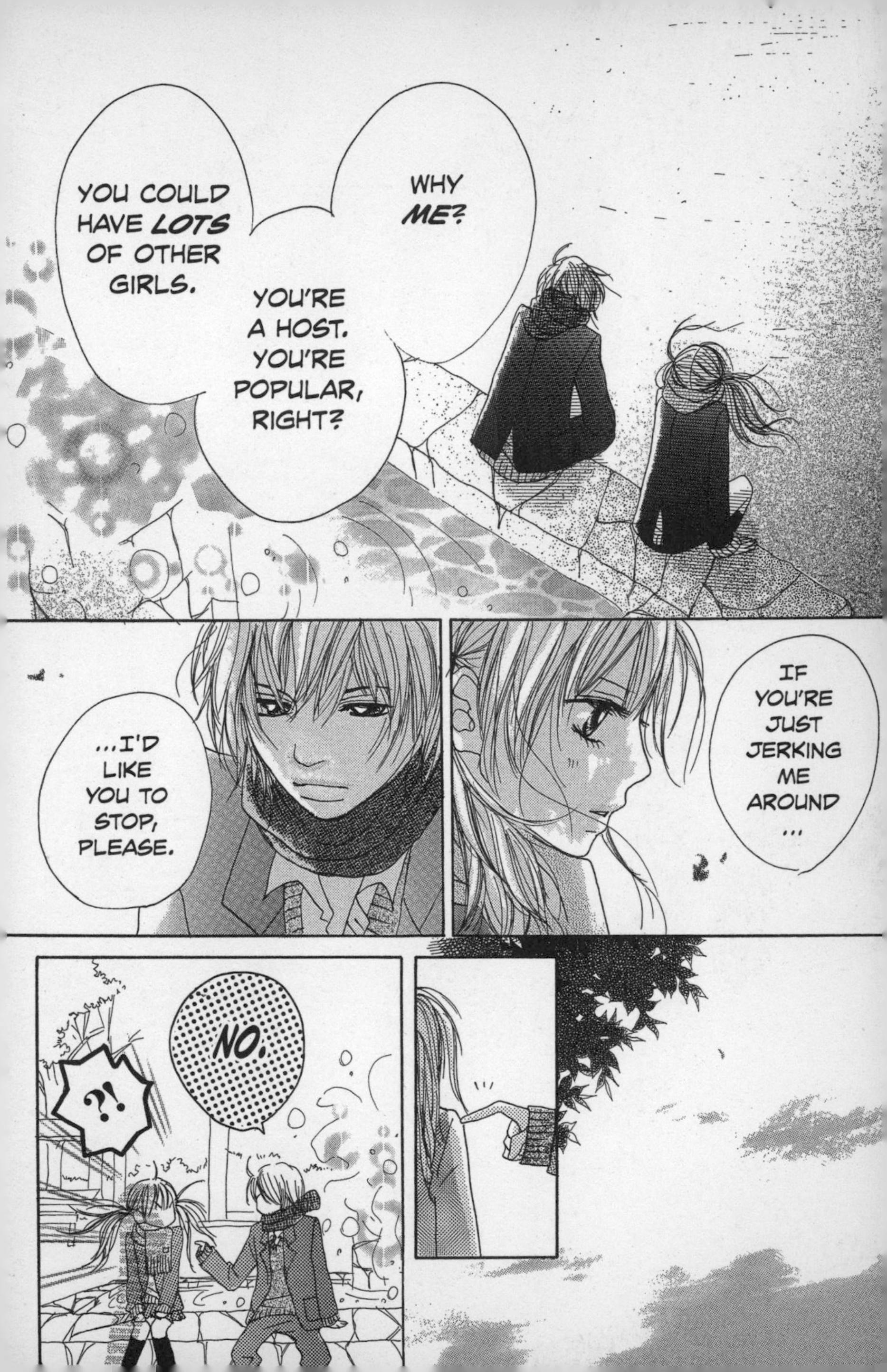
WHY ME?
YOU'RE A HOST. YOU'RE POPULAR, RIGHT?
YOU COULD HAVE LOTS OF OTHER GIRLS.
IF YOU'RE JUST JERKING ME AROUND...
...I'D LIKE YOU TO STOP, PLEASE.
NO.
?!

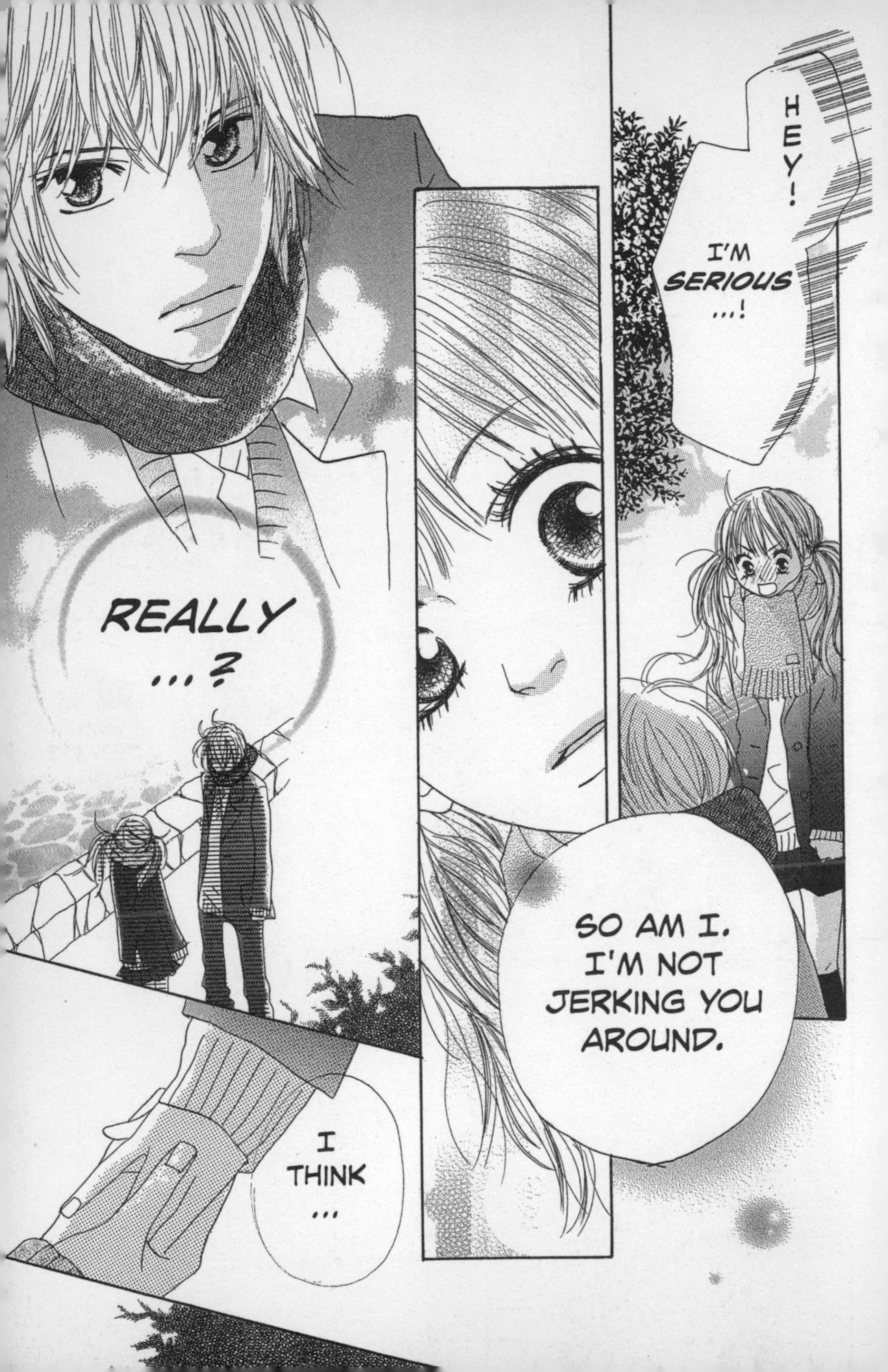
HEY!
I'M SERIOUS ...!
SO AM I. I'M NOT JERKING YOU AROUND.
REALLY ...?
I THINK ...

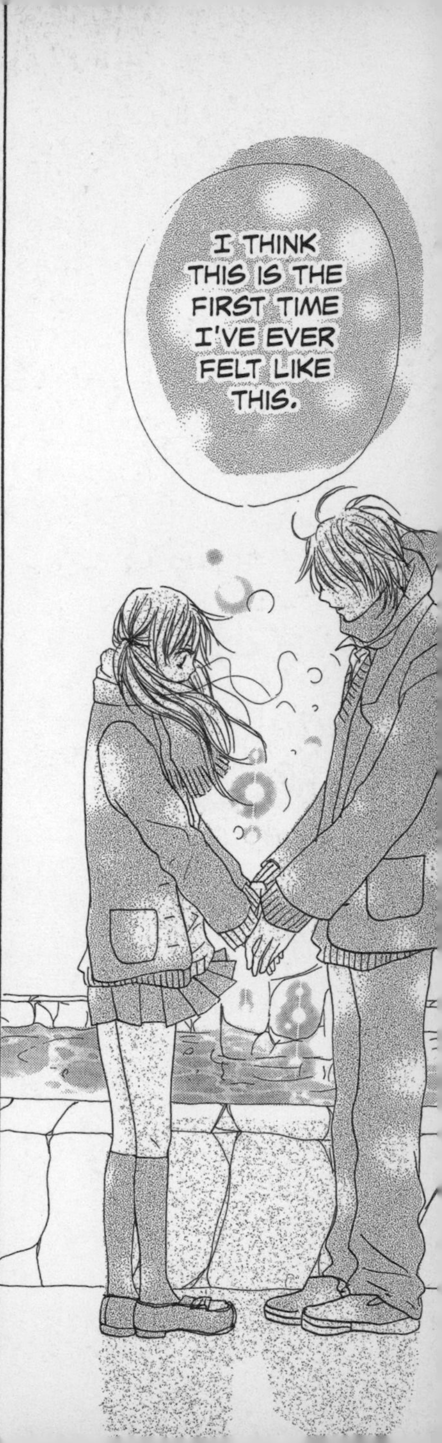
I THINK THIS IS THE FIRST TIME I'VE EVER FELT LIKE THIS.

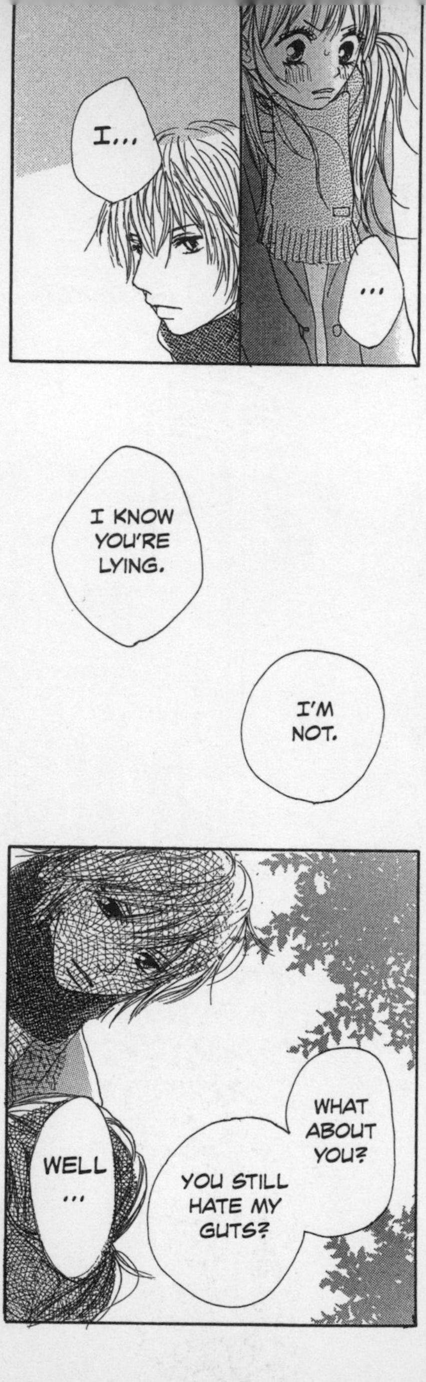
I...
...
I KNOW YOU'RE LYING.
I'M NOT.
WHAT ABOUT YOU?
YOU STILL HATE MY GUTS?
WELL...

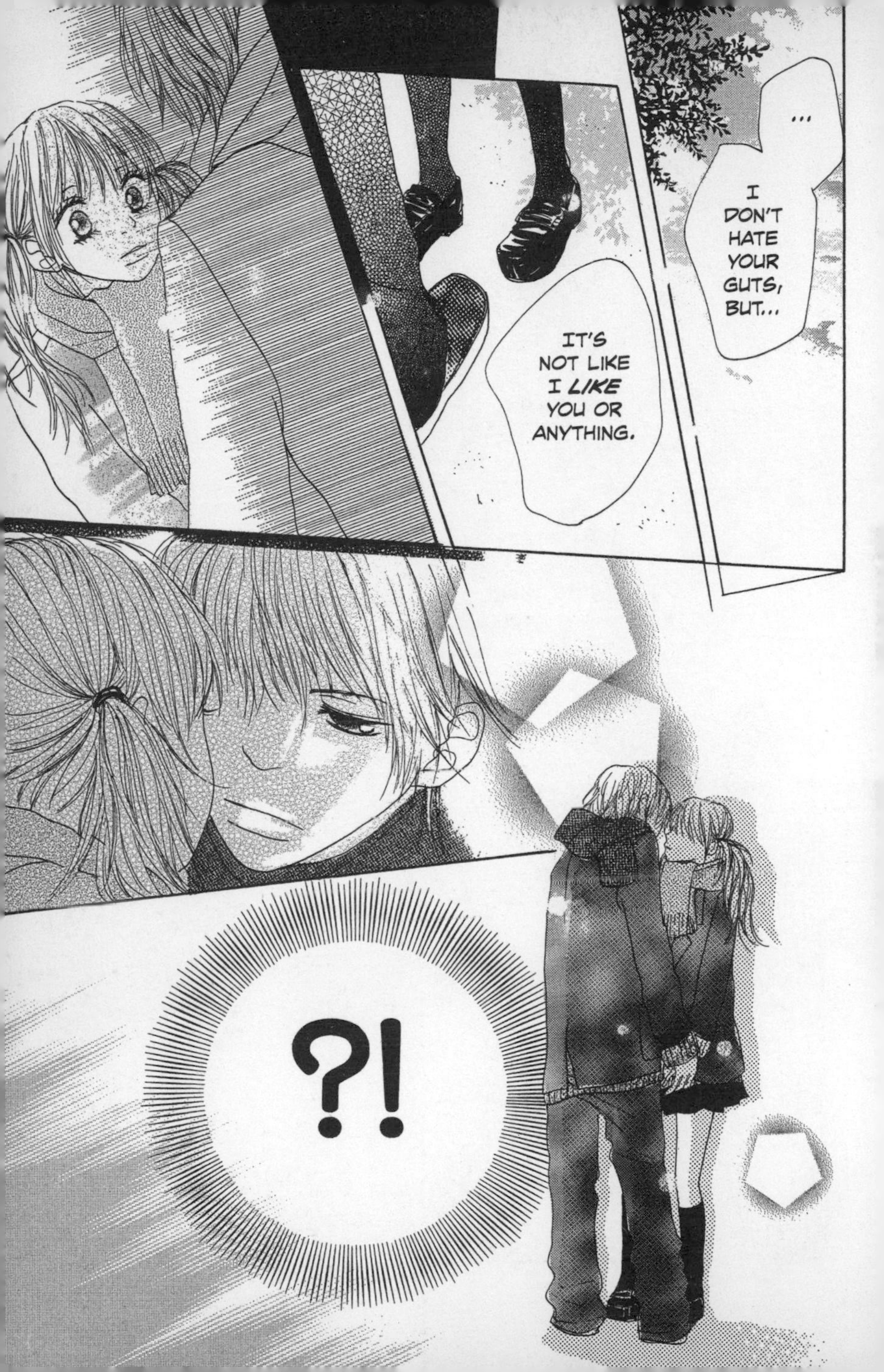
...
I DON'T HATE YOUR GUTS, BUT...
IT'S NOT LIKE I *LIKE* YOU OR ANYTHING.
?!

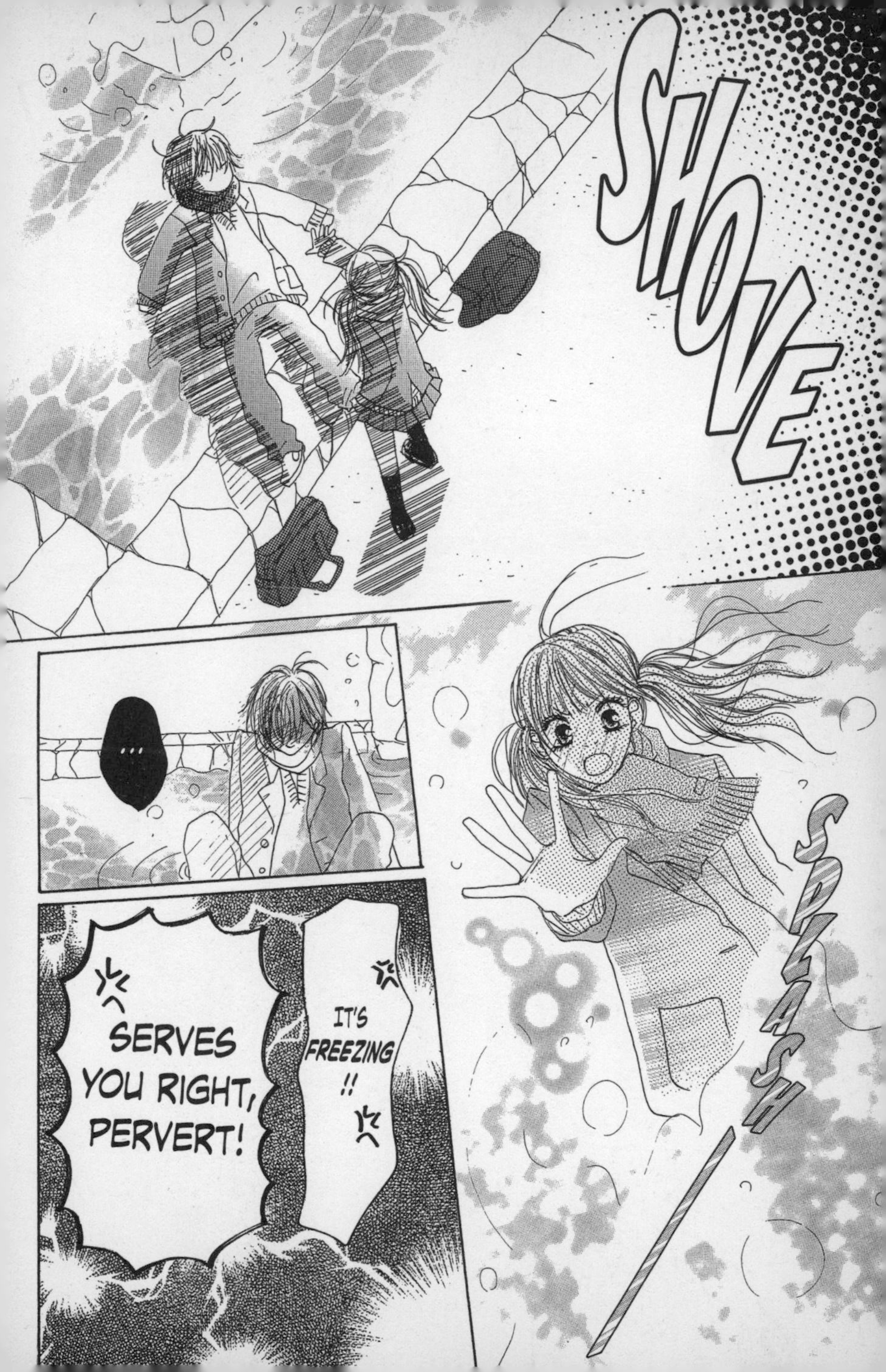
SHOVE
SPLASH
...
IT'S FREEZING!!
SERVES YOU RIGHT, PERVERT!

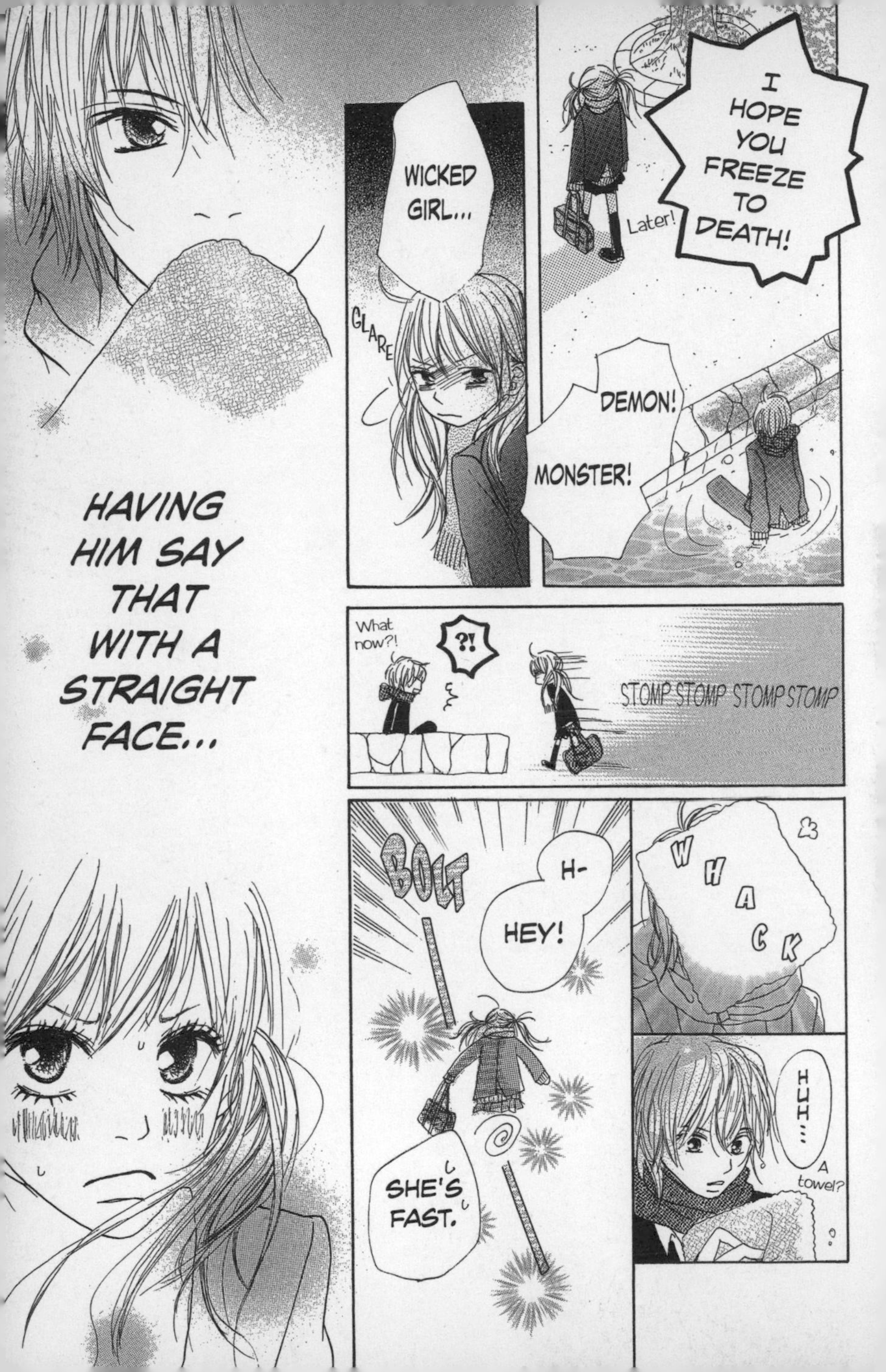
I HOPE YOU FREEZE TO DEATH!
Later!
DEMON!
MONSTER!
WICKED GIRL...
GLARE
STOMP STOMP STOMP STOMP
?!
What now?!
WHACK
HUH...
A towel?
BOLT
H- HEY!
SHE'S FAST.
HAVING HIM SAY THAT WITH A STRAIGHT FACE...

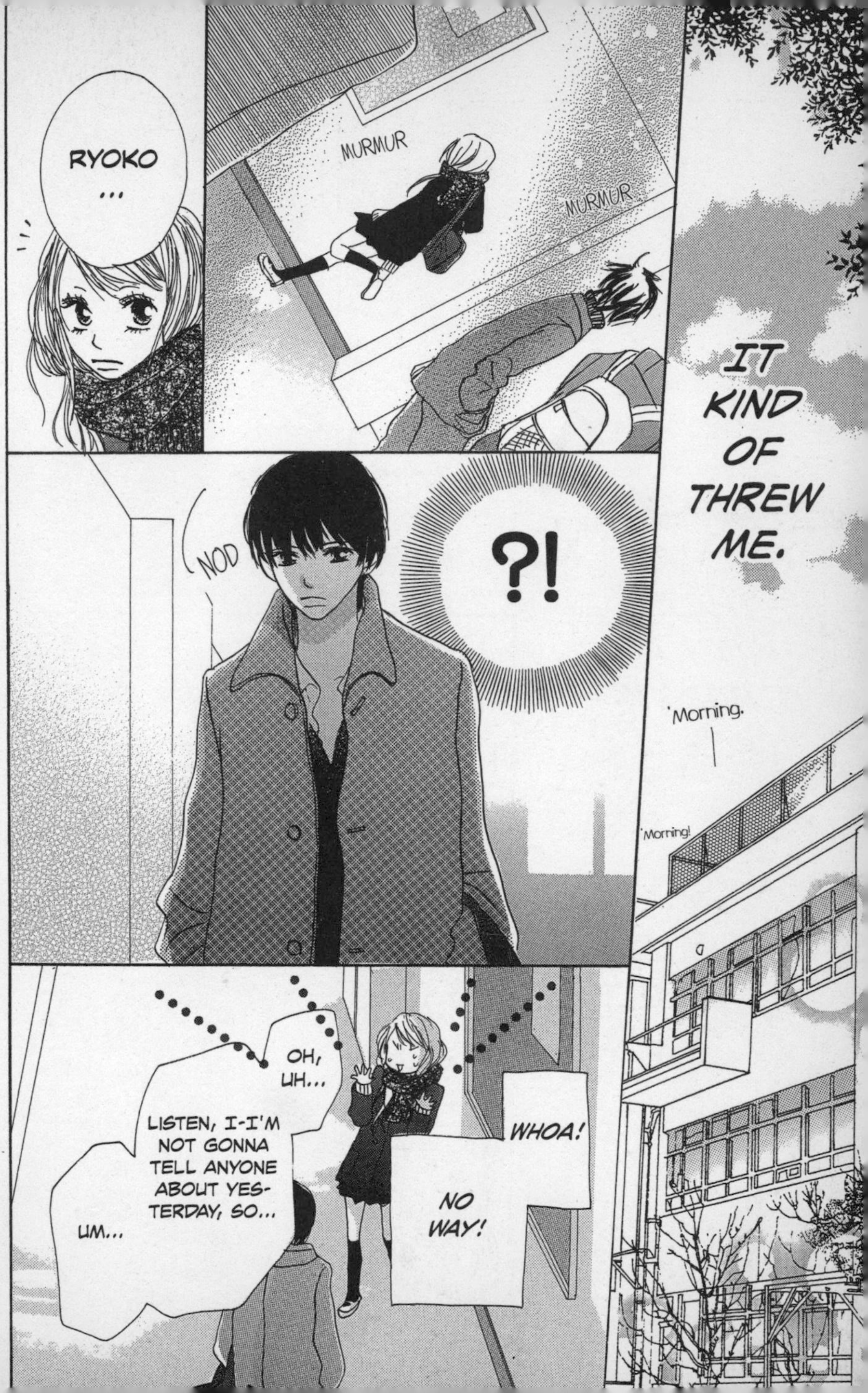
IT KIND OF THREW ME.
'Morning.
'Morning!
MURMUR
MURMUR
RYOKO ...
NOD
?!
WHOA!
NO WAY!
OH, UH...
LISTEN, I-I'M NOT GONNA TELL ANYONE ABOUT YES-TERDAY, SO...
UM...

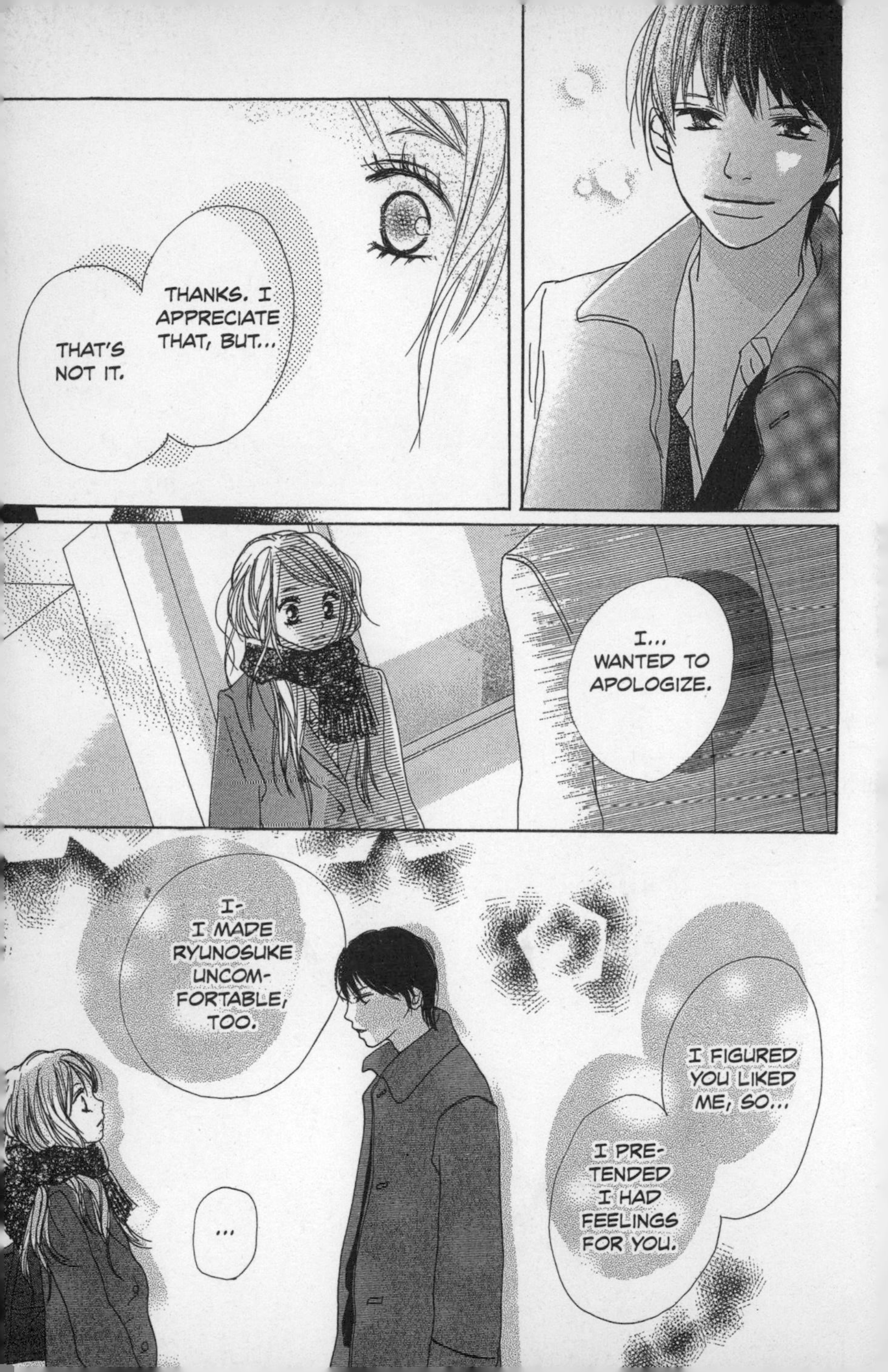
THANKS. I APPRECIATE THAT, BUT...
THAT'S NOT IT.
I... WANTED TO APOLOGIZE.
I FIGURED YOU LIKED ME, SO...
I PRE-TENDED I HAD FEELINGS FOR YOU.
...
I- I MADE RYUNOSUKE UNCOM-FORTABLE, TOO.

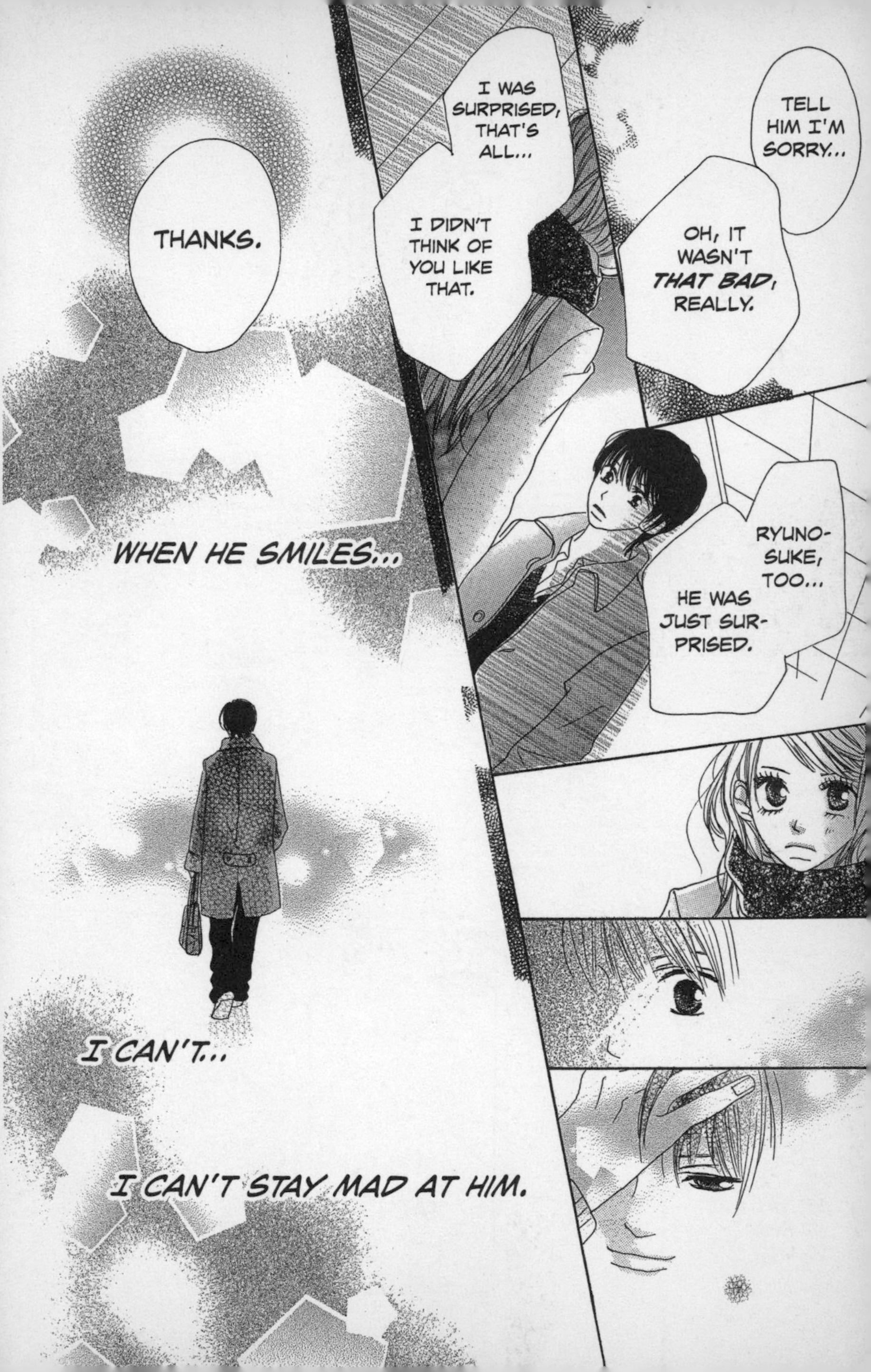
TELL HIM I'M SORRY...
OH, IT WASN'T *THAT BAD*, REALLY.
I WAS SURPRISED, THAT'S ALL...
I DIDN'T THINK OF YOU LIKE THAT.
RYUNOSUKE, TOO...
HE WAS JUST SURPRISED.
THANKS.
WHEN HE SMILES...
I CAN'T...
I CAN'T STAY MAD AT HIM.

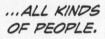

WHO'S THIS...?

BIP

HELLO?

BU RU RU RU

MM?

THIS WORLD IS FULL OF...

...ALL KINDS OF PEOPLE.

HEY.

IT'S ME.

HUH?

RYUNO-SUKE?!

'BOUT TIME.

ME WHO?

HOW... HOW DID YOU GET MY NUMBER?!

ME.

BU RU RU RU

Letters and E-Mail

Thank you for all the letters and e-mail! I read them all, I swear I do! I'm really, really sorry I don't have time to respond... GRUMBLE

The more mail I get, the happier I am. Keep 'em coming. Tell me what manga you're reading or, well, anything, really! Okay, wait—nothing too serious, please!

Address:
Ao Mimori/B.O.D.Y.
c/o Viz Media, LLC
P.O. BOX 77010
San Francisco, CA 94107

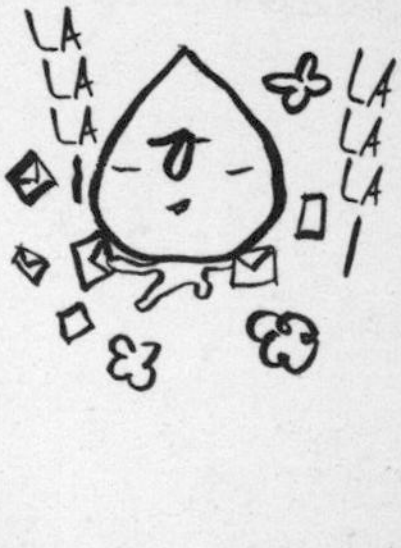
LA
LA
LA
!
LA
LA
LA
!

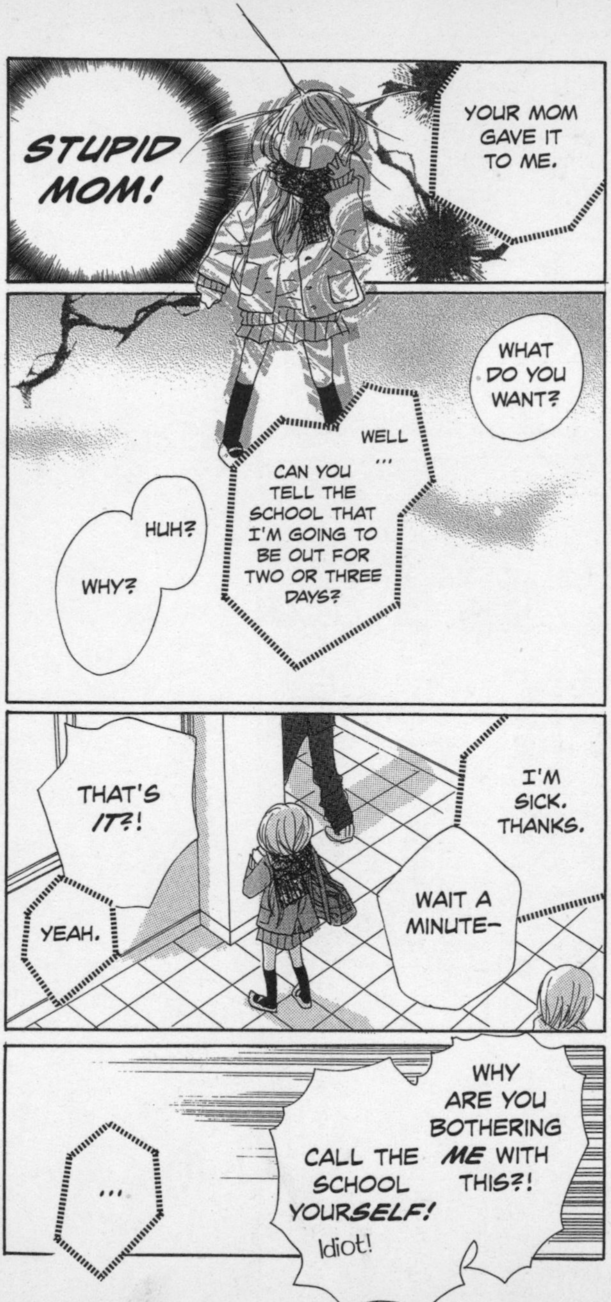
YOUR MOM GAVE IT TO ME.
STUPID MOM!
WHAT DO YOU WANT?
WELL ...
CAN YOU TELL THE SCHOOL THAT I'M GOING TO BE OUT FOR TWO OR THREE DAYS?
HUH?
WHY?
I'M SICK. THANKS.
WAIT A MINUTE-
THAT'S IT?!
YEAH.
WHY ARE YOU BOTHERING ME WITH THIS?!
CALL THE SCHOOL YOURSELF!
Idiot!
...

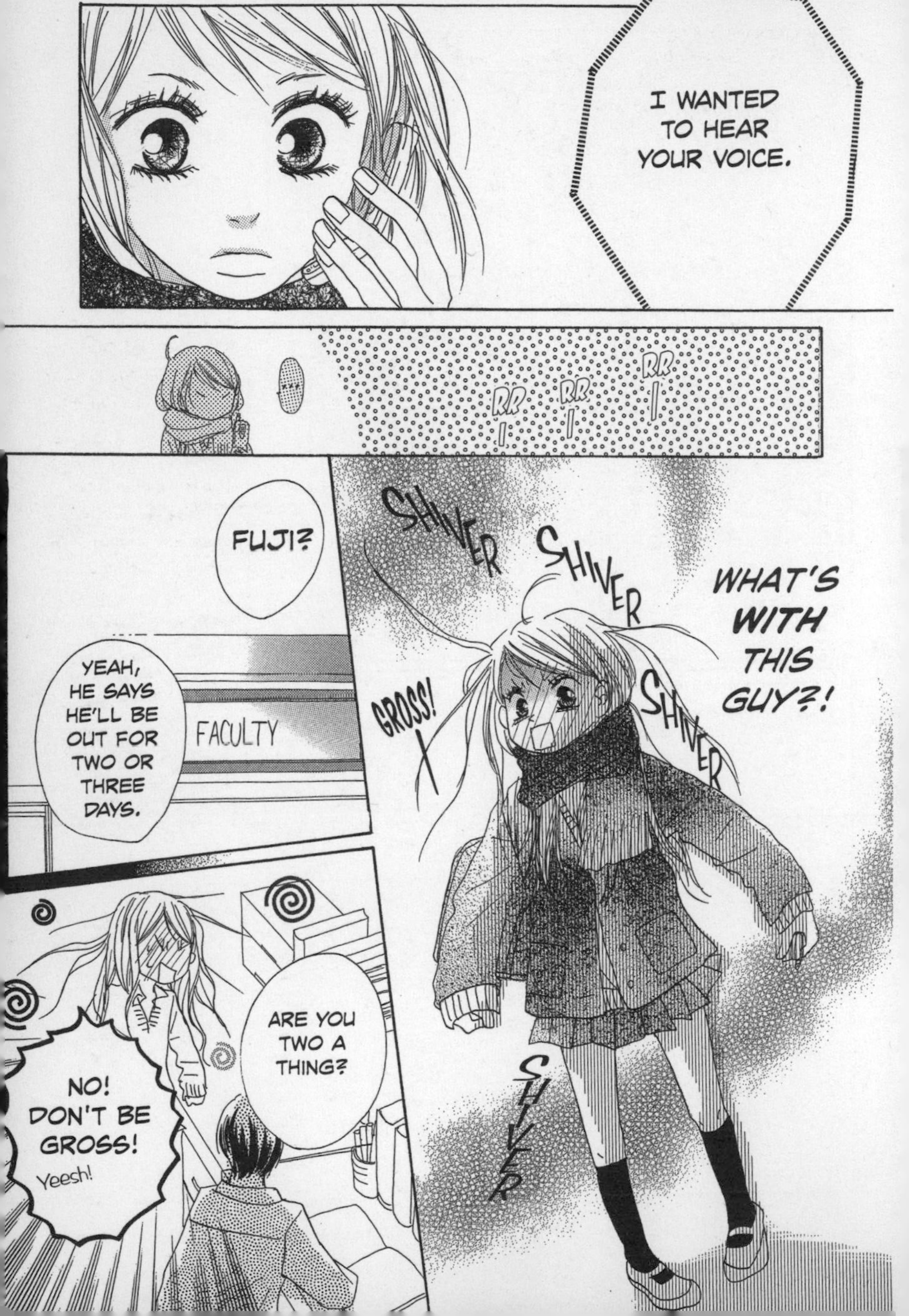
I WANTED TO HEAR YOUR VOICE.
RR RR RR
...
SHIVER SHIVER SHIVER SHIVER
WHAT'S WITH THIS GUY?!
GROSS!
FUJI?
YEAH, HE SAYS HE'LL BE OUT FOR TWO OR THREE DAYS.
FACULTY
ARE YOU TWO A THING?
NO! DON'T BE GROSS!
Yeesh!

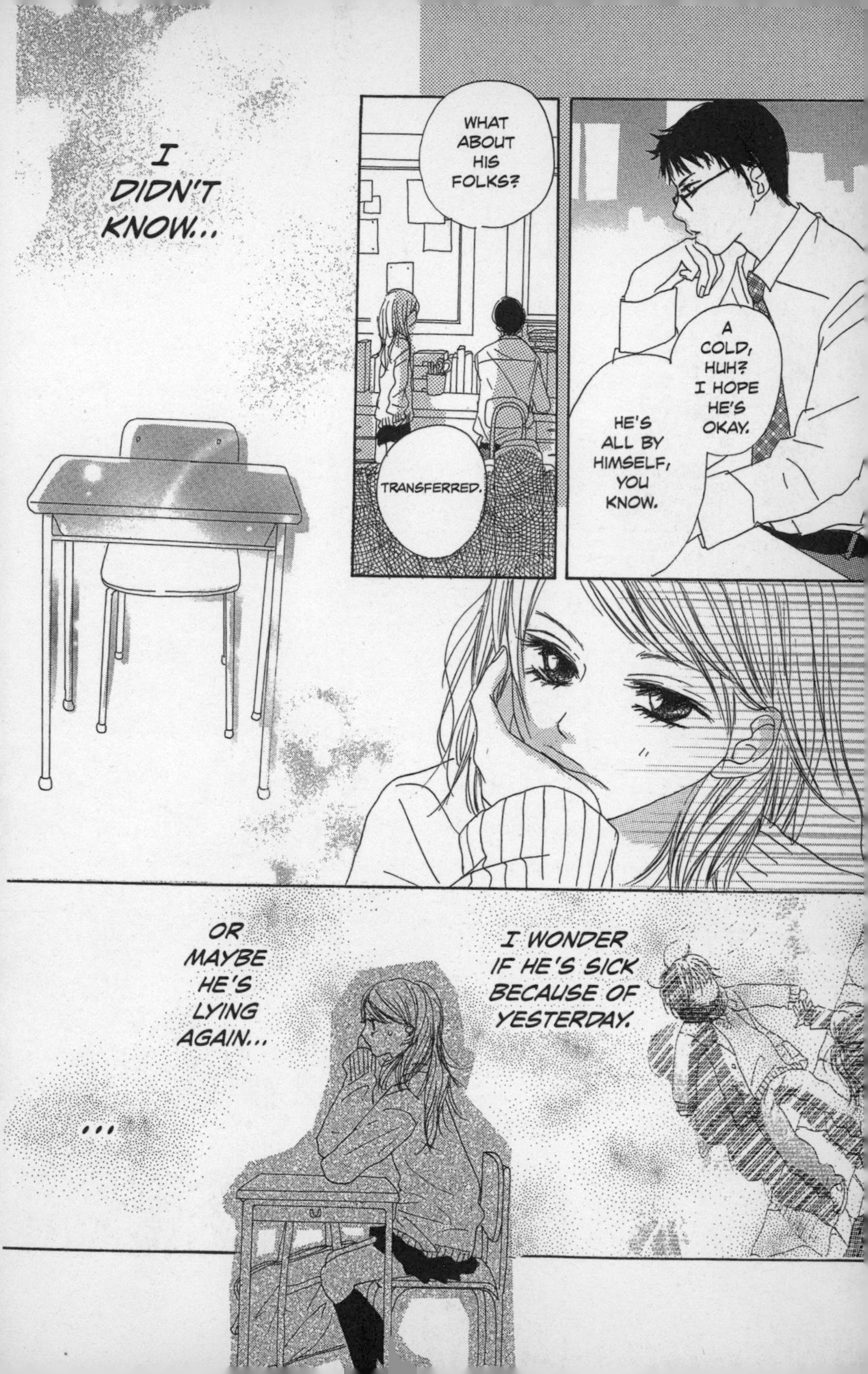
A COLD, HUH? I HOPE HE'S OKAY.
HE'S ALL BY HIMSELF, YOU KNOW.
WHAT ABOUT HIS FOLKS?
TRANSFERRED.
I DIDN'T KNOW...
I WONDER IF HE'S SICK BECAUSE OF YESTERDAY.
OR MAYBE HE'S LYING AGAIN...
...

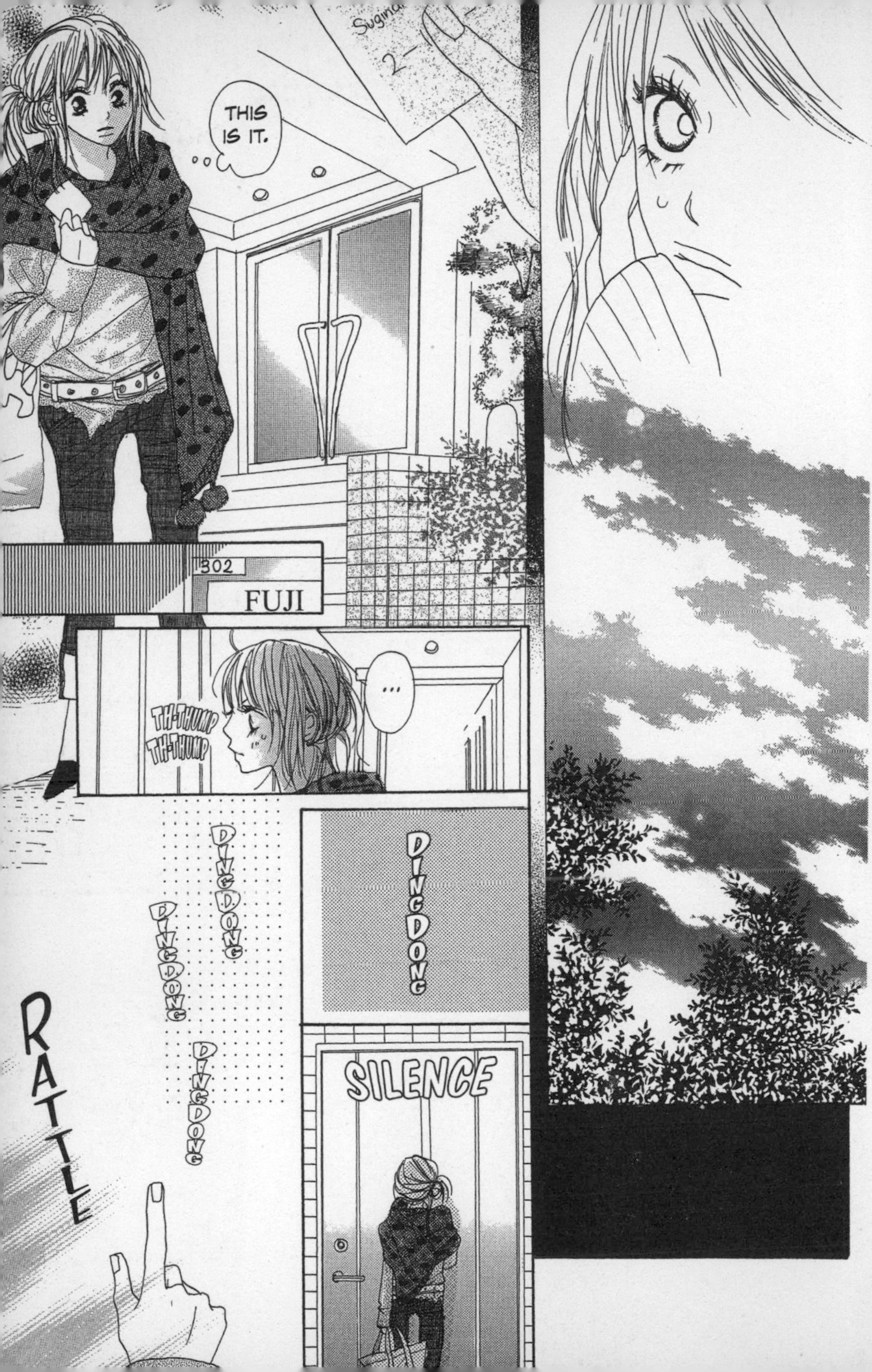

THIS IS IT.
302
FUJI
TH-THUMP TH-THUMP
...
DING DONG
DING DONG
DING DONG
DING DONG
SILENCE
RATTLE

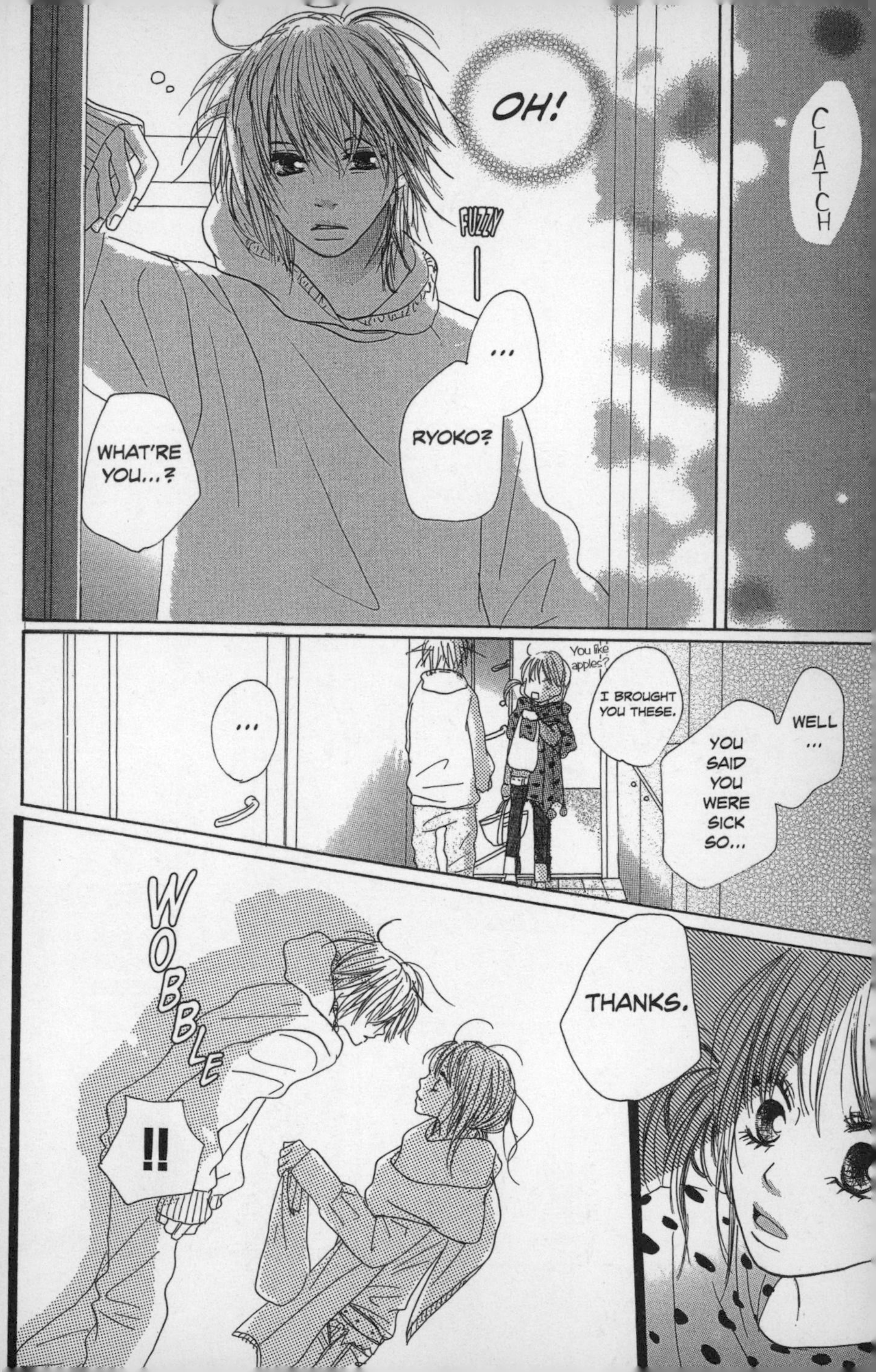
CLATCH
OH!
FUZZY
...
RYOKO?
WHAT'RE YOU...?
WELL...
YOU SAID YOU WERE SICK SO...
I BROUGHT YOU THESE.
You like apples?
...
THANKS.
WOBBLE
!!

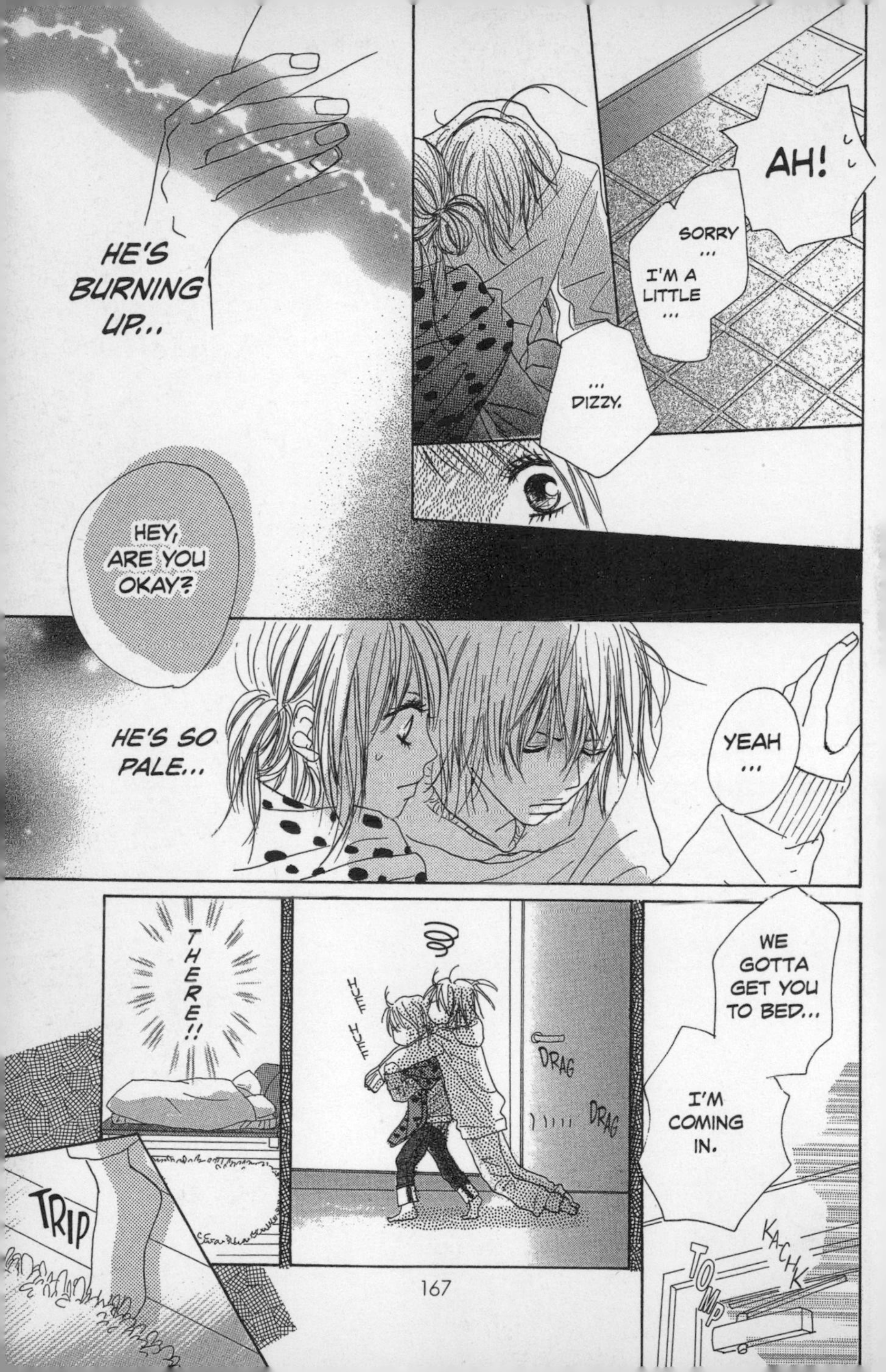
AH!
SORRY ... I'M A LITTLE ...
... DIZZY.
HE'S BURNING UP...
HEY, ARE YOU OKAY?
YEAH ...
HE'S SO PALE...
WE GOTTA GET YOU TO BED...
I'M COMING IN.
KA-CHK
TOMP
HUFF HUFF
DRAG
DRAG
THERE!!
TRIP

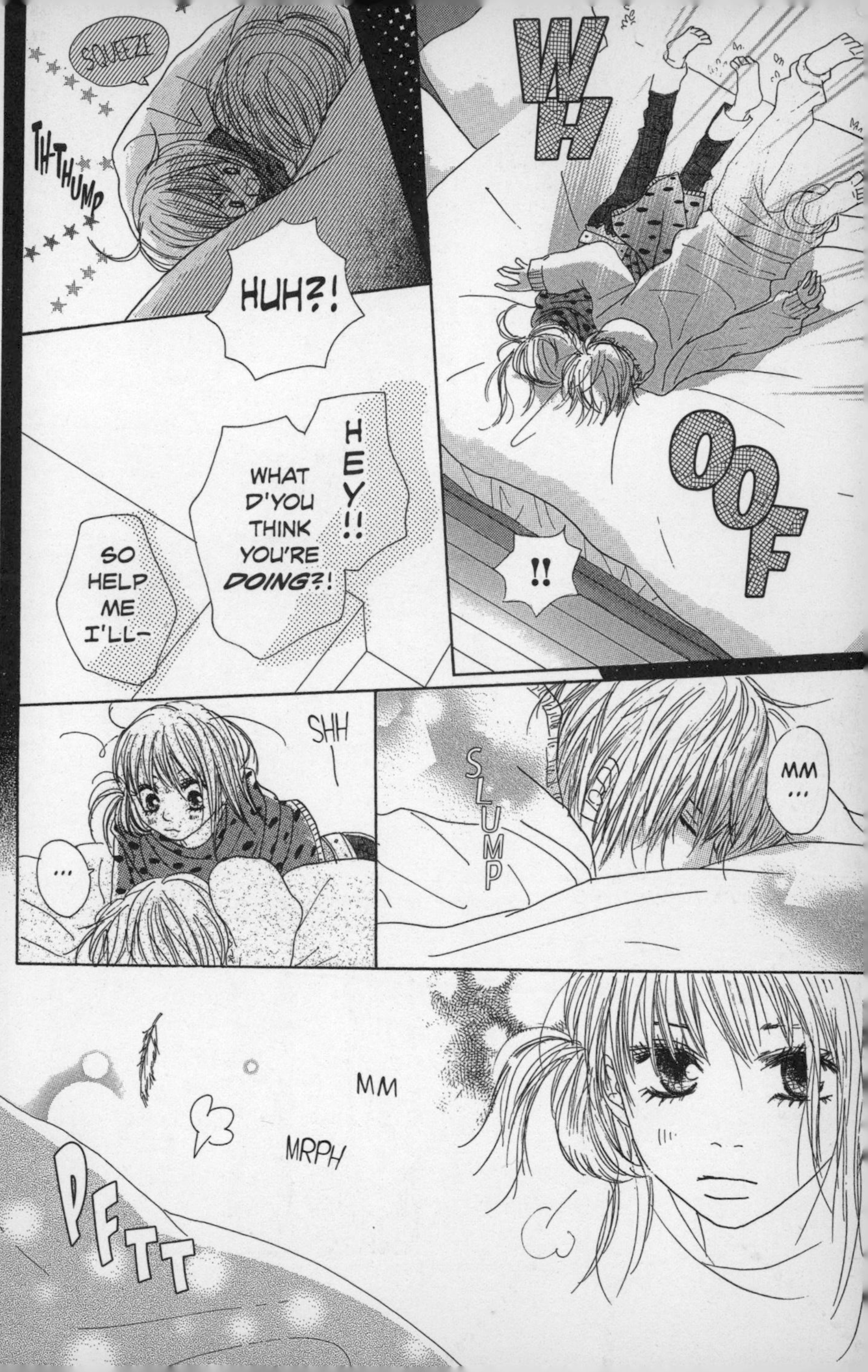

WH
OOF
!!
SQUEEZE
TH-THUMP
HUH?!
HEY!!
WHAT D'YOU THINK YOU'RE *DOING*?!
SO HELP ME I'LL—
MM ...
SLUMP
SHH
...
MM
MRPH
PFTT

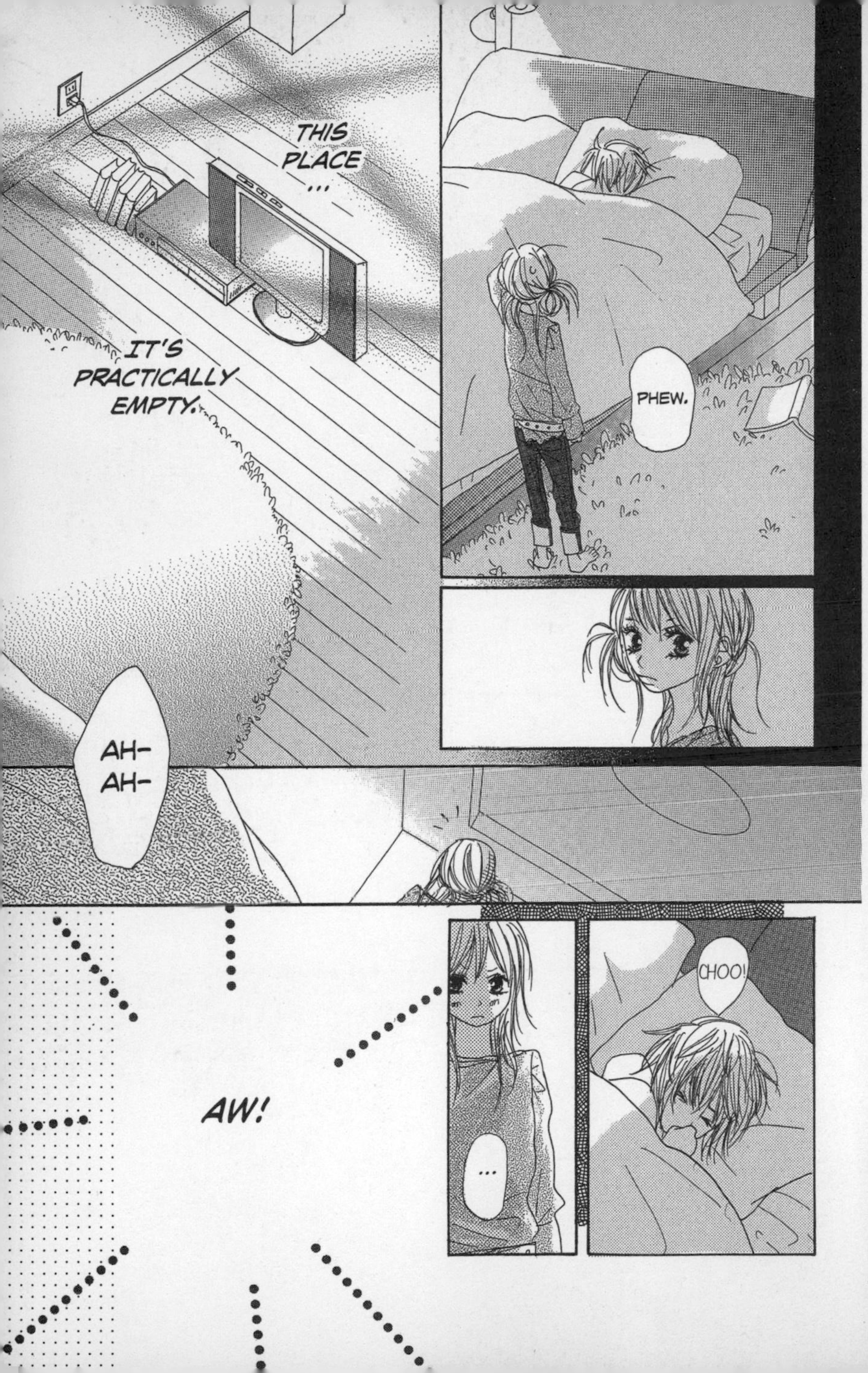
PHEW.
THIS PLACE ...
IT'S PRACTICALLY EMPTY.
AH-AH-
CHOO!
...
AW!

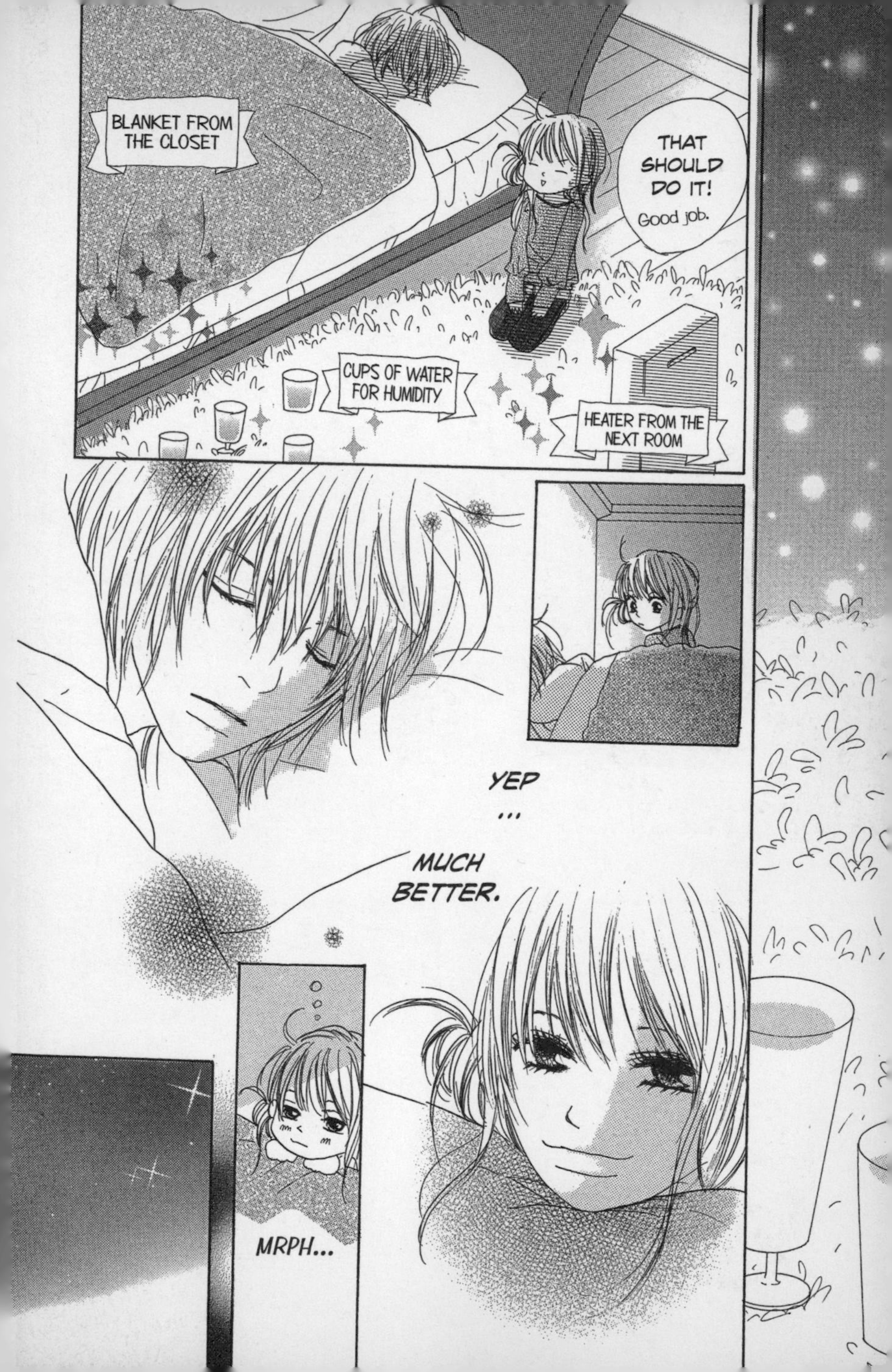

THAT SHOULD DO IT!
Good job.
BLANKET FROM THE CLOSET
HEATER FROM THE NEXT ROOM
CUPS OF WATER FOR HUMIDITY
YEP ...
MUCH BETTER.
MRPH...

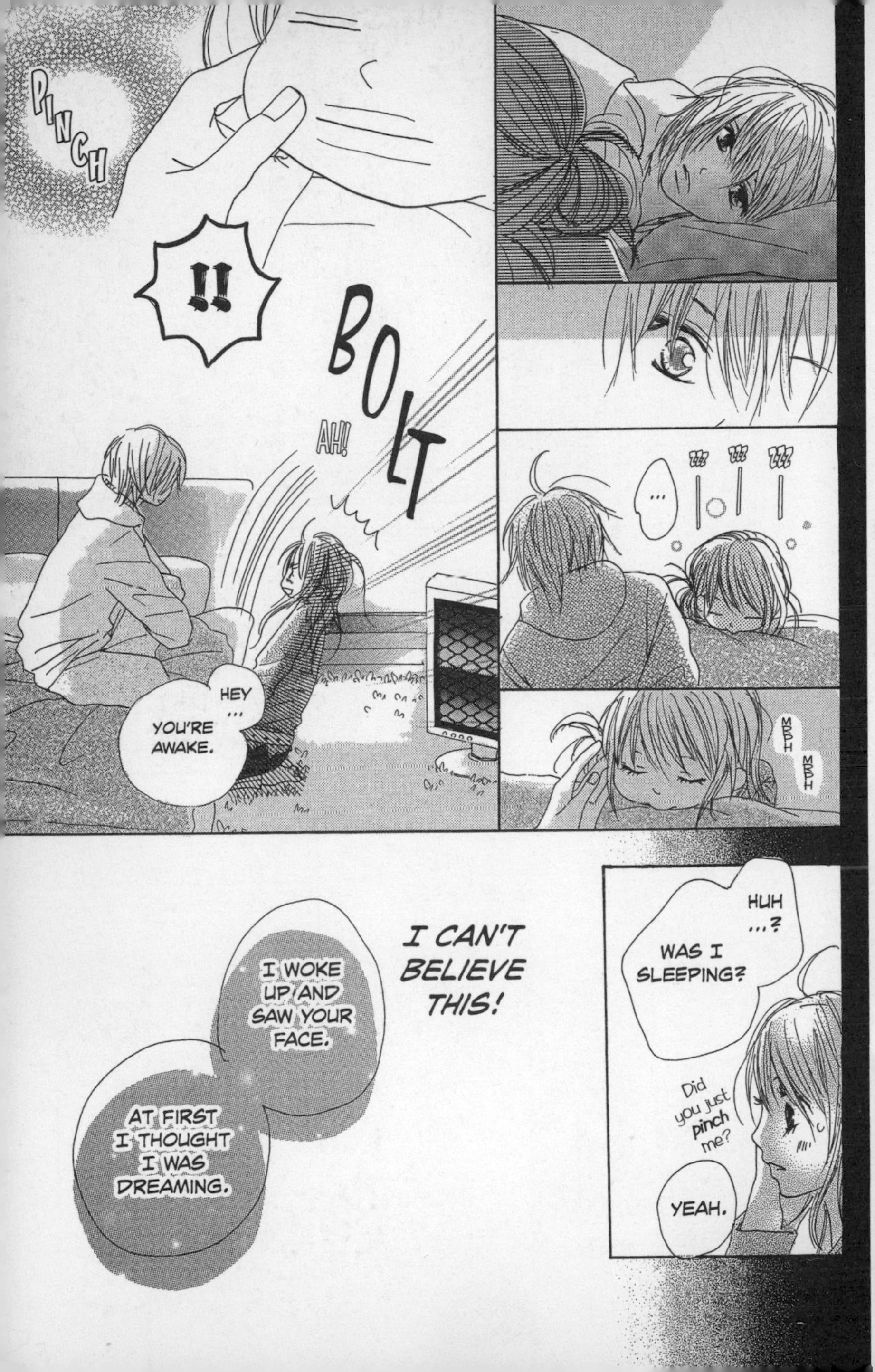
...
ZZZ ZZZ ZZZ
MRPH MRPH
PINCH
!!
BOLT
AH!
HEY... YOU'RE AWAKE.
HUH...?
WAS I SLEEPING?
Did you just pinch me?
YEAH.
I CAN'T BELIEVE THIS!
I WOKE UP AND SAW YOUR FACE.
AT FIRST I THOUGHT I WAS DREAMING.

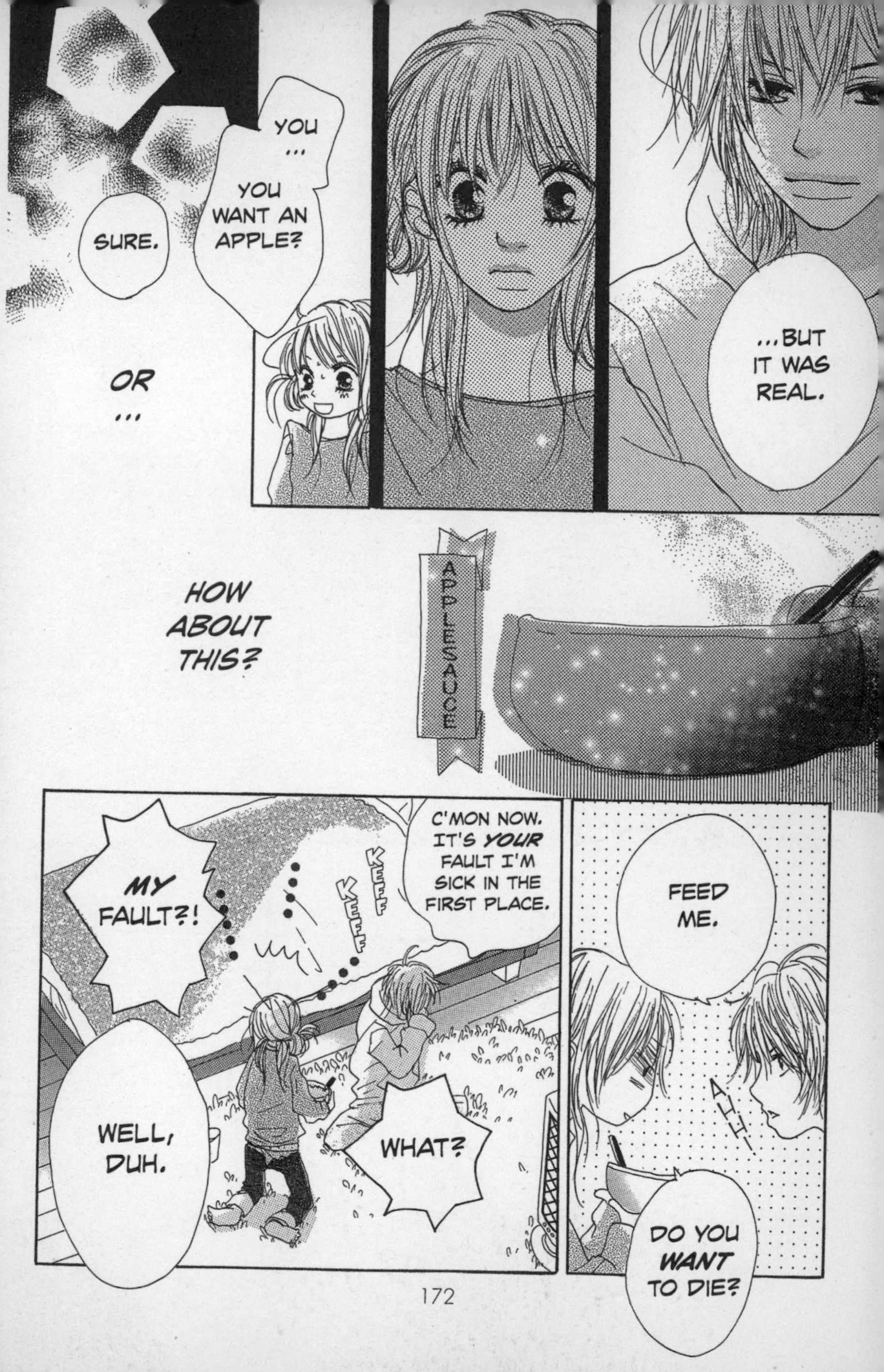
...BUT IT WAS REAL.
YOU ...
YOU WANT AN APPLE?
SURE.
OR ...
APPLESAUCE
HOW ABOUT THIS?
FEED ME.
AHH-
DO YOU WANT TO DIE?
C'MON NOW. IT'S YOUR FAULT I'M SICK IN THE FIRST PLACE.
KEFF
KEFF
MY FAULT?!
WHAT?
WELL, DUH.

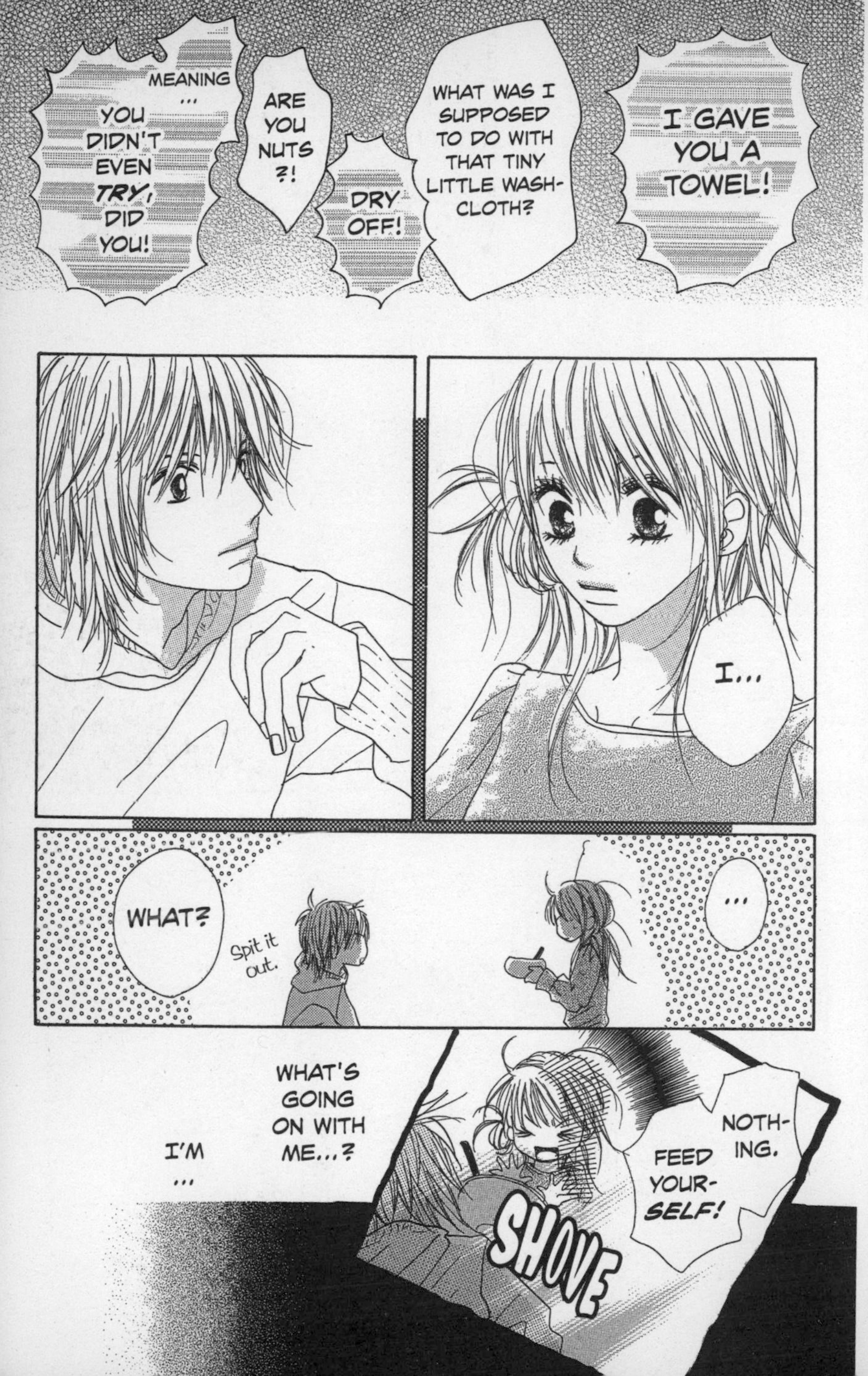
I GAVE YOU A TOWEL!
WHAT WAS I SUPPOSED TO DO WITH THAT TINY LITTLE WASH-CLOTH?
DRY OFF!
ARE YOU NUTS?!
MEANING... YOU DIDN'T EVEN TRY, DID YOU!
I...
...
WHAT?
Spit it out.
NOTH-ING.
FEED YOUR-SELF!
SHOVE
WHAT'S GOING ON WITH ME...?
I'M ...

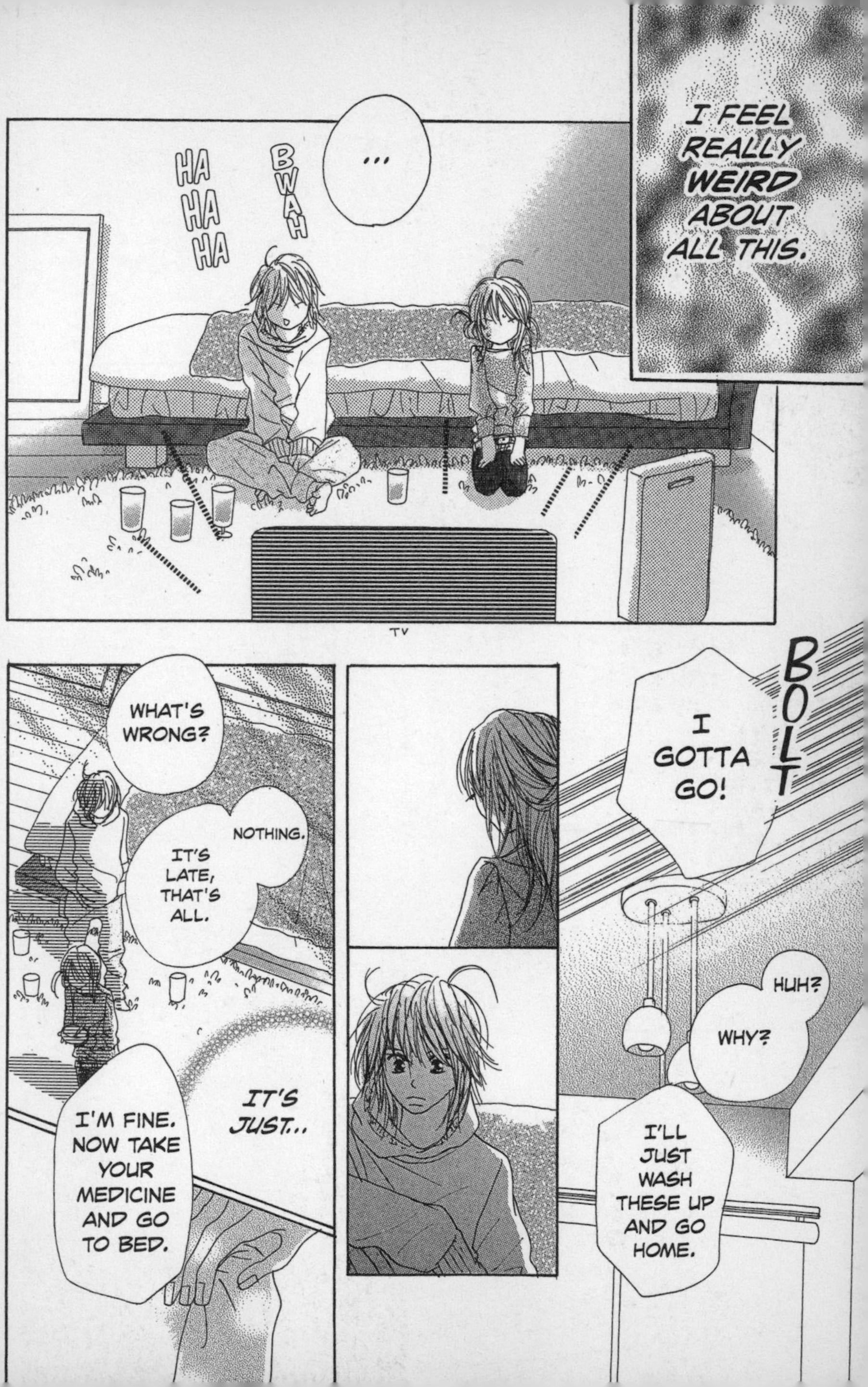
I FEEL REALLY WEIRD ABOUT ALL THIS.
...
BWAH
HA HA HA
TV
BOLT
I GOTTA GO!
HUH?
WHY?
I'LL JUST WASH THESE UP AND GO HOME.
WHAT'S WRONG?
NOTHING.
IT'S LATE, THAT'S ALL.
IT'S JUST...
I'M FINE. NOW TAKE YOUR MEDICINE AND GO TO BED.

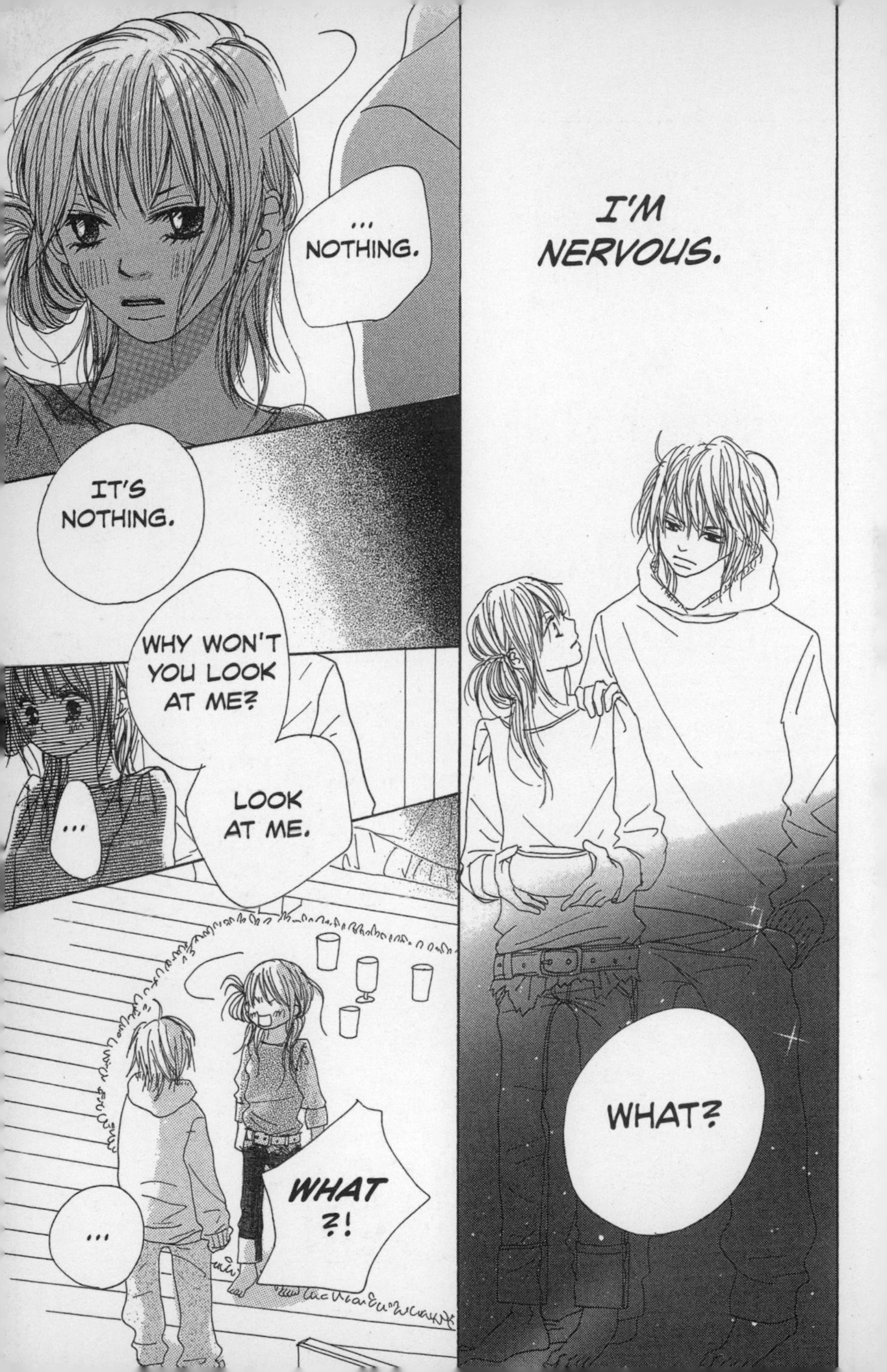
I'M NERVOUS.
WHAT?
... NOTHING.
IT'S NOTHING.
WHY WON'T YOU LOOK AT ME?
LOOK AT ME.
...
WHAT ?!
...

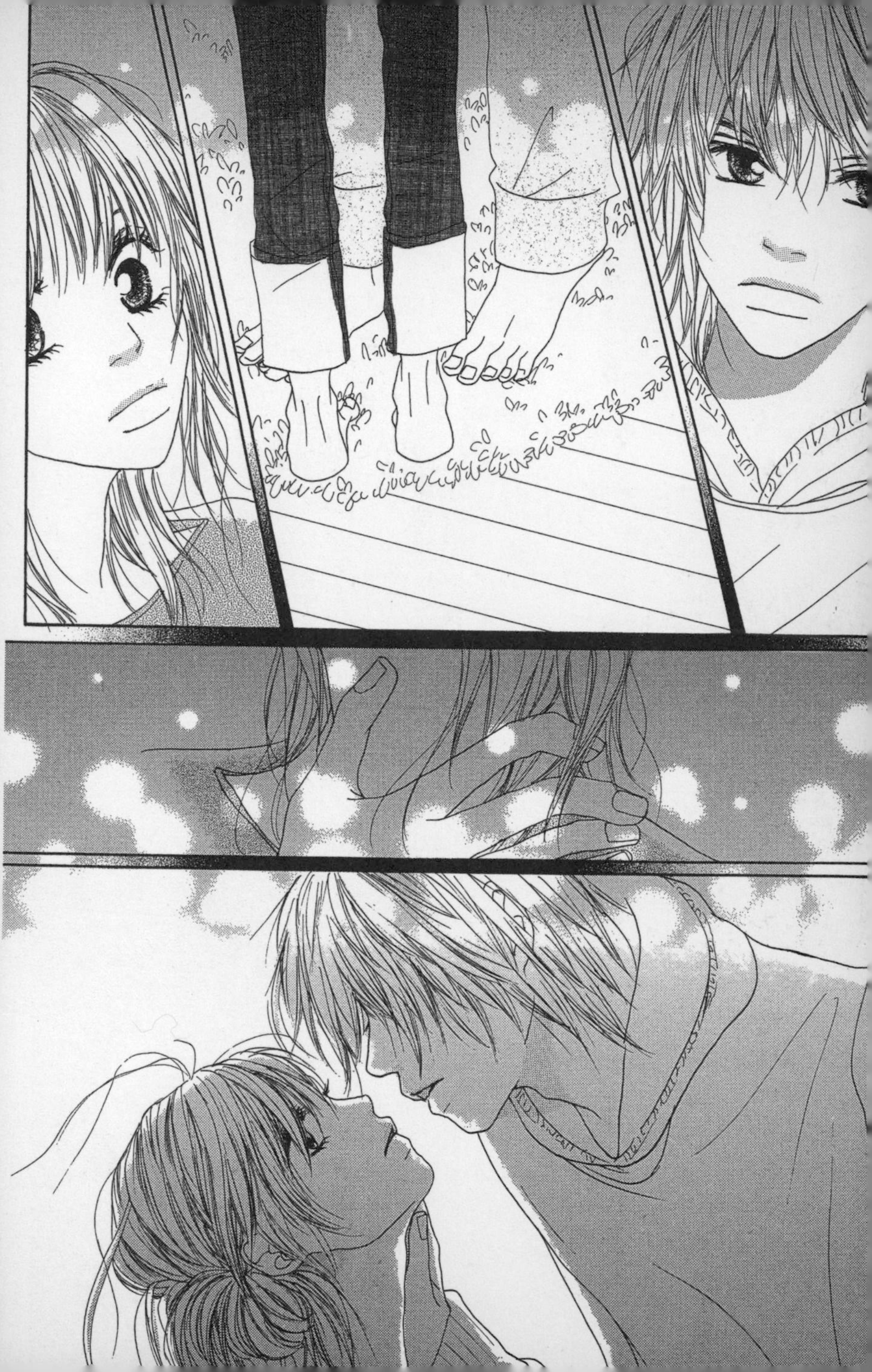

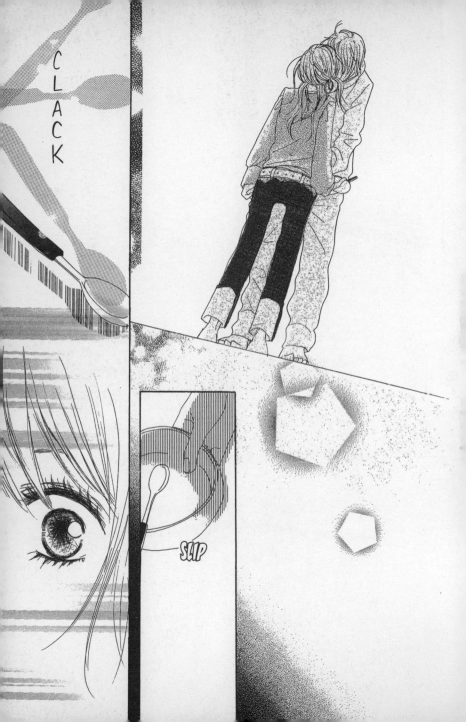

CLACK

SLIP

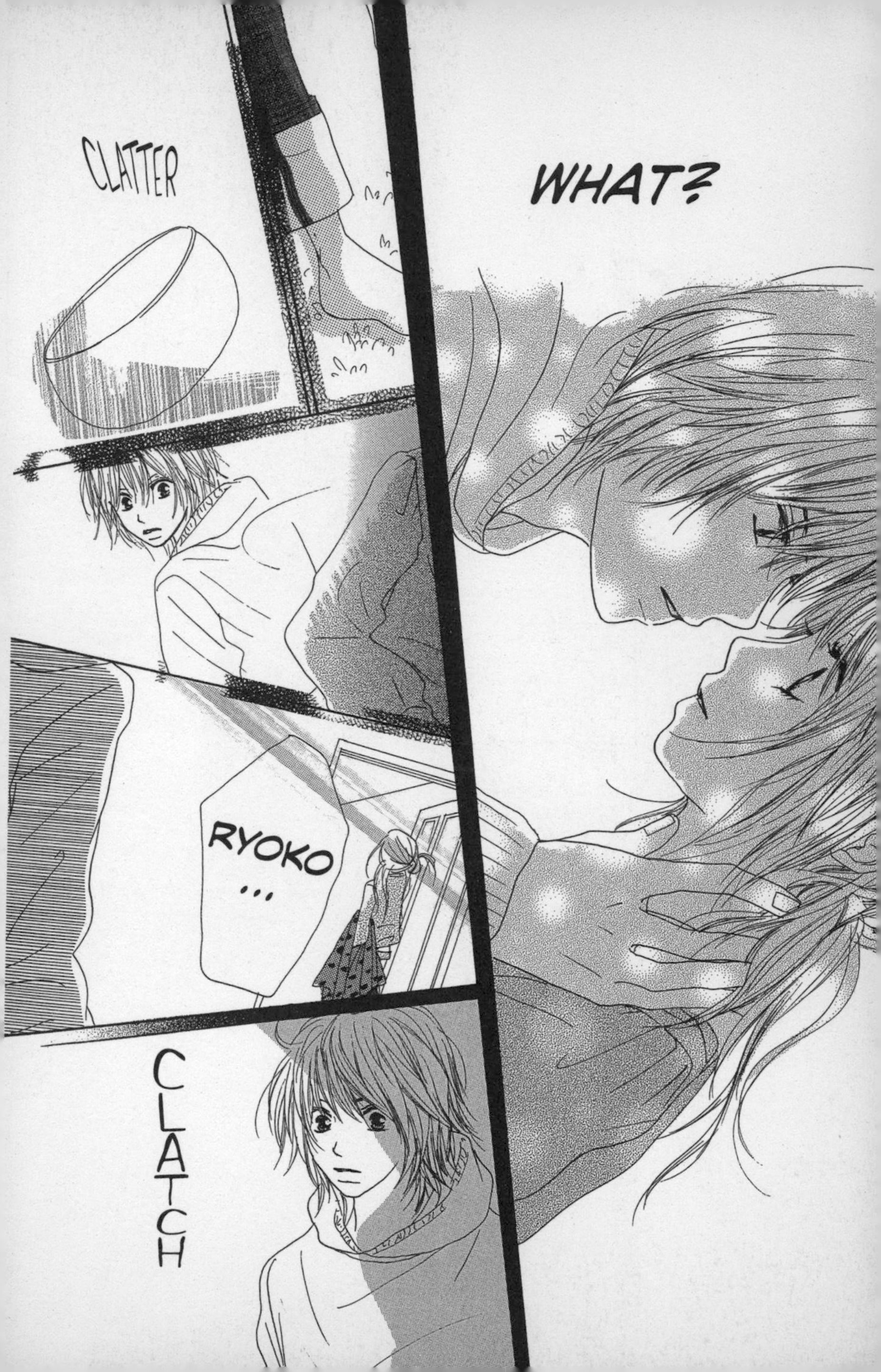
WHAT?
CLATTER
RYOKO...
CLATCH

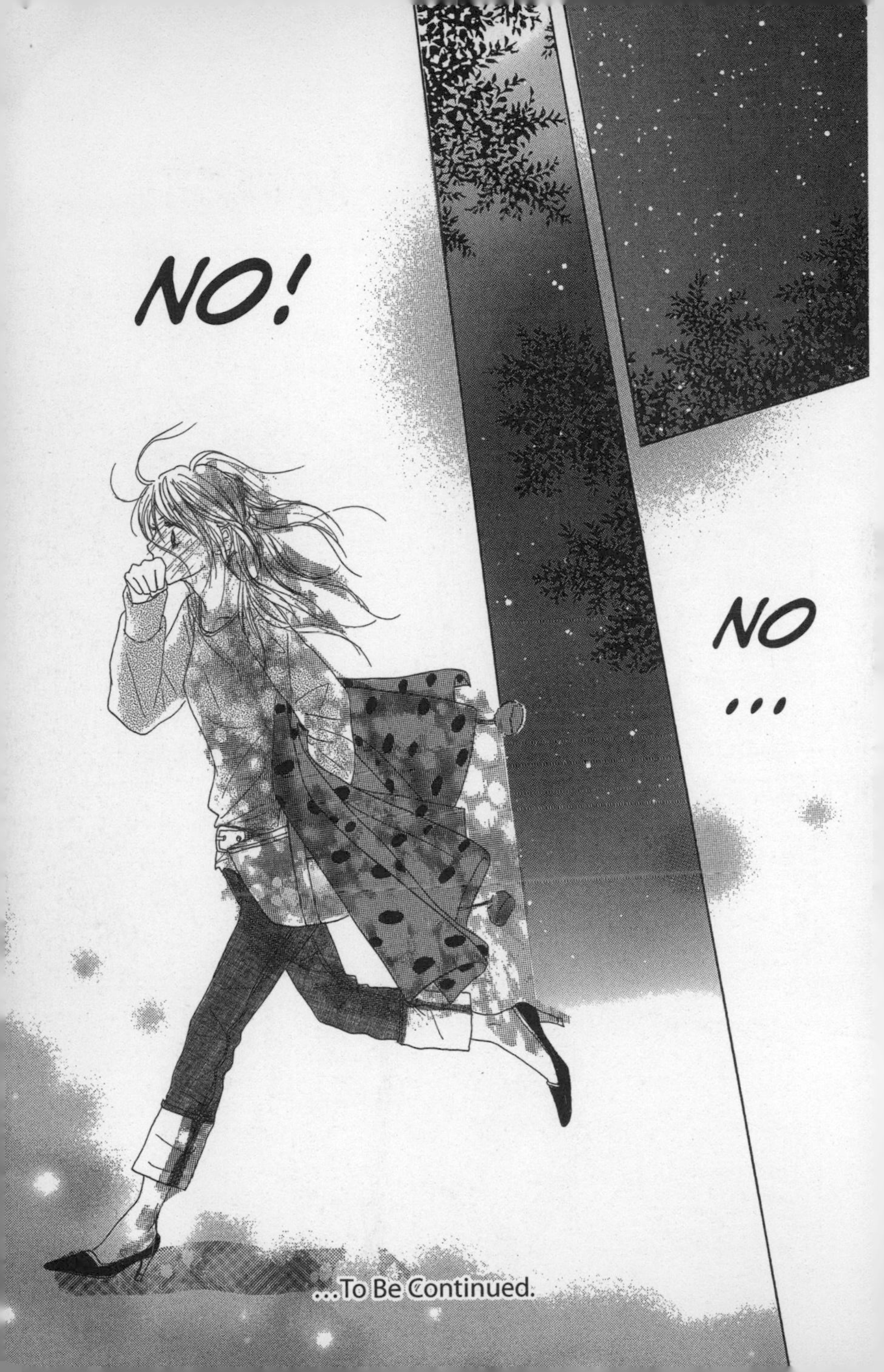
NO!
NO ...
...To Be Continued.

How B.O.D.Y. Got Its Title

Summer, 2003 A Pub in Asagaya

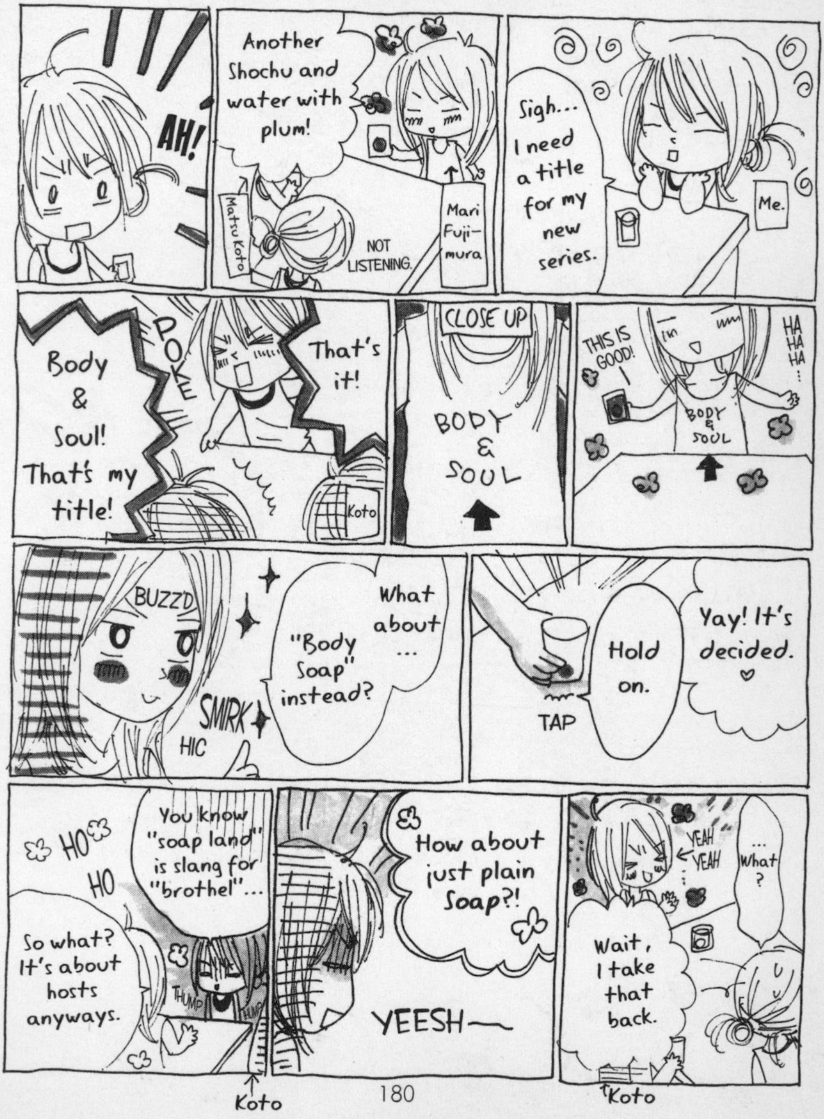

Sigh... I need a title for my new series.
Me.
Another Shochu and water with plum!
Mari Fuji-mura
Matsu Koto
NOT LISTENING.
AH!
THIS IS GOOD!
HA HA HA...
BODY & SOUL
CLOSE UP
BODY & SOUL
That's it!
POKE
Body & Soul! That's my title!
Koto
Yay! It's decided.
Hold on.
TAP
What about ... "Body Soap" instead?
BUZZ'D
SMIRK
HIC
...What?
YEAH YEAH
Wait, I take that back.
Koto
How about just plain Soap?!
YEESH—
You know "soap land" is slang for "brothel"...
HO HO
So what? It's about hosts anyways.
THUMP THUMP
Koto

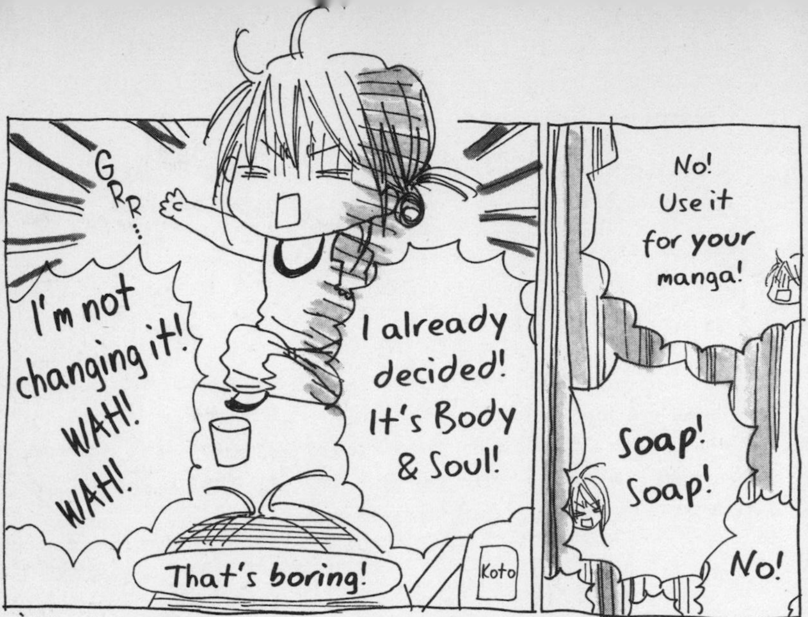
No! Use it for your manga!
Soap! Soap!
No!
GRR...
I already decided! It's Body & Soul!
I'm not changing it! WAH! WAH!
That's boring!
Koto

※ After this, on Ms. Fujimura's orders, we called my editor and went to his favorite pub...

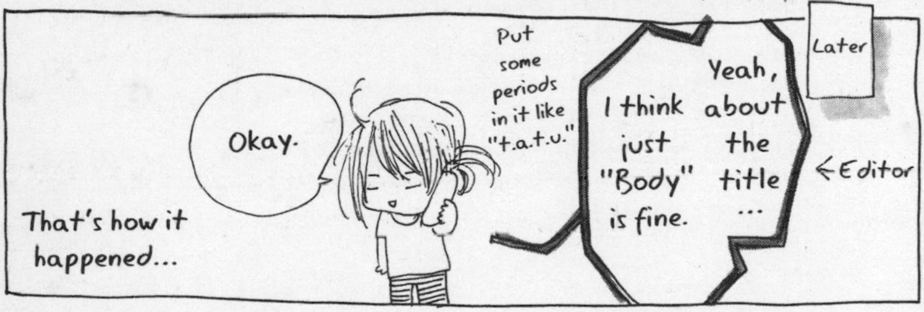
Later
← Editor
Yeah, about the title... I think just "Body" is fine.
Put some periods in it like "t.a.t.u."
Okay.
That's how it happened...

Did you think there was some hidden meaning behind it? There really isn't. Sorry to disappoint you! I'm sorry I'm so lame! Forgive me!

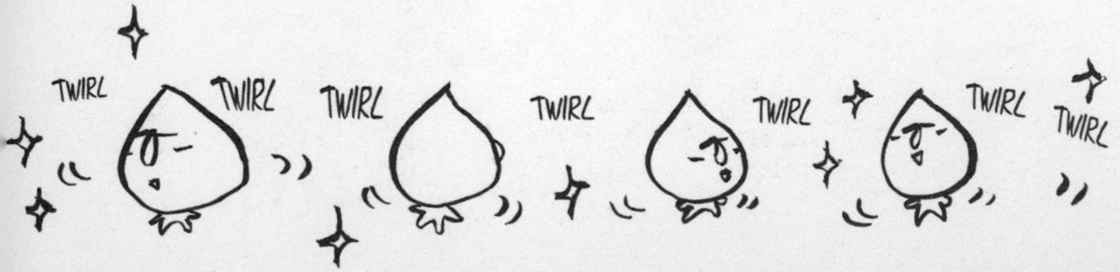
TWIRL
TWIRL
TWIRL
TWIRL
TWIRL
TWIRL
TWIRL

Something Touching

I just read *Maison Ikkoku* and I bawled like a baby! It was so moving.
I loved *Urusei Yatsura*, but this was amazing... Wow.

Ryunosuke's Glasses

Something's not right. They're bent or warped or something, aren't they?
It wasn't a conscious design choice. I get so into it when I'm drawing that
I didn't notice at the time—I was shocked when I saw it in the magazine.
I was like, "What the hell?" (Sigh.) I'll fix it in Volume 2. What's my point?
The point is, I'm sorry.

Monday's Television Line Up

Detective Conan! → *Uchimura Produce!* → *Ame Talk!* → *Robert Hall!*
                              Taikutsu Kizoku! ↵

I watch them every week. Especially *Conan* and *Uchimura Produce.*
I love *Uchimura Produce.* I hope it never goes off the air.

I'm running out   of things   to say...

Uniqlo Jacket →

The cat has a long tail!

Uniqlo Top

↑ Uniqlo Pants

TWIRL TWIRL TWIRL TWIRL TWIRL

Check it out!

The End.

This is it! Thank you for reading all the way to the last page. I hope you'll join us again for Volume 2! Volume 2... What will happen in Volume 2?! I'll still be sweating bullets, that's for sure. But I'll do my best, so please be kind!

Until then,

Ao Mimori

YAY!

YAY!

A Rough Sketch →

I was thinking about making him a model back then, but after a few meetings he became a host. I wonder why...

BONK

TWIRL

TWIRL TWIRL

TWIRL TWIRL

TWINKLE

My 7th volume!

BOII————IING!

Author's Commentary

This is my 3rd manga series. It's difficult as ever. This is my 7th volume, total. And I'm still struggling. I love the numbers 3 and 7. I hope something good is coming my way.

Ao Mimori began creating manga during her junior year of college, and her work debuted when she was only 23. *B.O.D.Y.*, her third series, was first published in *Bessatsu Margaret* in 2003 and is also available in Japanese as an audio CD. Her other work includes *Sonnano Koi Jyanai* (That's Not Love), *Anta Nanka Iranai* (I Don't Need You), *Dakishimetaiyo Motto* (I Want to Hold You More), *I LOVE YOU*, and *Kamisama no Iu Toori* (As the God of Death Dictates).

B.O.D.Y. VOL 1
The Shojo Beat Manga Edition

STORY & ART BY
AO MIMORI

English Adaptation/Kelly Sue DeConnick
Translation/Joe Yamazaki
Touch-up Art & Lettering/James Gaubatz
Design/Izumi Hirayama
Editor/Annette Roman

Editor in Chief, Books/Alvin Lu
Editor in Chief, Magazines/Marc Weidenbaum
VP of Publishing Licensing/Rika Inouye
VP of Sales/Gonzalo Ferreyra
Sr. VP of Marketing/Liza Coppola
Publisher/Hyoe Narita

B.O.D.Y. © 2003 by Ao Mimori
All rights reserved.
First published in Japan in 2003 by SHUEISHA Inc., Tokyo.
English translation rights arranged by SHUEISHA Inc.
The stories, characters and incidents mentioned in this
publication are entirely fictional.

Printed in Canada

Published by VIZ Media, LLC
P.O. Box 77010
San Francisco, CA 94107

Shojo Beat Manga Edition
10 9 8 7 6 5 4 3 2 1
First printing, May 2008

www.viz.com   store.viz.com

PARENTAL ADVISORY
B.O.D.Y. is rated T+ for Older Teen and
is recommended for ages 16 and up.
This volume contains mature themes.
ratings.viz.com

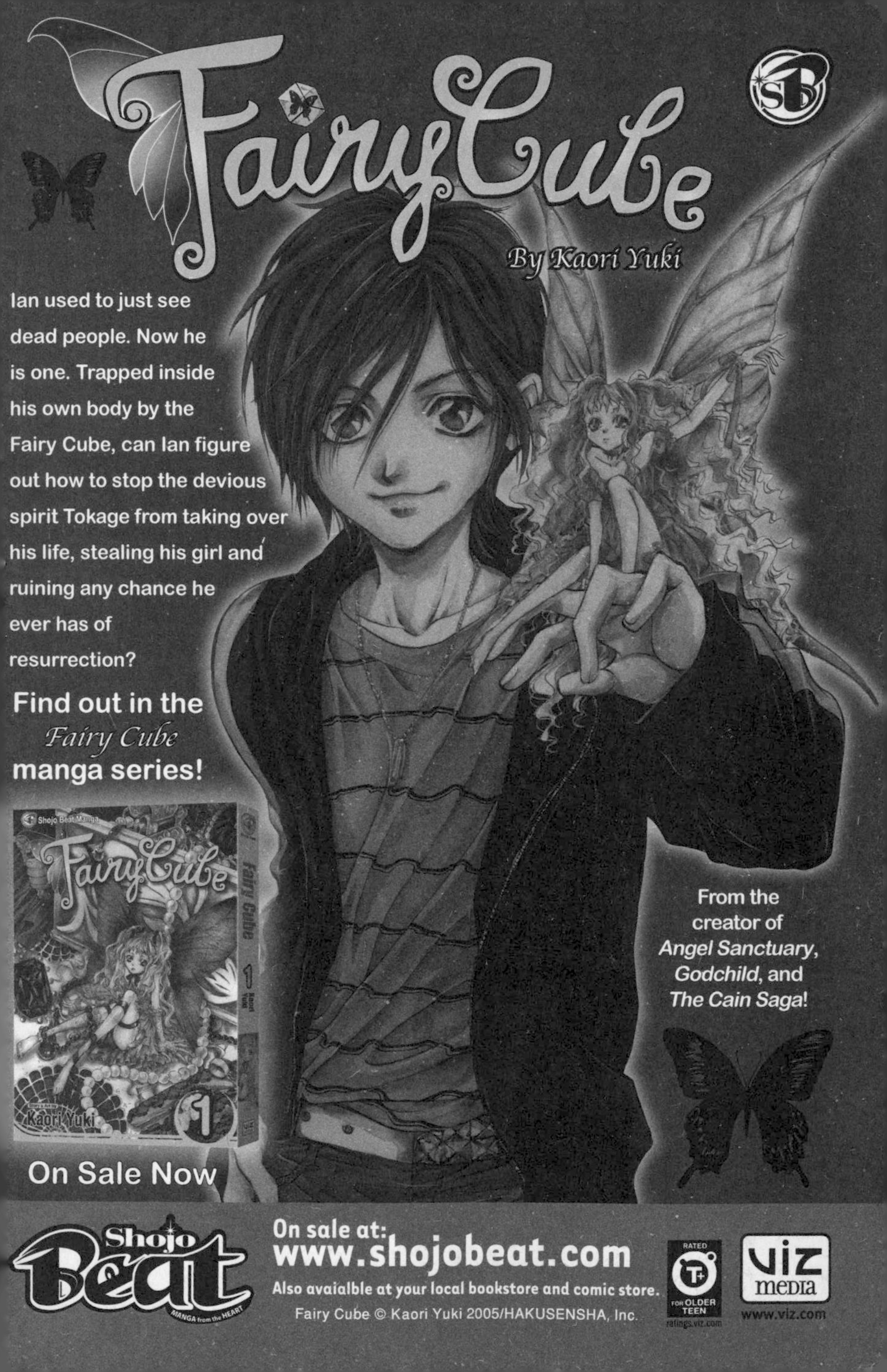
Fairy Cube
By Kaori Yuki
Ian used to just see dead people. Now he is one. Trapped inside his own body by the Fairy Cube, can Ian figure out how to stop the devious spirit Tokage from taking over his life, stealing his girl and ruining any chance he ever has of resurrection?
Find out in the Fairy Cube manga series!
Shojo Beat Manga
Fairy Cube
1
Kaori Yuki
On Sale Now
From the creator of Angel Sanctuary, Godchild, and The Cain Saga!
Shojo Beat
MANGA from the HEART
On sale at:
www.shojobeat.com
Also avaialble at your local bookstore and comic store.
Fairy Cube © Kaori Yuki 2005/HAKUSENSHA, Inc.
RATED
T+
FOR OLDER TEEN
ratings.viz.com
VIZ media
www.viz.com

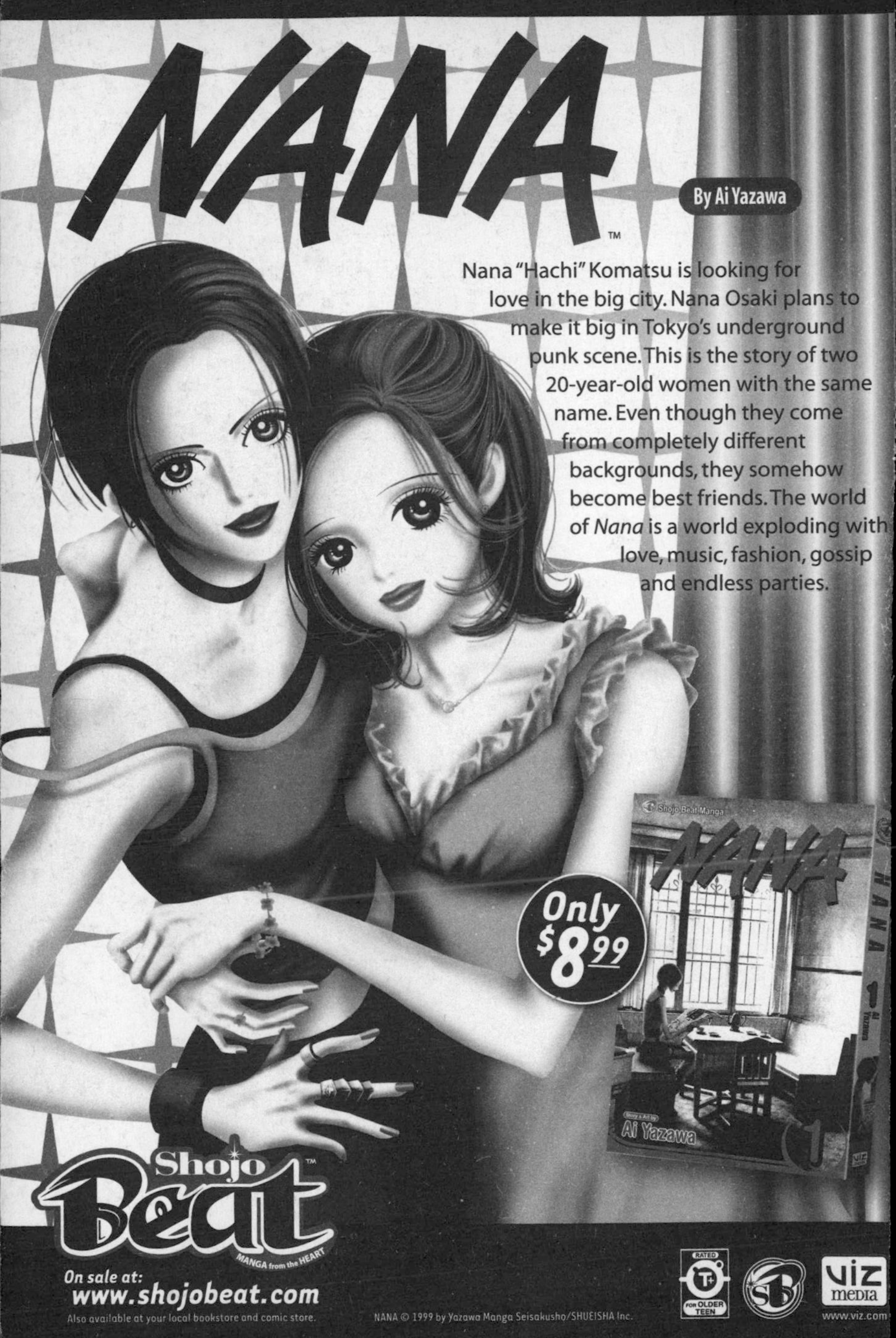

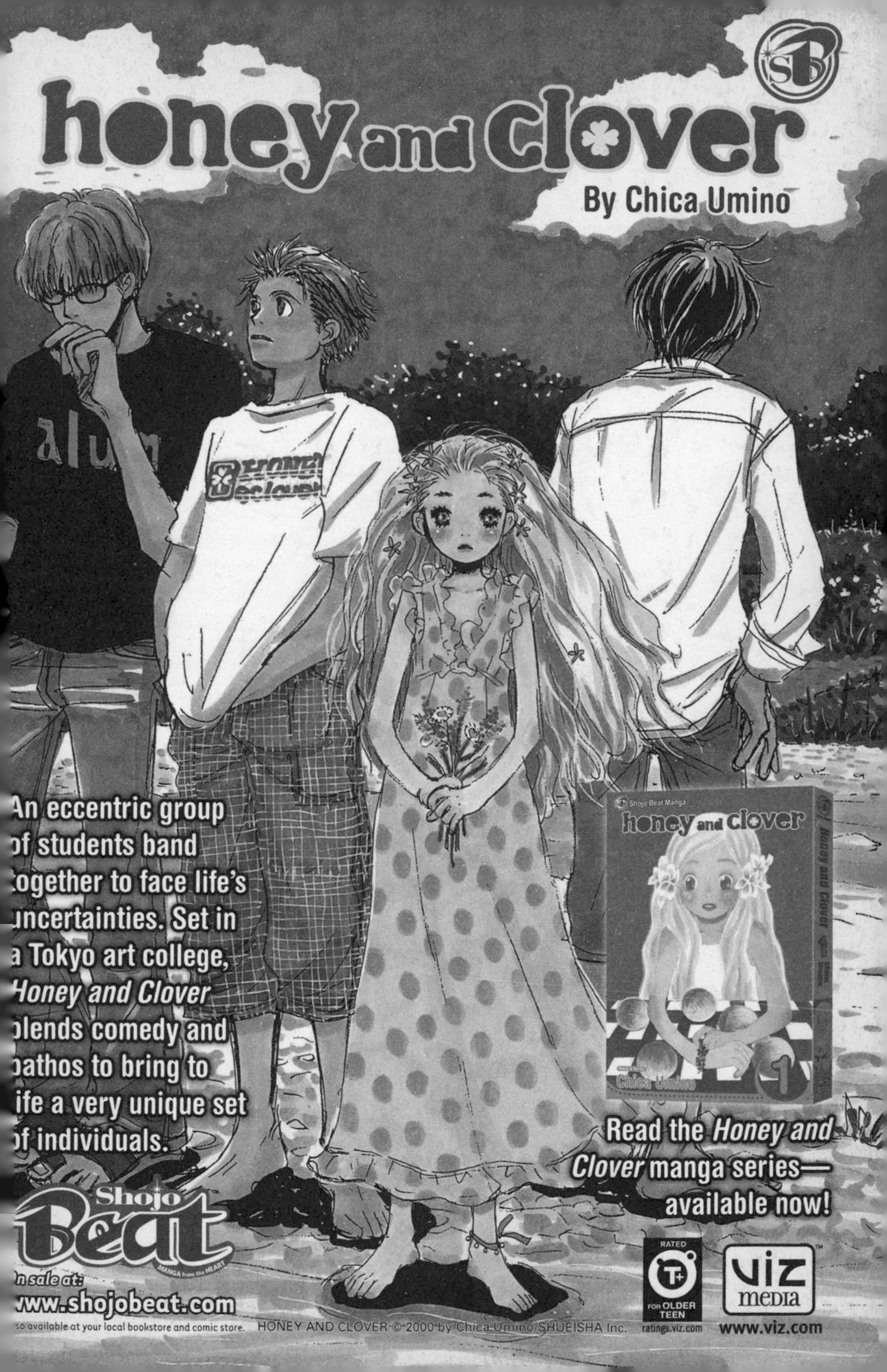
honey and clover
By Chica Umino
An eccentric group of students band together to face life's uncertainties. Set in a Tokyo art college, *Honey and Clover* blends comedy and pathos to bring to life a very unique set of individuals.
Shojo Beat Manga
honey and clover
Chica Umino
1
Read the *Honey and Clover* manga series—available now!
Shojo Beat
MANGA from the HEART
On sale at:
www.shojobeat.com
Also available at your local bookstore and comic store.
HONEY AND CLOVER © 2000 by Chica Umino/SHUEISHA Inc.
RATED T+ FOR OLDER TEEN
ratings.viz.com
VIZ media
www.viz.com

Find the Beat online!
Check us out at

www.shojobeat.com!